WINNING
DIRECT RESPONSE
ADVERTISING

WINNING DIRECT RESPONSE ADVERTISING

How to Recognize It, Evaluate It, Inspire It, Create It

Joan Throckmorton

Prentice-Hall, Inc.
Englewood Cliffs, New Jersey

Prentice-Hall International, Inc., *London*
Prentice-Hall of Australia, Pty. Ltd., *Sydney*
Prentice-Hall Canada, Inc., *Toronto*
Prentice-Hall of India Private Ltd., *New Delhi*
Prentice-Hall of Japan, Inc., *Tokyo*
Prentice-Hall of Southeast Asia Pte. Ltd., *Singapore*
Whitehall Books, Ltd., *Wellington, New Zealand*
Editora Prentice-Hall do Brasil Ltda., *Rio de Janeiro*
Prentice-Hall Hispanoamericana, S.A., *Mexico*

© 1986 *by*

Joan Throckmorton

Library of Congress Cataloging-in-Publication Data

Throckmorton, Joan.
  Winning direct response advertising.

  Includes index.
  1. Advertising, Direct-mail.   2. Direct marketing.
I. Title.
HF5861.T47   1986   659.13'3   85-31237
ISBN 0-13-960915-6
ISBN 0-13-960634-3 PBK
  Printed in the United States of America

This book is dedicated to my husband—
my toughest critic and dearest friend.

About the Author

Ms. Throckmorton is a direct marketing specialist with over twenty-five years' experience in direct mail and mail order. She is president of Joan Throckmorton, Inc., in New York.

Prior to establishing her own marketing and advertising agency in 1970, she was associated with such major publishers as Time Inc., Cowles Communications, Inc., Doubleday & Company, Inc. and American Heritage.

While at Time Inc., she was associated with *Life* Magazine where she helped introduce the first major Time Inc. book, *The Life Picture Cookbook.* She also worked on *Sports Illustrated* and later became Assistant to the Chairman of the Board of Time Inc.

At Cowles Communications, she helped set up the first merchandise and services operation for *Family Circle* and *Look* magazine readers. She ran her own promotion business in Mexico City in the early 1960s.

Since 1970, Joan Throckmorton, Inc. (formerly Throckmorton Associates) has worked on significant direct marketing projects for a broad variety of clients in consumer publishing, merchandising and services, and in education and manufacturing.

Among these clients were General Electric, McGraw-Hill Publications Company, AT&T, Citibank, Doubleday Book Clubs, Rodale Press, Inc., Time Inc. and several Cable TV systems.

Ms. Throckmorton was a member of the board of directors of the Direct Marketing Association, Inc. for six years; she is a former member of its executive committee and the long-range planning committee. She was one of the founding members of Women's Direct Response Group, a business women's organization that now has chapters in New York, Chicago, and Washington, D.C. She is a member of Women's Forum, Inc., New York.

She has been a speaker/lecturer before such groups as the Practising Law Institute, American Management Association, New York University graduate courses, the Mail Advertising Clubs of Chicago, Washington, Boston, Los Angeles, Kansas City, and Minneapolis and the Direct Marketing Association's national conventions 1971 to 1981. Under the sponsorship of the DMA, she currently conducts seminars on "Winning Direct Mail." In 1976 she was selected as one of the top 100 Corporate Women in America by *Business Week* magazine.

Acknowledgments

Acknowledgments are fearful things to write, not because of all the people you want to include, but because of the few you may leave out. One could start with parents and move on to teachers and early employers. True acknowledgments should probably include everyone who has ever influenced you—even those who have unconsciously had an effect. As there is no way to do this practically speaking, let's give them their due and get on to the present project.

Most immediately, I owe an acknowledgment to my editor, Bette Schwartzberg, and my two assistants, Debbie Carrano and Eileen Ryan, who were responsible for patiently holding things together and typing, typing, typing. Beyond this, I have a deep and sincere debt to those many professionals who gave me support and good counsel—Bob Stone for his helpful insights, Nat Ross for his patient support, Martin Baier for his thoughtful contributions, Dick Hodgson, Cecil Hoge, Pierre Passavant, Sandy Corpora, Tom Collins, Pete Hoke, Frank Johnson, John Yeck, Emily Soell, David Gordon, Jane Bryant Quinn, Chester Burger, T. George Harris, Rod Kilpatrick, Bill Jayme, Hank Burnett, Ken Sheck, Jim Punkre, Ed McLean and all the other fine writers who have proved that direct response advertising can be as creative as any advertising in America.

I'm also grateful for the assistance from my Direct Marketing Association friends (past and present), among them Bob and Bonnie DeLay, Bonnie Rodriguez, and Dick Montesi. Thanks, too, for the fine books from which I borrowed (rather than reinvent the proverbial wheel): Ed Nash's *Direct Marketing, Strategy/Planning/Execution*, Bob Stone's *Successful Direct Marketing Methods*, Jim Kob's *Profitable Direct Marketing*, John Caples' *Tested Advertising Methods*, John Witek's *Response Television* and Martin Baier's *Elements of Direct Marketing*.

My book belongs to all of them and to all of you.

Contents

chapter 5

Nurturing Creative Concepts: How to Sharpen Your Creative Judgment and Grow a Concept

chapter 6

Creating the Direct Mail Package

chapter 7

Deathless Prose

chapter 8

An Evening with the Good Stuff

Introduction

WHY YOU SHOULD READ THIS BOOK

This is a book for creative people or those people who are involved, one way or the other, in the creative process in direct response advertising.

Aha! you say—creative people—that means *writers*. Sure it does, and *Winning Direct Response Advertising* is for direct response writers (or aspiring writers), but it will also prove helpful for others whose jobs touch on the creative process:

- creative directors who must work with their staff to develop good advertising
- managers who must judge their agency's creative work or the work of their own promotion departments
- marketers who are in charge of developing advertising plans
- product managers and corporate directors who have to work with market planning
- artists and art directors who work with copywriters (and just about everyone else on the creative team)
- large companies, small companies, and individuals who wish to enter the field of direct marketing.

Not only will it enable writers to do a far better job in direct response advertising, but it will help management—in businesses large and small—to better understand what must go into good direct response advertising and how to work with creative people. (There are several fine books that can help individuals and companies entering direct marketing today, but nothing that enables them to participate in, evaluate, or judge good creative development and direct response advertising as a whole.)

This book will also help managers and supervisors encourage greater quality and creativity in direct response advertising. It will assist creative directors in guiding their creative people—artists as well as copywriters—to higher levels of direct response advertising.

As for you writers—take heart. This book gives you the solid basics of direct response advertising—and then some. It offers you a sound grounding in technique (the formulas, rules, and rules for breaking rules). Equally important, it will guide you through the creative process from beginning to end and set you on the way to creative reasoning. This is an area that will be crucial to your career—to your own creative growth and development. Once you master this aspect of direct response advertising, you will understand not only the fundamentals, but the heart and soul of direct marketing. You will be prepared to chart your own future, whether it be master craftsperson and creative star, or creative director and leader of others.

WINNING
DIRECT RESPONSE
ADVERTISING

chapter 1

Your Opportunity, Your Challenge

In New York City in the 1980s, surprising as it may sound, a direct response free-lance copywriter received upwards of $200,000 in royalties in one year alone, representing several successful direct mail promotions.

Another top writer asked *and* got over $15,000 to write *one* direct mail promotion. Still other writers received *bonuses* of $10,000 *and more* from major companies when their promotions won out over other promotions they tested against. Meanwhile, at major New York direct response agencies, full-time creative director jobs at $100,000 to $125,000 were unfilled, and senior copywriting or copy supervisor jobs went begging at $50,000 and $60,000 a year. Outside New York City, even *junior* copywriter jobs at $30,000 to $32,000 were easy to find! (Impressive, when you consider that standard agency creative directors averaged only $49,200 in 1984 and copywriters only $25,000.[1])

In a profession that can measure response to its advertising, the ability to understand, supervise, and execute winning direct response advertising pays off big. Proven top performers are treated royally, because time after time they help ensure the profitability of the businesses that hire them.

WHY SO FEW ARE MAKING SO MUCH

If top creative performers can do so well, you'd think there would be hundreds of individuals pushing to prove themselves in direct marketing. Many new people do keep popping up, claiming to be direct marketing specialists, but they come and go without making a name for themselves or proving very much. Top jobs are still unfilled, free-lance stars continue to ask exorbitant prices without challenge, and more and more competent direct response advertising professionals are going for those free-lance dollars.

The growth of direct marketing itself is phenomenal. The use of third-class (or bulk) mail tripled from 1976 to 1983 and mail order sales in 1984 rose to

---

[1] *Adweek* (June 4, 1984), pp. SS18-23.

over $171 billion.[2] According to *Direct Marketing* magazine, "Mail order accounts for as much sales as Catalog Showrooms, Direct Selling and Vending Machines combined ($43 billion), more than for all department stores ($30 billion), and as much as any single consumer selling channel except mass general merchandisers and supermarkets...."[3]

This unusual growth is also reflected in over twenty-five major direct response agencies that billed more than $20 million each in 1984 (and two of these billed over $100 million), and in scores of smaller agencies that are continually starting up. Nearly every major United States advertising agency has a direct response agency subsidiary or division and many of these have branches around the world. Add to this the entirely new or expanded corporate divisions among large and small companies that are moving into direct marketing; add individuals with new entrepreneurial mail order businesses; add the continually growing established direct marketing companies; then figure in the computer operations, printers, lettershops, listbrokers—all the service companies that rely on direct marketers—and the size of this business, or marketing form, is truly impressive.

A BUSINESS THAT'S BEGGING FOR CREATIVE LEADERS

All of this expansion takes people. In the creative area it takes marketers and product managers, promotion directors, creative directors, copywriters, artists, and art directors. And the people most desperately needed and hardest to find are those managers, marketers, directors, and creators with a solid understanding of the underlying creative principles of direct response advertising.

They are hard to find because, until recently, direct marketing (or mail order and direct mail, as it was known in the 1950s and 1960s) was neither an exciting nor a rewarding field for creative individuals. It wasn't even very respectable. To call yourself a mail order or direct mail writer meant that you wrote for catalogs or did "junk" mail (a derogatory but dying term, used only *outside* the industry today)—not very good for a writer's image, or for the paycheck. As you would expect, few talented individuals would go this route, so the inevitable happened.

Although the first direct mail agencies were founded in the early 1900s,[4] as direct response became a more acceptable form of advertising, a number of specializing agencies sprang up (Schwab and Beatty, Inc. was founded in 1928; Altman, Vos & Reichberg, Wunderman, Ricotta & Kline, Rapp & Collins, and

---

[2]Simmons Market Research Bureau, New York, 1984

[3]Interview with Arnold Fishman, "1983 Mail Order Sales Rise to Almost $100 Billion," *Direct Marketing*, (July, 1984), p. 60.

[4]Buckley-Dement, founded in Chicago in 1905 and Dickie-Raymond, established in 1921. Source: *Fact Book on Direct Marketing 1984 Edition* (New York Direct Marketing Association, Inc., Publications Division, 1984), p. 6.

Stone & Adler followed in the 1950s and early 1960s). As a consequence, demand grew for good creative practitioners, but there were very few creative leaders or teachers beyond the original masters: John Caples, Bob Stone, Tom Collins, the late Max Sackheim, the late Vic Schwab, and the late Edward N. Mayer, Jr.

This situation did not correct itself, but allowed, instead, a sort of free-lance "star" system to build up in the 1960s and 1970s—the kind of system that can develop only in a creative vacuum. By the 1980s it consisted of some twelve to fifteen creative stars or free-lancers who asked top dollar and worked for agencies and clients alike across the country.

As direct marketing continued to grow, experienced creative writers remained scarce, and today we have about the same situation we had ten years ago. The large direct response agencies have, however, gradually developed their own talented creative directors, artists, and copy technicians—but even here the more gifted often move out into the greener free-lance arena.

In 1965, the Direct Marketing Association established an Educational Foundation that offers five-day intensive courses to bright college students, but the courses handle fewer than 100 students a year. In 1982 the Direct Marketing Association membership raised over $1.2 million to establish a chair for a Direct Marketing Center in three major universities.

There is now a center for direct marketing at the University of Missouri, Kansas City, and one at New York University. There are courses at Boston University, Syracuse Newhouse School of Communications, the University of Cincinnati, and Alabama State among others. But direct marketers will have to wait some years for this to have an impact on the situation as the first waves of direct response students mature.

In a sense, direct marketing today represents a burgeoning field, with few qualified creative leaders in relation to its size and still fewer accomplished teachers with a sound background in the fundamentals of direct response advertising. The four outstanding leaders, who have shepherded the educational programs through twenty years of development and are largely responsible for today's achievements, are Bob Stone, chairman of Stone & Adler, who continues as a leading author and teacher in direct marketing; Martin Baier, senior vice-president of Old American Insurance Company, who wrote the first teaching text, *Elements of Direct Marketing;* Nat Ross, former vice-president of Lincoln Graphic Arts, who developed and nurtured the N.Y.U. School of Continuing Education direct marketing programs over the last eighteen years; John D. Yeck, Partner of Yeck Brothers Group, who has devoted his talents, time, and heart to the DMA's Direct Marketing Educational Foundation, Inc. (as trustee and chairman) for over 20 years.

BRING ON THE MARKETERS

Another major problem in developing top creative direct response talent has been the total lack of understanding of what is *required* to teach the creative process. Creative stars and leaders seemed to learn by instinct, but little if any formalized analysis was done to determine what methods they applied to creative problem solving or creative reasoning so that these methodologies might be taught or passed on.

Traditionally writers were expected merely to sit in a cubicle, take assignments, and ask few questions. Experience was the writer's and art director's primary teacher. The creative department as a whole was given little information and was continually left out of the marketing process. When they were let in, no one gave them training in using or applying marketing tools. People who supervised or bought creative work—or actively developed creative work—were often not privy to marketing formulas. On the other hand, few marketing people were trained to understand or judge good creative work.

This disastrous situation is only now beginning to change. Gradually marketers are beginning to understand that creative direct response practitioners must be privy to marketing data and planning long before a budget is determined or a word is put on paper. Today, in many of the best agencies, the marketing requirements have been overlaid on creative basics, and the result is structured creative strategies—the first step to successful promotions. This cooperation does not occur often enough, and where it does, creative people frequently participate without really understanding the process or how they are expected to contribute.

The standard direct marketing plan deals with sales goals. The creative strategy, an important part of the overall marketing strategy, deals with the development of winning promotions. The two areas *must* interrelate, and while the creative strategy relies heavily on the big plan, neither can succeed without the other. What's more, the creative strategy cannot be successfully developed without full input from the creative people—the writers, artists, art directors, creative directors—as well as the marketers.

Supervisors and marketing management need guidelines for helping creative people do their best. You, as a creative person, must request and receive the marketing cooperation that allows you to develop true creative concepts. The goal of this book is to make sure you know exactly what you need and how to use it.

UNLOCKING THE SECRETS OF SUCCESSFUL DIRECT RESPONSE ADVERTISING

Your training and the development of your creative talent are further compounded by the "mystique," or "mysteries," of direct marketing, perpetrated by its practitioners who often profess that years of experience are required before one is initiated into such mysteries.

"What are the mysteries?" you may ask. "There are no mysteries," I will answer and there never were. *But there are a lot of secrets—secrets of direct* marketing that only a relatively small number of people seem to understand, or share, or know how to put into practice. Those without solid direct response advertising training, without a clear understanding of the rules, techniques, and concept development—all the secrets—can neither teach nor practice successfully. You are going to learn the secrets in this book.

Perhaps the best kept secret of all is that there's no need for you to fail in direct response advertising! No marketing director, product manager, creative head, or copywriter need ever sponsor a "bomb" or create a dismal direct response promotion—not when you know the initial creative steps to follow. These are proven first steps that you can apply to a project to give you a solid idea of success or failure even before any copy is written. Protect yourself, if you need to, when these steps show the red light. Top creative stars turn down projects when their red lights start flashing. *You* can learn how to judge for yourself as they do.

Next, there is no excuse for you ever to produce direct response advertising that is not professional and, consequently, measuredly successful.

Good direct response advertising that pays out in dollars and cents sales can be executed if you understand the secrets (the techniques, rules, procedures), how to apply them professionally, and when to break them. *You* can take control of the basics and develop direct response advertising that is effective in its own right.

Finally, you can also learn the "secret" principles for executing direct response winners—advertising that beats out all comers!

In any situation that deals with accountable advertising, the advertiser is able to test your advertising against the best going ad or direct mail package. This testing is a continual process in good direct marketing, and the winners— the direct response promotions that *consistently* beat the competition—also have their secrets.

Here's where top creative talent comes into play. When you study the techniques of the pros, understand the rules they live by, and appreciate *the kind of creative reasoning that goes into their direct response promotions,* then you'll be ready to move out and develop your own stable of winners.

You may ask, "Why doesn't everyone in direct marketing do this?" Successful direct marketers *have* done this, and they are always looking for others who can.

Remember, there are few teachers to produce new leaders; few professionals to set down the steps that need to be followed; few marketers that involve artists and writers in their strategic planning; few creative people that even understand the disciplines required in creative concept development.

And no one yet has placed these steps or stages squarely at the door of the creative function in a form that creative people can follow and use—until now. In *Winning Direct Response Advertising* you have at your fingertips both the technical and the creative equipment you need.

CAN <u>YOU</u> MEET THE REQUIREMENTS?

If you break down the marketer's doors, become privy to the secrets of the planning, help develop creative strategies that will work, *how can you be sure that you can develop the skills and talents to carry them through to winning promotions?*

Possibly one more reason for the lack of top creative people in direct response advertising today is the heavy demands it makes on the skills and talents of its professionals. To begin with, creativity here is not pure inspiration. It is not "intuitive" or something you sense "innately" or any other way. It is something that can be taught and learned. More than any other form of advertising, direct response advertising also requires you to have a *diversity* of talents and skills. And these skills can be acquired; the talents can be honed; the systematic procedures and tested techniques can be assimilated.

In addition to being artistic or creative, for example, you also have to be a *technician*. Because direct response is filled with creative guidelines and tested do's and don'ts, over 50 percent of your basic work falls into the "technique" area. You have to incorporate certain rules and formulas and adapt certain guidelines as you plot every piece of direct response advertising copy and build your sales message. Then, as an artist, you have to apply all the creativity you can muster to your copy development and the framing of your selling proposition.

When it comes to basic writing requirements, you need the abilities of an advertising copywriter *and* you also need the skills of a good salesperson. There's a discernible difference between these two requirements, and two different temperaments are involved. One is the dream builder and sizzle-seller who uses words and pictures to make you long for things you never knew you needed. The other is the fast-talking circus barker, the typical traveling salesman who wants your money now—the sale-closer.

In direct marketing, you need a combination of both, because in direct response advertising, in one way or another, *you ask for the order.* Advertising that merely "influences," or gives you a better feeling about the product or creates a brand "awareness" is not for direct marketers.

As a direct response writer, you have to entice; cajole; promise wealth, health, and happiness—all for a very special price—if the customer "acts now." You have to advertise *and* sell. As with any good salesperson, you have to know your selling points and anticipate questions in advance. If your customer has one question unanswered, your entire sales talk is wasted, because you lose that customer.

Your writing must embody a variety of sales approaches, depending on the specific product you are promoting. You have to understand how a good salesperson makes the sale. You have to have a feeling for it. What's more, you have to develop your sales *dialogue* for each product all alone, without the use of interactive selling skills or trial-and-error practice on customers.

On the other hand, you'll also be expected to be a good, solid advertising copywriter. You have to know how to position your product, to extract benefits from features, to build images using the right words and pictures. You have to make your point and develop your selling platform with the efficient use of words and phrases that people will relate to.

We now have four skills for you to apply in your role as a direct response advertising creative person—the skills of the technician, the skills of the artist, the skills of the salesperson, and the skills of the advertising copywriter.

One more role or skill should be added; it grows logically out of the other four.

Because of the all-important letter in the basic direct mail package, you, as a creative person, are seldom exactly who *you* are. You must become other people at the same time. You must identify with them, and as you assume their roles, you must be credible. You must sound like them, feel the way they would feel and know the things they would know as you address your prospect market (or, in fact, *their* prospect market). And, of course, *as those other people,* you must empathize with *their* market.

You may be thinking, "Anyone can write a letter from a magazine publisher or an insurance executive or a merchant. Just put the name and title at the end." But that doesn't work—unless you want to sound like a faceless technician with neutralized copy. Each publisher reflects the tone of his product. Each insurance executive should have his or her own style and, certainly, every good direct response merchant has a distinct personality (from Richard Thalheimer of Sharper Image, to Harry and David of Bear Creek, to Duke Habernickel of Haband). Without this personality or point of view, you may write flat and faceless copy. Mediocre stuff. Sausage.

A top writer knows that insurance executives don't sound like lingerie salespeople, nor do they express themselves in the same words or use the same expressions or describe their product in the same glowing terms. To sound credible to the prospect, you have to get into the skin of the person signing your letter, the spokesperson.

What's more, you have to put yourself in the place of the prospect group you are addressing. You have to empathize with your market, understand its motives, aspirations, and drives. Above all, you must have respect and consideration for the people who make up that market.

So now let's add one more skill—the skill of speaking as someone else; the skill of the actor. You must speak in another's voice, or *the voice people would expect that speaker to have.* In each case, you have to learn to sound the way the customers imagine you *should* sound.

For example: Almost all of us can hear and readily recognize the differences between the voice of the football sportscaster and the voice of the minister speaking from the pulpit. They don't sound the same. Close your eyes and listen. You can *hear* the difference right now if you try.

Your job is to listen to different spokespeople and understand what makes that difference so that you can recreate it—recreate it and direct it *to a specific market with its own personality.* So now we add "actor" to your list, right under copywriter.

- technician
- artist
- salesperson
- advertising copywriter
- actor

Which leads us to the next requirements.

THREE IMPORTANT QUALITIES FOR YOU TO DEVELOP

So far, we have the skills of the technician and the artist. Next come the talents of the salesperson and advertising copywriter, and following these you have the charge (as actor) to speak credibly as a spokesperson other than yourself, to communicate positively to a specific type of audience. (As you may have guessed, we're working on an inverted pyramid here.)

Right under "actor" comes curiosity—a basic and very necessary quality, on which the five skills above must balance. Supporting curiosity are imagination and discipline. Curiosity is vital to artistic temperament or to the development of highly tuned skills, largely because no advertising copywriter can work in a vacuum. Curiosity gives you a storehouse of input to draw on when you need it, particularly if you are working on dialogue and letter writing (or broadcast, for that matter).

How do you start your mind-expanding curiosity, get it going? First, you listen to dialogue. You eavesdrop. Every passing conversation has something to tell you. On any given day you can learn how a busy career woman complains about her dry cleaning bill, how a threadbare old man inquires about a grocery purchase, how a clerk in a bookstore presents new books. You can get a small idea of trivia and lingo from two teenage girls on a park bench, or you can sense the loneliness of an out-of-town traveler as he or she strikes up a conversation with his or her waiter.

Curiosity also means asking questions and reading newspapers, magazines, journals, and books that you wouldn't ordinarily read. It means wanting to know how people feel about things (like asking a college freshman about world affairs or quizzing a senior citizen on the national budget). It means watching a broad assortment of television programs, especially things you haven't seen before. It does not mean escape reading, or mindless viewing, or playing radio or TV in the background.

The quality of your curiosity also contains something I call your *Renaissance Quotient* (R.Q.). Beginning in the fifteenth century the Italian nobles set the standards for the Renaissance Quotient by looking into practically everything. Wealthy, enlightened Italians spent their lives exploring and delving into the arts and sciences—everything known to man—just for the sake of knowing. (Remember Leonardo da Vinci—painter, inventor, engineer!) Today a high Renaissance Quotient usually means having a marvelous rampant curiosity about many aspects of life—a very important attribute for you to develop if you're aspiring to top status in *any* area of advertising.

Curiosity is particularly important for you here, however, because of that unique "actor" aspect of direct response advertising that requires you to speak as an expert on all sorts of products and services in someone else's voice, directly to your (or someone else's) prospect market.

Your R.Q., or curiosity, helps you be a good spokesperson or representative who is conversant with the market. It helps you understand how people (customers) feel, how they sound or talk, the things they enjoy, the values that are important to them, their particular lingo. Writers who don't really care about these things will most likely have a tough time developing the all-important creative skills of dialogue writing—they may even end up as mere technicians—if they don't have curiosity.

Curiosity leads logically to *imagination,* which visits your mental store-house to select and shape the fruits of your curiosity into something great and grand and beautifully, appropriately, creatively moving. Imagination grows from your desire to know more by inventing or imagining beyond what you *know,* utilizing your experiences. It enables you to create something meaningful and compelling *for others* from all you've observed and learned.

Imagination is a critical quality for everyone who plans to develop artistic skills of any kind, be it composer, writer, painter, wood carver, chef, architect, or direct response creative writer.

Last, and possibly most important of the three qualities, is *discipline.* Discipline is your ability to develop your curiosity and your imagination, then put them to work—and keep on doggedly working. Call it determination; in direct response advertising you need a lot of it. As Tom Collins, the creative head of Rapp & Collins says, "Advertising is hard!"[5] and, as you can see, direct response advertising is no exception.

But take heart. By mastering direct response advertising you assure yourself of a good future with many opportunities and growth options. You will be able to move into all other forms of advertising and promotion as well.

David Ogilvy, former chairman of Ogilvy & Mather and an early supporter and user of direct marketing, claims that the disciplines of direct response advertising are invaluable. "This elite corp ... knows more about the *realities* of advertising than anybody else."[6]

---

[5]Edward L. Nash, *Direct Marketing Strategy/Planning/Execution* (New York: McGraw-Hill, Inc., 1982), p. 231.

[6]David Ogilvy, excerpted from *Confessions of an Advertising Man.* Copyright ©1963 David Ogilvy. Reprinted with the permission of the author.

YOU'LL BE TESTED!

Before we get too far along, now is a good time for you to decide how you feel about being tested. Remember, direct response advertising is accountable. Everything you do will be *tested*. This may seem a little unnerving at first, but ultimately, your ability to do winning promotions will make your reputation. And give you highs. Exhilaration! Confidence!!

If you stick with it, you will actually learn to love testing. You'll know the rules, you'll know how to practice them professionally, and you'll be eager to prove yourself through your work—and win.

Speaking of winning—please bear in mind that there are two kinds of winning in our business. The promotions that win awards are not always the promotions that win tests. Everyone needs awards under his or her belt. But if winning awards is *all* you want, keep reading, then plan to stay with a company or ad agency. Top creative stars are very well paid, not because they win awards, but because they win tests and make money for their clients.

Whether you've already tried direct response copy or not, it will prove most helpful if you are now writing advertising copy, or have some experience writing, or experience in advertising or marketing. And if you are presently writing direct response copy, so much the better.

Direct response advertising desperately needs more creative talent, but up until now no one has shown potential stars how to go about developing and applying the full range of talents required.

Although you can find several books that offer fine instruction and rules on writing good copy,[7] there are very few guideposts to follow in developing good, solid professionalism-cum-creativity in direct marketing today.

This book can point the way, act as your mentor—teaching you...pushing you...challenging you...encouraging you. Its job is to give you the tools, the instruction, and the guidance—even the inspiration—you need to develop your creative skills and determine whether direct response advertising wealth and fame are ahead for you.

You *can* become a better creative person (and possibly one who understands writing a little more), and you might come away with a very solid, profitable, lifetime profession. Try it. And try hard. Remember, *direct marketing needs you, too.*

---

[7]John Caples, *Tested Advertising Methods*, © 1974 by John Caples, (Englewood Cliffs, N.J.: Prentice-Hall).

John Caples, *Make Your Advertising Make Money*, Englewood Cliffs, N.J.: Prentice-Hall, 1983.

David Ogilvy, *Ogilvy on Advertising*, (Crown Publishers, 1983).

Ed McLean, *The Basics of Copy: A Monograph on Direct Marketing* (Ryan Gilmore Publishing Co., Inc., 1975).

CHAPTER 1 EXERCISES

TEST YOUR CREATIVE POTENTIAL

A Self-Test to Help You Evaluate and Expand Your Creative Abilities
(Don't spend more than seven minutes on the answers.)

Add up your
cumulative
score here

1. Do you ever watch TV programs that you don't ordinarily watch,
   just to see what *other* people are watching?
   _____ yes (3)   _____ no (1)
2. Evaluate the magazines below; do you read them regularly,
   irregularly, or not at all? Check the boxes at the right.

	Regularly	Irregularly	Not at all
Mademoiselle			
Cosmopolitan			
Redbook			
McCall's			
Ladies' Home Journal			
Working Woman			
Working Mother			
Audubon			
Savvy			
Smithsonian			
Architectural Digest			
Esquire			
Bon Appétit			
GQ			
Horticulture			
U.S. News & World Report			
American Health			
Mother Jones			
The Mother Earth News			
Prevention			
Organic Gardening			
50 Plus			
Playboy			

(Score 3 points for regularly, 2 points for irregularly, and 0 for not at all.)
3. Have you ever ridden a rollercoaster? ___ Yes (3) ___ No (1)
4. Have you tried a Nautilus machine? ___ Yes (3) ___ No (1)
5. Do you know what book is #1 on the Fiction Bestseller list? ___
   Yes (3) ___ No. (1)
6. Nonfiction? ___ Yes (3) ___ No (1)

7. Do you know who is the biggest single record seller this week? ____ Yes (3) ____ No (1)
8. Can you name today's hottest recording group? ____ Yes (3) ____ No (1)
9. Have you watched MTV on Cable? (no excuses) ____ Yes (3) ____ No (1)
10. Do you eavesdrop on other people's conversations? ____ Yes (3) ____ No (1)
11. You see a poor man on a cold day in rags, unshaven, and with no coat, huddled in a doorway reading *The Wall Street Journal*. Do you feel inclined to make up a story about him? ____ Yes (3) ____ No (1)
12. A young, attractive couple is seated near you in a restaurant. He is talking rapidly and angrily and while he talks you notice that a tear rolls down her cheek.
    Do you ____ continue your conversation with your companion? (1)
    ____ try to figure out what might be happening between them while your companion talks on? (2)
    ____ get up and throw your glass of wine in the man's face? (3)
13. As you wait for the salesman, a middle-aged couple next to you is buying a product from him. They cannot agree. They argue. The woman seems to dominate the conversation.
    Do you ____ look at other items on display? (1)
    ____ make mental note of their decision and agree/disagree with the final choice? (2)
    ____ make up a story about the man and woman? (3)
14. Do you solve tough problems in the shower/shaving/brushing your teeth? ____ Yes (3) ____ No (1)
15. Do you daydream? ____ Yes (3) ____ No (1)
16. Do you have fantasies? ____ Yes (3) ____ (1)
17. Do you like to

Travel	____ Yes (2)	____ No (1)
Explore Ruins	____ Yes (2)	____ No (1)
Climb Mountains	____ Yes (2)	____ No (1)
Cross Country Ski	____ Yes (2)	____ No (1)
Sail	____ Yes (2)	____ No (1)
Birdwatch	____ Yes (2)	____ No (1)
Sailplane	____ Yes (2)	____ No (1)
Kayak or Canoe	____ Yes (2)	____ No (1)
Snorkel	____ Yes (2)	____ No (1)
Scuba	____ Yes (2)	____ No (1)
Hike	____ Yes (2)	____ No (1)
Camp	____ Yes (2)	____ No (1)
or take long walks	____ Yes (2)	____ No (1)

18. Do you like to read? ____ Yes (2) ____ No (1)
19. Do you write poems, stories, or articles (whether or not they've been published or even read by anyone)? ____ Yes (3) ____ No (1)

20. Have you studied anthropology? ___ Yes (3) ___ No (1)
21. Have you studied archaeology? ___ Yes (3) ___ No (1)
22. Have you studied semiotics? ___ Yes (4) ___ No (1)
23. Do you average more than one movie a month? (Don't count TV.) ___ Yes (2) ___ No (1)
24. Do you spend more than three hours a day watching TV? ___ Yes (2) ___ No (1)
25. Can you imagine what it would be like to be nineteen years old. Can you picture the clothes you'd wear, the three things you'd like most to buy, how you would feel about music, food, exercise, politics, money, sex? ___ Yes (3) ___ Sort of (2) ___ Hardly (1)
26. Now, think what it's like to be sixty-five. Imagine the kind of place you live in. The car you own. How do you feel about your health, food, the President, nuclear warfare, retirement, your children? Can you imagine what it's like to lose your hair, get paunchy, be chronically ill? ___ Yes (3) ___ Sort of (2) ___ Hardly (1)

After answering all questions, put each score in the far right-hand column, then add up all figures for a grand total.

Evaluations

If you scored from 110 to 170, you have an imaginative mind that jumps and bounces and peeks and pries and tries almost everything. In short, you are a constant source of entertainment and a joyful companion.

If you scored from 90 to 109, you, too, have a good imaginative mind and a potentially fine friend. Just give it a little more head—let it drift in the current—or maybe take it kite flying in the spring! Or to the Orient!

On the other hand, if your score fell between 75 and 89, your mind needs a diet—preferably one that's filled with light and airy flights of imagination, bubbling daydreams, champagne, lawn parties, yachts in the Aegean, treks through the Himalayas, safaris in darkest Africa. Get cracking!

Under 75? Put down this book. You should be pumping iron!

This self-test is really a reminder of the many ways you can exercise those little gray cells every day. Work them well. Let your curiosity build your reserves—a storehouse—for your imagination. Then if you're ever shipwrecked on a desert island, you'll never be lonely!

ADDENDUM TO CHAPTER 1:
SOME TERMS WE OUGHT TO GO OVER BEFORE YOU DIVE INTO CHAPTER 2

What Is Direct Mail?

It's easy enough to describe direct response magazine and newspaper advertising as well as direct response radio and television ads. You've seen these ads many times and, no doubt, recognize them for what they are with their obvious coupons and toll-free numbers. But direct mail needs clarification.

Coming from the outside with clear vision and perspective, you're liable to think that the term *direct mail* itself is somewhat redundant. After all, what is more direct than a letter from one person to another? Even a piece of mail addressed to "occupant" or "boxholder" goes direct to someone in a particular place. Mail is direct. Can it be *more* direct? If anything, isn't direct mail as *we* know it somewhat *less* direct?

If you have spent most of your business life in direct marketing, this is perfectly acceptable; direct marketers, when questioned on the term, give no valid reasons for it. Homer J. Buckley started it all back in 1902.[2] No one objected to it then and I suspect no one wants to change it at this stage. So for your sake, bear in mind that *mail* is a letter from mother to son, husband to wife, banker to client, doctor to patient, while *direct mail* is a promotion or communication from an institution, company, or business to a group of people—sometimes hundreds of them, or thousands, or even millions!

Direct Mail means postcards, self-mailers, folders, corrugated boxes, jiffy bags, tubes, booklets, envelopes large and small—anything that goes through the mails, mostly in "packages."

A *package* in this business is a term used to refer to an envelope and its contents or components. Components mean *always* a letter, almost always a reply form or card, sometimes a brochure, and often other things like stamps and stamp sheets, postpaid reply envelopes (or business reply envelopes), samples of one sort or another, buck slips (short messages on small papers to emphasize a selling point or a deadline, or to add "news"), and lift letters (short *second* letters or notes that we'll be discussing in Chapter 4. (See Figure 1-1.) A package can also be a self-mailer—a folded piece or folder that combines letter, brochure and order card in one piece without a real envelope. Be wary of self-mailers, however. Because of their economics, they have a strong appeal for many new direct marketers, and hundreds of professionals have tried to make them work, but they are consistently successful *only* for business conferences, seminar announcements, and business books and reports.

Where Do Names Come From?

Where do we get the names to write letters to hundreds, thousands, even millions of people? First know this: names (in all cases) come on *lists* (lists of names). Someone may ask you how many names you are mailing; this is the total count of your mailing—its overall size. If someone asks you, "What lists are you going to use?" he or she wants to know the specific categories or areas from which you are drawing your names—your market. There are magazine lists, catalog lists, good lists, bad lists, unavailable lists—all kinds of lists of names. Here are some you should know:

House Lists (internal, customer names). These are the *best* lists because

---

[2]Nat Ross, "A History of Direct Marketing," *DMA Factbook* (1984).

Figure 1-1

your own customers are always the finest prospects for additional purchases from you. Both business and consumer direct marketers work hard to develop and maintain these customer or house lists.

Rental Lists. These are lists of names that you *rent* for a one-time use (you don't buy them) from the list owner or from a *list broker* (someone who brokers lists, in most cases, for the owners).

Under rental lists there are

1. *Mail order buyer lists.* These are lists of people who respond to direct marketing: catalog customers, magazine subscribers, out-and-out purchasers, inquirers, trial acceptors. Many companies are wary about renting their lists to outsiders. None will rent to competitors and some refuse outright to rent at all. Those who do rent enjoy considerable net income from such rentals.

2. *Compiled lists.* These are lists of like or similar people: lists of doctors, lawyers, dentists, accountants, wealthy people, people belonging to special groups and societies, businesses and services of all kinds (broken out by size, business volume, number of employees, SIC classification), people owning cars, or people living in a defined geographic area. Traditionally, lists of current mail order buyers will generate far more response (nearly twice as much) than compiled lists of unqualified people, or companies with only business titles but no specific names, or householders addressed simply as "occupants". Whatever the quality, however, there can be no direct mail without lists and no lists without names or titles and addresses.

Is All Direct Mail Alike?

Direct mail comes in lots of different colors and sizes. It covers both products and services, and it goes to consumers, business clients, and prospects. Although it always looks for a response, sometimes this is no more than a request for information or approval for a salesman to call—or it may work to create a favorable impression that in the long run will result in a major sale.

Let's summarize the differences here, as they will apply to you in your creative function.

1. Business-to-business communications frequently have a far larger budget than does consumer direct mail.

2. Business mail frequently consists of a series of direct mail letters or an initial mailing with several follow-up mailings (or follow-up calls). Consumer mailings usually try to close a sale or get a commitment in one effort.

3. The primary objective of business promotions is often less to make a sale, more to create good will, interest, or an evidence of interest (a request for more information)—thus gathering qualified prospects for sales calls or further promotion. This makes an individual promotion harder to evaluate.

4. It is far more difficult to pinpoint *and reach* your prime customer or decision maker in business-to-business mail because

– more than one person in a company is often needed to make a major decision (so decision makers at two or three levels of influence must be reached).

– the names you need are frequently not available without costly research and/or list development costs (most business names are merely title-addressed on compiled lists—Purchasing Manager, X Corporation, Y address).

– your promotion will be screened in most businesses by mail rooms and/or secretaries. (When you mail only by title, it is very difficult to get past the screeners who are liable to throw out "unimportant" mail.)

5. Your major appeal to business prospects will differ from the appeal to consumer prospects as a business prospect is being asked to make a decision that is not directly personal; it will not benefit him or her personally. A consumer, on the other hand, is buying or considering something for herself or the family.

Now these are significant differences, but the similarities will far outweigh the differences for you as a creative person.

I *stress* this here, because much has been done to separate business and consumer. Trade groups or business groups in direct marketing divide themselves into business groups versus consumer groups; they say they are *one or the other*, but you should not do that. As a creative person, *you can be both*.

Once you understand the differences, you must remember that businessmen are also consumers—and they are human beings. You write and create direct mail for human beings—not business versus consumer categories. Don't let anyone label—or limit—you here. Ultimately, of course, you may gain more experience in one area than the other, but why not go for both, for now?

The same important rules, formulas, and guidelines apply to businesses and consumers. The research requirements are no different; creative concept methodologies (Chapter 5) work roughly the same for one market as for the other. Your writing guidelines in Chapters 6 and 7 apply to both.

Anyone who argues with this is unconsciously (or consciously) saying that a good creative person doesn't know the difference between a highly promotional consumer package and a business letter to a big industrial client. I think you do; or will after reading this book.

Products and Services—The Same?

While we're on this subject, I'd also like to put to rest some major reservations on products and services (and fund raising, while we're at it). Over the course of a long career in direct marketing, people have asked me if I was a "financial services" specialist or if I knew how to do insurance or fund raising.

Many financial and insurance mailings circulating these days could use an infusion of creative people with a fresh approach.

Granted, there are some definite legal no-no's and specific lingo or terminology that you'll have to digest in each area. But as long as you do your homework (which includes studying the competition), this shouldn't hold you back. As for fund raising, some of the top product professionals in our business slide easily into all sorts of successful fund-raising letters without a thought.

You may encounter many noncreative types along the way who like to surround their areas of direct marketing with an aura of mystery, but don't let them discourage you or deter you from a worthwhile experience. If you're good at products, you'll be good at services—and at fund raising. And vice versa.

chapter 2

Your Indispensables

If you are just starting, there is a lot to learn about direct marketing in general and there are general books that can take you there, from *A* to *Z*.[1]

You can't know too much about its workings—the role of the computer, the importance of fulfillment, distribution channels, pricing strategies, how the numbers work, the ratios and equations, model building, product selection, multivariate and regression analysis, ROI. All these things are important, but if need be, you can live without them and still do good work as a creative participant.

There are some things you can't live without, however—certain aspects of direct marketing that you *must* understand if you plan to arrive at a point where you plot your own creative course and make your own creative determinations.

Contrary to some expectations, your work as a creative direct response person starts long before you develop a copy platform, put one word on paper, or plan a mailing format. It will have to, unless you are willing to blindly accept the input of others, unquestioningly adopt their thinking, and follow their directions without any convictions or opinions of your own. Yuk!

Some copywriters in our business *are* willing to work this way. The assignment is plopped down before them, while (I assume) they accept what greater minds than theirs have decided. It's not for them to question. Well, so much for them. *You* won't accept that sort of dead-end mediocrity for a minute, and that is why you're going to want the tools that make sure you are in control from the start.

"The start" means that you'll need the abilities to understand and evaluate the basic marketing premises that are set down prior to every assignment you undertake. Otherwise, you're at the mercy of the marketers, and so is your reputation. Although you don't really need to follow probability charts or handle long-range planning, here are the essentials that you truly cannot live without if you want to be confident and succeed in direct response advertising.

---

[1]Martin Baier, *Elements of Direct Marketing*, (New York: McGraw-Hill, Inc., 1983).

Bob Stone, *Successful Direct Marketing Methods* (Lincolnwood, Illinois: Crain Books, an imprint of National Textbook Company, 1984).

Edward L. Nash, *Direct Marketing Strategy, Planning, Execution* (New York: McGraw-Hill, Inc., 1982).

THE BIG PICTURE—ARE YOU GETTING IT? ARE "THEY" SENDING IT?

Most of your assignments won't drop out of the blue; they won't be lonely, one-shot efforts to sell something or to get an inquiry. There is, or should be, solid reasoning behind every assignment. Something has gone before (except in the case of a new product introduction); something will follow.

If you don't know from the start, you have every right to ask where your assignment lies in the big picture, and most good marketing people will be happy to tell you. Whether they are happy or not, you'll do well to come prepared with questions of your own, just to make sure. (It also shows "them" you're not one of those cubicle dullards.)

Basic research aside (we'll come to that in a moment) you need to understand how the marketers see the overall promotion and its effects, how they set their objectives.

- Why do they feel direct marketing is appropriate for the product or service?
- Why has one specific medium been chosen over another (say, direct mail instead of print)?
- Is this part of a campaign, or one in a series of promotions?
- Does it make sense to pre-announce the promotion? To follow it up with additional promotions?
- Have they considered a media mix?
- Have they made reasonable commitment with a realistic budget? (This question's a doozy. No one seems to work with abundant funds these days, but some allocations are ridiculous. You'll learn to sort these out as you go along, with a little production experience.)
- Are their expectations reasonable? (This is not one for you to ask them, but to answer for yourself. It takes some experience to do this well, but you'll have solid evaluation guidelines to start you off in just a few pages.)

THE UNDERLYING LAW OF CREATIVITY

Now that you have a big picture, let's deal with the function and purpose of direct marketing as a whole. "That's simple," you may be thinking, and to some extent, you're right. But some things are so basic, so simple, so close to us that we actually run the risk of losing sight of them as we adjust our vision to more complicated aspects of the marketing process on the horizon—a reverse forest and trees situation. This happens every day with experienced marketers, and they pass it right on to the creative people.

To make sure it doesn't get passed on to you, you need the *Underlying Law of Creativity* for direct marketers. Follow me through it, digest it, make it part of your basic equipment. It will help you achieve your first step toward success.

If you don't carry it around somewhere in the back of your head, you'll be starting out on an important creative journey with a flat spare tire. Sooner or later, maybe not this week or next, it will catch up with you.

This law has five premises. The *first premise* deals with the basic function of direct marketing itself.

As direct marketers we're not here primarily to make a sale; we're here to get a customer.

Sales are important, of course. (Where would marketers be without them?) But the name of this game is *repeat* sales rather than one-shots. And to have that, you need a customer.

Some marketers today use a form of advertising that I call "response" advertising. It goes directly to customers who answer their promotions via coupons and telephone. But these marketers are *not* recording customer names and establishing a database, therefore, this is sampling—or coupon redemption or sales promotion. It is *not* direct marketing.

To capture yourself a customer (or prospect) you have to capture customer data in the computer so that you can build a relationship based on a growing knowledge of the customer and his or her habits. Once you have this, you're ready for the *second premise.*

We set up a positive dialogue with our customers via direct response techniques. Through this dialogue we constantly test and measure to determine what "pleases" or appeals to the customer. The customer is always right.

Smart direct marketers understand that they are dialogue marketers. Establishing a dialogue is, in fact, the name of the game, whether it is by mail or by phone.

Let me give you a sample of dialogue and see if you can hear it.

"Dear Reader: Here is an exciting new product. Act now and you can receive it..." "Yes. Send me...and charge it to my VISA card..." "Thank you for your order. Enclosed is a special offer for new customers and our new fall catalog..." "I want to exchange the green skirt, size ten for a size twelve..." "We have a green plaid blouse that matches your skirt on a private customer sale right now..."

And so it goes—on and on.

What could be more sensible once you have a number of customers by name and address, than to test and measure their likes and dislikes? If you want to keep your customers buying, ask them what they want.

You learned in Chapter 1 that this is a profession in which you will be tested (because your work can be measured). It is important to point out here that you will also be testing. While the direct marketers test media and markets and product, you will be expected to participate with constant creative testing. You'll be expected to test entire ads or promotions, copy concepts or approaches, creative devices, format changes, premiums or other offer variations, and graphics. Your job is to discover the strongest appeals, the most compelling presentations, the most involving formats through testing, or talking to the customers and prospects.

The wisdom of direct marketers is gained from customers. Listen to customers and they will tell you, as long as marketers test carefully and scientifically. (Which means in two brief sentences: Test only one thing at a time. Test in quantities or numbers of customers that are statistically valid and can therefore be projected.)

Your customers will even tell you when they've had enough or when a product needs changing. And certainly, they will tell you when they are unhappy or disillusioned. In this sense, your customer *is* always right—and, of course, what's best for your customer is ultimately best for you.

In the *third premise* the customer is always right in the old-fashioned sense.

Customer Service is an important aspect of our business. Properly treated, the customer will continue to tell us reliably not only what to sell, but when to sell, how much to sell, the best offer to use.

All marketers know this—don't they? Certainly they should. But no one is equipped to demonstrate it better and more precisely than direct marketers because direct marketers are the first to develop *and* utilize customer records (the database) to establish a productive customer dialogue or an ongoing, repeat purchase history. Frankly, we know (or should know) so much about our good customers that we can put the average retail sales clerk to shame!

In addition to this history, a well-run operation will record when an order was received, when it was shipped, how it was shipped, when and how it was billed and paid for. This is known as *fulfillment*—the complete operation of order processing—and it includes customer service. If order processing, or fulfillment, does its job, customer inquiries and complaints can be kept to a minimum and handled promptly and positively when they occur. (If it doesn't do its job, a good customer turns off, not just to one direct marketer, but often to direct marketing as a whole.)

By the way, not every marketer *does* put the customer first. Sadly, some very big manufacturing companies have come to direct marketing with a "quota-driven" approach, rather than "customer-driven" marketing: "We have to sell 100,000 of these widgets by spring. Find more customers. Roll out the advertising, cut the prices!" instead of "Find out how the customer will react to the new widget. What can he or she tell us about pricing preferences, increasing sales volume?" And so we have the *fourth premise.*

When we listen to the customer first, we can make money with considerable confidence. Our computers can take customer information and tell us not only where we are but also where we can logically expect to be over the years ahead.

You'll discover that every kind of direct marketing (magazine subscriptions, book clubs, continuity programs, catalogs, third-party mailings) not only has extensive testing programs all along the line, but also has established formulas based on consistent behavior of specific customer groups. The marketers develop entire computer models on these formulas and use them to draw up their long-range marketing plans.

Each magazine, book club, or catalog modifies or adapts the formulas to its own customer group, of course, and no two are exactly alike. Such formulas (or computer models) are not critical to your creative well-being, but if your R.Q. (Renaissance Quotient, remember?) is high, ask your marketing people about them.

Here is the *last premise*—and it *is* critical to your creative development. You probably gathered by now that the customer is pretty sacred in this business—or should be. Well, this is the place where *you* take an active role in developing and preserving this important relationship.

Nothing must destroy our credibility with the customer. The customer takes us very seriously. The customer listens to us. The customer remembers.

Sounds a little corny, doesn't it? Well, so does "A penny saved, a penny earned," "The best things in life are free," "Too soon old; too late smart!" These are all old-fashioned adages—truisms. They live on.

In direct marketing this premise should be the creative truism. For every time we forget it or ignore it, we suffer.

You, as a creative person, get the last cut on holding fast to this premise. It may not happen *every* time or all the time, but many managers and marketers, in their enthusiasm to structure a plan, forget about the very people who made all that planning possible. Their objectives, goals, and quotas take over and they lapse a little or get sloppy in terms of customer credibility. ("Who's going to remember that this is our *sixth* Final Sale this year?")

The Underlying Law of Creativity comes in here. It was established to help you help all those managers and marketers, and in the final analysis, to help you help yourself sort out the real story from all the hyperbole.

The Underlying Law of Creativity
(for All Aspiring Creative Types in Direct Response Advertising)

Whatever you say, however you say it, however you present it, first ask, "Does this make sense to the customer?"

You'll have plenty of opportunities to apply this law at several important stages as you move along through your creative development in the pages of this book. Neglect it, and you won't be protected from out-and-out failures. Use it and you'll be safe.

"Of course things have to make sense," you may be thinking. "Let's get off this track and get on with it." Not so! Not yet! Too many of us have gotten short-sighted on this point today. The industry needs more questioners and *you* should be among them. If you aren't, you might end up trying desperately to sell something to customers, realizing that you aren't making sense or that you aren't being honest. You may be faced with some unsolvable creative problems (including writer's block).

Today our customer base is growing and evolving right along with direct marketing. Customers now buy jewelry, expensive collectibles, boots, cosmetics, fine clothing, and furs through direct marketing. They are better educated and more sophisticated than customers of twenty years ago. They have more money to spend; they are more demanding.

You have to be pretty good to sell them, so protect yourself. Make sure before you even begin that you won't be forced to shake their credibility or try something on them that *you* don't believe in yourself. For example:

- Don't run the big sale into the ground (same goes for "Last Chance") or you'll end up like the boy who cried "Wolf!"
- Don't shout "Hurry" when a magazine subscription still has six months to go. (There *are* other things you can say to motivate your subscriber.)
- Don't tell a customer how important he or she is to you when your computer can't even tell the customer's sex. (Dear B. Fish, Esteemed H. Rock.)
- Don't claim "This invitation is not for everyone," when the "Official Invitation No. 1,318,149,975" is printed on the reply card.
- Don't promise something on your outer envelope or in a headline that you can't substantiate in the body copy. (Customers get mad, and so would you.)
- Don't try to hype a weak offer with deceptive phrases and weasel words.

These are all clear-cut no-no's—at least they should be. Here are two situations that illustrate the point in action. (Further subtleties in applying the Underlying Law will come in succeeding chapters.)

Example 1: A nationally known record club had a joining offer of some thirteen records free with a member commitment to purchase eight additional records over the following years. Ostensibly, members who fulfilled their commitment were free to leave the club any time thereafter.

This club was highly sophisticated in direct marketing techniques. Its people were (and still are) considered some of our industry's finest. It is likely that these marketers found that most or many of their members failed to purchase often (or at all) once the commitment was fulfilled.

To deal with this problem, the marketers decided it would be smart to get members who had fulfilled their commitment to recommit. How did they do it? They offered these members thirteen more free records if they would recommit for eight more purchases over the next three years.

All of this is fine. And if this is how it happened, it is logical enough, up to this point. However, not knowing how to put it to the members, someone suggested simply sending them the initial joining offer again. Now they couldn't do that while the member was still a member, obviously, so they simply wrote and asked the member to quit!

A headline read:

You are invited to cancel your membership—and then receive 13 albums FREE!

The letter began:

Dear Preferred Member:

Remember way back when you first decided to join the Club? What prompted you to do so? Undoubtedly it was the lure of getting a sizable number of albums all at once, at practically no cost!...

Well, how would you like to relive that exciting moment once again?...

If you tell us to, we'll cancel your present membership and then send you 13 albums of your own choice...Nothing for you to pay...

In exchange...you simply re-enroll in the Club and agree to buy 8 selections, at regular club prices, in the coming three years.

A close friend, not a direct marketer, had been a perfectly happy member of this record club. He'd finished his commitment and continued to buy now and then. When he received the promotion suggesting that he quit and rejoin, he thought the club had lost its mind. He was both confused and angry, certain he was being taken. He did not respond to the offer and has since stopped buying completely from the club.

The above-mentioned promotion is an example of smart marketers dealing intelligently with real problems, but they were dealing so intently with solving the problem that no one—right down to the copywriter—ever stepped back and asked, "Will this make sense to the customer?"

Example 2: This second example comes from a major American automobile manufacturer who mailed sophisticated, computerized letters to prime prospects for a new sports car.

The four-color brochure was exciting and the letter was a complimentary invitation to test drive the new car, but *nowhere* in the entire mailing was a phone number or address given! If you didn't know the address of a local dealer, you had to look it up. And that, somehow, didn't make sense after you had just received a *personal* invitation from the general marketing manager himself. A toll-free telephone number to call "headquarters" for the nearest dealer would have paid off in many more test drivers!

Just as some direct response advertising can fail to make sense in part—or totally—to customers and prospects, so other advertising seems to go out of its way to be both reasonable and logical.

The double-postcard magazine subscription solicitation is a particularly fine example of this.

These double-postcard mailings (used initially by Ziff-Davis Publications and *Newsweek)* make sense to both the prospect *and* the publication.

For the publication, they are economical to mail. For the prospect, they state simply (to paraphrase the offer), "You are busy. Why waste your time. Here's a good offer to a publication you know. Tell us if you're interested at this time."

This works (1) when the publication is a nationally known magazine, the assumption being that if it is necessary to explain the publication to the recipient, he or she cannot possibly be a good prospect (if you don't know what *Newsweek* is now, you're just not meant for *Newsweek);* or (2) when the magazine is a special-interest publication that is repeatedly promoted to a core group of individuals who are prime prospects because of their known interests. Here, again, if any of these prospects doesn't recognize the publication immediately, it's doubtful that he or she is a real prospect.

Figure 2-1 is a good example from *Inc.* magazine (a magazine for small

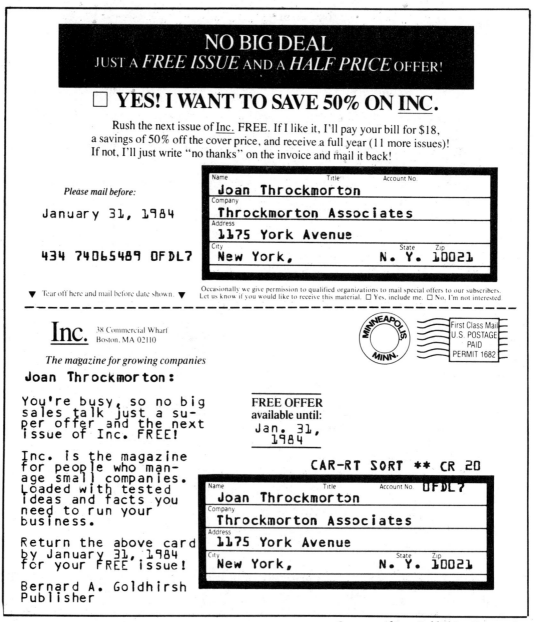

Figure 2-1

Courtesy of Inc. Publishing Corporation
Used by permission

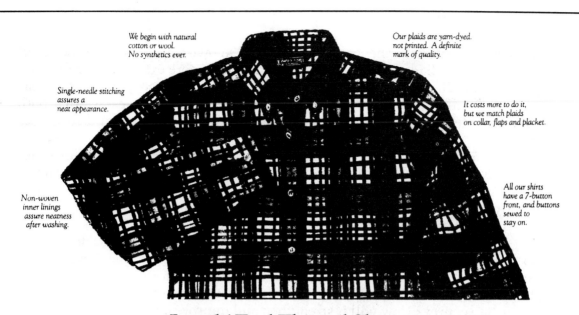

We begin with natural cotton or wool. No synthetics ever.

Our plaids are yarn-dyed, not printed. A definite mark of quality.

Single-needle stitching assures a neat appearance.

It costs more to do it, but we match plaids on collar, flaps and placket.

Non-woven inner linings assure neatness after washing.

All our shirts have a 7-button front, and buttons sewed to stay on.

Lands' End Flannel Shirts.
Easy to look at. Comfortable to wear.
Made with painstaking care.

We invite you to compare the features above, which are standard equipment on any Lands' End flannel shirt, with any other flannel shirt you like.

We don't think you can beat them, even for more money. We offer them in a heavy weight 100% cotton and, happily, for both men and women. You'll find them proudly displayed in full color in our Lands' End catalog.

No single breakthrough.
Frankly, the features above, which we insist on in our shirts, are not notable breakthroughs taken singly and separately. But finding all these features in a flannel shirt at Lands' End prices—that is exceptional.

It comes from a philosophy we apply to whatever we offer you at the time we either buy it or have it made. We don't ask,

"What can you leave out to make it cheaper?" We ask, "What can you put in to make it better?" You'd be surprised how unusual this attitude is, and how pleased our sources are to show us the full range of their talents.

Our buyers aren't the only fussy people.
Fussy as our Lands' End buyers are, even they get checked out by our Quality Control people, who have the last word at Lands' End.

If they nix a buy—in shirts or anything else we sell—there's no Supreme Court to grant a hearing. They *are* the Supreme

Court. And that's for your protection, along with our no-fine print guarantee:
GUARANTEED. PERIOD.
The price, of course, is determined only after we're sure we have the quality we want in the product. That way we are sure we offer you value.

Leaf through our catalog for full details. Fill in the coupon, send it in, and we'll mail you a free catalog. Better still, call us at 800-356-4444. It's toll free, 24 hours a day.

LANDS' END
DIRECT MERCHANTS
of fine wool and cotton sweaters, Oxford buttondown shirts, traditional dress clothing, snow wear, deck wear, original Lands' End soft luggage and a multitude of other quality goods from around the world.

Figure 2-2

business executives). The card was sent to known top executives of small companies who had already received several other, more extensive and detailed promotions. The opportunity to take advantage of a good joining offer was presented without editorial detail, but with a very succinct message that both complimented the prospect and allied the prospect with *Inc.* and its prime market.

The ad in Figure 2-2 from Lands' End Direct Merchants, a mail order company, is another beautiful example of making sense to the customer. The ad is low-key, but crystal clear and credible in telling the customer or prospect exactly everything he or she needs (and wants) to know about cotton flannel shirts and, most important, the company that makes them.

Both Lands' End and *Inc.* are demonstrating a creative approach that was formulated by asking "Will this make sense to our prospect? What have we said before? What questions or problems can we put to rest for our customers with this mailing or ad? Are we being consistent? Is this in keeping with the image we wish to convey? How will it strengthen and improve our image in the eyes of our good customers and prospects?" In short, does this make sense to the customer?

Now—on to your next essential!

RESEARCH—A BASIC INGREDIENT
IN LAYING THE GROUNDWORK FOR SUCCESS

One of the nice things about advertising is that it allows you to get intimately involved with all kinds of products and services. Creative people constantly change hats, selling beer to furs to spaghetti sauce to automobiles. That's why many advertising creative types have a strong Renaissance Quotient. They enjoy constantly learning about new products and markets. It's exciting and hardly deserves to be called *research*, yet that's exactly what it is.

It can offer you some opportunities for marketing insights that no other form of advertising can offer. And because of this, as important as research is in general advertising, it becomes far more important to creative people in direct response advertising. Here's how.

Test Research—Your Secret Weapon

You are in a measurable form of advertising now, so if your product or service isn't absolutely new to its market, you can look forward to some very exciting insights, by test research.

Any marketer worth his or her salt in direct response advertising keeps extensive and clear records of testing history. And this testing history can provide you with a lot of help, if you enjoy being a bit of a detective. For example:

Media: If you have media testing history available to you, see if you can get an accurate picture of the *list* history. (These are lists of names from different sources—mail order buyers, magazine subscribers, association members, professionals—that are rented, not sold, for a one-time use in a mailing.) Ask what lists of names are rented regularly because they consistently respond or "pull" well for the particular product or service. This can tell you a lot about the present prospect market.

If the following lists did exceptionally well for your product— subscribers to *Esquire, GQ, American Health, Runner,* and *Executive Fitness Newsletter,* plus Brooks Brothers catalog buyers—you might assume that you have an affluent, young to middle-aged male executive market, conservative business types with a strong interest in health and fitness. Clear enough.

Also, see if you can study list test responses over the past year for lists of names that *failed* to respond well. If *Field & Stream, Car and Driver,* and *Rod & Gun* subscribers all failed in the above grouping, your males are probably upper middle class, conservative, and affluent, with little interest in the workings of fast cars or in hunting and fishing. It gives you a familiar feeling about the market you'll be talking to, doesn't it? (Of course, all this testing history should jibe with the product's market as it is described to you by the marketers.)

List test history can also indicate possible shifts in the market or changes in the product perception as new lists become productive and old lists fall away into marginal profitability.

Space ads in magazines can be an indicator as well. Taking the affluent male market blocked out above, you can easily pick the three to four best magazines for your ads right now. This also works in reverse. If the magazines work well for you, so will their subscriber lists, *and so may other lists that work for each magazine in its own subscriber prospecting* (if you can find out what they are).

Offer: Another valuable piece of research for you will be the offer test history. Price, of course, is a part of offer. But good offers also take into consideration premiums, involvement devices (like tokens or stamps), guarantees, and trials. Some markets respond better to one offer than another, while certain products require certain offers to remain competitive. See what's worked well in the past and what hasn't had much success. It can give you a good idea of what offers to recommend and what to avoid. And ways to make your current offer even stronger. (For example: Your market may be a greedy bunch that needs a lot of premiums—or they may respond to razzmatazz and color—or they may have a passion for tokens and other involvement devices—or they may hate free books.)

Format: Format is still another possible history that may be available. Is a brochure important in direct mail? Does it pay to include extra flyers or promotional materials? Is an order card important or will a simple *800* number do better? Must you always use a jumbo envelope? What has happened up to now? You'll want to check it out if you can.

The control: One of the most important areas of your test history will be a study of what direct marketers call the *control.* This is the direct mail promotion (or ad or TV commercial) that out-pulled all the others. As good direct marketers are constantly testing against their control to develop still stronger controls (or replacements when the old control begins to slip), you have every right to ask about a *control history* as part of your initial research. (After all, if great minds all think along the same lines, you just might reinvent the last control without realizing it!)

Ideally, this history should give you a nice little pile of direct mail promotions (or ads, or packages, or whatever), along with data sheets showing when each promotion was control, for how long, which one beat what, controls that were later retested (and, possibly, reinstated), controls that were hard to beat, and so on.

It's also important here that you're able to examine losers in the control history, as they, too, have a story for you. (The only thing worse than reinventing a wheel is reinventing a square wheel.) In some cases, it may be easy to see why a mailing was a loser. In other cases, not so easy. Try to figure out why one failed where another succeeded. It may tell you something useful about the market and your product or service, and it can surely give you ideas on what to do *or not to do* with your own promotion.

I was recently lucky enough to be able to study over five years of winning and losing mailings from a new client. The results were unexpected but consistent and forced me to reverse my entire creative attitude regarding the market. This kept me from repeating the mistakes of the past.

Direct marketers are also likely to have testing results on such things as seasonality (best time of year for promoting the product), the use of four-color versus two-color for their products or services, and so on. You must ask for this information in many cases. Not everyone gives much importance to test results, unfortunately.

Altogether, *good* testing history can be an invaluable guide. "Good" testing history, by the way, assumes that the testers have taken into consideration such things as backend performance as it relates to joining offers and return on investment (ROI).

This means that the marketers measure the *quality* (as well as the *quantity)* of the prospects or new customers brought in by one test versus another—their ability to continue to purchase or renew the relationship. Anyone can design a sleazy offer that hypes upfront response by giving away the store. Such offers attract a large proportion of freeloading deadbeats. (This, of course, dilutes response and makes it a costly way to prospect.)

Overcoming Test Research Resistance

Here's a word of caution that may be helpful to you in all this information gathering: if you're an outsider—working for an advertising agency or as an independent freelancer—don't be surprised if the client feels wary (if not downright hostile) about sharing test information with you.

Direct marketers are notoriously cagey and devious when talking about their own results. After all, the best direct marketers put a fortune into testing and learning and applying what they learn. It's a major corporate investment—and a most valuable asset. Why should they risk sharing their breakthroughs and discoveries with competitors?

Today, there is more openness and industry wide cooperation among companies than there has ever been before (this means more sophistication and more general sharing), but does this mean talking numbers from current test results or the present seasonal response to a big promotion? You'd better believe it doesn't. Openness or no openness, direct marketers are pretty smart about knowing when to share and when to pass on passing it along.

So if you're not on the payroll, you may encounter some resistance to divulging test results. You may be told, "You don't need to know that." or, "That's not important to you." or, "No one's ever asked for that before." Don't let them put you down! It is important and you do need to know it—if you're going to do professional work.

If they don't have the information you want, you should make it clear that having no testing history to refer to also puts you at a disadvantage. (Protect yourself.) Now, if they do have it, but won't divulge it, here's one way of enlisting cooperation. Rather than ask for actual response, have them index for you. For example, say you have an eight-part test:

A – Control Package

B – Control Package with Premium

C – Control Package with Special Brochure

D – Control Package with Free Trial

E – New Creative Package 1—Control Offer

F – New Creative Package 1—Premium Offer

G – New Creative Package 2—Control Offer

Take 100 as the score for the control; everything else is in relation, doing either better or worse by degree. In the list below, for example, although E, a new creative package, barely beat the control, it moved ahead considerably when the premium was added. G, meanwhile, did poorly against the control. And both the special brochure and free trial offer failed to raise response to the control sufficiently to justify a change.

F – 105

B – 103

E – 101

Control A – 100

D – 99

C – 94

G – 90

You may have to give a little and sacrifice pure accuracy for such rankings. Do it anyway. It will still serve your purpose—and it will show that you're working in good faith, on the same team.

Product Research

It's impossible for you to be too familiar with the product or service. After all, *you're not creating awareness advertising here. You are the salesperson.*

When promoting subscriptions by direct mail, top direct response writers read *at least* one to two years' worth of the magazine; when selling products, many writers will go out and buy or borrow the product, use it or sample it, try it out on family and friends, and visit the manufacturer. *All* of them also read up on and study the competition.

You'll want to know how the marketers perceive a product or service, too— how they position it. Ask questions and listen.

Try to determine why the company is particularly qualified to make or offer this product or service. (You may find ideas here for a story that helps establish credibility.) Ask for a history of the product or service, how and why it came about. (More ideas.)

How do the various principals (owner/founder/editor) describe their product and its benefits? Do they agree with the marketers? How do they perceive the competition?

Don't trust yourself entirely to the marketers when you're doing product research. Some of your most valuable input may come from others (designer/inventor/builder), and from your own relationship to the product or service itself.

THE MARKET

You will want to know as much as possible about the people to whom you'll be "talking," and you have a good start once you've reviewed a media history. You will also want a clear definition of the primary (and secondary) market profile from the marketers. (If anyone fudges on this, consider it a dangerous sign.)

Nat Ross, one of the great teachers and founders of the educational movement in direct marketing, says "Our culture changes every hour. Our biology has remained the same for millions of years." This means you'll need full demographics, geographics, *and* psychographics as well, where they are available. Your marketing people must have a precise knowledge of the market, based largely on an analysis of those customers already on the books (or in the database), and they should willingly share this with you.

In business-to-business direct response advertising, rather than get into demographics and psychographics, you'll want to pinpoint the decision maker or makers. This is very important when it is likely that more than one person is involved in making the buying decision. (In a family where a decision requires more than one person, your selling proposition won't change as long as all members of the family are included in the market profile.) In big business purchases there may be different areas or levels of interest, requiring totally different advertising approaches.

For example; your sales message to the president of a company or the head of a division would not be the same message you'd send to the engineer who might actually use your product—or to the purchasing agent who might approve the equipment purchase. Each of these groups has different interests and different responsibilities. Sometimes you'll have to go out to *all* three before you get an inside line.

As you'll see later on, there's no way you can proceed without a clear customer picture (whether it's pinpointing your decision makers in the corporate structure or defining your market's lifestyles). As a matter of fact, without a good market definition, there's no way *anyone* will proceed in this customer-driven form of marketing.

Another Secret Weapon

In a form of marketing where customers call the shots, it's one thing to know who this customer is and still another to understand how this customer (or customer prospect) *already* perceives the product or service, or the company that is offering it.

Here, if you can get it, is your most valuable research in developing a strong, convincing dialogue with the customer or prospect. It's not always available, of course, but there are three places to look for it. Try. You may discover a pot of gold (or a pot of problems).

1. *Customer Correspondence:* As we discussed before, direct marketers aim at developing a dialogue with customers and prospects. See if you can cut in and listen on the line. Chances are, you'll pick up new impressions of the customer and how he or she perceives the product and/or the company.

Every direct marketer who deals with the public has some sort of fulfillment and customer service area where customer inquiries, complaints, and requests (that are not simple orders) are handled. Borrow as many of these different kinds of correspondence as you can get your hands on. Read it all. It may give you some valuable insights. It will certainly do so *if there are problems that you should know about.*

For example: Several years ago a large Midwestern mail order company was having an unusual problem with bad pay and customer cancellations on a certain product line. Before repromoting the line, the company then decided to do some customer research by reviewing cancellations on the product. An extensive study of customer correspondence (where literally hundreds of letters were read) indicated cancellations and failures to pay were based largely on a broad misconception regarding the product line and its performance.

This was not evident at first. Few, if any, customers came right out and stated the problem. Only after listening to the tone, the words and the phrases used to justify the cancellation action, did a pattern or direction emerge. It was there, nonetheless, and happily, it offered a clear, creative solution. The product was repositioned and its benefits in the joining offer were clarified.

2. *Focus Groups:* These are scientifically planned groups of ten or twelve, led by a professional interviewer (who follows an outline). The members are all prime prospects or users of a specific product or service. The participants speak out candidly. The leader keeps things going and on track.

Good marketers are wary of overinterpreting focus groups, because they know that a small, intimate number of individuals interacting with each other cannot give a good reading on quantitative product appeal (or how many people will or will not buy the product or service). It does give marketers a pretty good picture of how their prime prospects might respond to the quality (features and benefits) of the product or service as a whole.

For you, it should be a gold mine of ideas. Smart creative people jump at an opportunity to observe (unseen behind a one-way window) a focus group in action—or as a second choice, to listen to a tape recording of the focus group conversation.

If you have never heard a focus group at work, you have every reason to ask, "Why so important?" The answer is simply, "The dialogue! The ideas! These people can write your copy!" (They can also show you dangerous areas or weak places in the product or service where your copy will have to work hard to make its points.) Sure, there's a lot of useless talk, but when the participants get turned on they'll say things you might never think of—and in an ingenuous style that you might never develop all alone.

It's not unusual for a smart copywriter to pick up several big headlines, copy leads—entire creative approaches—just from listening to a good focus group.

Be sure to ask about focus groups when you start your research. Your timing may be good and you may be in luck!

3. *The Telephone:* Professional direct marketers know that there is no mystery in direct response advertising. There is a reason for everything. But sometimes explanations are hard to come by.

For example: In a regular customer mailing, say many customers fail to respond. The mailing is so far below its expected or budgeted return that it looks suspicious. After checking to make sure all mail was delivered, a smart marketer may turn to the telephone and ask customers if they received the promotion and why they failed to place their regular orders. Only a dozen or so of these calls can yield valuable information.

If you come up against a situation where basic research is scanty, if there seems to be a customer problem, if the marketers are not convincing (or convinced), you can suggest that they first consider taking the proposition to a customer sample by phone—a sort of quick-and-dirty way to determine whether your promotion will have a chance to make it at all in the big lonely world.

You'll find this particularly helpful when you're asked to resurrect, or reactivate, a dormant customer group with a new promotion. They may be gone, moved away, apathetic; they may even hate the company. If there's doubt, and you're uneasy, often all it takes is fifteen to twenty customer calls to get a reading.

At this point you have every right to wonder how you got bogged down with all this research business. You were promised creativity—and all I've done is pile on caveats about data gathering.

But I also promised you no failures, right? O.K. You're about to apply your first test to assure success. And you can't do it without research, the big picture and the Underlying Law.

YOUR EARLY PAYOFF—MAKING IT ALL WORTHWHILE

If you've ever wondered why top creative people always end up good, better, or best *but never worst*, here's your answer: they know when (and how) to bow out or say "No thank you" (or tactfully suggest a little remarketing).

There's a primary rule for creative stars and other winners that says "Take no dogs." If the product or service concept is elusive, if the market is hazy, if benefits aren't clear and credible, if you can't get all the information you need— no amount of fine writing will help. Make this your rule, too. Why should your name be leashed to a preordained "dog?"

How can you be *sure* it is a dog—and how do you explain this to others without making enemies or losing your job? It's one thing to say "No" as a free-lancer, quite another to do it as an employee or an agency. The free-lancer is able to take the easy way out. (He or she can say there's a conflict or no time left in the schedule.)

You, on the other hand may have to explain your reservations clearly and constructively to a boss who is expecting the work to be done, or to a team that's raring to move ahead.

To do this effectively, it's good business if you can demonstrate your concerns by testing out the proposition. Once you know how to do this little exercise, you'll know when your assignment is sound or when it's time to blow the dog whistle. You'll also know how to explain it all impartially and positively.

TESTING YOUR SELLING PROPOSITION

Before you even accept the fact that a creative piece of direct response advertising is required, or desirable, you have to be comfortable with the basic selling proposition; you have to be sure it's sound. Here's how you do this:

- *First,* how is the product or service described and how is it positioned in the market?

- *Second,* what is the offer? What is the objective of the offer? More than one objective?

- *Third,* what is the market definition?

- *Fourth,* is this a single promotion or part of a "big picture?"
  – How does it fit in the marketing plan?
  – Has the plan been thought through, covering all bases? (Ask what happens if the prospect does this? What if he or she does that? Then what?)

- *Fifth,* apply the Underlying Law of Creativity.
  – Does this product or service sound reasonable?
  – Why is the product targeted to this market?
  – Will this product make sense to this customer market?
  – What is the competition's proposition?
  – What are your product's advantages?
  – Is the offer solid?
  – Will you feel comfortable offering this to the defined market?
  – Is there another market?

Here are some examples that show you how this works. (Try to decide each one for yourself before looking at the analysis; it's good practice!)

1. *Example:* Your product is a book club on home care, maintenance, and improvement. It offers two new selections every month, plus dozens of bonus or special books. The books are hard to find, as few book stores offer such a wide variety of home improvement publications. The club can be positioned as an exclusive service for those who are interested in home improvement. The joining offer is three books for a dollar, with no membership commitment. The initial market is 500,000 subscribers to a home improvement magazine.

Analysis: On all counts, the book club sounds like a reasonable project. It has a clearly defined market; it is a unique club aimed at that market; it is going out with a popular (and proven) book club offer.

2. *Example:* You're asked to help a new magazine that will be the first magazine ever to focus on work. It will deal with unusual jobs that people do, new job opportunity areas, examples of successful workers from all kinds of jobs, and so on. The subscription offer is one year for fifteen dollars. The initial market is entrepreneurs, professionals, graduating college students, American Express cardholders.

Analysis: You study the product and find that the magazine concept is poor. "Work" is much too large and amorphous a topic for a magazine. Because it means something different to everyone, it won't make sense to anyone. As a result, there is no targeted or efficient way to reach its market and no real market to target. The entire concept should be reworked.

3. *Example:* Your assignment is to offer several luxury liner cruises to the customer list of a large travel agent. The cruises last sixty days and thirty days. They are the finest luxury cruises offered. The prices are competitive but on the

high side. The promotion's job is to generate inquiries for the agent. It will mail to customer lists of which 50 percent are over age fifty-five.

Analysis: You agree that the idea is a good one, but over 50 percent of the agent's customers are *under* fifty-five years of age. A sixty-day cruise (or even a thirty-day cruise) is something few executives and few families (with one or two working members) could afford in terms of time.

You recommend cutting the list in half, using only those over fifty-five who may be affluent *and* retired because they show an active travel history. You also suggest mailing to outside lists with older, affluent demographics.

4. *Example:* A famous sports supplies company with a reputation for good quality at high prices asks you to design a mailing for 200,000 catalog customers.

It has been losing a considerable amount of customer business in its shoe and boot division over the last year because its products (although of the finest quality) are priced considerably higher than the competition.

The company wants you to announce a permanent 33 ⅓ percent price *decrease* to its customers on almost all the major shoe lines. They see this as a big new promotion.

Analysis: At first it sounds like a good idea, but then you shake your head and decline. Although they have the right product and market, this cannot make sense to the customer. A *sale* is one thing, but you need solid reasons for a major price *cut*. Without them, it will certainly appear that the company has been overcharging its customers all along!

5. *Example:* A manufacturer of office equipment wants to establish a customer base of mail order buyers. He has a large, elaborate catalog filled with his product lines. He wants to get this catalog to the proper decision makers at small and medium-sized businesses. Since this is his first entry into direct marketing, he's not sure exactly how much appeal the products will have or at what business level the appeal will be strongest. He would like you to do a direct mail test to find this out, using lists of small to medium companies.

Analysis: If the product lines are attractive and competitively priced, you accept the assignment, but with the stipulation that he consider inquiry generation first in small space or print advertising. Then use direct mail on qualified prospects who request the catalog, because

– the catalog is too costly to send out to unqualified prospects

– the market is ill defined and amorphous.

A lead-generating print ad in several large business publications is the most economical way to build a list and to determine the market composition and size.

This may sound a little tricky, but once you start applying your proposition-testing formula to your own work, backed up by your big picture and research, you'll see how easy it is to walk others through this with you. It's your best defense when you see a danger signal popping up, because it approaches the problem logically and removes you from the stigma of personal prejudices.

You can save yourself time, and maybe even reputation, if you move through the research process and into this test of your proposition humming, "Take no dogs." Be a skeptic—until you feel comfortable. Now's the time to do it—not later.

Don't get complacent or too cautious, of course. Feel comfortable with your selling proposition, but allow it to challenge *you* at the same time.

CHAPTER 2 EXERCISES

Using Test Research

Let's say you've been asked to do a test mailing for a big, nationally known travel magazine called *Sunrise.* You've asked for test history and you've been given the following seven mailings, along with their indexed ratings. You can assume all were properly tested and all went to the same or similar markets. What is your conclusion from the history? (What formats and offers might you suggest for *your* new test based on this?)

Package 1—Current Control: Index 100. This was a jumbo package (9" × 12") offering a year's subscription for eighteen dollars (billing later) and the ability to cancel on the first bill if not satisfied. The letter was two pages, back and front. The brochure was four-color showing magazine covers, life size, and many large pictures from the magazine. There was an order card, a token, and a postpaid reply envelope.

Package 2—Test 1: Index 91. This was also a jumbo package and it had the same offer as the control. However, it contained a short, one-page letter and the brochure was filled with many more colorful pictures than the control but they were reduced in size. There was no picture of magazine covers in the brochure. The order card had a token. There was a postpaid reply envelope.

Package 3—Test 2: Index 107. This package was identical to the control, except that the offer included a small calculator as a premium.

Package 4—Test 3: Index 99. This package was identical to the control except that there was no token on the order card. And there was no postpaid envelope. The order card itself was postpaid.

Package 5—Test 4: Index 94. This was a four-color package measuring 6" × 9" (outer envelope). Inside was the same letter as in the control, a slightly smaller version of the control brochure, the control offer, and a reply card with token and postpaid reply envelope.

Package 6—Test 5: Index 103. This package was identical to the control, except that instead of a token there was a stamp that had to be affixed to the order card. No postpaid reply envelope was included, but the order card itself was postpaid.

Package 7—Text 6: Index 89. This package was identical to the control except that there was no cancellation guarantee after receipt of the first issue.

Conclusions

1. Jumbo (9″ × 12″) packages seem to do best with this market.
2. The use of a premium (or at least a calculator premium) raises response considerably.
3. Long descriptive copy is preferable to shorter copy.
4. Large, attractive pictures seemed to have more appeal than a large number of smaller pictures. Readers liked the many large pictures in the magazine itself and these were most representative of the product.
5. Use of a token is not justified.
6. A stamp seems to be an effective involvement device.
7. The clause allowing cancellation on first bill is very important to response.

Based on these indications, you'd be playing it safe to consider a package that incorporated :

- a jumbo format.
- a calculator premium.
- a four-page letter and brochure with large, colorful pictures.
- a stamp that has to be affixed to a postpaid order card.
- an offer that allows cancellation on first bill.

chapter 3

Direct Response Technique: How to Get It and Where to Start

THE SINK-OR-SWIM METHOD

Direct response advertisers used to take aspiring creative types with little or no previous training and give them on-line creative assignments. A little like throwing the baby into the pond, certain that it will innately demonstrate a love of the water and a natural talent to stay afloat.

You may agree that this sink-or-swim method is a brutal way to acquire a love of anything, particularly in direct response advertising, where the young writer's first plunge may well bring forth some chilling responses. As you come out dripping with your first soggy offering, you'll begin to hear, "You never start a letter with...," "Don't ever put the whoozis before the whazzis," "Don't even think about parking here..." and so on.

Take heart. Today things are better. For one, you now have some good books on direct marketing and almost all of them offer solid guidelines to producing effective direct response advertising. As a matter of fact, as you start to look around today, you can find an amazing number of rules, guidelines, formulas, and do's and don'ts for creative promotion in general. They appear regularly in trade publications like *DM News; Direct Marketing; Advertising Age; Catalog Age; Folio;* and the Direct Marketing Association's manual, its monographs, and its newsletters.

Every time direct marketers move into new media these days (like the telephone and broadcast), new rules and formulas seem to spring up. If you try to follow everything, you might even begin to feel a little overwhelmed. You could take your first plunge and sink right to the bottom, weighted down with iron-clad rules and formulas. After all, what is this—a form of advertising that is composed predominantly of do's and don'ts instead of pure creative panache? Advertising that eschews intuition and inspiration in favor of rules and formulas?

You bet it is! And as a matter of fact, you could find it quite comforting for starters. You'll know exactly what to do. You have rules to help you keep your head up. In a form of marketing that tests, tests, and tests everything, certain creative guidelines will evolve; rules will proliferate. Finally someone will start to record all these rules in one place. Remember, no marketer made these up arbitrarily. The customers dictated the guidelines by saying, "All things considered, this is the way I like to be promoted; this is what makes me respond."

As people change with the times, so the appeals to which they respond change and must, therefore, be constantly checked and adjusted. The result is a vast body of shifting knowledge made up of years of experience, testing, and retesting.

In direct response advertising this vast body of knowledge is called *technique*, and you can't put one word to paper without it.

All right. You've heard *that* before, but this is creative progression. Here's where you are on the scale.

- You're honing your creative skills and letting your imagination grow. Check.
- You've made the Underlying Law (and its premises) *your* law. Check.
- You've lined up your research requirements and refused to take "no data" for an answer. Check.
- You'll "take no dogs" because you can test your selling proposition. Check.

Now you're ready for the big "T"—technique. *Some professionals claim that 75 to 80 percent of direct response advertising is technique, and that the balance is creativity!*

This may be a bit of an exaggeration, but—courage—it shows you're really moving along on the percentage scale. Even if good direct response advertising is only 50 percent technique and 50 percent creativity, you have to get your techniques down pat to be a competent direct response creative person.

You can't be a professional without the big T simply because this amalgam of formulas and rules, representing a vast body of direct marketing experience, makes sure you don't repeat the mistakes of the past. Eventually your own experience in applying these formulas and rules (often to the point where your application is automatic and unconscious) enables you to break the rules from time to time—but not until you have a reasonably long and intimate relationship with them. (More about this later.)

FIRST THE FORMULAS—NO ONE BREAKS THESE

What's the difference between formulas and rules? Formulas are all-encompassing. They are structures or frameworks for the entire direct response promotion, whether it is a direct mail package, a newspaper ad, a radio commercial, or an egg carton coupon. They tell you what your promotion *must* accomplish and how it should do this, in logical progression from start to finish.

A lot of people like to write formulas, so you have several to choose from. Some pertain to all direct response advertising, others concentrate on direct mail.

First, there is *P-P-P-P*, created by Henry Hoke, Sr.[1]

Picture: Get attention early in the copy to create desire.

Promise: Tell what the product or service will do; describe its benefits to the reader.

Prove: Show value, backed up with personal testimonials or endorsements.

Push: Ask for the order.

The second, *Star-Chain-Hook*, was invented by Frank Dignan. L.E. "Cy" Frailey described the "Star, the Chain, and the Hook" as follows:[2]

First, get the reader's favorable attention. Do it deliberately with an opening paragraph which is bright and brisk—the Star. Second, follow quickly with a flow of facts, reasons, benefits, all selected and placed in the best order to transform attention to real interest and finally desire—that's the Chain. Third, suggest action and make it easy as possible—the Hook.

A third formula is William Steinhardt's A-B-C Checklist.[3]

*A*ttain attention.

*B*ang out benefits.

*C*reate verbal pictures.

*D*escribe success incidents.

*E*ndorse with testimonials.

*F*eature special details.

*G*ild with values.

*H*onor claims with guarantees.

*I*nject action in reader.

*J*ell with postscript.

One of the most popular and widely used formulas is called **AIDA** (pronounced like Verdi's well-known opera).

A – Attract *A*ttention.

I – Arouse *I*nterest.

D – Stimulate *D*esire.

A – Call for *A*ction.

---

[1]Martin Baier, *Elements of Direct Marketing*, (New York: McGraw-Hill, Inc., 1983), p. 306.

[2]Ibid.

[3]Ibid., p. 308.

AIDA is the broadest in application and is probably all you'll need to carry you through years of good direct response writing. (There is, however, something to be said for each of them, so use what makes you comfortable.) Most people know AIDA simply because it is easy to remember.

The best way to digest a formula is to practice by applying it to existing promotions. Figure 3-1 shows a good example of a bad promotion—one that never met AIDA:

In direct mail, AIDA starts on the outer envelope, and this washed-out outer here needs all the AIDA it can get.

Whether the designer was aware of formula or not, he or she failed to use one of the best attention-getters in the world. (The magic word "free.") And yet—the writer had it all along, hidden inside the envelope. AIDA makes modesty of this sort highly unbecoming. The short and obvious answer is—a free gift offer inside an envelope deserves a "FREE GIFT" on the outside.

AIDA is best demonstrated in mail order ads. Figures 3-2 and 3-3 show two fine examples. Every time you run across ads like these, try AIDA. Sometimes, by the way, it may not work. If this happens, you can be pretty sure the ad didn't work either.

As you move along, you'll become more and more expert at spotting good or effective direct response advertising. And you may be surprised at the number of promotions that could clearly have been improved by following AIDA.

The best examples of AIDA are the promotions you see repeated over and over. (As everything is measured, the ones that keep running are obviously the ones that keep getting strong response.)

In addition to the formulas, or in conjunction with the formulas, you have the four big rules and the Underlying Law that work for you in all media. There are also five sales guidelines with which the copywriter within you creates a salesperson's presentation.

> *Establish Credibility:* Who is the seller and why is he or she qualified to make this offer? (Would you buy a used car from this person?)
>
> *Get Involvement:* This means use the "you" and sing the benefits. It could be a song titled "You, You, You."
>
> *Motivate Your Prospect:* Why *now,* not later. (Most prospects who put it off never return.)
>
> *Structure a Strong Offer:* Unless your product is unique, you'll need all the competitive ammunition you can muster.
>
> *Apply the Underlying Law:* Don't let "them" convince you it makes sense if it doesn't!

Follow these five guidelines along with six other rules and guidelines in the next chapter that pertain exclusively to the direct mail package. They are just too important to miss. I didn't invent them. The customer invented them. Of all the things the customer has taught direct marketers, these are the most

UNIVERSAL SAFE DEPOSIT CORP.

115 East 57th Street, New York, New York 10022 / (212) 644-0124

I HAVE A FREE GIFT FOR YOU!

Here is an offer you will not want to pass up! UNI-VAULT, the
private safe deposit company, is promoting its facility by
offering FREE GIFTS to all new customers for a limited time only!

Now you can rent your safe deposit box at UNI-VAULT and choose
from a wide selection of FREE GIFTS.

stomers by pro-
the vault area.

r guards manning
ghline central
Mosler will give
essions at our

days a year service
RANCE IS PROVIDED
ge of arts and

e of computer tapes

all, near the
644-0124!

A FREE GIFT FOR YOU

WHEN YOU RENT CONFIDENTIALITY AND SECURITY WITH A UNI-VAULT SAFE DEPOSIT BOX

PERSONAL & STANDARD SIZE

A101

A102

A103

A104

YOUR CHOICE OF...

A101
APF Desk Top Calculator
A102
Shetland Can Opener/
Knife Sharpener
A103
GE Light 'n Easy®
Spray, Steam & Dry Iron
A104
GE De Luxe FM/AM Portable
Radio with TV Sound
B201
Emerson AM-FM Digital
Clock Radio
B202
Waring Eight Speed Blender
B203
3-piece Corning Ware Set
with Glass Covers.
B204
Proctor-Silex Coffee Maker
C301
Emerson Black & White
Television
C302
Sony Micro Cassette
Recorder
C303
GE Toast-R-Oven™ Broiler
C304
Sony Walkman, FM Stereo
LL604
Zenith Portable Color
Television

OVERSIZE &

B201

JUMBO SIZE

C301

UNI-VAULT — SAFE D

CONFIDENTIALITY: It is important
tents of your safe deposit box kept
bank records? *UNI-VAULT using a
provides maximum privacy.* We
Security Numbers, and provide acce
coupled with signature and/or picture identification if
so desired.

SECURITY: Advanced security system including vibration,
heat, motion and smoke alarm sensors, 24 hours a day, 365
days a year manned closed circuit TV and professionally
trained armed guards.

ing or directly across the street from the 58th Street entrance.

BULK STORAGE: Do you have objects d'art or antiques
which are too large for a safe deposit box and much to valuable to be left unprotected at your home? UNI-VAULT provides large lockers or bulk storage areas expressly designed for this purpose. Here you can be assured of convenient access to your belongings in a high security facility.

plus — personal service

UNI-VAULT
UNIVERSAL SAFE DEPOSIT CORP.
115 EAST 57TH STREET • NEW YORK, N.Y. 10022

(212) 644-0124

Located between Park Avenue and Madison Avenue in the mall of the Galleria — from 8:00 A.M. till 8:00 P.M.
OPEN 365 DAYS A YEAR.

 SEE REVERSE SIDE FOR DETAILS ▶

UNIVERSAL SAFE DEPOSIT CORP.

115 East 57th Street, New York, New York 10022

J THROCKMORTON
1175 YORK AV
NEW YORK NY 10021

Figure 3-1

44

Attention → # Treat yourself.

Choose one of these five sets and save up to $305⁵⁰

You simply agree to buy 4 books within the next two years.

Interest ↗

Remembrance of Things Past
for $12 (Pub. price $75)

The major new translation of Proust's masterpiece includes six new segments and many other passages that were not in the original version. All seven parts of the work—*Swann's Way, Within a Budding Grove, The Guermantes Way, Cities of the Plain, The Captive, The Fugitive* and *Time Regained*—have been combined into three elegant, boxed volumes. "An extraordinary venture...brilliantly effected at last" —*The New York Times Book Review.*

Desire →

The Metropolitan Museum of Art & The National Gallery of Art
for $17.95 (Pub. prices total $110)

The Metropolitan Museum of Art surveys the Met's entire collection, with more than 1050 plates (602 in full color). *The National Gallery of Art* reproduces the gallery's greatest treasures with 1120 illustrations, including 1028 plates in full color, many printed with gold.

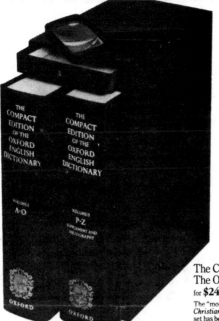

The Compact Edition of The Oxford English Dictionary
for $24.95 (Pub. price $175)

The "most complete, most scholarly dictionary of the English language"—*The Christian Science Monitor.* Through photoreduction, the original 13-volume set has been reproduced in this two-volume *Compact Edition.* A Bausch & Lomb magnifying glass is included.

The Encyclopedia of Philosophy
for $24.95 (Pub. price $225)

Regarded as the most comprehensive encyclopedia of philosophy ever published, this superb set—compiled in collaboration with the world's foremost philosophers—encompasses all aspects of ancient, medieval, modern, Eastern and Western thought. The four volumes represent an essential aid for students and a rewarding reference source for home libraries.

The Story of Civilization by Will and Ariel Durant
for $29.95 (Pub. prices total $335.45)

For almost half a century Will and Ariel Durant traced the continuity of world history—the religions and philosophies, the political and economic tides, the arts and sciences, the customs and conquests—to show the foundations of society today. A Book-of-the-Month Club exclusive for almost 50 years, the Durants' 11-volume illustrated masterwork is history come alive in all its dimensions.

Action ↖

Benefits of Membership. Membership in the Book-of-the-Month Club begins with your choice of the extraordinary works offered here. Because our prices are always lower than the publishers' prices, you will save on works such as these throughout your membership, as well as on the finest new fiction and nonfiction titles. In fact, the longer you remain a member, the greater your savings can be. Our Book-Dividend® plan offers a variety of fine new books at savings of up to 50% or more. All Book-of-the-Month Club books are well-made, durably bound, quality editions; they are not condensed versions or cheaply made reprints.

As a member you will receive the *Book-of-the-Month Club News*® 15 times a year (about every 3½ weeks). Every issue reviews a Selection and more than 125 other books that we call Alternates, which are carefully chosen by our editors. If you want the Selection, do nothing. It will be shipped to you automatically. If you want one or more Alternates—or no book at all—indicate your decision on the Reply Form and return it by the specified date. *Return Privilege:* If the *News* is delayed and you receive the Selection without having had 10 days to notify us, you may return it for credit at our expense. *Cancellations:* Membership may be discontinued, either by you or by the Club, at any time after you have bought four additional books. Join today. With savings and choices like these, no wonder Book-of-the-Month Club is America's Bookstore.

BOOK-OF-THE-MONTH CLUB®
America's Bookstore® since 1926.

Figure 3-2

Figure 3-3

important. And if you *don't* want to reinvent the wheel, follow the additional guidelines and checklists from others who have gone before; you'll find them at the end of this chapter and at the end of Chapters 4 and 7.

THE FOUR BASIC SALES GUIDELINES

Guideline 1: How to Establish and Maintain Credibility

You can't establish a relationship with a prospect or sustain a dialogue with a customer without credibility. This guideline applies in all areas of direct response advertising and all media. If they don't believe you and believe *in* you (your company and product), forget it. No need to worry about benefits, involvement, motivation, or offer.

Once you've got the credibility going for you, maintaining it is largely a question of constantly applying the Underlying Law. Be consistent. Make sense.

But how do you start? How do you go about *establishing* credibility?

Imagine you've knocked on a stranger's door...you're holding a wonderful product (or service) with honest-to-goodness values. The first question the prospect asks is, *"Who* are you?"

Once you've explained this satisfactorily and the prospect shows an interest in your product, the next question is "What qualifies you (or your company) to make this product?"

Looking back to Chapter 2, if you've done your research, you should be able to handle these questions. Fast. Effectively. Right? Wrong.

If it were only as simple as that! Here's the curve. There's credibility *and* there's credibility. How you handle it depends largely on the company or person you represent in each case.

It sounds convoluted, I know. But here are some examples that will clear it up.

If you ring a stranger's doorbell wearing the uniform of the local telephone company, and your truck, clearly marked, is out in front, will anyone ask, "Who are you?" Of course not. You've established an instant identification that carries with it all the trappings of the telephone system, good and bad. You carry its image around on the side of your truck and the front of your shirt. It opens a lot of doors. (So does the identification that goes with the Good Humor truck, the local grocery, UPS, the post office. All are operations that are known, familiar.)

Imagine, for a minute, the customer response if you ring that bell wearing a gray suit and carrying a small black case. You'd better be fast—and convincing—when the prospect asks, "Who are you?"

In direct response advertising (and most particularly in direct mail) you'll have to deal with this all the time because you go out to the customer; the customer is not referred to you. This means you must establish credibility in every element of your package, beginning with the outer envelope.

Often you'll represent a nationally known and respected operation. More often, you'll probably represent someone or some company that does not command immediate recognition (and, consequently, credibility). Each situation has its guidelines for establishing credibility. In some cases, it's a question of degree.

To illustrate this let's take an example of two extremes—a company with instant credibility (like AT&T, Sears, IBM, or American Express) and a little-known, small company like Sam's Suit Company.

Direct response advertising from well-recognized, big companies must attempt to humanize the cold, impersonal image and *maintain* credibility by setting their particular "corporate" tone throughout, while Sam's Suit Company must fight to *establish* credibility and stature. (Why is it qualified to do what it promises?) And then it must go on to *build* credibility in every part of the mailing.

Major U.S. Corporation	**Sam's Suit Company**
1. Recognition	1. Recognition
• Instant logotype identification	• No "Recognition" factor
• Company image immediately conveyed	• Need to establish the company in the prospect's mind, explain corporate policies, years in business, size
	• Good photography helpful (Example: Our new warehouse and fulfillment center, pictured here)
2. Spokesperson	2. Spokesperson
• President or chairman *not* credible unless he or she is addressing the soundness of the company's stock	• Needs president, chief executive or owner—the person most logically to be trusted, most credible
• Must be a department or service executive (marketer, salesperson, engineer), preferably a peer of the prospect	
• *Someone with whom the reader can identify*	
3. Guarantee	3. Guarantee
• Expected as part of the corporate image	• Absolutely necessary
	• Must be clear, carefully worded, strong, and visually reinforced with equally strong graphics

4. Testimonials
   - Needed only for an unusual new service

4. Testimonials
   - Very important, but must use real people with real names (Photographs help)

5. Endorsements
   - If used at all, must be carefully chosen to represent product, market, and corporate image (Big companies are often wary of "personality" endorsers)

5. Endorsements
   - Helpful if the endorser is credible and has a good image in the company's marketplace

6. Tone of Promotion
   - In accord with corporate image; but a friendly and accessible tone is suggested for the letter so the prospect feels he or she has someone to relate to in the big company

6. Tone of Promotion
   - Strong, straightforward in the style that best represents the company image
   - Hard, persuasive selling is acceptable

7. Offer
   - Conservatively stated proposition

7. Offer
   - Strong sell with absolute satisfaction guaranteed
   - Use of motivators and incentives wherever possible

As you can see, there's quite a difference in the optimum requirements for the two extremes. The little company has to *prove its right* to do business. The big company has to show that it is warm and human and not too big to care about individual customers.

Guideline 2: How to Create and Sustain Involvement

You don't need a Dale Carnegie course to know that the best way to get people involved is to concentrate on the "you". What wonderful attention-getters and attention-holders the following are:

"Enough of me. Let's talk about *you*."

"Tell me, Mr. Jones, what did *you* think of the movie?"

"My, what lovely eyes *you* have, Miss Smith."

"Take this test to see how *you* rate in attracting the opposite sex."

"Have I got something for *you!*"

"Can *you* answer these important questions?"

We all like to talk about ourselves; express opinions; see how our skills, knowledge, or abilities stack up; receive compliments; and learn about things that will benefit us, please us, and fulfill our needs, wants, and desires. You can boil this down to involvement by benefits-to-you, questions, quizzes, and flattery, but it's so much more—and more exciting—that that.

If you're going to be a top creative person, with every job you take on, you'll want to think of the many ways to say, "let's talk about you." *Use them all!*

This is particularly important in the direct mail letter where you speak directly to your prospect or customer. Use the "you" generously; use the "I" sparingly. And remember, your readers are human; we all like to be stroked.

Most professionals will tell you that the best way to do this is by promoting benefits (and we'll deal with this in detail in the next two chapters). This is true, of course, but *don't stop there.* How else can you sidle up to your prospects? Can you ask them some questions? Give them some quizzes? Flatter them? Make them smile? Have some fun? Why not, as long as it makes sense and relates to the subject? (But remember, to do this well, you must know your market well. You *must* know how they have been treated by the company in the past, what has gone before.)

Q. How else can good direct marketers create involvement?

A. Give your prospect something fun *to do.* Gimmicks or involvement devices work.

Q. Can you list ten involvement commands?

A. Insert token   Scratch the panel
Peel off the seal   Lift here
Paste stamps here   Detach here
Choose the color   Fill in here
Check the box   Initial here

Used properly, such involvement devices can increase your response because humans enjoy lifting, peeling, and pasting, especially during the act of ordering. It's fun.

Figure 3-4 represents a group of involvement devices at work on order cards.

The token, which is now over twenty-five years old, is still one of the most effective devices you can use—and it is particularly good in book mailings and magazine subscriber marketing. (It seems to have special appeal to well-educated readers!) Use it if you can link it to the offer and, graphically, with the product.

Stamps are even older than tokens and can be used in much the same way. (Another way is the stamp sheet, from which your prospect makes a selection.) Peel-off stamps or seals can also go out affixed to the letter ("peel off and affix to your order card") or even to the outer envelope.

If your product's smell is a big selling point, scratch-and-sniff (fragrant inks) can play a role in your promotion; or if you're promoting a sweepstakes, prizes, or gifts, a scratch-off covering on winning numbers offers you another involvement device.

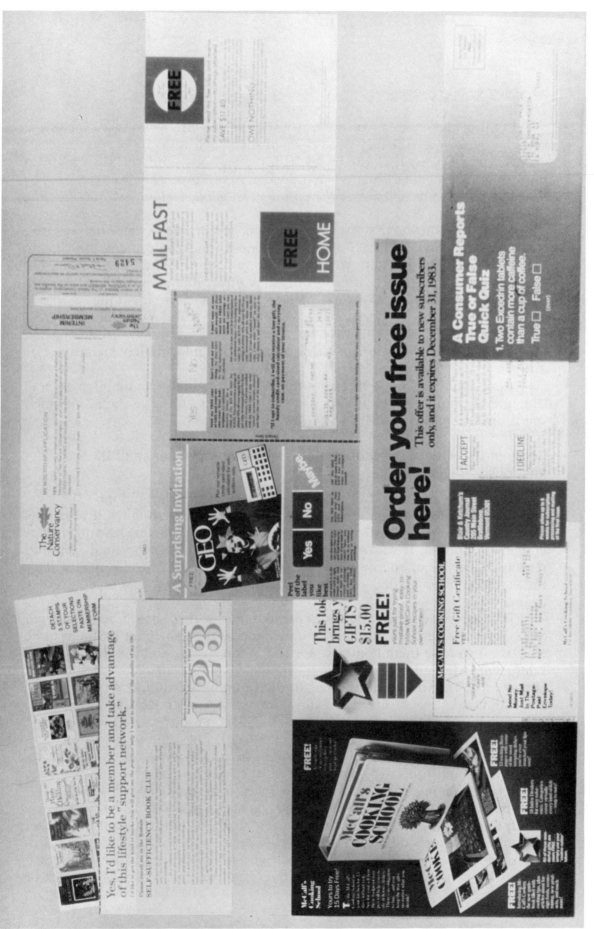

Figure 3-4

In all of these cases, you should test to make sure response is increased sufficiently to cover the increased costs of such devices.

When you use check-off boxes, fill-ins, tear-offs, and the like, it's also important to remember this: When ordering, *your prospects may be confused by too many choices or options. If the options create indecision, you may lose the order.*

Tests have shown that two options are acceptable (a one- or two-year subscription, a gold or green recipe box). More than two options may create inertia through indecision. You walk a thin line here between the fun of involvement and the fear of indecision. Many direct marketers are shying away *completely* from choices-as-involvement today and keeping it simple.

In some magazine solicitations marketers have found a continued interest in playing with stamps and tokens, but a decided fall-off in response when prospects are asked to choose or check boxes, or add information, signatures, or initials.

What could this be saying about our society? About our inability to act? Our love of dumb tokens? It says one thing for you—this is an area in which you'll want to move carefully and test, test, test.

Guideline 3: How to Overcome Inertia—The Dread Disease of Direct Response

The final command of all direct response formulas is "Action!"

The opposite of action is inertia (and that's what can happen if prospects have too many choices!). All your smooth phrases, benefits, tokens, and stamps amount to nothing if you can't get your prospect to take the final step and respond. Once he or she puts your promotion aside (to consider it at a later time) you're pigeonholded—and few promotions that get pigeonholed ever fly again.

There are several techniques to prevent inertia that should be considered even under the best promotional circumstances. You can count on them to be effective if you use them honestly. Actually, they are used all the time by good salespeople who capitalize on the very human fear of losing out or missing a hot opportunity. They are: limited offer; limited supply; a deadline; and a *free* gift.

The word "free" itself is probably the greatest motivator (or incentive to respond) in all direct response advertising. The phrase "free gift" (although redundant) is even stronger. Some top copywriters hesitate to take an assignment without the word "free" in the offer. It can be important for you, too. (We'll talk about this later when we build the offer.)

If you are going to use a deadline, two measures should be considered: (1) It must be close enough to incite the prospect to act; and (2) it must be sufficiently far off to allow the promotion to reach the prospect and to give the prospect enough time to respond. (About four to five weeks from your *drop date* in third-class direct mail is considered tight but right, taking into consideration third-class delivery time. With first-class delivery, you can easily lop off a week or more.)

As for "limited supply," here's a good example of human psychology: A wig distributor was offering his product at a 30 percent savings in small space ads. Almost *all* prospects ordered only one wig. He added the headline "Strictly Limited—Only Two Per Customer," and immediately over 45 percent of his orders doubled in size.

You will also want to employ action words and phrases to combat inertia (like "let us know now," "hurry," "act now," "don't delay," "send your answer by return mail," "call today," and so on). And you may want to vary your tone or pace a little, by speeding up the rhythm or pacing at the end of your letter (using very brief sentences and paragraphs with lots of action phrases on the last page). It is also important to give your order form or coupon a *valuable* look that urges, "Process me now."

A little of this rousing motivation goes a long way, however; and I'd rather you concentrate here on the causes of inertia so you'll never by guilty of *slowing down your own response rate.* (What a horrible thought!) There are two major mistakes to avoid (and even top professionals have to watch out for these).

First—a lack of full information regarding your product or service (all the benefits in the world can't prevent inertia if your prospect still needs to know one tiny little bit more about the product—like whether the product is over eight inches high).

Second—a general lack of clarity regarding the offer for the product or service. "Clarity" means a lot more than stating the full sales story clearly and including all the features and benefits. A lack of clarity can mean a cloudy guarantee or complex offer terms. (*You* can understand it, and so can the marketing director, but does it really make sense to your prospect? Try it out on the cleaning man or the delivery girl.) A lack of "clarity" can also mean too many check boxes and choices. As you saw with involvement devices, when your prospect or customer can't make up his or her mind, inertia sets in.

To compound the problem, people just don't read very carefully. (No surprise.) As the old saying goes, you have to tell them what you're going to tell them, then tell them—then tell them what you've just told them.

In direct mail this in itself is good enough reason to have the letter and the brochure (if you have one), as well as the order card or order form, all repeat the offer *and* the major selling points or benefits. Wherever your prospect starts in, it will all be there, as clear as one-two-three.

Guideline 4: How to Structure a Compelling Offer

Credibility, involvement, and a call to action (or motivation)—these three basics interrelate and contribute to the fourth: a compelling offer. The ability to recognize or develop a strong offer and to present it creatively will be critical to your success in all forms of direct marketing. You simply cannot create involvement, and motivate your prospect, in this competitive world without a sound offer.

Of course, strong offers aren't important if you are the only one on the block with an unusual product that everyone wants. But how often is that going to happen—and how long will it last?

You don't have to remind me at this point that you are creative material and that creative stuff doesn't usually control the offers. This unfortunate situation is precisely why I'm dragging you into "offer."

You must be able to spot a weak offer. You owe it to yourself. (If you can't recognize one, you'll prepare a promotion that, no matter how good it is, will dive for the circular file.)

Thanks to your research, you should know immediately whether your offer is highly promotional, barely competitive—or trouble ahead. Equally important, *you must know how to make recommendations for strengthening the offer.* And that's what you'll pick up here. A lot has been written on this, but I've set down those most important elements for creative people like you.

When it comes to major financial decisions, there is not much you can do about weak offers and noncompetitive pricing other than to clearly point out where the competition is coming from (and the powers that be should know this anyway).

But offer is not just price. Price is only one term or part of the offer. And there are a lot of creative ways you can make a dull or barely competitive offer much stronger. Such creative offer structuring can make a large difference in response (as much as 100 percent difference!).

WHAT MAKES UP AN OFFER?

In addition to the product or service, your offer is composed of the price, the credit or payment terms, the commitment, the guarantee, the response motivators and incentives, and any other conditions.

Terms may be set legally or they may merely reflect the competition in a particular business, but for established products and services, most of the offer's terms have been carefully tested and retested. (New products have a lot of testing to do.) The terms represent the commitment on both sides, the agreement. ("If you do this, we'll do that.") For example:

- This catalog purchase may be made by cash, credit card, or C.O.D. There's an extra charge for C.O.D. and 5 percent discount for cash. Returns are accepted if received within thirty days of delivery, and so on and so on....

- When the prospect joins the book club he or she gets four books for three dollars with the understanding that the prospect will also purchase at least four club selections over the next two years. Every purchase is also worth member bonus points. Every month or so the member will receive an announcement, and so on and so on....

- When the prospect enters a subscription to this new magazine, he or she will be billed after receipt of the first issue. He or she may cancel and owe nothing by simply writing "cancel" on the invoice and returning it, and so on....

Strengthening Your Terms

You'll want to go over all your terms carefully to find out first where changes can be made (tested) and where they can't. If it's a new offer, you'll probably have much more latitude. Look for ways to enhance credibility, build involvement, and create motivation to act.

There is one major way to build credibility that should be in every offer as one of its basic terms and that's the guarantee. If someone tosses you an offer without a guarantee, put one in. If your offer already has a guarantee, see if you can strengthen it. If it's a new product, don't even consider letting it out without one. For example:

- *Strong:* If for any reason you're not satisfied with your magazine subscription, just let us know and we'll promptly refund all monies due on unmailed copies.
- *Stronger:* If for any reason, at any time during the first year of your magazine subscription, you're not satisfied—just let us know and we'll promptly refund your initial payment in full.
- *Strongest:* 100% Money-Back Guarantee (Add this headline to the above.)

Another important aspect of the terms is payment. It's unlikely you'll get heavily involved with this, but it's good to understand what's available to help you further evaluate your offers as they come along.

- "Bill me later" represents optimum terms. (Response can rise 30 percent or more with this credit option.) It is extended primarily to customers with an established credit standing; or it is confined to magazines, club plans, and financial services (all things that can be suspended if payment does not eventually go through).
- Credit card charges (usually a choice of two or three cards) are used by most mail order companies.
- Installment billing is common for large ticket items.
- "Check or money order enclosed," and even cash payment incentives, may be used.
- Last, and least desirable, is C.O.D. (Cash on Delivery).

Usually, several options are included (like "payment enclosed" or "bill me later," or "payment enclosed" or "credit card" or "C.O.D."). Wherever you can, work to effect ease of payment. And remember, next to "free," the best terms are, "we'll bill you later" and "100% money-back guarantee."

Determining the Objective of Your Offer

Before you get too tangled in the terms of your offer, however, you might find it helpful to reestablish your objectives first.

Step back from the product, stretch, relax your shoulders, roll your head, shake your wrists, and ask yourself, "What is the offer out to accomplish?" Out to get new subscribers? Out to get business inquiries? Or do you simply want the prospect to buy something?

Here are some possibilities:

- Make a purchase
- Subscribe (to a publication)
- Join a program (book or record club)
- Enter a continuity agreement (to buy a set or series of products over a period of time)
- Accept a trial
- Make an inquiry (send more information)
- Make a contribution (fund raising)
- Become a regular customer (make repeat purchases)

If your perspective is clear and you're feeling especially creative, you may be able to strengthen your offer *right at this point* by combining two objectives:

- Instead of one purchase, how about adding something to motivate repeat purchases. ("A $5 credit coupon comes with your purchase to apply to future purchases!")
- Instead of just an inquiry or a trial offer, perhaps you could combine the two. ("Send me the gidget widget for 30 days' free examination under your unconditional guarantee," or, "Send me more information on your new gidget widget.")

What Kind of Offer Will You Select?

If you had your druthers—and who knows, you *should* be called in to help develop the offer—what kind of prospecting offer would you favor? (Yes, there is one answer!)

If you said "FREE" or "PREMIUM" offer—right on! (Remember, some top copywriters won't take on a highly competitive product without a premium.) There are seven broad offer categories here and the premium ranks #1 for testing to acquire new customers.

1. The Offer with Premium: A premium can do wonders for a lackluster offer; use it to motivate response to trial offers, to increase order size in mail order, or to generate inquiries and sales leads.

There are two big caveats, however: *First,* if the premium overshadows the product or service, you may get a lot of takers but few stickers. Premiums do build response (they can even double it), but often the new customers are only bargain hunters who fall away quickly. *Second*, premiums are habit forming. There's a saying that goes "Premium sold means premium renewed" (or premium resold) in future promotions. Once you've started, your customers logically come to expect it every time you go back to them.

To avoid forming bad habits in consumer and business-to-business direct response, try to encourage selection or development of a premium that is closely related to the product or service you are promoting. (Some of the best premiums are booklets, demonstrations, or surveys that directly relate to the product or service and, therefore, help you by qualifying respondents and reselling the need for your product or service.) In business it may also be something that can be used in the office or at home, like a tape recorder. Consumer premiums can cover a wide range of products including mystery gifts. Do not overpromote the premium at the expense of your main product's selling story. The premium belongs with the offer every time the offer is stated. It is *not* the offer.

2. Introductory Offers: These can be trial offers or sample offers—or one-time joining offers.

a. The Charter Offer. If you're launching a new magazine, newsletter, or other subscription publication be sure to structure a *charter offer.* Subscribers signing on during the early months of the publication will be called charter subscribers, entitled to the lowest going rates (in perpetuity), first word, and best price on new projects and publications for as long as their subscriptions continue without interruption. This may not sound like much to you, but the offer alone can make a full 1 percent difference in response. Charter offers have an unceasing appeal—so far.

b. Trial or Sample Offers: Here's where you try to get your product into your prospects' hands at all costs, under the assumption that they will be pleased and impressed enough to purchase. Trial offers usually have low prices or (in the case of subscriptions) a shorter term or subscription period and low price.

With 100 percent money-back guarantees, there is less and less sampling these days, except with some magazines that have a "first issue free" offer. (You write "cancel" on your bill if you don't wish to continue after your first issue—and you keep the issue.)

Such free sampling offers tend to generate at least 30 percent to 50 percent more response than regular offers when the "free" is heavily promoted; they also generate nearly the same percentage of additional bad pay or "cancels." It pays to test.

Newsletters used to be promoted by sending out sample issues; it was an inexpensive way to get the product into the hands of the prospect. Smart promoters are shying away from this, however, as few specific issue samples can live up to the broader promises of the promotion regarding the overall subscription.

3. Club and Continuity Plans: Book and record clubs and collectors' groups have joining offers that require significant commitment. Some of them ship product automatically every month or so until you cancel (Til Forbid); others ship unless you tell them *not* to (Negative Option); and still others ship *only* when you say "yes" (Positive Option). These are offers you won't be able to change, as they are carefully tested and even more carefully worded—often by the legal staff. You can police them for clairty, however, as they do tend to run on. And when premiums are used (which is often, with such joining offers), you can shine with your contribution.

4. Sale or Discount Offers: Here are the good, old-fashioned savings promotions, based on the notion that all the world loves a bargain (save $50, 30% off, all products on this page reduced 25%, use this coupon to get $10 off any product, etc.). It's common practice to have regular sales for mail order customers when there's a reason—time of year, specific holiday, anniversary, back-to-school sale, or warehouse clearance. These sales work if there's an established retail price against which the sale price is compared, and you can often do some nice footwork on price comparisons.

Take this offer for a monthly magazine that sells for $1.75 on the newsstands: "Your Price, only $7.97 for one year!" This can be compared with the newsstand cost (12 Issues, $21.00) and the regular subscription price (12 issues, $15.94). "Your price is *half* the regular subscription price!"

There's really a lot you can do with your offer when you apply a little creativity to the basic bargain or sale statement. See what you can do with this sale challenge: *Let's say you're selling wigs (yes, wigs again) and you are able to give fifteen dollars off on any one or all of three popular wigs that ordinarily retail for forty-five dollars each.*

How many promotional offers can you come up with here?
Answer:

a. One-third off on any of these wigs

b. Save up to $45 (buy three at one-third off each)

c. Buy two wigs and get a third wig FREE!

d. $10 discount on all three wigs and get a free wig brush with each purchase of two wigs or more

Which of these are the stronger and why? The two strongest offers are "c," because it has the magic word, and "d" because it has the magic word, plus a premium, *and* a discount.

Can you come up with another offer here? Remember the earlier wig example? "Who needs more than one wig?" you may ask. No one, probably, *until* you put a "limited" in the offer. And so you have:

Take any of these 3 wigs for $30 each (Save $15 on each wig!)
Purchase Limited—only 2 to a customer.

Also, go back to the premium offer with a wig brush—a highly related premium. Your creative offer structuring can dare to ask, "If $15 off is feasible, why not lessen the discount and spend a little on a good premium for an offer with *both* discount and premium?" Be inventive!

If you've got a good price story, feature it, and feature it creatively. Embellish it with guarantees and a premium where you can. Use the magic word. Make comparisons. State your savings in different ways. "Limit" your product. Add a deadline. And keep with it! Your offer is getting stronger at every step.

Your price—a penny can make the difference! A word about numbers here: Most direct marketers (and magazine publishers in particular) find that

a. There are price breaks above which there is resistance.

$9.99–o.k.	$10.00–n.g.
$49.99–o.k.	$50.00–n.g.
$99.99–o.k.	$100.00–n.g.

b. Odd numbers are more credible than even.

$7.97–o.k.	$7.90–n.g.
$2.77–o.k.	$2.80–n.g.
$5.59–o.k.	$5.50–n.g.

To carry this even further, many publishers believe in "the law of the seven." That is, prices that end in 7 (and, if possible, also have another 7 in the first or second number) get a greater response than simple odd number pricing—$7.97 is stronger than $7.99! None of this is conjecture—it is the result of years of repeated testing.

You have been carried outside your area of required expertise at this point only so you can throw in a *99¢* or a *7¢* now and then, when you have the opportunity. Most good direct marketers (and fortune tellers) already understand all about this.

5. Sweepstakes Offers: Advocates of sweepstakes claim they can raise order response up to 100 percent. Maybe so, but the power of the sweepstakes is so strong, that I marvel anyone remembers what they've ordered after they respond. Other than a chance at a dream.

Whatever your R.Q. (Renaissance Quotient) on sweepstakes, here are a few important offer aspects to remember.

- You have two offers with a sweepstakes, the overpowering one to participate in the sweeps *and* your basic product or service offer (which is really what it's all about).

- You probably know (by virtue of pure bombardment) that you "need not order anything to win." That's a fact in every legal sweepstakes. Yet people *will* order anyway just to be safe. To encourage this, many

sweepstakes have two reply envelopes—one for orderers and another for nonorderers. The entry-with-order is hyped on the reply form and made to look more official.
This sort of thing obviously contributes to the belief that it's necessary to order (even though the small print says it ain't so).

- Although you cannot legally combine the sweeps offer and your main offer, see if you can get your prospect to combine the two mentally in other ways than "fear of not winning." For example:
  - Lobby to get a sweepstakes that is themed to tie in with your product (or that has product-related prizes).
  - Try for a sweepstakes name that incorporates the name of your product or service or its theme.
  - Fight hard to keep enough space in the sweepstakes package to present and sell your product or service properly.

6. The Inquiry Offer: This is most common in business-to-business direct mail although it has been used for unusually large ticket consumer purchases and services (homes, cars, loans, financial planning assistance).

The objectives here are to prequalify the prospect (a) for a sales call or visit, or (b) for a more elaborate promotional mailing, or (c) for a prospect visit to a showroom, office, or plant. It is often called a two-step promotion, as it works to make sure that only the strongest, best qualified prospects receive step two: an expensive direct mail promotion or an equally expensive sales call or visit.

All steps should have been carefully thought through by the time you get involved, but this is a good place for you to apply the Underlying Law and be sure the progression will make sense to the customer or prospect.

For example:

- Be sure to include a toll-free *800* telephone option.
- Use price and other terms as a qualifier only (the offer itself comes in at step two); for example: "If you believe a good car's performance is relative to its cost...."

7. Fund Raising: Fund raising offers are a breed apart and are based on the concept of a perceived need—for starving families or for a politician who is looking for campaign funds. Ostensibly, people contribute for altruistic reasons, expecting no tangible reward. (The underlying reason for political contributions is good government.)

There are several things to remember here when you formulate a fundraising offer.

1. People must perceive a clear and imminent need to give—a strong reason to contribute *now.*

2. They must be encouraged to "give all they can," while being told that "no amount is too small."

3. Prospects need to be told *how* to contribute and what their contribution will do. (Here—and only here—choice can be a plus. In some cases, established levels of giving are absolutely necessary. Rather than create inertia via indecision, several choices can encourage response.)

4. Today, many nonprofit groups use membership and membership benefits as well as related premiums (or token gifts) for contributors (bumper stickers, tote bags).

Look over the seven possible offer types for a minute. How about combining them? A lot of direct marketers do—all the time. You should try to combine two or *even three* if you can. For example:

- a business inquiry solicitation with a premium
- a straight purchase offer with option for more information
- a charter offer and a FREE sample issue
- a club offer with a discount or savings offer
- a fund raising offer with membership and a premium

This gives you more opportunities for strengthening your offer. Compelling offer structuring can't be passed off lightly. Look how far you've come already.

- You have an offer that is clear and easy to understand.
- You have defined objectives and have developed an offer with more than one objective.
- You have an offer that combines other offers for strength (premium offer, joining offer, sale or discount, inquiry).
- You have credibility with a strong guarantee.
- You have financial terms that are attractive.
- You use numbers and price comparisons promotionally.

Now use your creative tools—the motivators and involvement devices!
Here's where you hark back to the basics of involvement and motivation.

Fear of losing out:
- Offer deadlines (limited-time offer for enrollment or membership)
- Limited supply

Pure fun of involvement (devices that let the prospect participate):
- Tokens to insert
- Labels or seals to peel off
- Stamps to lick and paste
- Colors to choose

- Boxes to check
- Panels to scratch
- Space to initial
- Perforations to tear

You have fun here, too, but please remember to use caution on choices. Moving a "yes" or "free" token is one thing. Asking your prospect to decide between three alternatives is quite another. Play it safe!

Well, here we are. You have now covered the 4 Basic Sales Guidelines (along with the Underlying Law) and I hope you've noticed how they interrelate and overlay. To have a strong offer, for example, you need credibility, involvement, and motivation. You can't have motivation without involvement. You won't get involvement without establishing credibility. And you won't have any of this, of course, without the Underlying Law. So! Now on to the specific direct mail guidelines.

The Guidelines:
Now You've Started, Will It
Ever End?

Not if you get involved and start testing and learning with the other professionals—and what's more—you won't want it to end. Rules and guidelines are always changing or being modified as times change and people change. This is exciting stuff, and vitally important to you.

Right now, for example, you are about to learn all those wonderful secrets and tricks that top writers use to get the envelope opened. And much, much more, my friend. You're going to learn *why* people open envelopes and *how* envelopes are perceived—all the tools you need, not just to copy, but to create on your own.

A lot of space is devoted to creating envelopes, letters, and brochures here for a good reason (I promised not to reinvent the wheel for you). I'm giving you things that haven't been covered—or haven't been adequately covered before. Maybe no one thought writers needed to know … maybe they assumed you'd osmos it. Maybe not. But for sure, understanding these techniques *and* understanding the how and why of them puts you ahead of the pack.

DIRECT MAIL—WHY START HERE?

Why not television—isn't it more glamorous, more fun? Or print ads? Why mail?

If you feel that way (even a little), I'm going to do all in my power to prove to you that direct mail is every bit as exciting … far more complicated and more challenging *and* more fun than any other medium in the world!

Starting anywhere else is like building a house without a foundation … jumping without a parachute or high diving when you can't swim (not only dumb, but impossible to conceive). You're right, I feel strongly about this, because quite simply, *direct mail is the learning ground that unlocks all the creative secrets.*

- It embodies the majority of all direct response technique (all the formulas and nearly all the rules).
- It is not confining or limited (no 60 seconds of air time or an 8″ × 10″ page to hold it back).
- Its format is flexible (a letter, a postcard, a folder—even a box).
- It is a pure one-on-one communication (the only other medium that can make this claim at present is the telephone, and its cost and flexibility can't compare with direct mail).
- It is discreet and highly efficient because of its precise ability to target its market, and it is therefore the most effective medium for serious testing.
- The direct mail letter itself is a true test for the direct response writer. It initiates dialogue with the prospect; it maintains dialogue with the customer.

So when we talk about rules, we're going to concentrate on direct mail first. The big rules that apply across the board are best represented here. The specific rules for other media will fall easily into place in later chapters. You'll see.

YOUR FIRST DIRECT MAIL GUIDELINE: GET THE ENVELOPE OPENED

If it weren't for the big four, this would just naturally be the first creative rule of direct mail. Doing this well is so important that everywhere you look in direct marketing you'll find guidelines for effective outer envelopes. (Notice we call the envelope the *outer* envelope, because there's often an *inner* envelope or Business Reply Envelope (BRE). The BRE is generally a postpaid envelope used to return an order form or an order card that doesn't carry return postage. A card that has a postpaid side is a BRC or Business Reply Card.)

The outer envelope may prove to be your greatest challenge, because no matter how carefully you plot and plan, *one small detail* can make a big difference. Sometimes it's the stock...sometimes the size of the envelope *or* the type...sometimes it's the use of color...sometimes it's *one word* in the teaser copy or the promise...sometimes it's what I call "mailbox ennui"—just too much stuff for your prospect to assimilate.

I have polled literally hundreds of professionals regarding effective envelopes in my direct marketing classes over the years, and the constant disagreement over successful envelopes still amazes me. Imagine—many of us in this business have trouble spotting, or understanding, winners and losers. Perhaps we're too close and too analytical. Certainly most envelopes walk a thin line—and you do, too, until you can distinguish between the winners and the losers.

To understand how to go about getting *your* outer envelopes (or folders, or self-mailers, or boxes) opened, it's important to consider first *what makes people open some envelopes in the first place*—and why do they throw others away? Today's mail boxes are crowded with envelopes competing for your prospect's dollar. Your envelope must gain attention *first*. What will make it stand out?

At one time you could certainly get attention with an oversized envelope in bright colors. But that's no longer enough—many of your prospects (and their mail boxes) have had their fill of big, bright envelopes. Your real job is to create positive involvement—fast (Chapter 3, Guideline 2) and to do that, you'll have to work on one of two things: your envelope will get opened (1) if it gains immediate recognition (positive recognition) or (2) if it arouses significant curiosity.

Gain Immediate Recognition

Let's take recognition first, because it's important that you understand both the positive and negative aspects of this kind of involvement.

"Wow, a check from Dad!" (Positive)

"A letter from my wife!" (Positive)

"The phone bill." (Sort of positive)

"Ugh. Who needs an encyclopedia?" (Negative)

"No need to bother the boss with *this* kind of mail." (Negative)

There are some cases where corporate recognition is a plus: when the prospect is already a customer, when the company is well known and respected (credibility) and when the envelope itself is fully personalized, carries first-class postage, and looks very important. (And this is the way good business-to-business mail works best, if you can afford it.)

You can see that recognition has its good and bad sides, however. The negative side leads to the circular file. And here's where direct marketers go crazy. They'll use all sorts of involvement devices and disguises to prevent *negative* recognition.

Since you may have few opportunities to bask in the unqualified positive recognition of "Wow, a check from Dad!" you'll want to concentrate on this second strong form of involvement.

Arouse Significant Curiosity

The Important Envelope: This is a disguise technique used in business when recognition may have a negative effect. The goal is to make sure the envelope looks impressive or important enough to get by the mailroom, or whoever screens the prospect's mail, by averting negative recognition and arousing curiosity. ("Hmm, looks important. Sounds important. Maybe I'd better keep it for the boss.") See Figure 4-1.

The Envelope that Carries a Promise: In consumer and business direct mail, perhaps the most popular way to arouse curiosity is to make a strong promise. A promise on your outer envelope can be as simple as "You are invited..." or as

```
100 West County Road C
Little Canada, MN  55117
```

```
Ms Joan Throckmorton
Joan Throckmorton Inc.
1175 York Avenue
New York, NY  10021
```

Figure 4-1 *The Important Envelope*

complex as "Respond to this special 50% off introductory offer by April 30th and get a FREE Gift." You can set down one big benefit, "How to regain the vitality of youth...see inside" or lay out the three basics of your package right on the outer envelope:

A Special FREE gift offer (offer)
that can bring *you* (involvement)
the vitality of youth (big benefit)
—from the Smith Company (credibility)

As sophisticated as we all are about direct mail, the promise of something free is almost always the best bet, however you use it. Remember, premium on the inside rates a FREE on the outer. So if you have it, flaunt it.

The Questioning or Challenging Envelope: You can hook the curious by asking a question ("Hard boiled eggs, bedroom slippers, and oil tankers. How are they going to affect your income? See inside.") or by making a challenging statement ("Only one person in four will qualify for this opportunity. See inside.").

The Tell-It-All Envelope: This one pulls no punches. It immediately states exactly what's inside. Just by opening it, the recipient becomes a qualified prospect. In many cases, particularly business-to-business, this can ensure that it gets to the right person and gets opened. (Figure 4-2.)

The Mysterious Envelope: In consumer advertising when third-class postage is used, or when the name of the company is not well known or known at all, you may also want to consider developing an outer envelope that teases

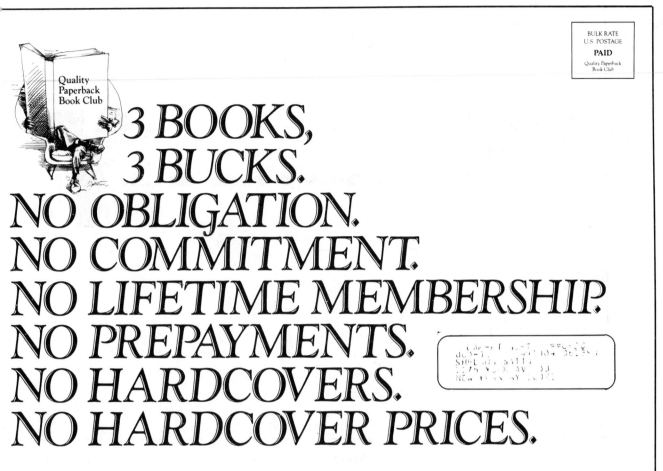

Figure 4-2 *The Tell-It-All Envelope*

the recipient, that uses copy and/or art and format to tickle the imagination and arouse curiosity without a direct promise.

This might be an envelope with a distinctive look and a simple corner card with a very well-known name. ("Now, why is Harvard writing me?") Or you might start an exciting story on your outer (to be finished inside, of course). Or state simply RSVP, leaving the prospect to wonder what kind of invitation might be enclosed. Or put one large, attention-getting word in two-inch letters across the envelope from side to side. (Figure 4-3.)

The blind envelope: The ultimate teaser is something called a blind envelope. Blind to your eyes, really, because it carries virtually no identification. ("What might this be?")

Use this very carefully for blind envelopes can cheat. They try to involve the prospect without qualifying him or her. (Like "If you are a gardener," or "If you enjoy fine cooking...") and without setting down a promise (Like "A free

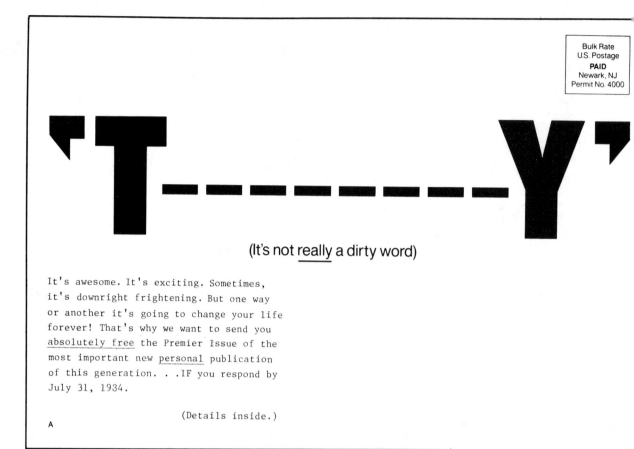

Figure 4-3 *The Teaser*

book offer..." "You'll have fresher, clearer skin..."). They therefore run the risk of disappointing—or even irritating your prospects. ("You jerks—you tricked me into opening ·this!") Blind envelopes are safest when the offer inside has broad appeal, like a sweepstakes or a cable television installation.

Aside from making copy promises and sending out teasers, you also arouse curiosity by the way you use envelope format, paper and color, personalization, and postage.

Let's stop a minute. I've slipped in some involvement tools on you. We've been building another pyramid here from top down and it goes something like this.

Effective envelopes
get attention (*AIDA*)
via involvement (Big Guideline 2)
through recognition or curiosity/promises
using copy/format/personalization/postage/art/die cuts/folds/perforations/distinctive stock.

By now you're no doubt getting a good idea why recognition is *not* the key route for you as a direct marketer. Not always, anyway.

Why You Must Consider More Than Pure Copy in Planning Your Envelope

Positive recognition, you'll remember, is most often the pure personal letter—hand-addressed on pale blue stock or hand-typed on a fine white #10 (4⅛″ × 9½″) business envelope—both with a first-class stamp. Of course, in our business (or any business), it's also a logotype or corner card that identifies a company or professional firm with whom we already do business. There's no fighting in the mailbox among these fine aristocrats.

Your challenge falls outside this sacred arena among all those other outers hustling and scrounging—and sometimes even cheating—for attention.

In the business-to-business competition you must rise with dignity and importance above the rubble and get past the guardian at the gate, be it mailroom clerk or secretary, nurse or assistant—and you'll need more than pure copy to do it.

In consumer competition you must shout when the others whisper, whisper when the others shout—and out-guess them all with a shining, deathless, delightfully compelling appeal that cannot—just cannot—go unopened. Again, it is much more than just copy.

As a copywriter you must understand how to use these three tools creatively to arouse curiosity: format, personalization, and postage.

1. *Format:* Envelopes come in all different sizes but due to U.S. Postal Service regulations and budgetary limitations, much of your work in third-class mail may be confined to only two or three sizes: the #10 (4⅛″ × 9½″), the 6″ × 9″, and the jumbo (9″ × 12″). Unless you're mailing unusually large quantities and are well equipped to process jumbo envelopes, it's safer to stay smaller.

If you're not on a budget and can travel first class, the world is your oyster from small (minimum size, according to UPS, is 3 ½″ × 5″) to a monarch (3⅞″ × 7½″) up to the jumbo, and all variations in between. (Permissible envelope maximum sizes vary somewhat between first-class and third-class.)

A business-to-business envelope should look important and businesslike. That doesn't mean it can't go to a jumbo size or use a colored or kraft stock. And, since you want to attract attention with your consumer-directed outer, you'll also want to consider colored stock and die cuts (or windows) in your envelope that show graphics from the brochure or a token from the order card. Or you may want a four-color drawing or photograph right on the outer. Or, if everyone else in the mailbox is shouting, you may want to whisper with a plain white envelope and just one or two strong words in heavy type. (Better *be* strong, though.)

There are other devices, like all-plastic envelopes (polybags), snap packs, envelopes with "tear here" flaps that pull down to open "windows." Some envelopes even self-destruct. This is where copy, art, *and* production come together to see what can be done and how far you can go within the budget.

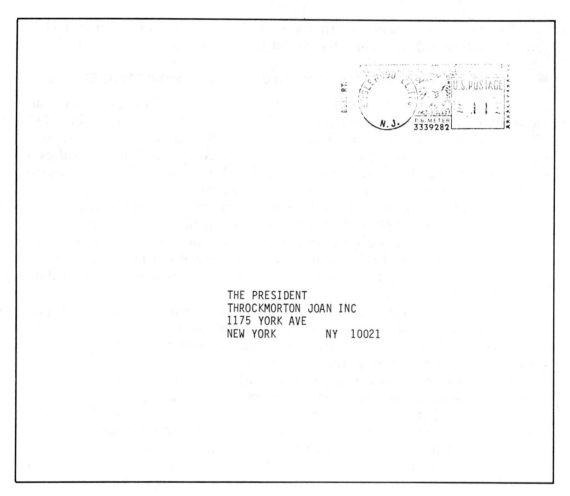

THE PRESIDENT
THROCKMORTON JOAN INC
1175 YORK AVE
NEW YORK   NY 10021

Figure 4-4 *Almost as Bad as "Occupant"*

But remember—all of these are your *tools*. They are a means to an end. You have a story to tell. It starts on the outer. You must make sure that the tools work *for* you to tease or start your story and get the envelope opened.

2. *Addressing and Personalization on the Outer Envelope:* The *least* effective form of addressing is a label addressed to "Occupant" or "Boxholder," stuck on the outside of an envelope. (Figure 4-4.) The *most* effective form for direct marketers is a hand-typed address (three or four lines) to the individual with a full title (Ms., Mrs., Mr., Dr., and so on).

Everything else falls in between, as will most of your work. Certainly budget and production will again have a large say regarding which end of the spectrum you work in, but here are some things to remember:

a. Few direct marketers can afford the luxury of hand-typed outers (unless you have a very classy, big-ticket promotion).

b. Response is *always* stronger if the order form goes out already filled in with the prospect's name and address.

c. Computer-personalized reply forms are a popular way to do this. Computerized labels or printout name-and-address strips are affixed to the form. The name and address then show through a *window* (or die cut) on the outer envelope. This enables the mailer to use one label or address form instead of double-addressing (on both the order card and outer envelope). This is particularly popular with test mailings where rented names are set up on computer tape, presorted in Zip sequence for mail delivery and affixed to order cards in sequence.

d. Now, however, entire order cards can also be directly addressed by computer. In some cases, outer envelopes, order cards, letters, and even business reply envelopes can all be economically computerized within one package. As it becomes less expensive, good computer personalization will be used more and more, so it's important for you to understand it and to understand that there are times to use it extensively and times to use it sparingly.

The least you should expect today (if your envelope is to do its job), is addressing to the card or reply form with a window outer. If you feel strongly about more personalized addressing directly on the reply form—and/or directly on the outer itself—you will want to consider other sophisticated forms of computerization. These are just a few bare possibilities to whet your appetite and get you talking to the artist and production person.

3. *Postage:* To understand postage, you have to understand a little of the economics of postage. After all, it can take up 30 percent *or more* of your total direct mail budget! If you have a high R.Q., check the DMA *Fact Book.*[1] Otherwise, here are three major points to remember:

a. First-class is just about double the cost of third-class. (You get certain discounts for presorting or separating your mail when you mail in quantities in both groups.)

b. First-class as its much higher cost is priced by the ounce, while third-class gives you over three ounces right up front at its much lower rate. (One ounce of first-class is more than double the cost of three ounces of third-class.)

c. At some point you pay the piper for all of these third-class advantages, however. This is it: Third-class is true third-class travel. It is segregated from first-class; it seldom rides as well and, most important, it travels like a snail—and unevenly. Sometimes it's slow; usually it's slower; often it's slowest. Hard to predict. A third-class letter can go from Long Island, N.Y. to San Francisco in six days or sixteen (and sometimes a lot more).

---

[1] *Fact Book on Direct Marketing* (1985 Edition.) (New York, Direct Marketing Association, Inc., Publication Division, 1985). To order, inquire at the DMA, 6 E. 43rd St. New York 10017.

People notice postage. A standard #10 envelope with a first-class stamp has a better chance of getting opened than a standard #10 with a third-class indicia (or preprinted permit with postal number). And it gets there faster and surer. However, a precancelled third-class stamp has a pretty fair chance against the first-class stamp on a white envelope.

In consumer communications where third-class is popular because of the savings, you have to learn to use it well. The plain #10 envelope with a third-class indicia doesn't stand much chance against a 9″ × 12″ jumbo envelope with the same indicia and with four-color photography and strong involvement copy.

If you are clearly promotional—don't just sit there. Use promotional tools to create involvement and stimulate curiosity, teasing the prospect into opening the envelope.

In consumer direct mail, a first-class letter can be effective and is worth testing if it fits the budget and the product's image. To use first-class postage on an envelope that is obviously and blatantly promotional (or third-class) is a waste of money.

Since business-to-business mail is usually screened, as I've said, your objective here is to create something that the screener will be afraid to throw away or decline to throw away because of its implied value. Postage helps. However, since Pitney Bowes' first-class metered mail looks very much like its third-class, the difference narrows, because secretaries and mail rooms don't or can't read the meter carefully. This is well worth testing.

The advantages of first-class and third-class are continually being argued. This is an area where you *must* test unless your market and product *clearly* require one or the other. (Mass appeal products that drop millions of pieces of mail at a time always mail third-class because of the immense savings.)

When considering postage, *in relation to format,* it's smart to apply the Underlying Law. "What will make sense to your prospects or customers?" What will look "right" or logical or interesting to them? For example: If you must use third-class postage (and most of us must), try a Pitney-Bowes meter for a serious, businesslike approach and use a preprinted indicia for a clear consumer promotion with color art and pizazz and/or a big copy teaser on your outer. If you can justify first-class—and if you're blessed with a stamp—keep it pure and pristine with only a return address and possibly a hand-typed name above that. If it's first-class Pitney-Bowes, you might want to call attention to it by stating something "official" like "First-Class Mail" on the envelope itself. It may sound corny but it helps.

The outer should always be in keeping with the tone and appearance of the direct mail package as a whole. If your market is sophisticated and your product is high-brow, your message and the format that carries it will be sophisticated. (Remember your Underlying Law.)

A small change in your envelope can and will affect your entire mailing. So, go carefully here; test as much as you can. Don't try to be cute or clever or funny on your outer—not until you're very, very good. Spend a lot of time. Think it through and never cheat by promising something outside that you don't carry through on the inside.

This is a lot of envelope business to digest all at one sitting, but here's something that can help you. Every day when you collect your mail, before you open your envelopes, test them out. First, set aside the ones you open on pure recognition (bills, letters from friends and family). Then look at the rest and rate them. What does each one do to catch your attention? How does each succeed (or fail) in involving you through copy promises, teasers, and involvement devices? Analyze an envelope. Then open it up. Look at the offer. Was the outer honest? Could you have devised a stronger outer? Did you like it or did it irritate you?

After a week or so, this evaluation process becomes automatic *and* very valuable because you're actually applying and learning and remembering— and getting some good ideas for future use while you're about it.

Now before you move on from the envelope to the letter, there's one brief stop you should make.

YOUR SECOND DIRECT MAIL GUIDELINE:
HOW TO SET THE TONE...THE VOICE OF THE LOGICAL SPOKESPERSON

Remember when we discussed credibility as one of the first guidelines? I talked about the most credible spokesperson. Hand in hand with credibility goes *tone*—or you might say, establishing the voice of the logical spokesperson.

Not everyone in our business does this well, and some don't even bother. Their letters are signed simply J. Smith for *X* magazine or B. Jones for *Y* company.

If you really believe in direct response as dialogue marketing how can you support such bland anonymity? Every direct mail letter should come from someone (even a pseudo someone), the person who, *in the customer's mind*, is logically suited to make the offer.

What's more, you as the writer will find it much easier to develop your dialogue *if you know who you are.* Imagine being shoved out in front of an audience to make a spontaneous presentation on a new product without knowing who you are supposed to be. (Manufacturer, inventor, salesman, user— what's your point of view?) A salesman does not present like an inventor or sound like a consumer. Your tone in presentation will be largely determined by the kind of person you are speaking for and by the prospect audience to whom you are speaking.

To determine who you are, first define your audience. You'll want to know what kind of individuals, what kind of families make up your market. In the case of business-to-business markets, you could have two or even three levels of decision makers. (You won't talk to the corporate division head or president in the same tone as the purchasing manager or chief engineer, and you might want to use a different executive as your spokesperson to represent the company at each level.) So check out the audience (you've done your Chapter 2 research, of course), then select your logical spokesperson or persons.

Once you decide who you are, develop that individual's point of view and stick with it. And sound the same throughout the letter. (If you start off like Howard Cosell, don't end up like Norman Vincent Peale.) *Sound the way your readers think you should sound.*

For example: A business executive writing to other business men and women will be serious and to the point; a doctor writing to colleagues will sound technical and authoritative; a sportswear and camping catalog owner might sound like a friendly camper who understands the outdoors; a woman cookbook author will sound like a woman who knows and enjoys good food when discussing her book; a fashion designer will use the terms and jargon of someone who understands flair and style when describing clothes. And, interestingly, an editor or publisher of a magazine should sound *like the magazine* when he or she describes it.

What does all of this role playing do for you, the creative person? First, it enables you to dramatize, to set up an imaginary dialogue in your head before you even get started. Act out your sale with your imaginary prospect. Empathize with your spokesperson. Now empathize with one individual in the spokesperson's market. Back and forth. One on one. You're writing dialogue!

There are many logical spokespersons—real people—who have become legends in mail order, like Harry and David Holmes of Bear Creek Orchards, Lillian Vernon of Lillian Vernon, Max and Duke Habernickel of Haband, Mrs. Miriam B. Loo of Current, Inc., and Richard Thalheimer of Sharper Image, to name a few.

You don't have to immortalize the boss here, but you should know who you are if you're going for continuity with credibility. And if you're a small company—what's wrong with the boss?

So get the envelope open and set the tone … and let's do the letter.

GUIDELINE 3: THE BASIC ELEMENTS OF A SUCCESSFUL LETTER

You've now arrived at the center or heart of the direct mail package: the letter. It can be one paragraph, one page, four or eight pages. It can be a postcard, or a note, or a full 8½″ × 11″. Whatever format it takes…*always* a letter. This is important for you to understand, because a few Philistines who claim you *don't* always need a letter have crept into this business. Letters are important. They are the most important part of the package besides the outer envelope. (If your outer envelope doesn't get opened, what use is your letter anyway?)

You'll find letters in "packages" as well as part of all other direct mail formats from postcard to carton. You'll find two-line letters and even eight-page letters. (In some cases, you may find that all you need is two paragraphs or two sentences. Look at the double postcard on page 26.)

By the way, as you move ahead in direct response advertising you're going to hear a lot of comment about long letters. The gist of it generally goes like this: "No one reads a four-page letter." "Long letters are old-fashioned. Today's readers want a short, one-page message."

Don't believe it! The customer or prospect who's interested needs *all* the facts. You're a salesperson, remember. You have to present these facts and even if it takes eight pages, the customer will stay with you happily, as long as you're telling a good story and presenting a case that appeals. (The only person you'll bore is the one who is clearly not your prospect.)

So how long should a letter be? *As long as necessary to get the story across.*

Follow this rule, write a good tight letter, and anyone who says it's too long is either a Philistine, or no prospect for your product, or both. In keeping the letter tight, consider the product/market first. If it's a product for *doers* (and a market of doers) work to keep the letter as short as possible. (If it's a product for readers, don't worry.) Business letters, especially if they're inquiry seekers, can afford to be short and tight because the message *is* short— "Send for more information."

The letter, more than any other medium or media segment in direct response advertising, is loaded with rules. Sink-or-swim on the letter is unforgivable. You can't jump off the dock or wade to your ankles without getting tangled up in a network of guidelines.

Before we move through this network at close range, let's review the basic elements that make up the structure of a successful letter by examining what the letter must accomplish—every time—all by itself. Again, it's important to remember that sometimes it does this in a few sentences and sometimes it takes eight pages.

All right. What does go into a letter? Your big benefits, your offer, your qualifications, other benefits, all the features, involvement devices, motivation to respond—all belong in your letter.

I've shown this in Figure 4-5 in the form of a framework and it relates the seven major elements of the letter to each other in descending order. The first four frames are grouped together. You've already seen how the three outermost frames work to create the initial impact of every piece of direct response advertising:

Offer for you—with benefits to you—equal involvement from you.

That's how you start to gain attention. But before you can say "free" or "50 percent off" credibility also comes in. (Who are you? What qualifies you to make this offer?) Credibility can even beat out the other three if it's offered in the form of a well-known corporate logotype on the letterhead.

What's more, they can all precede the letter, if you decide to put them on your outer envelope as you saw in the envelope guidelines. And when your prospect goes inside, the letter should immediately take over the same theme, embellish it with secondary benefits and features, then add motivation to act. That's what your letter has *to do* in one form or another. That's your structure or formula.

Now how do you go about it? To begin with, your letter should look like a

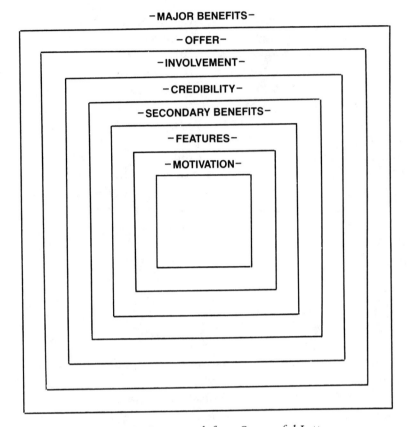

Figure 4-5 *Framework for a Successful Letter*

letter. It should look typed. It should have indented, short paragraphs, under-lines, marginal notes—a variety of visual devices to make it easy to read, spacious, friendly. In other words, it should be designed. You are not fooling your prospect into thinking you've typed a letter, certainly, but you are producing a familiar, friendly format conducive to a one-on-one dialogue to which your prospect will relate. (You'll find an example of the right way to set this up in Chapter 7.)

How to Sound Like a Professional in One Easy Lesson

- Know where your offer goes in a four-page letter?
- Know what a Johnson box is and when to use one?
- Where do "nuts 'n' bolts" go?
- How about the P.S.?

Of course, I'm not playing fair. Why should you know these things? But in less than five minutes you *will* and that puts you ahead of 50 percent of the striving direct response beginners.

Let's start on page one and work our way through a pretty standard two-to-four-page letter.

1. Your offer *must* go on the first page and on the last page, near the end. (If you bury your offer and big benefit, you lose your prospect right off the bat!)

2. It can go in your letter copy or in a Johnson box on page one. A Johnson Box is a sentence or two preceding the salutation giving the high points of the offer. Originally it was centered on the page right under the letterhead and surrounded by a border of typed asterisks. It was invented by a great direct mail letterwriter. His name is Frank (you guessed it) Johnson. Frank devised this "box" because he's a fine storyteller. He likes to start right off in the first paragraph of his letter and carry the reader along with a totally involving sales tale. Just as he gets to the best part, he breaks the action with an "over please" to the next page (another rule). Frequently there is just *no way* to fit the offer in the first page—without ruining a good story. The Johnson box is his compromise. It gives him flexibility and it works. And it's been working for others, in one form or another, ever since. (Strangely, while scores of other writers have adopted—and adapted—it, Frank doesn't use it much anymore.)

3. The first page should also have a letterhead and a salutation. (Always use a salutation. This *is* a letter.) When you can't personalize here, many writers choose "Dear Reader" or "Dear Friend" ("Friend" may be a little presumptuous for unknown prospects). "Dear Customer" is always good for customers if you're not using computerization. And often you can personalize to job, profession, or hobby, depending on the lists you are using (Dear Architect, Dear Bird Lover, Dear Collector, Dear College Graduate). One salutation to women 18-34 years old went like this: "Dear Career Woman, Professional Person, Wife, Sweetheart, Mother, Economist, Gardener, Cook, Interior Designer, Chauffeur, Buyer of Most Consumer Goods—Friend."

4. Your very first paragraph must grab your prospect by the eyelashes—and hold on! The first few lines of your letter will make or break the success of the letter itself. Why? Because almost everyone's eyes start reading there. You want to make sure those eyes continue.

5. Whether you use a Johnson box or not, don't end your first page with a period. Try to break your thought and entice the reader to turn the page. (You know what I mean: "She looked up fearfully and saw the curtain move. Suddenly...over please.")

6. In between the opening and the close of your letter (whether it's one page, two pages, four, or whatever) you'll be working your benefits, adding all features, reinforcing credibility (if need be). And this can mean such things as a list of features, customer testimonials, descriptions with *specific* examples (specifics sell), and always to you, you, you.

7. Before closing, go back to your big benefit and major selling points once again, and tie it in with your original lead.

8. Just before you close (in the wrap-up) you'll also want to state the full details of your offer. It's part of your call to action. This section, where you restate the offer, emphasize haste, and provide an easy way to respond, is called "Nuts and Bolts."

9. If you use involvement devices, motivators, and incentives be sure to bring them in up front *and* when you wrap up in Nuts and Bolts.

10. Please don't think that direct response copywriters are absent-minded just because many, if not most, good letters carry a P.S. It's just another rule or technique that always seems to work. People *read* the P.S. Even when the first few lines of the letter itself can't hold on to them, the P.S. offers another chance. This makes it a good place to repeat an important selling point or to pop in a new or different benefit. Some of us even resort to P.P.S. on occasion. I can't prove to you that it always works but, like chicken soup—it can't hurt!

That was simple. A few of the familiar basics, then ten rules and you've wrapped up the letter, right? Wrong.

There'll be even more guidelines that apply to letters as we move along and I've excerpted some good ones from two more of our finest letter writers, Tom Collins and Bob Stone, at the end of this chapter. To top it off, remember that some of these guidelines and rules can be twisted or broken from time to time, but only if you're *very* good.

GUIDELINE 4: THE LIFT LETTER—WHEN AND HOW TO USE IT

It's time for you to meet one of the most valuable friends you can have in developing a direct mail package—the lift letter. And it does just that; reliably, consistently, dependably it can "lift" response for you almost every time, if you use it correctly. Bless its heart.

But first a word of history because the lift letter has actually evolved over the years, so you'll find this helpful in understanding and using it.

Back in the 1960s, the Greystone Press, a company that handled mail order book sales, did a promotion that added a *second*, shorter letter to the other direct mail components. It was folded and carried teaser copy on its outside that said "...Do not open this envelope unless you have already decided *not* to send in for...." (Curiosity being what it is, you can be sure most prospects opened it.)

This second letter was *not* from the person who signed the longer letter. In this case, it was from the publisher, Paul M. Greystone, and it began, "As the publisher of this encyclopedia I am puzzled. Frankly, I do not understand why *everyone* does not send in for free Volume 1...." The writer went on to express amazement that everyone would not take advantage of this exciting, no-risk offer. It ended by urging the reader to reconsider.

And scores of readers did so—every time the little letter was used. Some of us called it the "Frankly, I'm puzzled" letter, but it was no puzzle why and how this brought in additional response.

1. It allowed a second promotional point of view.
2. It strengthened the credibility of the offer.
3. It permitted new benefits, or different selling points, to be highlighted.

After Greystone, "Frankly, I'm puzzled" was used effectively by dozens of astute practitioners. By the 1970s Time-Life Books began using a version that started out from their publisher. (The Editor wrote the main letter.)

Guess what they called it? The Publisher's Lift Letter (or Pub Lift Letter), because it carried a message from the publisher. This was only the beginning of its evolution. Other voices, other points of view were added. Celebrities or individuals who contributed to the Time-Life Books series were used in lift letters to provide a particular point of view regarding the excellence of a specific book or series (for example, how the unusual photography was executed, how carefully recipes were checked).

From here in, the lift letter, as it became widely known in the late seventies, was in a no-holds-barred situation. Anything was feasible for testing. And most sensible creative utilizations struck responsive gold.

Outer teaser copy went from "Open only if you don't plan to respond" to "Open only after you've dropped your order card in the mail," or "Read this side if you've decided to respond, read the other side if you've decided not to respond," or "Here are three more good reasons to respond now."

The letter can come from any logical person with a strong, promotional point of view, including an editor, a customer service supervisor, a museum director, or a happy husband. *(Happy Husband?* Yes, speaking for his wife's new cookbook.)

Some say the lift letter has been overused and has, therefore, lost its effectiveness (i.e., lift). I say it's been *mis*used rather than overused. A Lift Letter written for the sake of being cute or presenting a charming point of view (POV) that doesn't directly reinforce or enhance the sales message is misuse, and it may even detract from the main message. Hold back. Don't use it frivolously. Use it widely and it'll "lift" for you, too.

It is my sincere hope that you learn to love the lift as I do. It will solve many of your letter-writing problems by giving you a good stage for a big selling point that just doesn't fit in the main letter. It will enable you to introduce a new point of view and change your character (and your tone) a little. It will give your package more interest, and strengthen your offer. It can also be one of the most enjoyable parts of the promotion if you use it creatively. (Frankly, *I'm* puzzled that more writers don't add a lift letter.)

GUIDELINE 5: WHEN AND HOW TO BROCHURE

Whoever said, "A brochure is nice—if you can afford it," was slightly dotty, and people say this all the time. Brochures aren't *nice.* They are absolutely necessary or absolutely unnecessary.

A brochure's mission is to dramatize the benefits and illustrate the features. Please don't expect it to do a lot more than this for your product. This *is* a lot.

Brochures are not necessary

- when you have a product or service with features that don't require illustration, like a newsletter or newspaper.
- when you have a product so well known that it doesn't need visual description for most prospects—like *Time* or *Newsweek* magazines, or your expired membership or subscription to whatever.
- when you have a business-to-business promotion geared to *qualify* prospects by creating inquiries for "more information" ("more information" will include the expensive brochures, charts, and diagrams).
- when you have the ability to write so well that your description does a *better* job than words and pictures because it lets your prospect draw upon his or her own imagination! (This works best when you're selling services like travel and entertainment, or educational books and programs that help individuals achieve goals and aspirations. It doesn't work if you're selling widgets.)

Brochures are necessary almost all other times—and you cannot afford to go without them.

A word of caution. Brochure (or "folder" or "flyer" or "booklet" or "broadside") shouldn't mean just pictures and words. A brochure can be represented by a game board, a travel folder, a life-size shot of a table spread with food, a minature magazine that fits in the palm of your hand, a page "torn" from a book, a sales kit or manual, a printer's proof sheet. It can be all four-color photography or two-color charts and graphs and columns of words and lists of figures—particularly in financial promotions.

How you see your brochure is limited only by your creativity and cost constraints. Creativity and cost constraints are unlikely bedfellows, however, so in most cases (particularly in consumer advertising) you'll have to hold your soaring imagination to a piece of paper that folds nicely into a #10 or 6″ × 9″ or 9″ × 12″ outer envelope.

There are standard paper weights as well—and efficient paper sizes and logical folds. Learn about all of these from your art director and the production specialists before you plunge ahead with plans for a design that exceeds your budget and production's capabilities. (More about this in Guideline 6.)

When to Put a Coupon in Your Brochure

Every piece in your direct mail package has a job to do. The brochure, order card, and letter have to work together, but they also stand alone. (No one is exactly sure how many prospects read which first and why, but it is definitely established that our society is composed of order-card-first readers as well as brochure and letter-first readers.)

Think about it this way: Good prospects are often tempted to *save* the brochure or pass it on to a friend. This can generate more business and enable one direct mail package to reach two prospects or more. But for this process to work, creative people must include a coupon *with an offer* on the back of the brochure itself. This is hard to do when you're testing several different offers on the order card, as you'll also have to repeat those offers on the brochure coupon (and then make sure the right brochure is enclosed with the right order card!).

Today, with prices subject to frequent testing and changing, direct marketers often develop generic brochures that can be used in a variety of packages over and over because they do not spell out the offer at all. They refer the reader to the order card instead. As you get to understand printing costs, you'll see that this is often a necessary economy. On the other hand, something is lost.

Try to test the brochure coupon whenever the cost is not prohibitive. It can bring you a serendipity of extra (unbudgeted) orders. How many? The better your offer, the better your serendipity.

The Requirements for Your Brochure

Whether it stands alone, or limps a little without its offer, the brochure must work with your other components.

1. It must *dramatize* the benefits.
2. It must use all the basic techniques applied in the letter to do this: big benefits/credibility/involvement/motivation.
3. It must illustrate the features (here's where every single bit of basic information and detail goes—the sort of detail that reinforces the letter's sell and answers all possible questions).
4. It must create its *own* tone. A golden-tongued orator or a folksy cook may speak in the letter, but the brochure is neutral ground—a credible straightforward presentation without the intimate or impassioned one-on-one dialogue of a letter.
5. It must *track*. If you don't know what "track" means, you can probably guess. Just envision your prospect at the "gate" of the racetrack. This is your cover. A good brochure leads the prospects gently around the curves and corners to the first fold (in an orderly fashion), then to the next spread, then right down the main stretch to the finish line (inside spread).

Instead of wandering aimlessly, unfolding, and turning the paper (and how many times have we all gotten lost in the maze of a poorly designed brochure?), your prospect moves along with your message in pictures and words—following closely as the story develops—right up to the big finale. That's tracking!

Some Help on Illustration

In any talk of brochures, you're liable to run into arguments on illustration. Some art directors swear by photography, others stick to drawings or commercial illustrations. A few (and they have to be *very* good) combine the two effectively. This happens most often with photographs of the product and small *drawings* or diagrams to show detail or specific parts or sections of the product at work.[2]

Here are some thoughts when you're confronted with illustration decisions:

1. Most art directors prefer good four-color photography. It works particularly well for

food and cooking	"picture" publications
travel	hard goods
gardening	soft goods
sweepstakes	entertainment

2. But drawings have a place, too, and every art director has opinions here. I suggest you consider drawings for

- light and heavy industrial machinery
- technical product details or enlarged areas
- shots that are expensive and difficult to set up (aerial views; groups of buildings; large groups of people, children, or animals; period pieces and historical settings)
- mood shots (to express strong feelings of sentiment, mystery, horror, nostalgia, and fantasy)

3. Your illustrations show your product's major benefits and features and, if it is appropriate, they show the product in use as well. For example: If it is a service like a travel program, show people enjoying a ship or a plane (the product or service at work), then show specific pictures of planning the trip, destinations, and featured places on the itinerary. Services, rather than products, are easier shown in use, as use itself is part of the benefit structure. If it is a sewing machine, show the benefits (all the clothes it made), and possibly some close-up shots of important features. Showing the product at work is not appropriate here; it will add nothing to your story as motion or moving parts obviously cannot translate to still photography.

4. People illustrations in direct response advertising can make or break your story. Photography has a stronger impact, but offers more dangers than drawings in big benefit situations. People often identify readily with benefit illustrations, drawings, and cartoons. On the other hand, given one or two

---

[2]If you're interested in the art of combination, I'd recommend you get your hands on a *Smith & Hawken Catalog for Gardeners*, (Smith & Hawken, 25 Conte Madera, Mill Valley, CA 94941).

close-up photographs, showing real people and benefits, many people are likely to say, "That's not *me*. My family doesn't look like that!" or "I'm not even married!" or "I'm not that old," and so on.

When you use a wide variety of photographs, with different people groupings in benefit situations, your prospects are more likely to identify with them, and photography in such cases is preferable. If you have room for only one picture, be careful. Your prospect must be able to identify with these benefit dramatizations.

For example: I've seen major book clubs with broad appeal to both men and women try the two different benefit presentations. One presentation showed a large photograph of a "family" reading together. There was a father, a mother, and two children. The other used a cartoon drawing of a nondescript but pleasant man reading. The cartoon survived. Moral: When you can't photograph all the types that make up your prospect market (or aren't sure what they all are), try drawings, sketches, or cartoons that anyone can and will relate to without saying, "That's not me...this isn't real."

5. If your illustrations aren't self-explanatory and don't have headlines, make sure they have strong captions. *Captions get read.*

6. Push hard for color. Your alternative to four-color is two-color, which is fine for many financial services and business promotions. In some cases, if you *must* compromise, two-color can even be used for soft goods, hard goods, and travel—but not for food! We know four-color improves response, but you won't be able to quantify this precisely until you test with it and without it. Most professionals, when including a brochure, opt for four-color if their product needs it.

Organizing Your Brochure Copy

In talking about direct mail packages, good direct marketers tend to gloss over guidelines and assistance in developing brochures. They get lost in the excitement of outers, letters, and order cards—and many direct marketers probably never sit down and really analyze the brochure.

This may happen because the brochure's job is tough and thankless. In addition to dramatizing the benefits, it must list all features without leaving out one detail or specification; it must anticipate and field all questions. An effective brochure is the result of good research and organization. It can be grueling work. It can also be enjoyable. Here are some techniques to help you organize and present, and to make it more enjoyable.

- A "standard" brochure uses headlines and illustrations to guide your prospect through a logical story from benefits to features—from what it will do for you to precisely how it will do this.
- The main headline restates your big benefit(s).
- The secondary headlines point up secondary benefits and features.

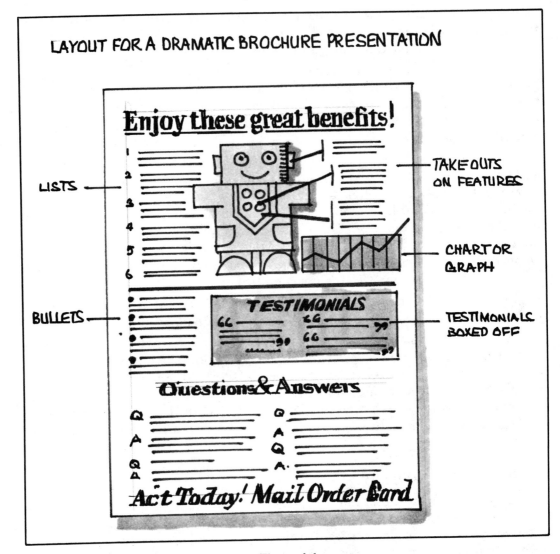

Figure 4-6

- Your first block of body copy usually starts with a broad, overall benefit sell.
- Use lots of subheads to hold the reader and pull the waverer back into your body copy.
- Use "throwover" heads at the bottom of each spread to help tracking and to guide your reader to turn the page (for example, "See other side for your special offer").
- Your back cover is a good place to restate your offer and/or to dramatize your guarantee.

Organize your data and make it more interesting with these graphic devices.

- Use takeouts around the photograph or drawing of your product, underlining features and benefits.
- Use the question-and-answer technique—the best way to anticipate sales resistance and dissolve it.
- List benefits numerically, using the old countdown method.
- Line your features up in a column and bullet them.
- Include a boxed-off section of testimonials (with pictures, if you have them).
- Add charts and graphs to dramatize the numerical aspects of your story.

Your good prospects will want *all* of your information, but they'll take it better if you sugar-coat it where you can. And remember, if you enjoy bringing it together, they'll enjoy tracking through it with you! (Figure 4-6 illustrates this.)

GUIDELINE 6: HOW TO WIN ON CPO—A RULE FOR THE NEXT DECADE

CPO means *cost per order* and most creative people never really had to know what this meant before inflation. Back then, when a creative team or several writers were asked to do test packages to beat the control, they were usually told to pull all stops, not to worry about cost, just be creative. If the new packages got more responses than the old control, well, the costs could always be honed down by gradually testing production efficiencies.

It was so simple then. Gross response or pull was all that counted. When you won—you *won*.

That's not the case today. Thanks to the high cost of getting into the mail, every package is judged by its cost in relation to its pull, not by its pull alone.

Marketing managers are apt to challenge their creative people on the cost per thousand (cost to produce, print, obtain lists, label, insert, stamp, and mail). This is known as CPM. In our business, printing, lettershop, lists, and postage are all estimated in terms of thousands produced. That is to say, each of your components is costed out by the thousands, postage is added in by the thousands, then list rental and lettershop are plugged in—still by the thousands. Look at it this way: $250M equals $.25 per piece, $400M equals $.40 and so on.

Cost per order (CPO) can be figured in much the same way. If you paid $250M going into the mail, and you received twenty orders per thousand (or 2 percent response) coming back, you would have paid $12.50 to get each of your customers. If you spent $300M on your mailing and received the same number of customers, you would have spent $15.00 to get each of your customers.

All other things being equal, imagine the cost differential if you were mailing 3,000,000 pieces at 2 percent! On one hand you'd have 60,000 customers at $12.50 each; on the other, 60,000 customers at $15.00 each—only a 5¢ difference in the cost of the individual mailings (25¢ versus 30¢), but overall a $150,000 difference!

You can see that if the present control costs only $250M in the mail, you can't very well design a test package that costs $300M in the mail unless you're awfully certain it will outpull the control *enough to more than offset the higher cost.* Otherwise, why change the control?

I'm sorry about this CPM-CPO business. I expect you're mumbling humorlessly about these meaningless acronyms and your relationship to them right now, and actually you're right to resist—to a point. Somewhere along the line we all have to fight accounting-controlled creativity. When you're told you can't use odd-sized envelopes or big brochures, or order cards with paste and patch and peel-off, it takes a lot of fuel out of your imagination. And when you're constantly saddled with #10 and 6″ × 9″ envelopes, 11″ × 17″ two-color brochures and simple two-color order cards with a BRC back, it can take all the creative challenge out of the job. It also promises that everything will soon start to look the same.

But numbers must have their due; after all, the increased costs can be *big.* If you're going to be a smart creative type today, you'll have to fight the numbers people with their own numbers, learn to understand costs, and argue effectively. When you run over in one area of your planning, know it, and compensate by cutting back in another.

For example: You don't *have* to live with #10, 6″ × 9″ and 9″ # 12″ outer envelopes. There are seven other standard sizes with windows, like a Monarch or a 5″ × 11½″ (a #14). An 11″ × 17″ brochure may be economical, but so are 25″ × 8½″, 12½″ × 8½″, 8½″ × 7″. Take a look at some of your low-budget alternatives. They can be absolutely inspiring!

You can't do this kind of creative juggling without the help of a good artist or art director with some grounding in production. Although you should be aware of certain basics yourself, any good direct mail production person should be able to give you input on the following. Digest it. In addition, try to arrange trips to a printer and to lettershops, and visits with computer printing representatives. (You may feel now that once will be more than enough for you, but you'll find once is really barely beginning.)

Here are the minimum production basics you should digest for creative planning in a CPO-oriented business.

- United States Postal Service specifications and charges for first- and third-class mail (to include *weight* and *size* limitations, return addresses, and outer envelope requirements such as window placement and "white space").

- Lettershop inserting capabilities and limitations (number of pieces, envelope sizes, and how papers must be folded or nested for inserting).

- Economical brochure formats (what makes them economical, how do special sizes and folds increase costs?).

- Cost differentials between a #10 envelope, a 6 × 9 envelope and a jumbo (9 × 12) envelope. (When are plastic or polybag envelopes practical?)

- The difference between 100 pound stock, 90, 80, 70, 60, and 50. Why are some papers too heavy for brochures? When will some lack opacity? What is a matte finish?

- How to quickly guesstimate the increased cost of four-color over two-color. What do you need to know?

- The cost of an average two-color order card (BRC) for a #10 or a 6 × 9 envelope. (25M, 50M, and 100M quantity).

- The lightest reply card stock to make it safely through the return mail (smallest permissible size, largest size).

- The average cost of a four-page folded letter, two-colors on 60 pound offset (25M, 50M, and 100M quantity).

- Computer printing—Ink Jet, Impact, and Laser: Which is best for what? What minimum quantities are required? What new things are being introduced? (There's *always* something new in this field.)

The Golden Age of Direct Mail is past. You can no longer totally separate creativity from cost. But once you've established your rules of thumb, move on to create and dream and imagine. If you go too far, somewhere in your mind a little warning bell will sound—and back on track you go!

GUIDELINE 7: THE UNDERLYING LAW REVISITED

The final guideline for everything you do is a reminder to question. Don't get too close. Step back. Think first, second, and finally about the customer. *Be* the customer. Does it make sense to you? Will it make sense to the customer? Could it make *more* sense to the customer?

The Technically Correct Letter or "Is That All There Is?"

Now that you're moving into the big T, you'll be able to spot technique in every direct mail package. You'll also spot a lot of packages that are 99 percent technique.

You've seen them. We've all seen them. They are direct mail packages that are patently uncreative, boring, ho-hum, untalented stringing together of "Here," "Now," "Act today," all lined up with an equally unsophisticated offer presentation and a letter that sounds strangely familiar—totally impersonal—and embarrassing to those of us who care about bad images and lingering accusations of junk mail. And yet, most of these packages incorporate all the rules and formulas!

Look closely at these uninspired offerings. The products or services may vary, but the mailings persistently go on and on and on in the same way with the same tone, or lack of it. Two or three of the products could even be interchanged and one might never notice. Flat, humdrum sales spiels.

This bad image is being perpetrated by the new practioners who have indeed come upon the rules and formulas and are applying them in megadoses. They have the big T down pat; if you dissect and analyze their promotions you'll find there's nothing actually wrong with them. They follow the rules. They represent the formulas. *They are technically correct.*

There's nothing creatively right with them either. They are totally lacking in individuality of expression and any hint of creative excellence. Their authors have copied "success" and applied all the do's and don'ts you've learned in this chapter. Period. Not a thing more. Even more distressing, this technically correct, mediocre direct response works! Yes, you'll find that such advertising can indeed pay off—*but only under optimum conditions.*

It works with an exclusive market or an unusual, new product or an unbeatable offer. Given these optimum situations, the promotion supplies only what is required in a form that is technically acceptable. And as long as it has a hold on an exclusive product, the prime market, and the best possible offer, it will continue to work.

But once the competition gets in, once the price is no longer competitive, once the market erodes or becomes marginal, these mailings cease to work, because they don't know how to *sell.* Direct marketers know that selling starts the minute the prospect says no. Once the mailbox is full of offers, these technically correct packages can't even get through, much less hold their own with strong selling appeals.

Small solace to you…here you are at least 50 percent on your way; you've got the big T down and are ready to graduate, and I'm talking about the *other* 50 percent. Sure, you can go out and be a technician right now, today. But you'll never make creative director or promotion manager, or leader or teacher or top banana *without the creative part.*

Creativity adds style and tone. Creativity uses its tools to grab the reader and carry the reader through a direct mail package or ad until the reader gets to a point where it makes more sense to say yes than no. Creativity sells!

We'll be doing some important creative work in the chapters ahead to give you the missing 50 percent—creativity as it relates to concept development, creativity in determining the benefits and copy strategy, your approach, and your layout—creativity in pulling together the big ideas and writing them down.

Before you move on, however, be sure to check out the additional rules and guidelines here. And have fun with the fictitious Jim-Jam letter. It's technically correct. It follows all the rules. It's ugh, repulsive.

And I shall devote the rest of this book to helping make sure you never get involved with this kind of nauseous mediocrity.

ADDITIONAL RULES AND GUIDELINES

Bob Stone's Seven-Step Formula for Good Letters[3]

1. Promise a benefit in your headline or first paragraph, your most important benefit.
2. Immediately enlarge upon your most important benefit.
3. Tell the reader specifically what he or she is going to get.
4. Back up your statements with proofs and endorsements.
5. Tell the reader what will be lost by not acting.
6. Rephrase your prominent benefits in the closing offer.
7. Incite action now.

28 Rules from Tom Collins (Chairman, Rapp & Collins)[4]

Apply this checklist to each package you examine.

It won't be long before you understand exactly what makes direct mail packages work, why some are effective and why others aren't.

Creative Checklist

1. Do you have a good proposition?
2. Do you have a good offer?
3. Does your outside envelope select the prospect?
4. Does your outside envelope put your best foot forward?
5. Does your outside envelope provide reading motivation?
6. Does your copy provide instant orientation?
7. Does your mailing visually reinforce the message?
8. Does it employ readable typography?
9. Is it written in readable, concrete language?
10. Is it personal?
11. Does it strike a responsive chord?
12. Is it dramatic?

---

[3]Bob Stone, *Successful Direct Marketing Methods* (Lincolnwood, Illinois: Crain Books, an imprint of National Textbook Company, c/r, 1984) p. 192.

[4]Ibid., p. 205.

13. Does it talk in the language of life, not "advertise at?"
14. Is it credible?
15. Is it structured?
16. Does it leave no stone unturned?
17. Does it present an ultimate benefit?
18. Are details presented as advantages?
19. Does it use, if possible, the power of disinterestedness?
20. Does it use, if possible, the power of negative selling?
21. Does it touch on the reader's deepest relevant daydreams?
22. Does it use subtle flattery?
23. Does it prove and dramatize the value?
24. Does it provide strong assurances of satisfaction?
25. Does it repeat key points?
26. Is it backed by authority?
27. Does it give a reason for immediate response?
28. Do you make it easy to order?

CHAPTER 4 EXERCISES

Anatomy of a Successful Letter

Here are some of the elements that make up a successful direct mail letter. (You may be able to come up with still more points; if so, just add them in. The rules are always expanding and changing.)

Meanwhile take a look at the Jim-Jam letter to see how these elements can be combined to make up a technically correct promotion that's almost pure technique. (Figure 4-7.)

− Use a salutation.
− Use a logical spokesperson.
− Use the "You."
− State offer on p.1.
− Use a Johnson box to introduce offer and emphasize it.
− Use Charter or Membership in a Club when you can (exclusivity).
− Introduce a premium (use the word "Free").
− Emphasize dollar savings; use price comparisons.
− Have an offer deadline.
− Use odd numbers, 9's and 7's in particular.
− Indent first line of each paragraph.

– Use a broken sentence structure at the end of each page to carry over to next page.

– State major benefit(s) up front.

– List features.

– Use specifics; don't generalize.

– Use takeouts or margin notes to emphasize points in the letter.

– Involve your reader with dramatizations.

– Offer a deluxe version to increase order size.

– Promise fast delivery—immediate gratification.

– Use a strong guarantee to build credibility.

– Include testimonials to build credibility.

– Use call to action.

– Offer charge convenience or installment purchases.

– Offer cash payment incentives.

– "Limit" supplies—set tone of urgency.

– Use an *800* number to facilitate ordering.

– Use stamp or token for involvement.

– Use "P.S." to restate a major selling point.

I could suggest you practice combining pure techniques yourself here, but I can't encourage you to duplicate such garbage. So on to the next chapter.

A 4-page Technically Correct Letter

Immediacy

Premium Motivator

Magic Word

Personalization & Qualification

Invitational/Exclusivity Approach

Specific Offer Rephrased

Bargain Restated

Motivation -- Overcome Inertia

Premium

Carry over page break

```
* * * * * * * * * * * * * * * * * * *
*                                   *
*        Now, for the first time,   *
*   an Exclusive Charter Opportunity *
*          for you to try the       *
*             all-new Jim-Jam       *
*      at 40% Off Its Regular Price *
*         -- and get a free gift!   *
*                                   *
* * * * * * * * * * * * * * * * * * *
```

Dear Friend:

We are pleased to announce that because you have been a good customer in the past, now -- for a short time only, you are privileged to purchase the newest Jim-Jams at the low Charter rates of only $94.97.

Ordinary Jim-Jams alone sell for as much as $145 or more. Yet, you have this special Charter opportunity to purchase the Jim-Jam's latest model at a savings of 40%!

And, if you act quickly and respond before May 24, we will send you a hand-tailored Smersh with every Jim-Jam purchase.

What makes our Charter Jim-Jam so special?

Every one comes complete with

● 4 color interiors and

Johnson Box -- Offer Emphasis

"Charter" Exclusivity

Discount

Dialogue Begins

Odd Number (9 and 7)

Savings

Urgency

Deadline

Selling Points (Description)

Figure 4-7 *A 4-page Technically Correct Letter*

92

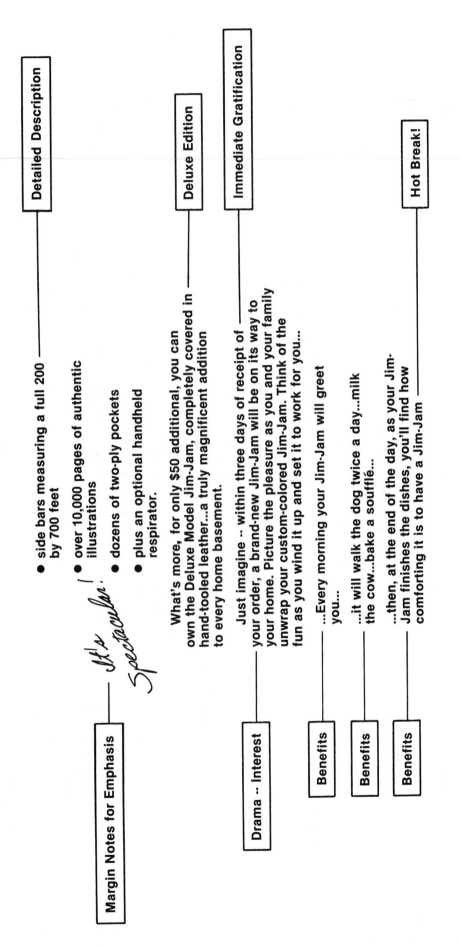

Detailed Description

- side bars measuring a full 200 by 700 feet
- over 10,000 pages of authentic illustrations
- dozens of two-ply pockets
- plus an optional handheld respirator.

It's Spectacular!

Margin Notes for Emphasis

Deluxe Edition

What's more, for only $50 additional, you can own the Deluxe Model Jim-Jam, completely covered in hand-tooled leather...a truly magnificent addition to every home basement.

Immediate Gratification

Just imagine -- within three days of receipt of your order, a brand-new Jim-Jam will be on its way to your home. Picture the pleasure as you and your family unwrap your custom-colored Jim-Jam. Think of the fun as you wind it up and set it to work for you...

Drama -- Interest

...Every morning your Jim-Jam will greet you...

Benefits

...it will walk the dog twice a day...milk the cow...bake a soufflé...

Benefits

Hot Break!

...then, at the end of the day, as your Jim-Jam finishes the dishes, you'll find how comforting it is to have a Jim-Jam

Benefits

Figure 4-7, *continued*

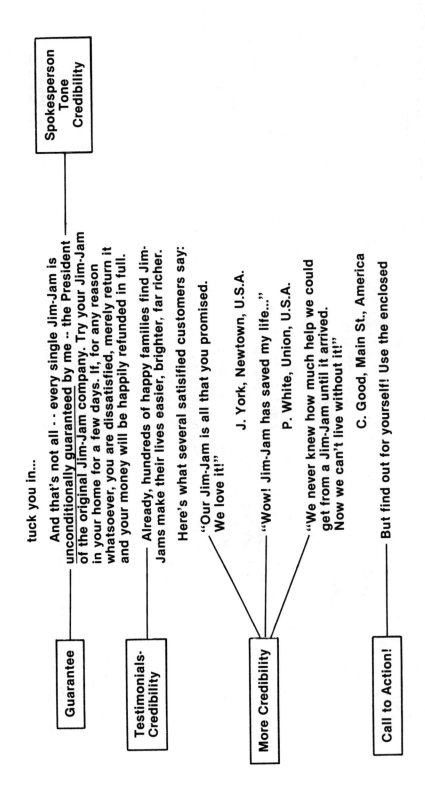

Spokesperson
Tone
Credibility

tuck you in...

Guarantee

And that's not all -- every single Jim-Jam is unconditionally guaranteed by me -- the President of the original Jim-Jam company. Try your Jim-Jam in your home for a few days. If, for any reason whatsoever, you are dissatisfied, merely return it and your money will be happily refunded in full.

Testimonials-
Credibility

Already, hundreds of happy families find Jim-Jams make their lives easier, brighter, far richer.

Here's what several satisfied customers say:

"Our Jim-Jam is all that you promised.
We love it!"

More Credibility

J. York, Newtown, U.S.A.

"Wow! Jim-Jam has saved my life..."

P. White, Union, U.S.A.

"We never knew how much help we could get from a Jim-Jam until it arrived. Now we can't live without it!"

C. Good, Main St., America

Call to Action!

But find out for yourself! Use the enclosed

Figure 4-7, *continued*

94

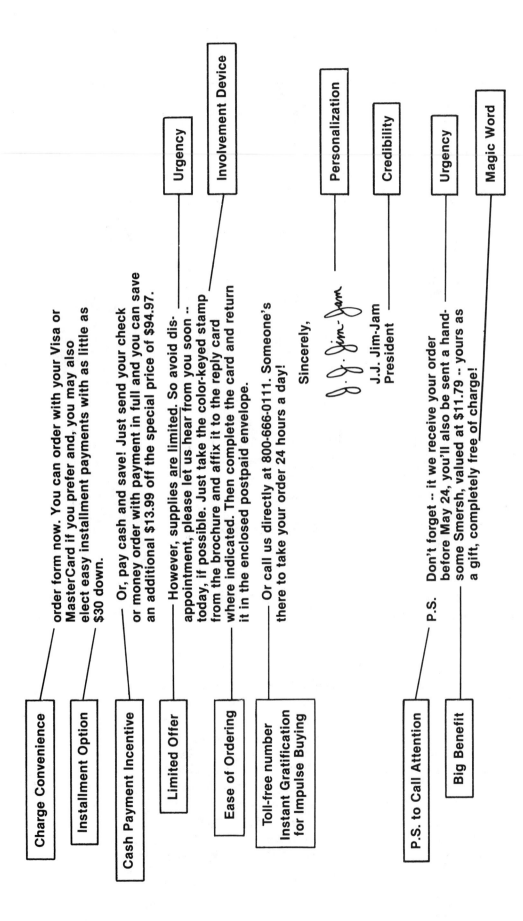

Charge Convenience

Installment Option

Cash Payment Incentive

Limited Offer

Ease of Ordering

Toll-free number
Instant Gratification
for Impulse Buying

P.S. to Call Attention

Big Benefit

Urgency

Involvement Device

Personalization

Credibility

Urgency

Magic Word

order form now. You can order with your Visa or MasterCard if you prefer and, you may also elect easy installment payments with as little as $30 down.

Or, pay cash and save! Just send your check or money order with payment in full and you can save an additional $13.99 off the special price of $94.97.

However, supplies are limited. So avoid dis-appointment, please let us hear from you soon -- today, if possible. Just take the color-keyed stamp from the brochure and affix it to the reply card where indicated. Then complete the card and return it in the enclosed postpaid envelope.

Or call us directly at 800-666-0111. Someone's there to take your order 24 hours a day!

Sincerely,

J.J. Jim-Jam
President

P.S.   Don't forget -- it we receive your order before May 24, you'll also be sent a hand-some Smersh, valued at $11.79 -- yours as a gift, completely free of charge!

Figure 4-7, *continued*

95

Nurturing Creative Concepts: How to Sharpen Your Creative Judgment and Grow a Concept

I can hear you say it now, "Oh boy, here we go—into the obtuse stuff."

I'll make you a promise. This is a very important chapter for you. I can't let you feel the least bit bored, confused, irritated or disinterested. This chapter can make the difference between a technician and (quite simply) a creative leader.

Its job is to help *you* identify the essence of what sells in every product or service that comes your way. It will enable you to play an important role in creative teamwork. It will help you take the lead and decide in what directions the creative appeal will move, what benefits will be promised, what moral imperatives will be used. Learn to to this—and do it well—and you'll be equipped to rise through the ranks to top advertising and marketing positions. Pass it by and it's back to the cubicles with you!

To help you through, I promise to be clear, concise and not take the easy outs of ambiguity. I'll stick with you; you stick with me.

The first step is to agree on definitions. Like what is a creative concept anyway? And what does it have to do with creative strategies?

According to *The American Heritage Dictionary of the English Language,* a concept is simply "a general idea or understanding, especially one derived from specific instances or occurrences. A thought or notion."

Although it's somewhat redundant, a *creative concept* is a creative idea, thought, or notion. A strategy, on the other hand, is a plan of action with military connotations. In marketing, it's an aggressive plan. Creative strategy is that part of the marketing strategy that applies to the creative development. Tactics (according to *American Heritage)* is "the technique or science of securing the objectives designated by strategy." Pretty simple, right?

If you agree, you're already ahead at this point, because many direct marketers have never acknowledged that they even *need* a creative strategy or plan as such. I say, you most certainly do, and it's going to be immensely important to you, whether the strategy development is a group effort or you go it alone.

A standard, well-known rule for all direct marketers is "sell the benefits!" But few people stop to wonder

- How do you decide *what* the benefits are?
- How do you know how many benefits to use?
- Does the benefit always go in the headline?
- How do you determine *which* benefits to use?
- Are all benefits equal or are some benefits more important than others?
- Once you have benefits, exactly how do you set them forward or present them?
- Is the offer the most important benefit?

Answering such questions is hard work every time, and without a clear creative strategy the answers can in fact be disastrously misleading.

Your creative strategy, as part of the marketing plan, is set up to incorporate all the input from research and marketing with logical step-by-step creative planning and tactics, culminating in a definite, creative direction. Before you can begin to develop your strategy, however, several preliminary steps are necessary.

THE SELLING PROPOSITION

Let's look back a minute and review the first steps you picked up in Chapter 2.

1. We'll assume you've done your research thoroughly. This means that to the best of your ability you understand the product positioning; you have a complete understanding of what the product or service is, how it works, how it looks, and what it does; you understand the competition and the company that produces your product and why that company is particularly qualified to do so; you know the market or customer; and you know the offer.

2. At this point you have also tested the soundness of your selling proposition. As we discussed in Chapter 2, this is your first critical go, no-go step in the creative process—the mission possible/mission impossible stage (your last chance to say "No Thanks"). Remember a 60-day cruise for busy executives? You had serious reservations, of course. Remember a 30 percent price cut for good customers? You declined. Take no dogs. Have no failures.

We're going to start off this time with a positive example, however, a brand new monthly magazine called *Vital Woman*. It's the first comprehensive magazine devoted to women's health and fitness, designed to appeal to active, busy women between the ages of 18 and 34. It will be priced competitively (one year, 12 issues, $15 by subscription) and published by a company with considerable experience in publishing, particularly in health and fitness publishing (credibility).

Check out your product's positioning and the offer, look over the market. Does the product make sense to the market? Do you feel comfortable with the market and the offer? Sound O.K.? Let's accept then, and take this project with us to serve as one example of how you'll go about developing your own creative strategies, starting with benefits and features.

HOW TO EXTRACT YOUR BENEFITS FROM YOUR FEATURES

"Extracting" sounds tooth-painful somehow and it should. "Pulling" the benefits is not easy and in many cases, you may feel you have to pry them out. If your selling proposition holds, however, you've already avoided a major problem. If you *had* been uncomfortable with the basic proposition, but took it on anyway, here's where you'd start to get into trouble.

For example, you could have ended up with a benefit that didn't fit the market, like promising a group of *young* women that your product would make them look *younger,* or offering a group of busy executives a two-month cruise! In the case of the one-third price cut offer, you might have ended up discovering that the benefit was in fact a creative person's curse, because it indicated that the product was overpriced all along.

Let's assume that our *Vital Woman* proposition holds, and before we do any real extracting, we need definitions for *features* and *benefits.*

Features are the physical characteristics of your product or service—the *facts* about the product: It is 10″ high; it comes in three colors; it is bound in leather; it has dozens of gourmet recipes; it has an unconditional guarantee.

Benefits are the promises of your product or service for the prospect—the involving *you* is ever present: It is easy for you to use; it will color-coordinate with your room; its fine quality is a reflection of your good taste; people will admire your cooking; it offers you security because it is a safe, sound investment.

Because most of us need all the help we can get with benefit extraction, let's crystal clear this with a slightly different illustration.

- The copier mechanism moves 10 copies through per second (how this saves time for the customer is a benefit).
- The computer weighs 15 pounds and measures 18″ × 12″ × 10″ (how this allows the customer to move it easily and store it conveniently in small space is a benefit).
- The course has four workbooks and eight audio tapes (how this material will enable you to move ahead in your profession is a benefit).
- The insurance policy pays its holder $70 a day for every day he is in the

hospital (how he can use the money to relieve worry and anxiety is a benefit).

- The book club offers a selection of six books a month at 30 percent off publisher's price (the ability to be up-to-date and well-read, plus save money, are the benefits).

Offer as Benefit

Wait a minute, you may be thinking; isn't the offer really a benefit in the last two examples here? (Get $70 a Day...Save 30% off...) Good point—and the answer is tricky. Certainly, price or savings and money gained are out-and-out benefits. When you have a product or service that's similar to others but offers a clear financial advantage, or when you have a group of products with an established price and you offer them to customers at a significant savings, price or savings can clearly be the primary benefit.

But when you introduce a new product or service to your market or a known product or service to a *new* market—as long as price is competitive with that of similar products and services—it is not a benefit. (Even if it isn't competitive, remember that nothing is a bargain if you don't want it!) If your product itself can't be compared, because there is no other product quite like it, price can hardly be considered a benefit.

In any situation where you have a big price advantage, where the saving is significant or where money itself is the focus, then the money or the offer does become the big benefit—and how the product or service will enhance your life becomes secondary to this. For example:

Primary: "Save $1,000 with this sensational offer"
Secondary: "And enjoy all the advantages of having a deluxe Jim-Jam in your home."

These differences will become clearer as we move forward, but let's go back now to the project we've just accepted and see how *Vital Woman* figures its features and benefits.

Vital Woman is a new monthly magazine devoted to women's health and fitness. Since it is the first (only) magazine to do this, the price or offer will not be the major benefit.

> It has ninety-six pages, many illustrated articles in color, two major features in each issue concerning major health issues and women, nine regular departments covering the art of self-care, fitness and exercise, nutrition, natural healing, reader questions and answers, preventive medicine, family assistance, advice on healthy relationships, and controversial topics.
> The magazine has ten editorial advisors, all prominent woman physicians, who will contribute from time to time as well as advise.
> Subscribers will be invited to send in questions and to share their experiences with other subscribers. The editorial board will digest current information, give both sides, then offer its point of view.
> As a new publication, it will be priced at $15 for the first year.

You've just read a long list of features. How many benefits can you extract?

This sounds easy enough, but once you actually try it, a lot of questions can come up, like "Is this *really* a benefit?"... "Isn't this benefit too small?" "Isn't this benefit too large—too amorphous?" Let's work it through together.

First, go back to your selling proposition. Who is the market? (Active, busy women between the ages of 18 and 34.) All right. Be 25 and female for a while. Now look at the features again and make a pass, using raw data. For example:

- *Vital Woman* can help you take better care of your health and overall well-being because of its information.
- *Vital Woman* will help you be well informed on medical topics that pertain to women. Then, when you go to your doctor, you will be able to communicate better regarding your own personal health problems.
- *Vital Woman* will give you current medical and health advice that you can count on because it comes from (or is reviewed by) a board of prominent physicians.
- *Vital Woman* is qualified to cover important medical and health topics for women because it is directed by a board of prominent *woman* physicians.
- *Vital Woman* is enjoyable and easy to read because it has many illustrations in color.
- If you sign on now, you will be able to take advantage of a special offer.

Not bad—for a first pass. (*You* may even have more than I've shown here. Good!)

You'll be able to pull a variety of nice specific benefits from the departments, too.

- *Vital Woman* enables you to talk about your health problems and get answers from top physicians (with Q and A sections).
- *Vital Woman* shows you how to diet and exercise for a healthy, well-tuned body.
- *Vital Woman* gives you guidance on a healthy outlook and positive relations with others.
- *Vital Woman* enables you to apply the principles of natural healing so you can keep medicines and drugs to a minimum.
- *Vital Woman* affords you an open information exchange so you'll be informed on controversial health topics.

If the editors are generous with their information, you can expand considerably in all of these areas with specifics. But how about the major benefits. Are they true benefits? Which are more important? Which should be subordinated? How might they be strengthened? Enlarged?

GROWING AND PRUNING BENEFITS

On your first pass, your benefits may seem pretty obvious—even mundane. For example, look at the first benefit, *"Vital Woman* can help you take better care of your health and overall well-being because of its information." So what? I don't know about you but this leaves me ho-hum. How can you turn a broad, blah statement like this into a big benefit—even a moral imperative?

Here's where you'll have to start employing your imagination (and your salesmanship). Some benefits are blah because they are too broad or too big. Others need dramatization. Most can gain by honing in on a basic human desire or aspiration.

To help you start thinking, here are some examples of how easily blah benefits can be reworked.

Blah benefit:

It will make your hair curly.

Rah benefit:

Have the beautiful soft curls you've always dreamed about!

Blah benefit:

You'll be able to make more money.

Rah benefit:

Never worry about money again!

-or-

Make $100,000 a year—even more!

Blah benefit:

You'll feel better with this vitamin compound.

Rah benefit:

Regain the vitality of youth!

Blah benefit:

This course will help you in business.

Rah benefit:

How to make it to the top in a rough job market!

-or-

If only one person is promoted—make sure it's you!

Blah benefit:

Win a new car.

Rah benefit:

Win the car of your dreams!

Blah benefit:

Improve your complexion.

Rah benefit:

Youth market: Banish ugly blackheads and pimples forever!

Mature market: Enjoy the soft smooth skin of youth!

Two things should become apparent as you play around with benefits and the many ways they can be stated.

1. You can expand or contract your benefits throughout your promotion, rephrasing them and regrouping them to tell your story from several different angles.

2. Your basic benefit development and the hierarchy of benefits (or relationship of one benefit to another) depend heavily on the specific values and aspirations of your target market.

You cannot determine your big benefit or major benefit until you develop a hypothesis upon which you will build your promotion and order your benefits.

DETERMINING YOUR HYPOTHESIS

The word *hypothesis* may be a little off-putting at first, but remember, just like *concept*, it's easy when it's defined. A hypothesis is merely an assumption or a proposition. (Tom Collins, of Rapp & Collins, first used this term in creative concept development. He applied the term in developing a group of testable space ads, each embodying a different assumption, or hypothesis.) For our purpose, it's an assumption regarding the market and what it wants or desires, and how this ties in to your product and its benefits.

When copy or concept testing is conducted in direct response advertising, it is, in truth, hypothesis or assumption testing.

A hypothesis is grown, or determined, by overlaying your product's big benefits on your market profile (demographics, geographics, and psychographics) and the corresponding values of that market. From this you nurture the one assumption that is based on the broadest and strongest appeal to your defined market. Once you have grown your hypothesis, you will be able to sort and order all your benefits in a proper hierarchical or descending/ascending order, and you will be able to theme your promotion and develop your "hooks," headlines, and leads.

Stop! Don't get concerned. I know I've introduced a new element here without warning. Let's back up for a minute and do a checklist:

Benefits? O.K.

Hypothesis? O.K.

Market profile? O.K.

Corresponding Values? TILT

I owe you an explanation of *corresponding values?* Big benefits are big because they hit certain deep-seated human nerves or drives. Basic drives, desires, and aspirations rule every one of us to a degree. They're not just the big drives like sex, greed, and fear (as some oversimplifiers may think they are), but a whole range of desires and concerns that change and shuffle around inside people depending on (1) how old they are, (2) how much income they have, (3) where they live (geographically), (4) their education, (5) the socioeconomic structure they come from, (6) their life style, (7) whether they're single or married, parent or childless, and (8) the tempo of the times.

SRI International, Menlo Park, California, is one of several research groups to make an extensive study to develop or categorize people by a combination of Values, Attitudes, and Life Styles (VALS). According to their research, there are outer-directed people, inner-directed people, and need-driven people, with a total of nine subgroups under these three categories. Every one of the groups has different mixtures of desires, aspirations, and values. They have different purchase patterns: they buy different things for different reasons.

Market *segmentation* is a big buzz word in direct marketing today. Thanks to the computer and the availability of vast data banks, we are able to target our prospects with far more scientific techniques than ever before, and these life styles selectors figure heavily in it.

If you're lucky, you'll have access to such research. Use it. You will know a lot about your prospect market, what is important to it, what it aspires to, what motivates it. Understanding these things is crucial to developing your hypothesis, for it gives you the key to your emotional appeals. It shows you how to couch your benefits and mold them to your market. Your ability to choose and develop those approaches with the greatest potential appeal (what I call the moral imperatives) will determine the success or failure of your promotion.

If you don't have access to scientific segmentation, take the clearest profile you can get of your market from your research and from media selection and media profiles (demographics from the lists that work, and readership studies from publications whose subscribers respond well). Also, get a subscription to *American Demographics*,[1] one of the finest profile sources for marketing and media people, and for smart copywriters.

In determining the drives and needs and aspirations of your market, be wary of the business market and the split appeals mentioned in Chapter 2. The basic drive in all such cases should be corporate recognition or advancement, whether one person or several people (or several levels of decision makers) are involved. At the same time, business and industrial direct response advertising today is targeted to incorporate the different needs and desires at various levels of decision makers in any one company, personalized to each level's specific requirements. (More about this strategy at the end of the chapter.)

Here are several fine examples of the appeals and promises that have been

---

[1] *American Demographics* (American Demographics, Inc., Box 68, Ithaca, New York 14851).

used by direct response specialists. This first group, by Vic Schwab, cofounder of Schwab/Beatty direct response advertising agency and a true pioneer of direct response, is as valid today as it was in 1942.

A CHECKLIST GUIDE TO SOME OF THE ADVANTAGES THAT PEOPLE WANT TO GAIN[2]

Better Health

Greater strength, vigor, endurance.

The possibility of longer life.

More Money

For spending, saving, or giving to others

Greater Popularity

Through a more attractive personality.

Through personal accomplishments.

Improved Appearance

Beauty. Style. Better Physical Build. Cleanliness

Security in Old Age

Independence. Provision for age or adversity.

Praise from Others

For one's intelligence, knowledge, appearance, or other evidences of superiority.

People also want to:

Be good parents
Have influence over others
Be sociable, hospitable
Be gregarious
Express their personalities

More Comfort

Ease. Luxury. Self-Indulgences.

Convenience.

More Leisure

For travel, hobbies, rest, play, self-development, etc.

Pride of Accomplishment

Overcoming obstacles and competition.

Desire to "do things well."

Business Advancement

Better job. Success. "Be your own boss." Reward for merit.

Social Advancement

Moving in better circles. Social acceptance. "Keep up with Joneses."

Increased Enjoyment

From entertainment, food, drink, and other physical contacts.

Win others' affection
Be "first" in things
Improve themselves mentally
Be recognized as authorities
Be creative

---

[2] Vic Schwab, *How To Write a Good Advertisement* (New York: Marsteller Inc., 1976), pp. 20-21.

Resist domination by others
Satisfy their curiosity
Be up-to-date
Emulate the admirable
Appreciate beauty
Be proud of their possessions
Be efficient

Acquire or collect things

And they want to save:

Money, Time, Work, Discomfort, Worry, Doubts, Risks, Embarrassment, Offense to Others, Boredom, Personal Self-Respect, and Prestige

Vic Schwab warned, however, that trends and times themselves change our aspirations and desires; appeals and values come and go in popularity, and this, too, must be taken into account. (When you consider the youth of the fifties, sixties, seventies, and eighties, it's clear that there can indeed be extreme value swings every decade.)

The second list comes from Bob Stone[3]

BASIC HUMAN WANTS

The desire to gain:

To make money

To save time

To avoid effort

To have health

To be popular

Enjoyment

Cleanliness

Praise

To be in style

To gratify curiosity

To satisfy appetite

To have beautiful possessions

To attract the opposite sex

To be an individual

To emulate others

To take advantage of opportunities

The desire to avoid loss:

Avoid criticism

Loss of possessions

Physical pain

Reputation

Danger in buying

Loss of money

Trouble

---

[3] Bob Stone, *Successful Direct Marketing Methods* (Lincolnwood, Illinois: Crain Books, an imprint of National Textbook Company, 1984), p. 173.

Andi Emerson, President of the Emerson Marketing Agency, lists human needs.[4]

EIGHT BASIC HUMAN NEEDS TO INCREASE MAILING RESPONSE

1. Making Money
   a. Improve job skills, increase pay
   b. Learn new job skills, get better paying jobs
   c. Outside spare-time income

2. Saving Money
   a. Sales, close-outs, discount operations, factory-direct, introductory offers, pre-pub offers, charter member offers
   b. Longer-wearing, less replacement cost
   c. Elimination of expense (do-it-yourself, reduce overhead, cut down consumption)

3. Winning Praise
   a. Improve homemaking, gardening, etc. skills
   b. Awards, citations, certificates for generous or meritorious actions
   c. Get better grades in high school or college

4. Helping Children and/or Family
   a. Health appeals (food, vitamins, medicines, exercise)
   b. Education
   c. Recreation

5. Saving Time and Effort
   a. Physical drudgery
   b. Instant results, overnight benefits
   c. Carefree maintenance

6. Impressing Others
   a. Specific status symbols (possessions)
   b. Indirect status symbols (memberships, certificates, awards, speeches, chairmanships, etc.)
   c. Education and knowledge (traveling, speech, courses, degrees, books, art, music)

7. Having Fun
   a. Traveling
   b. Family outings, picnics, etc.
   c. Nightclubs, race tracks, movies, bowling, dancing, etc.

8. Self-Improvement
   a. Physical (weight, muscles, hair, clothes, makeup, sex appeal)

---

[4] Andi Emerson, "8 Basic Human Needs to Increase Mailing Response," *DMA Manual*, Release #6102 (New York: Direct Marketing Association, Inc., January, 1978).

    b. Mental (education, philosophy, psychology, controlling others, influencing others)

    c. Spiritual (religion, helping others, self-control)

Andi Emerson cautions that the strongest motivations are unconscious motivations that must be directly tapped to work most effectively. (After all, you can't come right out and say that this is a way your prospect can impress others!)

Richard Shaver, President, Response Imperatives, Ltd., has added six basic drives to the eight basic human needs from Andi Emerson.[5]

1. Self-preservation

2. Love

3. Gain

4. Duty

5. Pride

6. Self-indulgence

Dick Shaver stresses the importance of distinguishing between the needs and the wants that your product or service will satisfy as you apply the two groups to your market.

Enough! You have your benefits, you know your market, you're able to extract the market's corresponding values (desires, needs, aspirations), and you can now formulate your hypothesis, based on strong, emotional appeals that will reach the greatest possible number of people in your market.

All you need now is a diagram showing this, but how about a sandwich instead? Follow this recipe:

- Take one slice of market, clearly segmented and defined.
- Spread it liberally with a thick paste mix of values, aspirations, and desires or drives.
- Take one fine slice of appropriate prime benefit and place it carefully on top.
- Sprinkle with creative thinking and heat well for 1 to 2 hours.
- Serve up garnished with secondary benefits.

What you get is one hot hypothesis, the quality of which may vary depending largely on the big benefit you use and the mix of your value paste.

This recipe can work in reverse as well. When marketers have a product and are trying to define the prime market for that product, they use a similar recipe to determine first the needs or desires that can be served by the product or service. Then the marketers find the market that best embodies these established needs and desires.

---

[5] Richard W. Shaver, "The Planning Process," *The Direct Marketing Handbook,* Edward L. Nash (New York: McGraw-Hill, Inc., 1984), pp. 29 and 30.

This product produces more attractive skin because it softens dry skin and removes wrinkles. Everyone wants to look better, have a better complexion. But only older people (and most particularly older women) are concerned with dry skin and wrinkles. Ergo—the prime market (you guessed it)—older women.

Easy as the hypothesis recipe sounds backward and forward, I hope you'll agree that this is something you should practice before moving along, because in application, it is *hard work.*

APPLYING WHAT YOU'VE LEARNED

Now that you have learned about benefit growing and hypothesis development, we can return to *Vital Woman.* Let's apply our knowledge and make a second pass at the primary benefits of *Vital Woman.* Don't forget, our market is active, busy women between 18 and 34. If you spread the values or aspirations on here, using Vic Schwab's listings, you'll opt for "better health" and "improved appearance" first off. But you might also consider (1) increased enjoyment, (2) pride of accomplishment, (3) resisting domination by others (i.e., the medical profession), (4) being up-to-date, and (5) saving yourself from worry, doubts, and risks. Then add "helping children and/or family," "self-improvement," "pride," and "self-preservation" from the other lists.

Here it is particularly important for you to understand your market in relation to the times and current lifestyles. While Vic Schwab was looking at housewives, you're dealing with a market of greater variety—probably women at home and women who work outside the home. They will also be representative of the times by having interests in health and fitness and self-improvement that are so typical of young *and* middle-aged people in the 1980s.

Let's go back to the first benefit again: *"Vital Woman* can help you take better care of your health and overall well-being because of its information."

Although good health and well-being are primary benefits, this benefit is too vague and all-encompassing. You should be able to state it more succinctly by tailoring it right to its prime market. For example, if the market were older women 55 to 60, you might say that *Vital Woman* would help restore vitality and a new enthusiasm for living and doing (under Schwab's listings). As we're talking to women 18 to 34, however, we have to consider what's more important to them.

Here is one theory or potential hypothesis: Young, active, women today want to be in charge (pride or self-preservation?). Taking control or resisting domination by others is important to today's women, particularly in the areas of health and medicine. They question doctors and expect explanations. Less and less do they accept medical instructions on blind faith.

They are most comfortable when they can obtain qualified medical and fitness input so *they* can decide (at least in part), what is best for them.

Let's take another of the benefits for a moment: *"Vital Woman* will help you be well informed on medical topics that pertain to women. Then, when you go to your doctor, you will be able to communicate better regarding your own personal health problems."

Here is another hypothesis that might apply: Many women are uncomfortable talking to male doctors about their female-related problems. Many of them feel doctors are unsympathetic, do not listen carefully or answer questions fully. If these women were better informed, they could have a better relationship with their doctors. Vic Schwab might have said they want to be recognized as authorities, or Bob Stone might say they want to be recognized as individuals.

There is still another possible hypothesis and it has to do with confidence and medicine. Today there are so many changes, new treatments and new drugs, that doctors are deluged with information. Many of them fail to keep up. To prevent doubts or fears about good health and good treatment, many women take it upon themselves to keep up with medical developments (self-preservation). This is all right, but in fact it seems to take us right back to the first benefit: *"Vital Woman* can help you take better care of your health and overall fitness because of its information."

The hypothesis that we set up first applies here, and this hypothesis can be enlarged and strengthened.

Earlier hypothesis: Young, active women today want to take charge. Being in control, or resisting domination by others, is important to today's women, particularly in the areas of health and medicine. They question doctors and expect explanations. Less and less do they accept medical instructions on blind faith.

Revised hypothesis: Today's women want to be informed on important health and fitness issues so that they can begin to take control of their lives *and* improve their relationships with their doctors.

However, we have still *two other* benefits that come into play.

Vital Woman will give you current fitness and health advice that you can count on because it comes from (or is reviewed by) a board of prominent woman physicians.

Vital Woman is qualified to cover important medical and health topics for women because it is directed by a board of prominent woman physicians.

Under the need for competent information to avoid risk, worry, or fears about lack of health data, you now have another hypothesis: Women feel more confident when they know their health and medical information is screened by a group of prominent physicians—and preferably woman physicians (the implication here being that they better empathize with other women who understand their problems).

Obtaining the information comes before who gives it. So now we're beginning to build a pyramid—to establish a hierarchy of benefits and hypotheses. And obtaining information is the base.

At this point, everything seems to flow from the statement, "When women are better informed they can take control, make decisions wisely, ask good questions, evaluate answers."

...This enables them to avoid risk and worry because they can understand and solve or prevent many health problems and live a more healthy life.

...This allows them to better communicate with their doctors (be recognized as individuals, not dominated).

Let's stick with this for now and see where it takes us on the next leg.

CONSTRUCTING THE COPY PLATFORM

Surprise! You have just laid the base for a copy platform.

If you've been following closely up to here, you've already accumulated enough material to start playing with your major headlines and subheads (and, no doubt, if you have a strong creative bent you've already been doing just that).

Up to this point, by the way, this may all be part of a group effort and you may be part of the group. There is no reason why creative meetings, or brainstorming sessions, synectics or creative planning groups consisting of writers, artists, creative directors, product managers, marketers and production people, can't get together to hammer out what we're going through.

There is also no reason that you can't go it alone, but this is where two heads can be better than one. If you are working with a publication, its editors may already have worked out some benefits and a hypothesis in structuring their editorial plan. (Let's hope!)

Authors, inventors, and manufacturers all have strong ideas about their own products or services and what they'll do for people. Marketers, managers, and well-wishers of all kinds will add their two cents as well. You'd be smart to listen carefully. You *might* pick up valuable ideas; then again, maybe not. *You* must be the judge. From here on in, your role in the group becomes more and more important. You're approaching the place where one head (*your* head) may be better than two. The copy platform belongs to you.

Again, we'll start with a definition to be absolutely sure we're together on this one. Your *copy platform* is simply a restatement of your hypothesis and your sub or secondary assumptions in direct response advertising jargon, or deathless promotional terms that incorporate the "you."

Let's line up the hypothesis and benefits on the left and extract the copy platform on the right.

1. *Main hypothesis*	1. *Main platform statement*
Women want to be better informed about their health and fitness so that they can	You are the primary diagnostician. Let *Vital Woman* help ensure that the

take control, make wiser decisions. This enables them to avoid risk and worry because they can understand and solve or prevent many health problems and live a more healthy life.

2. *Secondary (or alternative) hypothesis*

Good information allows women to better communicate with their doctors (be recognized as individuals, not be dominated), ask good questions, evaluate answers.

3. *Major benefits*

Vital Woman gives women current medical and health information that they can count on because it comes from (or is reviewed by) a board of prominent physicians.

Vital Woman is qualified to cover important medical and health topics for women because it is directed by a board of prominent *woman* physicians.

4. *Secondary Benefits*

• *Vital Woman* is enjoyable and easy to read because it has many illustrations in color.

• *Vital Woman* has top physicians to answer reader questions (Q and A sections).

one person who can take care of you best does a good job.

• Take charge of your own health with *Vital Woman*.

• Put your health in the best hands—your own.

• Save the time and cost of unnecessary doctor visits.

2. *Secondary platform statement*

You can make sure your doctor takes you seriously. (Why should you feel neurotic every time you feel sick?)

• Your doctor will listen when you ask, explain when you question.

3. *Major copy points*

Every month you are invited to sit in on your own private physician's council on health and fitness.

or

Join a round table of foremost woman physicians. Sit down every month and listen. Ask questions.

Women doctors understand.

4. *Secondary Copy Points*

• Over 10 pages of color illustrations, dozens of charts, drawings and graphs make every issue of *Vital Woman* an enjoyable and informative experience.

• Let's talk about *your* health problems. When you have questions, ask *Vital Woman's* board of physicians.

- *Vital Woman* has diet and exercise information.

- *Vital Woman* offers guidance on a healthy outlook and positive relations with others.

- *Vital Woman* presents principles of natural healing thay keep medicines and drugs to a minimum

- *Vital Woman* provides an open information exchange on controversial health topics.

- Keep in shape the right way with *Vital Woman*'s medically approved diet methods and exercises.

- Let *Vital Woman* help keep your head *and* heart in balance.

- Get sound information on natural healing. Keep medicines and drugs to a minimum. Save money.

- Understand the pros and cons of important issues like abortion, your legal rights in the hospital, a birth plan. Contribute your opinions.

Under your secondary benefits (and copy points) will come all the specifics (the "as ifs," "likes" and "for examples") that strengthen your copy.

You'll find there's *more* than enough material for your basic copy platform here. You also have two possible hypotheses. So you'll want to decide beforehand which one you'll be featuring or how you might combine them. Or, because you have *two* hypotheses, you can also suggest a concept test here.

A FEW GOOD THINGS TO SETTLE BEFORE THE FINAL STRATEGY STATEMENT

If you're on your toes, you may be wondering at this point why I've neglected to mention one major benefit: "If you sign on now, you will be able to take advantage of a special offer."

I've saved it for last because this is the offer and, as your offer, it's too important to go in with the other benefits. It is a benefit, but not the *big* benefit; that comes from the product itself. (Think about it—the offer is not a benefit until the product is a benefit!)

Because *offer* is important, whether or not you are in charge of its formulation, it is critical that you know how to judge a good one, and how to recognize a weak one. And now that you've been through Chapter 3, you can do just that.

Take the *Vital Woman* offer of $15 for the first year, for example. How might you strengthen it? Thanks to Chapter 3, you know this is a perfect place to use the initial "Charter Invitation," enabling your prospect to be "first on" and a "privileged" subscriber.

How else can you strengthen this offer? A guarantee? Of course. The product is untried and virtually unknown. This is a natural place for a one-hundred percent money-back guarantee. (If this sounds daringly generous to you, relax. Your prospects will appreciate it and few, *if any*, will ever take advantage of the guarantee. How do *I* know? Heh, heh—can't you guess?)

Something else? A response incentive? Sure. If you can convince the powers-that-be that this will justify the added expense, you might suggest a highly related, *qualifying* premium—something that's inexpensive but appealing. How about a low-budget booklet: *Answers to 24 of Women's Most Serious Medical Questions?* It has good copy potential for you.

Now you have (1) charter invitation, (2) special subscription price, (3) premium incentive, and (4) full guarantee. You might also want to apply another response motivator to your offer—a deadline, that is, so suggest this, too.

Now you have a strong offer. It means that your promotion has a good chance of success. What else might you consider before you lock up your creative strategy? Now's the time for miscellaneous recommendations or ideas that in some cases, may need consensus, or the approval of others. Remember: *voice* (who's talking) and *credibility* (why qualified).

Decide, for example, who should sign the letter—the editor—the publisher? In this case, since your market is women and your subject is women's health, you'd do well to choose a woman. Recommend that your spokesperson be a *credible, logical* woman. (A woman doctor? Publisher? Editor?) Consider a woman publisher in this case. Publishers can speak logically and glowingly about *Vital Woman's* editorial merits. And since *Vital Woman* is a medically oriented publication, how about adding your medical advisory board—right up front on the letterhead?

Go back to Chapters 3 and 4 and see if you've thought through all the major techniques and guidelines that apply here. Although more may come out as you write, it's good to try to pin down as many aspects of the package as you can at this point. Don't go overboard on motivators and involvement devices, however. Remember—credibility *and* the Underlying Law!

Your Format Options—Keep Them Loose

In the case of *Vital Woman*, you'll want to recommend a standard direct mail consumer package *with* brochure (since your specs indicate that *Vital Woman* will be heavily illustrated). Also, a brochure can give additional credibility to a new, as yet unpublished product. You may not need all four pages to tell your story in the letter; you may not want a lift letter, but it's good to know it's in the budget if you do.

Before creativity carries you too far, however, get a clear feeling for budget—"sky's the limit" or "standard and small." Pin it down *before* you move beyond this stage. But don't let *them* pin *you* down on format. Hold out! Hedge! You're not ready to finalize any format decisions yet, whether you have a $15,000 budget or a $500,000 budget.

Consider the Computer

Speaking of budget, at this stage you should also think about computerization. Good computerization can change the way you plan your package or packages. It will affect copy, design, and format, as well as costs.

Computer letters have considerable appeal if they're done properly. Sweepstakes, for example, often use dramatic computerized components because everyone likes to see his or her name in print (up in lights, with dramatic headlines and value certificates that claim the prospect may have won a million dollars or more). On the other hand, people also respond well to the more intimate, personal feeling of a dignified, computerized letter. (This does not mean simply computer-printing a name on the front page of a letter four or five times. That is a dull and tacky use of computerization and it impresses no one.)

Certain kinds of situations lend themselves to good computerization, however. Here's how to determine your course. Use computer formats only

1. If you have a package in which several components, in addition to your outer envelope, should carry the prospect's name and address for dramatization and credibility.
   - membership cards or personal invitations
   - sweepstakes components
   - financial applications, insurance certificates, and plastic cards
   - business letters that require personal salutations
   - warranties and service contracts

2. If you have customer data in your computer that can be used for a very personalized selling story.
   - last purchase date
   - product or category of product purchased
   - specific deadlines
   - serial or warranty numbers
   - appropriate personal information—birthday, anniversary, number of children

3. If your quantities and/or budget will be large enough on your test rollouts to make computerization cost-effective.

4. If you have up-to-date, accurate computer data. For example: you may not want to computerize your mailing if the computer can't give you sex or first names.

When Is a Direct Mail Format More than a Direct Mail Package?

We've been breezing along under the assumption that we want a direct mail package here. That may not be the strategy at all! A direct mail package may be just fine for *Vital Woman*, but you may want more than this for your next assignment. You may be thinking, "How about another mailing as a follow-up? Or a telephone call? How about an advance postcard to alert the prospect to expect my mailing?"

CAR-RT SORT **CR 20

MS. JOAN H THROCKMORTON
1175 YORK AVENUE
NEW YORK, NY 10021

INVITATION NO. SI-27047

NEW YORK CITY POSTMASTER:
PLEASE DELIVER THIS OFFICIAL
INVITATION PROMPTLY.

SMITHSONIAN INSTITUTION
WASHINGTON, D.C. 20560

MS. JOAN H THROCKMORTON

YOU ARE ONE OF A SMALL GROUP OF

NEW YORK CITY RESIDENTS

INVITED TO BECOME NATIONAL ASSOCIATES

OF THE SMITHSONIAN INSTITUTION

I know you receive many "personal" (i.e. computer-printed) invitations
but this is special.

By accepting this particular invitation you will join a special group of
Americans whose importance to our national culture I'll explain later.

The current enrollment program ends May 31. We can only hold the
enclosed Registration Number in your name until then. Let me review
the benefits of membership reserved for you:

Chief among them is SMITHSONIAN magazine -- perhaps the most talked-about
periodical of recent years. A monthly journal of science, history,
technology and the arts, it is handsomely printed, lavishly illustrated,
compellingly written -- and published especially for Smithsonian
Associate members.

SMITHSONIAN glows with color photographs -- of bobcat kittens, miming
clowns, renaissance clocks, illuminated manuscripts, jewel-like fish.

SMITHSONIAN also gleams with thought-provoking articles -- about how
computers are re-creating reality, how exercises can re-program the
mind, how mothers impart diverse social skills to newborn infants.

This splendid magazine is but the first of many pleasures in store for
you. Among the others:

Money-saving opportunities to travel and study abroad -- in Alpine
villages, Welsh manor houses, Portuguese fortified towns, African
game parks, the Himalayas.

Invitations to stimulating events at home. Concerts, lectures,
seminars on 18th and 19th century horticulture, Byzantine splendors,
Chinese ceramics, World War I aviation. Scenic hiking expeditions,
Grand Canyon rafting trips, Washington weekends.

(over, please)

Figure 5-1 *An Excellent Use of the Computer. The package is designed by David Gordon and written by John Francis Tighe.*

<u>Members' Discounts</u> up to 40% on books; 10% on records, jewelry, crafts, museum reproductions, and much more. Classic Smithsonian recordings, from Handel's Concerti Grossi to classic jazz by Jelly Roll Morton, Louis Armstrong, Fats Waller. Model airplane kits from the National Air and Space Museum. Authentic folk instruments such as the Sweet Dulcimer.

Membership in the National Associates Program is $18, and includes all the benefits mentioned above -- a subscription to SMITHSONIAN, group rates on overseas and domestic study tours, substantial savings on books, records and a variety of gifts from the Smithsonian shops and catalogs -- plus "members-only" dining privileges in our Associates Court restaurant whenever you visit Washington, D.C.

I know of few investments that offer so much for so little.

But there are also <u>intangible</u> benefits to becoming a Smithsonian National Associate, which in the long run may be of more value to you than the tangible ones.

Your membership fee will assist the Smithsonian Institution -- its price-less collections of human achievements from the prehistoric to contemporary American history, its magnificent art galleries, its continuing research in energy, the environment, space.

<u>Your National Museum</u>

You may not have realized that the Smithsonian is your National Museum, chartered by Congress in 1846 and dedicated to "the increase and diffusion of knowledge."

What a lofty goal it sets! And what a testimony to our form of government that it grows and flourishes to provide so much that gives meaning to the American experience.

It isn't often one gets a chance to participate personally in such a grand adventure. As a National Associate you not only contribute to the Smithsonian and its continuing mission; you help assure the future of one of the world's finest historical, scientific, educational and cultural experiments.

It's easy to begin your personal adventure with the Smithsonian. Simply check the box on the enclosed Enrollment Form and return it in the postage-paid envelope. No need to send money now. We'll bill you $18 annual dues at the same time we send your membership card.

Sincerely yours,

Anne Keating

Anne Keating
for the Smithsonian

AK:hv

P.S. The enclosed Interim Membership Card will immediately make you eligible for several benefits that only Smithsonian Associates enjoy. Your official annual card will be sent when we receive the Invitation Form.

Figure 5-1, *continued*

Smithsonian Institution
WASHINGTON, D.C. 20560

INVITATION NO: SI-27047

Detach the Interim Membership Card and slip it into your wallet. It immediately entitles you to the discount and special dining privileges mentioned on the attached invitation form.

(Detach on dotted line)

THE SMITHSONIAN ASSOCIATES
Interim Membership

NONTRANSFERABLE

JOAN H THROCKMORTON

6/30/85
Date of Expiration

Secretary, Smithsonian Institution
Washington, D.C. 20560

Smithsonian Institution
WASHINGTON, D.C. 20560

OFFICIAL INVITATION NO:
SI-27047

ISSUED TO:

60404227047

MS. JOAN H THROCKMORTON
1175 YORK AVENUE   OGYL1
NEW YORK, NY 10021

☐ **I accept your invitation to become a Smithsonian National Associate.**
My annual dues (for which you will bill me later) are only $18, and membership includes all benefits listed below:

• 12 monthly issues of SMITHSONIAN magazine.
• Discounts on books, records, museum reproductions and other Smithsonian gifts.
• Special dining and other members'

privileges in Washington, D.C.
• Opportunities to attend seminars and regional exhibitions.
• Eligibility for all Smithsonian foreign and domestic study tours at National Associates' group rates.

OF-20

---

*From the desk of
the Publisher*

To: MS. JOAN H THROCKMORTON

From: JOSEPH BONSIGNORE

Smithsonian Magazine
Smithsonian Institution • Washington, D.C. 20560

As one of the founders of SMITHSONIAN, I wanted to add a word of my own about this magazine that means so much in my life and which, I believe, can play an important role in yours.

Perhaps you've seen Josef Albers' colorful painting of a succession of squares progressing to infinity, captioned, "Learning Never Ends".

That comes close to visualizing our concept of SMITHSONIAN. Issue after issue, it's a continuing extension of our knowledge, ideas and appreciation of everything under the sun from art to zoology. No limits on what it covers, no stinting on the most colorful and compelling presentation.

Every month SMITHSONIAN is an exciting new learning experience for me -- as I hope it will prove for you. I look forward to welcoming you as a Smithsonian Associate, and a SMITHSONIAN reader.

-- J.B.

BR-21

FROM: MS. JOAN H THROCKMORTON
1175 YORK AVENUE
NEW YORK, NY 10021

INVITATION NO. SI-27047

BUSINESS REPLY MAIL
FIRST CLASS   PERMIT NO. 156   BOULDER, CO

POSTAGE WILL BE PAID BY ADDRESSEE:

Smithsonian Institution
Membership Data Center
P.O. Box 2949
Boulder, CO 80321

Figure 5-1, *continued*

Interpreted broadly, format can cover the shape of the entire promotion. In a few customer direct response programs, this can mean an additional effort. In almost all business-to-business programs, format includes more than one mailing or promotion.

Major format planning, a series of mailings, two-part promotions, and so on, are generally part of the big picture or the main marketing plan and therefore precede the creative strategy planning. It's important that you understand these formats nonetheless, because each embodies a promotional strategy. They will also affect your creative strategy development, particularly in business-to-business creative planning.

If the budget allows, testing a follow-up or announcement postcard is perfectly legitimate *if* you have good reason. (An announcement of importance is coming—watch for it! Since we cannot repeat this offer, we're extending our deadline to make sure you don't miss this one last chance.)

Such components should go into your creative strategy as extra steps with clear statements of objective. You should spell out their role in relation to your main package, name your spokesperson, set down your timing *(justify* it) and justify your reasons for the medium. For example:

- Use the telephone as a follow-up so that we can find out why people didn't respond.

- Use local billboards to announce the coming mailing since we're saturating a defined geographical area.

The Good Old-Fashioned Two-Step Format—When to Use It

Follow-up reminders and advance announcements are used to draw attention to your original or primary package. Their job is to help you get the most response from your prospect lists in a well-targeted market.

But in markets that are diffuse or difficult to target, a two-step process is often used. This is a very popular form of direct response for business-to-business mail and for large-ticket consumer products. It is generally known as inquiry generation.

Step One: Prospect Qualification

Step Two: Inquiry Fulfillment

No doubt you see dozens of ads all the time—in magazines and newspapers, on the radio, even on TV—that end with, "Write us or call for more information." Sometimes it's a simple direct mail package with an invitation to write or call. These are all lead getters, to be used

- when you have an expensive product and expensive promotion package that you don't want to waste on unqualified prospects (people who are very likely to throw it away).

- when you do not have a good, reliable list of prospects (by name, title, and address) and you want to build one.

The two-step's job is to produce *qualified* leads. There's no room for teasers here. You want to turn away unqualified prospects. ("For the discerning individual who is prepared to invest in the finest automobile ever made..." "If this is the kind of office equipment that can help your company increase productivity....")

Step two is the information that fulfills the inquiry: "Enclosed is the information you requested."

This step represents a second component in your format and it must also fulfill the requirements of your creative strategy whether its objective is to make a sale, open the door for a sales call, or initiate a request for more information.

Your fulfillment package or information kit can now be considerably personalized if you wish *and* if your budget allows. You and the art director can do wonderful things with envelopes, brochures or booklets, letters, reply devices, and motivators with the knowledge that you will be speaking to prime prospects.

Also (budget permitting), you can add a third step to the two-step for nonrespondents—a follow-up for "more information" requests—and on and on, for that matter. *Strategy* must work hand in hand with *timing* here. It should become part of your overall format plan as well. Without it, *you can't create.* (Just try to do a credible follow-up or an inquiry fulfillment letter when you have only a vague idea of the last time the prospect heard from you.)

Walk through your procedures carefully. Overlay your timing scheme. What do you want your prospect to *do?* What do *you* do next (a) if the prospect responds, or (b) if the prospect fails to respond? Is your timing realistic? (Don't keep your inquiry waiting more than a few days. Hot inquiries cool off quickly.)

Bear two things in mind at all times while you are plotting your strategy: the budget (stay within it) and the Underlying Law. (Is all this going *to make sense* to the prospect? Stop. Let it cool. Step back and reexamine it with a clear eye.)

Four steps, five steps, six steps, three levels, and your creative strategy: Once you're out of the old two-step formula you're into pure business-to-business creative strategy development and in many cases your format planning can go on and on and your creative strategy can become a little more complex. Not a lot—remember, you'll still have just one *basic* objective, to acquire and cultivate (sell) customers.

Budgets are generally pretty liberal in this area, as many businesses are playing for some very large stakes. (What's a small $500,000 direct mail investment played off against a $10,000,000 contract?)

You may end up strategizing a whole series of informational mailings. Some may not even require immediate response. All will require creative strategy statements. (Remember the Comparative Business/Consumer Objectives from Chapter 2?) Some may be real packages or dimensional mailings instead of standard direct mail packages. Dimensional mailings are usually gifts or premiums in tubes, envelopes, or boxes that dramatize a promotional theme. They can run in a series of three, four, five, six, or more, and can go on for a year. They raise awareness and generally work to pave the way for the salesperson's call.

For example, a coffee cake, sent to customers to highlight a new sunrise pick-up service, a fireman's hat to dramatize new solutions for the man who's always "putting out fires," or a miniature paper weight or pencil cup or pen holder to remind the prospect of the company. Good dimensional mailings should carry a letter and the gift should be closely related to the product or service and its sales story or theme.

This pretty well exhausts your format possibilities in both business and consumer direct mail. Before you draw up your strategy (or strategies), however, there is one more consideration: how to set up testing strategies against an established control.

Strategizing to "Beat the Control"

If you're developing your creative strategies to test against an established control, be very sure of your objectives and hypotheses.

Analyze the hypothesis underlying the control along with the basic selling concepts so you don't unconsciously repeat it in another format or a new copy presentation. (You can, of course, always capitalize on what works by improving on it!)

Make sure you are testing a specific creative idea that you can explain in the context of every single component in your package.

New offers, premiums, involvement devices (tokens, stamps) and motivators (deadlines), should all be tested in the control package, not in a new, untested package. *An untested package should carry the same offer and motivators as those of the control.*

The rule for testing: No test can incorporate and measure more than *one* variable. For example: Let's say you're testing a concept based on a new hypothesis and you also add a token (when a token has not been used before). It works wonders. You win the test. But *what* won? Your execution of the new concept? Or the token? Or both? Worse still—if it lost, what was responsible for the loss? Perhaps the loss would have been far wose without the token. Perhaps not. This is no way to learn.

A smart creative person sets testing sights clearly and specifically and defines objectives and how these can be realized with the test package. The test then is a pure test of yes or no. Yes, the creative concept worked; no, the creative concept did not work. You learn either way. A gray test (in which you learn nothing) is the only bad or poorly executed test.

When to break the testing rule: Many professional free-lancers, when challenged to beat the control, execute mailings that pull out all stops: new creative concepts for new hypotheses, new involvement devices and motivators, new graphics, new formats—all in one package.

Their job is to win, not to learn. Besides, they've already learned what makes winners and if they go up against a control that doesn't know better, anything goes. If they do win, this is good for the free-lancers' business, their clients will call on them again. If they don't outdistance the control, however, their clients lose doubly: no new, stronger control, and no clear, usable testing data as to why something failed.

It's safe and scientific to go for a yes or no, "let's find out" test. It's heroic (and *maybe* foolish) to go for broke unless the testing history and/or the present control has blatantly ignored sound direct response technique and, particularly, the use of proven motivators and response devices. Here's some sound guidance from Jim Kobs and Sol Blumenfeld:

An Organized Approach for Beating the Control[6]

Top creative people are not always able to verbalize their approach to creativity. An exception is Sol Blumenfeld of Sol Blumenfeld & Associates. I like his organized method for idea generation, which he calls a five-track approach to beating the control:

1. *The subtractive approach.* This seeks to improve the effectiveness of a given mailing by reducing costs, thereby reducing the cost per inquiry or sale. One way to do this is by using a "stripped down" version of a winning package such as going from a 6 × 9 size to a number 10 size, using a smaller circular, eliminating one element from the package, and so on. Another way to accomplish the same thing is to develop a new mailing that's more economical such as a self-mailer. These approaches usually won't outpull the control in percent response, but they can often produce a lower cost per order.

2. *The additive technique.* This means adding something to a control package that may increase its efficiency in excess ratio to any increased costs. Usually it involves inserts. A classic example is the so-called publisher's letter, which was originated by Paul Michaels when he was with Greystone Press. At other times the mere addition of a token, stamp, or other involvement device can provide a substantial boost in results.

3. *The extractive approach.* This technique entails drawing on the contents of an established ad or mailing and extracting a thought or idea that can be built up as the main appeal. Blumenfeld cites an example for a publication's subscription campaign in which he picked up a very human appeal that was buried in the body copy of their control ad. He developed it into a new headline, which substantially beat the control.

4. *The segmentive technique.* As you might guess, this one entails segmenting your market and developing one or more special promotions aimed at those different segments. Blumenfeld points out that correspondence schools often use a special women's package, because they have found that their normal

---

[6] Jim Kobs, *Profitable Direct Marketing* (Lincolnwood, Illinois: Crain Books, an imprint of National Textbook Company, c/r, 1981), p. 92.

packages simply don't work as well with the female market. Likewise, record clubs often use separate packages for country music, teen and classical market segments. Understandably, this technique requires that the copywriter be familiar with the list universe to which he or she is writing and its customer profile.

5. *The innovative approach.* This category is characterized by Blumenfeld as being highly original, even wild. He believes that every test series should contain at least one or two ideas that fall into this category, because they can often produce more dramatic improvements in results than the other approaches.

THE CREATIVE STRATEGY—FINALLY

Where such things as creative strategies exist, they often exist under different names. Like creative plan, creative work plan, copy strategy. Sometimes it's just a yellow pad with a free-lancer's notes. And sometimes it's a structured presentation by the creative director or the copywriter for a group of peers.

Some are shorter than the creative strategy outline I'm giving you here. But the considerable detail of your creative strategy is your assurance that you've covered your bases, thought through all the points, and cleared the concepts *before* you start to execute your promotion.

Let's go over the elements of a good creative strategy again.

From the original selling proposition you should have (1) your product and its positioning, (2) the market (its demographics and psychographics), and (3) the offer; (4) your hypothesis, then (5) your copy platform, starting with your major benefit, working down through your secondary benefits, and ending with a list of features.

It's also good to include a brief statement regarding the competition, which in the case of *Vital Woman* is nonexistent, and you'll want to set down your recommendations regarding motivators, spokesperson, and credibility.

Finally, you'll want to have some idea of format and, in the case of direct mail, postage, then testing considerations, if they apply. And that's it! "Format" should also take into consideration the *entire* program or promotion format. In our case this means only one direct mail package and its components, but as you've seen in some business-to-business promotions and some high-ticket consumer programs, you'll want more than one effort or package. And you may need to develop substrategies or separate plans for the details of the longer, more complicated programs. This may also be necessary if you have more than one level of decision makers (or market) in business-to-business promotions. We'll cover this in a minute.

These strategies may seem like a lot of work, but take heart. Once you've gone through all the steps, you can be comfortable with your creative direction and confident that you have the creative tools to execute a successful direct response promotion.

Let's pick up where we left off with *Vital Woman.*

Creative Strategy Outline

Title of Job: Vital Woman magazine, the first comprehensive magazine devoted to women's health and fitness.

Competition:	None. This is the first such publication.
Market:	Active, busy women between the ages of 18 and 34. (Women who have shown an interest in health and fitness publications, exercise book buyers, etc.)
Offer:	Charter Offer, 1 year for $15; full money-back guarantee. Premium ("Answers to 24 of Women's Most Troublesome Health Questions").
Hypothesis:	Women want to be better informed about their health and general well-being so they can take control of their lives, make wiser decisions, and improve their relationships with their doctors. This enables them to avoid risk and worry because they can understand and solve or prevent many problems and live a more healthy life.
Copy Platform/ Benefits:	*Vital Woman,* the first magazine devoted to women's health and fitness, will enable you to take more responsibility for your own health — via expert medical advice on health and fitness. — via a better understanding of women's health and fitness problems. — via a natural approach to health. The result will be — a better relationship with your doctor. — a healthier, happier life.
First Copy Statement:	You are the primary diagnostician. Let *Vital Woman* help make sure that the *one* person who can take care of you best does a good job. — Take charge of your own health with *Vital Woman.* — Put your health in the best hands—your own. — Don't waste time and money on unnecessary doctor visits.
Second Copy Statement:	Make sure your doctor takes you seriously. (Why should you feel neurotic every time you feel sick?)
Third Copy Statement:	Join a round table of foremost women's physicians every month. Sit down and listen. Ask questions.
Secondary Benefits/Features	— Sound information on natural healing (keep medicine and drugs to a minimum) — Pros and cons of major women's health issues — Reader Q's and A's — Medically approved diets and exercise

	– Emotional and interpersonal advice
	– 10 pages of color, many illustrations in every issue
Recommendations	– Use deadline for offer.
	– List full advisory board on first page of letter.
	– Make the spokesperson a credible woman (female publisher).
Format:	Direct Mail Package/Third-Class Mail

Outer Envelope
4-page letter (2-color)
Brochure (4-color)
Order card
1-page lift letter

DEVELOPMENT OF THE CREATIVE STRATEGY IN A BUSINESS-TO-BUSINESS SITUATION

Your creative methodology and your strategy outline work the same for your business market as for your consumer market, with one major difference.

In Chapter 2, I mentioned that businesspeople are human and that your appeals to them should take this into consideration. However (and here's the big "however"), they are usually not buying for themselves. They are purchasing for a business, probably one that is owned by someone else, and their needs and desires are tricky, as you'll see in the next chapter.

In a sense, you have a relatively easy hypothesis that, in one form or another, will apply to all business promotions. It is based on the appeal to do a better job for the company and help the company make more money, with the hope that personal recognition will follow, and with it, the opportunity to make more money.

This can be accepted as your hypothesis in most cases, but it must be carefully couched in terms that are not self-serving, and your benefits must represent primarily benefits *to the business* or to the people whom the business serves. You must honestly convince your decision maker that his or her action will indeed help the company, and thereby draw positive recognition. Then you must provide (through a careful presentation of benefits and features) the tools that your decision maker can use to present the case to a superior for approval.

If you have several levels of decision maker, you'll need separate creative strategies for each level. For example: You have major research equipment for sale. Engineers in the research department must be convinced of the need for such equipment. Top management must understand that your company makes the best in the world. The purchasing agents must feel that your company is a good company with which to do business. Here you might consider a three-level program.

– an ongoing corporate image-building campaign for top management that runs every month for a year

– the old two-step (qualification and fulfillment kit) for delivering extensive information to a middle-level executive

– a two- or three-step with an incentive to request a sales call on the third level, the agent

You'll need *three* strategy outlines because you have three markets, three slightly different hypotheses, three different formats, and three different spokespersons (CEO to CEO...Inventor to Engineer...Sales Rep to Purchasing Agent).

Benefits, hypotheses, copy platforms, multiple formats, and test situations—with all these converging possibilities, you can see how important it is to execute your creative strategies with your heart beating on the inspirational level and your feet firmly grounded in budget, timing and pacing, and the Underlying Law.

You will have to bring together harmoniously (and creatively) a group of separate elements. At all points as you develop your copy, you'll have to remember these elements and know when to pull them in or push them into the background. Some, of course, will always be up front, others will come and go, a few just come on once. It's a little like an orchestra—and you're the conductor! Avoid cacophony!

CHAPTER 5 EXERCISES

Review the following exercises before you go on to Chapter 6. Study them carefully. Work them out and don't peek at the solutions until you've given them your best try. When you feel comfortable with them move on to the next chapter—and the w-r-i-t-i-n-g! But please don't skip the exercises in this chapter—for your sake. They aren't easy; they are hard, but they are also very important for your understanding and growth. Mastering them (even a little) frees you to devote your creative energies to good writing as you'll see in the chapters ahead.

1. Benefit Extraction

The product is a collection of art sculptures of American songbirds from the Smith Mint. See how many benefits you can pull.

Features

- There are 6 songbirds in the collection; it is limited to 7,500 sets.
- They are designed by Arnold Fox, a well-known bird artist.
- They are all 10″ high, life-size.

- They are handpainted.
- They cost $100 each. You may pay in installments.
- They will be shipped at the rate of 1 every 3 months.

The birds are
Bluebird
Tufted Titmouse
Chickadee
Finch
Goldfinch
Tree Swallow

How did you fare? Miss any of these? Do you have additional benefits?

Features

- There are 6 songbirds in the collection; it is limited to 7,500 sets.
- They are designed by Arnold Fox, a well-known bird artist.

- They are all 10″ high, life-size.
- The birds are
Bluebird;
Tufted Titmouse;
Chicakee;
Finch;
Goldfinch;
Tree Swallow.
- They are handpainted.

- They cost $100 each. You may pay in installments.
- They will be shipped at the rate of 1 every 3 months.

- You will own a unique collection that increases in value with time.
- You can enjoy the artistic excellence of the collection in your own home.

- The natural beauty of the collection will enhance your home and give you personal pleasure and joy.

- Your friends will be impressed.
- No one else in the world will have another set exactly like yours.
- You belong to an exclusive group of collectors.
- You can pay for the collection easily.

2. Hypothesis Recognition

Each of the five ads shown in Figures 5-2, 5-3, 5-4, 5-5, and 5-6 has a strong hypothesis. What do you think it is? Remember, your hypothesis is not a promotional statement, but an *assumption* about the prospect, based on recognized human needs, drives, and desires. (You'll find the answers at the end of the exercises.)

Giorgio
Hair Formula
Lands' End (Sharon)

Walk with Kings
American Garden Guild

Courtesy of Giorgio, Inc.

Figure 5-2

Figure 5-3

Courtesy of Oleda Unlimited, Inc.

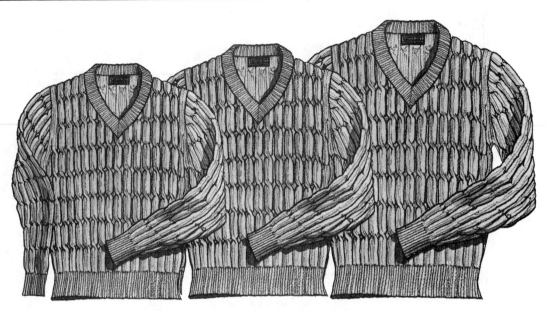

If you're not sure what size sweater to order, ask for Sharon.

She'll make sure you get the one that fits.

Sharon supervises the 90 friendly, well-informed operators who answer the phone when you dial the toll-free Lands' End number: 800-356-4444.

If she doesn't answer the phone herself, the person who does will be able to tell you what you want to know—about size, fit, material, color, availability—whatever. Including our unconditional, two-word guarantee:

GUARANTEED. PERIOD.

If you already have one of our catalogs, you will find it convenient to have it at hand when you call. If not, why not ask for one. Or, if you prefer, mail the coupon below. It's free.

Remember, you can call us toll-free

any hour of the day or night. One of us will answer. We certainly don't want you to talk to a machine.

Lands' End Cable V-Neck

We've found considerable interest in the cotton sweaters we have offered for summer wear—on those evenings, for example, when dusk brings a chill with it. This particular model is our new Lands' End Cable V-Neck of 100% cotton. It's a sweater basic to any traditional wardrobe. Yet, it is a natural extension from basic crew, providing value. And a colorful one, too—in red, kelly, yellow, blue, lavender and natural. Discuss your selection with Sharon, why don't you?

of fine wool and cotton sweaters, Oxford button-down shirts, traditional dress clothing, snow wear, deck wear, original Lands' End soft luggage and a multitude of other quality goods from around the world.

□ **Please send free catalog.**
Lands' End   Dept. L-05
Dodgeville, WI 53595

Name_____

Address_____

City_____

State_____Zip_____

Or call Toll-free:
800-356-4444
(Except Alaska and Hawaii call 608-935-2788)

Figure 5-4

Come, walk with Kings

Come, walk with Kings and let the ancient gates of London's Tower creak shut behind you.

Walk with King Edward III as he sallies forth from the Tower cell where he's been locked up for years. He has vowed to avenge the murder of his father and to seize the kingdom from his mother and her lover.

Wasting little time, Edward threw his mother into a dungeon and tossed away the key. Then he had her lover beheaded.

Walk with the boy-king, Richard II. Stand fast with him as he faces an army of 100,000 rebels on Tower Hill and refuses to surrender his jeweled sword to their leader, Wat Tyler.

Tyler was executed on the spot. Then Richard rode forth, alone, into the howling mob and, in a child's voice, commanded the rebels to go home. And they did.

Walk with King Henry VI, a gentle and retiring man who doesn't even want to be King. He is a helpless pawn in a power struggle between his son and the sensual, violent Duke of York.

Arrested by the Duke's men, Henry was brought as a prisoner to the Tower with his golden spurs struck off and his feet bound under his horse by leather thongs. When his son was killed battle years later and his value as a hostage w gone, Henry was murdered in his cell as knelt, praying.

Come, walk with Kings. Walk with Kir Edward the Confessor as he sees a comet strea across the sky and predicts that a time of gre. evil was coming over the land. *With that pr diction he died and his death set off such bloody struggle for his crown that his predi tion came true.*

Walk with King Henry V as he hurri about London, pawning the Crown Jewels an even the altar linen from his private chapel raise money for the invasion of France tha would result in his astonishing victory at Agin court. *It proved to be an empty triumph. Aft Henry's death a few years later, his son lost a that Henry had won.*

Walk with King Charles I as he accept the fate decreed by Oliver Cromwell. "I fea not death," he says as he kisses his childre goodbye, forgives his executioner, and tuck his long hair up under his cap so it will not de flect the axe. *Cromwell called his death "a cru necessity."*

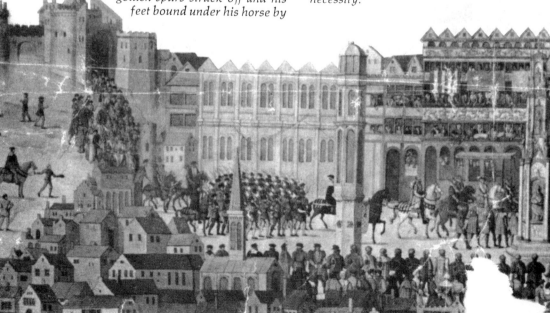

Figure 5-5

ACTUAL SIZE: 9¼" x 11½"

More than a book.
A memorable experience.

To walk with Kings, you need only two things:
1. imagination
2. your own copy—for $6.95—of a new, richly-illustrated volume called Tower of London.

Tower of London is one of a new and exciting series by Newsweek called Wonders of Man. You can sample this beautiful volume—and the series—without obligating yourself to buy anything.

Simply fill in the postpaid reply form that accompanies this advertisement. Then tear it out and mail it. Send no money. Your copy of *Tower of London* is yours to examine for 10 days in your own home.

When your free examination copy of Tower of London arrives in the mail, open the handsomely bound volume to any page.

You'll find lots of color. (More than half of the 100 illustrations are in color.) Modern photographs, especially commis-

sioned for this volume, have been juxtaposed with historical portraits, manuscript illuminations, old engravings, sketches, and paintings.

You'll read a fascinating 40,000 word narrative about the Tower of London and the role it played in royal intrigues and rebellions.

And you'll get a valuable reference chapter, including a chronology of English history ...a guide to the Tower of London itself... a genealogical chart of the Royal Houses of England...a selected bibliography...a selection of poems, travel diaries, and stories from those who have written about the famous Tower—including Shakespeare, Maxwell Anderson, Samuel Pepys, Sir Walter Scott and Alfred Lord Tennyson.

Tower of London is truly a panoramic sweep of nine hundred years of English history. And it's yours to explore and enjoy in your own home for 10 days—free!

Send for the *Tower of London* today!

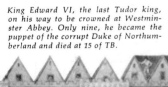

King Edward VI, the last Tudor king, on his way to be crowned at Westminster Abbey. Only nine, he became the puppet of the corrupt Duke of Northumberland and died at 15 of TB.

Courtesy of Newsweek

Figure 5-6

The above ad is created and owned by Literary Guild of America, Inc., which is owned by Doubleday & Company, Inc. All rights granted herein are owned by Literary Guild of America, Inc.

3. Case Study

Here are two other cases. Like *Vital Woman* their basic promotion format is a single direct mail package. One is to a consumer market, the other to a business market. Review them, then respond to the following points.

1. What is the hypothesis or creative concept underlying your overall promotion?
2. What is the primary or big benefit?
3. How will you establish credibility?
4. State your *offer.* How can you make it stronger?
5. What kind of outer envelope do you recommend? Describe your outer.
6. Paraphrase the outer envelope copy line.
7. What is your postage?
8. Who is speaking?
9. Paraphrase at least the first paragraph of the letter.
10. If you decide you need a brochure, explain why and paraphrase your main headline. What illustrations will you use (if any)? How will you use them?
11. Should you have a lift letter? Who is the speaker? What is the proposition or new point of view?
12. Order card: How does it present the offer? What motivates response? Does it have an involvement device?

The following outline of your Creative Strategy Statement should help you with your strategy.

1. Title and product positioning
2. Competition
3. Market
4. Offer (price & terms)
5. Rationale or hypothesis
6. Major benefit(s)
7. Secondary benefits & features
8. Copy platform
9. Recommendations (for credibility, motivation, involvement)
10. Direct mail format/postage
    Outer envelope
    Letter
    Brochure
    Lift letter
    Order form
    Other

Two Case Studies

CASE STUDY I

Situation: A large, well-known mail order company, the Homemakers Corporation, wants to test launch a new magazine called *America's Cooking.*

They will send direct mail to 350,000 names.

From the test, they hope to learn which are the best lists and offers and whether the overall magazine concept can grow at an affordable CPO.

You have been invited to participate in the test by developing a package to run against the control. The control is straightforward and basic.

Product Data: America's Cooking will be the first magazine to represent the many American groups with ethnic cooking traditions all across the United States. It will focus on native American cooking and family traditions, cooking passed on to us by our mothers and grandmothers. There will be particular emphasis on "easy" and "quick" meals throughout, *and* on *inexpensive* ideas for meals as well.

Each monthly issue will contain a lead story about an American town, its people, how they eat, their favorite local dishes, their traditions, their "community cookbook." There will be features on money-saving seasonal specials, quick and easy meals for modern American families on the go, fancy cooking for special entertaining.

Each issue carries lots of four-color pictures and over fifty recipes. The recipes are bound in a center section (to cut out and save).

One of the mainstays of the magazine will be its executive editor, the woman who founded the Homemakers Corporation, and who is well known to the catalog customers because of her cookbooks and recipes. She is affectionately known to the catalog customers as Mrs. Annie Morris. (Every time a catalog order is filled, a free recipe card from "Mrs. Annie" is included.)

Market Description: Homemakers Corporation's own catalog customers are the inspiration for the magazine. They are almost 100 percent female, aged 25-50. Well over 70 percent are married. More than two-thirds of the market work—generally in clerical or factory jobs (some do part-time work). Their families are all in the middle-income category.

Some 250,000 of these customers will be tested along with 100,000 names from women's magazines like *Ladies' Home Journal, Good Housekeeping, McCalls,* and *Better Homes and Gardens.*

Frequency and Price: America's Cooking will be published 12 times a year for $15 a year when it starts. After a year, the price will go up.

CASE STUDY II

Situation: A nationally known bank publishes a weekly economic forecast newsletter, *The Finance Bulletin.* Eight black-and-white pages of typewriter type, it is distributed exclusively to bank officers and their clients. The bank now wishes to test mail a promotion soliciting paid subscribers outside its immediate banking circle. You have been invited to design one of the test packages for this mailing.

Product Data: The newsletter goes to press Friday night so that it reaches its subscribers on Monday via first-class mail. This means that its board of senior economists sit down on Friday and review the week with the editor, who then finalizes all items and closes out the issue at the printer. These senior economists are all well known in finance and banking; one of them has written a book on a new economic theory.

The newsletter itself covers the stock market, bond market, commodities markets, interest rates and the "Fed," international banking and money movement, GNP, wage and employment statistics—all data (everywhere in the world) that can affect investments and monetary affairs. It does this with the help and contributions of six senior bank economists, forty staff economists, and an editor and research staff of three.

The Finance Bulletin works not only to spot major economic trends first (and to call them to its readers' attention) but also to reveal the stories behind much of the economic news today. *The Finance Bulletin* gives hard-to-find data on which financial officers can make sound business decisions. It tells *why* things happen, not *what* has happened. This kind of information is not readily available in the newspapers and magazines.

Market Description: The Finance Bulletin will be test mailed to 100,000 top business executives, largely CEOs and chairmen of small to medium companies, chief financial officers at larger companies, treasurers, division heads, brokerage firm executives, financial consultants, and money managers of all kinds.

Frequency and Price: The Finance Bulletin will be published weekly, 52 times a year. It costs $769 for 52 issues.

Answers to Hypothesis Recognition

1. Giorgio: This is identification, not imitation. You can be one of the "Beverly Hills Crowd" with Giorgio. Join the Elite of America. (P.S. The ad and Giorgio were a smashing success!)

2. Hair Formula: This hard-hitting ad worked very well on the assumption that after a specific age (40) women (and men) begin to notice changes (problems) in their hair...that at this time they will be particularly sensitive to reversing or stopping such changes.

3. The Lands' End ad assumes that many people don't try mail order software because they are afraid they will not be satisfied and that there will be no one to help solve or prevent their problems.

4. This ad for a historical book series is out to qualify the reader immediately by titillating the history buff. What could be more exciting than to move in the company of kings, privy to the secrets, the intrigues, the fears and

triumphs of the monarchy? (Everyone who's ever gone to the movies knows that kings don't make momentous decisions from thrones. They make them walking the cloistered halls of the palace with their most trusted advisors, of course!)

5. The American Garden Guild promises people that their plants can thrive and be healthy if they have good information. People need the assurance that plants will not reject them (by dying) and the ad works off this hypothesis.

chapter 6

Creating the Direct Mail Package

Ah—it's been a long journey, but here we are at last. It's inspiration time—the moment of truth.

You've done your research—*thoroughly*. You know the rules. You have a handle on your market and a list of moral imperatives. You've pulled your big benefit, created a hypothesis, and squared off the proposition with a good offer. You've locked in your creative strategy (except for format requirements) and you're nurturing a concept. Good. But now things change.

Many of you have been working as a team up to this point with your product managers, marketing directors, creative supervisors, production managers, art directors, artists. From here on, you go it alone. Well—not entirely. If *you* are a writer, you can't cut out your art director or artist.

But the rest of the team—what say, writers? Shall we let them come along—or ask them to tear these pages out of the book?

Not too fast. I almost hesitate to say this, but if they come along, they will certainly develop a great respect for the work you do, the sheer effort you put into your creation. And that's not all bad. They'll be more understanding—and less likely to nit pick. Perhaps. Worth a try? O.K.

WHAT WILL BE EXPECTED OF YOU, THE WRITER

Until now, you've been in the catbird seat, asking a lot of questions, making a lot of assumptions. Listening. Thinking. Planning your strategies. (And taking notes, I hope.) Now it's your turn to produce.

Just what is expected? First, that you will write, and that you will do so along the lines set down in your strategy, employing all the direct response technique you have learned.

You are also expected to develop creative ideas and full copy for a direct mail package that can be visually executed. This means you must relate at some point to the chosen artist or art director during this process.

SOME TERMS YOU MUST KNOW BEFORE WE MOVE AHEAD!

Artist/Art Director: Many free-lance artists refer to themselves as designers. When they execute layouts, they call themselves the art directors or designers, but in many agencies and companies artists working under an art director do the layouts while art directors supervise the design. For the purpose of much-needed clarity, I will use the term *artist* in the future to signify the person who designs the package *and* executes the layouts.

Finished Copy: Even though it may have to move through layers of approval, and you may ultimately have to make some changes, this is *your* final copy for all parts or components of the direct mail package as you first present it.

Layouts or Comprehensive Art: The design of the direct mail package is executed by the artist or art director. "Rough" layouts are the first pass and good artists will want to start conferring with you prior to this first pass. Layouts for direct mail are full size and cut and folded into a *dummy* package that closely resembles the proposed real thing. Headlines are hand-drawn or lettered to scale, subheads are usually indicated by heavy lines. Body copy is done in lighter lines or is represented by boxed-off areas with *X*'s in them. Illustrations are clearly blocked out and sketched in; die cuts, tokens, stamps, and seals are all simulated. The objective of the layout is to show precisely how the finished direct mail package will look, how the parts of the package will interrelate and come together, how colors, special designs and visual effects will be employed in conjunction with your finished copy. The layout is presented along with the finished copy. Once layouts and copy are approved (and all changes or modifications are incorporated), the artist moves into *mechanicals*. These are the finished composition boards (with set type, photography, illustrations) from which the printer works. Mechanicals are sometimes called camera-ready art.

Copywriter's roughs: Here, *rough* means a *very* rough layout or a preliminary laying out of the package, done by a writer. (Figure 6–1.) It is customary for you as the writer, when presenting finished copy executed *without* an artist's collaboration, to accompany the copy with your own miniature layouts, or a folded paper dummy of the direct mail package, as you envisage it. This is also a good way to work with artists, as this rough pen-and-pencil layout is done primarily *for the artist.* No one expects you to draw, but it should indicate your thoughts about format, illustrations you'd like to use in your brochure, where your headlines go, the general feeling and layout of the promotion, suggestions for tokens on the order form, layouts for the letterhead, envelope size, die cuts, and copy positioning.

You always knew you'd be writing copy; but I didn't mention you'd also be designing packages or visualizing formats. I encourage you—as a writer—to visualize your entire package and set down these ideas along with your copy. Chances are you won't be able to help yourself from doing so anyway. You'll find

Figure 6-1 *A Very Rough Copywriter's Rough for a Three-Panel Brochure*

your words create a picture in your mind. And, after all, these are only starting points that a good artist will bend and rework in creating his or her designs—designs that please you both.

HOW SHOULD YOU WORK WITH THE ARTIST?

Your final product depends a lot on how you prefer to work with the artist, or how your company or client wants you to work. There are two extremes, and there are degrees in between.

1. If you go it alone, without a team (or without an artist on your team), you may be expected to produce only finished copy with copywriter's roughs. Hopefully, at some point, you'll be able to discuss such roughs with an artist or art director. Even more important, you'll want an opportunity to see and discuss the artist's own roughs and final treatment of your ideas and suggestions.

2. If you're working closely with an artist from the start, you may not need your copywriter's roughs. It depends on how you're most comfortable and how well you and the artist communicate.

Some possible working scenarios for artists and writers:

- You amble off to your lair like a grizzly bear preparing for hibernation, only to return some days later with creative direction and solid copy ideas to discuss with the artist.

- You immediately sit down with the artist (alone at last) and start comparing ideas, trying out copy approaches and formats together.

- You and the artist meet (circling each other carefully) to discuss ground rules and procedures. You set goals and plan a meeting for the next steps.

My advice to you is, *open up! Don't hold back.* Explain your concepts, your reasons, your concerns, your fears, your problem areas, your precious big idea. Let the artist know exactly how you attack the problem. *Let the artist join you in the creative process.*

Keep an open mind! You may already see it, but the artist may give you something far better. Don't push the artist into your visuals. (Artists are known for their own, remember?) Give the artist the input *and* the opportunity. If the artist has followed your creative process closely, it's likely that he or she will be excited and eager to jump in with ideas.

Kick the ideas around together. Ask participatory questions: Can we show the theme on the outer? How can we tie the offer into the letterhead visually? Should this be a standard #10 package on this budget, or do you feel the need for something bigger? Given this kind of headline and the picture requirements, should we go to a really big brochure or stick with a miniature treatment?

Listen. Of course you already see it in your head. But you may learn something here. The artist may see it better and if you click, the two of you can go off into the sunset building beautiful direct mail castles, each of you inspiring the other, and spurring each other on to even greater heights. This can and does happen often (and it becomes a purely personal reward of good creative work for both of you).

However, it can happen *only* if you open your creative doors and let the artist in. Whether you're just starting out or meeting with copywriter roughs after you've finished writing, you must allow the artist to join your team. Otherwise, you're the solitary player, looking for the mundane, lazy artist who will take directions from you without question, who will try to develop the visuals in *your* head to suit *you.* What a loss.

You and your ideas lose good graphic input, the artist loses the inspiring challenge and opportunity to contribute, and the client (or your boss) loses a shot at a strong, graphically compelling package.

No one can really tell you much more about working with an artist. A lot of it is chemistry, but your relationship at least will get off on the right foot if you can pull together most of the following for the artist as soon as possible:

- Your outer envelope copy ideas
- Your order card copy
- Your letter leads
- Your brochure heads
- Your visual requirements (pictures, graphs, charts)
- Any sketches you may have made; other packages, ads or pictures that demonstrate your ideas
- Your reasearch—particularly samples of past control packages and tests that worked and/or failed

In the course of your meetings, the artist should be able to come up with as many rough layouts as you both feel are necessary before proceeding into final layouts.

One more point, how long should it take—all this writing and artist business? (I thought you'd never ask.) No one can tell you how long inspiration takes, but there certainly are reasonable guidelines for getting a package out and plotting your time.

YOUR WORK MAP (HOW TO BUDGET YOUR TIME)

There are two considerations here: (1) how much time you *need,* and (2) how much time you *are given.*

The Variables: Although you and the artist may be working together, before the two of you can start to work out illustrations and ideas for rough layouts, you may want to come up with some kind of creative noodling on your own.

Assuming you are given proper research materials, and that you and your creative strategy planning team can bone up and meet at least twice *before* you cut loose (whether the team is you—solo, you and your boss or client, or six to eight well-intentioned co-workers from the art, marketing, research, and production departments), it is not unreasonable for you and the artist to produce final copy and layouts (or comprehensive art) for a full direct mail package in three weeks from fully prepped cut loose time.

If you include research and planning, however, you'll need a total of at least four to five weeks. It's nice if you can get a little more than five weeks, say a week or two more. In most cases, however, you may be given a little less—a lot less in a few instances.

When do you cry "Uncle"? Some free-lance copywriters *never* say "Uncle." They take on jobs that most writers do in three weeks and whip them out in a week—even less—and they do competent work. How? Why? First, they're very experienced. Next, most free-lancers don't have the luxury of controlling work flow. They must work when they can get it and store up the dollars for a dry period. (And direct response advertising *can* have dry periods.) These free-lancers must be willing to work nights and weekends when the work is there, and yes, they do get exhausted. And yes, it can ultimately affect their work. And no, it's no great fun either.

As for you—you first need to know what is unreasonable as well as what is reasonable before you even consider the absurd. Here are some guidelines to apply for starters, whether you're working on your own or in a company.

1. In making all of these decisions you have to estimate how much time is open. What else is on your schedule? Do you have two or three other assignments? Are you taking the kids to school, or gardening, or having a house guest or going to the opera? Are you willing (or expected) to work late? Weekends?

2. When you are approached with a totally new package for a new product and asked to do full copy and comps, you should be given a minimum of five weeks from the start. (You'll need *at least* a week of this for the research and strategizing.)

3. You may not get your grand total of five or more weeks from the client or your boss; you may get only three to four weeks, including all your prework. This is not *madly* unreasonable, if you have quick access to all the background material and get your creative planning down within a week. But it's tight, particularly for a beginner.

4. Now let's say you're asked to do the job in two weeks. Feel free to do it, if you know your product and you are comfortable about the schedule. On the other hand, be aware that this is bordering on the madly unreasonable.

Whatever your work load or personal life style, at this point you have every right to express concern regarding your ability to do your best work on such a tight schedule. (Even if you do take it on, you should make this point.)

Make sure you have *everything* you need to move into the job. Every single day counts. You can't afford to wait even twenty-four hours to get a full look at the product line or testing history.

A word of caution: Clients will promise *anything* to get you to accept an unreasonably tight schedule, including twenty-four-hour approvals. Don't believe it. Their hearts may be in the right place, but I have yet to find a client (or company) that can come through with full data in twenty-four hours *or* overnight approvals.

Let me draw up an optimum time frame for you, showing places you can scrimp a little while keeping a small safety margin. A game plan like this can also help you deal with several jobs at once, each in different stages of development. Please note that your creative development needn't wait until the client says "Go!" It can start at any time—even in your first meeting. So take notes from day one!

Time Frame for Copy and Layout Development of a Direct Mail Package

	Best Case	Options
Week 1	a. Assignment is given b. Research is received and studied (Creative juices start.)	These three weeks can be combined into one week, especially if you are working alone (and if background material is readily available).
Week 2	First creative strategy meeting.	
Week 3	Final creative strategy meeting.	
Week 4	a. You start writing. b. Have first meeting with the artist (start roughs.)	
Week 5	a. You continue to write, revise, rework. b. Meet with art director or artist. (present your visual ideas, heads, leads, all thoughts for format and involvement devices. Here the outer envelope should be firmed up in your mind. So should the brochure concept and order card. The letter can be finalized later, as it requires little work from the artist.) Artist should be working on rough layouts.	Weeks four and five can be condensed by a few days, but use caution here or your work may suffer.
Week 6	This week, you and the artist hammer out all the details and finalize all the visuals and copy. Major changes can still be made, but you should use the time primarily for reworking and polishing your copy and for your final layout lockup.	Crucial week. Don't cut a minute—even if you are working alone and doing a copywriter's rough.

Totals: 6 + weeks to presentation of copy   3 + weeks to presentation of copy
         and layouts   and layouts

Now, to get you started writing! (This should come as no surprise, dear writer, but you *have* started. If you've done all the prework, sat through the meetings and made notes, your head should be bursting with ideas. So how about a few deathless words on paper?)

GETTING YOU OFF ON THE WRITE FOOT

You're sitting there, pen poised or pencil sharpened, electronic keyboard humming, or CRT staring you down and your artist is already starting to visualize. So…write! There's no longer any excuse to put it off. Or is there? Most writers can give you a dozen good excuses at this point: The garbage has to go out. Someone (any living creature) should be fed (the writer, most likely). A magazine or newspaper must be read…a letter answered…a friend called…a bill paid…a file drawer cleaned. No task is too onerous or too small, as long as it keeps you from getting started.

This is normal behavior, no matter how much (or little) you enjoy writing. Don't let it discourage you, but don't let it deter you, either. After all, you have your copy strategy and copy platform. And you have all that research behind you. You have a schedule—and the artist is waiting (not to mention the client)!

If the storehouse of experience has fueled your imagination properly it should be humming. And your subconscious should be mulling over the creative opportunities before you—ready to telegraph a great idea while you are in the shower, shaving, eating, trying to sleep, or even talking with your mother-in-law.

I personally have never been able to drum up anything inspiring by staring at a roaring fire or looking out to sea. Maybe you can. But whenever and however you get your inspiration (and it may come at the strangest times and in the strangest places), *write down your ideas.* Many writers carry paper and pencil (or a pocket recorder) with them or keep a pad by the bed for just this reason.

SOME HELPFUL POINTERS TO GET YOU STARTED

You're moving into an area that requires great discipline and determination. Don't feel guilty if you hold back or procrastinate. Every writer does, but every writer also develops little rituals or disciplines that start the creative juices flowing. Let me pass a few on to you.

1. William North Jayme, one of our best writers says, "A writer should be in a cold room because chill quickens the brain, should be hungry as an incentive to earn, and should dress only in underwear so as to place an obstacle in the way of chucking the job at hand in favor of heading for the neighborhood bar."

2. If you're not in the mood, good exercise like jogging or calisthenics—or even a long walk—can put you there. After a half hour's workout, you'll be relaxed but wide awake. (Then again, just the threat of exercise is enough to get some writers going.) Suit yourself.

3. Learn to recognize your most productive hours. Understand your mind and your body. Every good writer can tell you his or her best hours for writing. Some are morning people, some are evening. Find out when you work best, then save those hours for the hard stuff.

4. Discipline yourself. If you don't have a deadline, *set one*. Then do *not* put off until the last minute or claim "I write best under pressure." No one writes best under pressure. This is a cop out. You will write best when you have enough time to let your original work cool off a bit. Then come back to it cold. You'll be amazed at what a little time and a new perspective will do.

5. Start a dialogue in your head. You've decided who you'll be. You know to whom you're talking. Imagine one person representing this market. Be an actor, sit down and talk to this person. You can do it anywhere. Every time you like what you hear, write it down, wherever you are.

6. Do an outline for your brochure and for your letter. Be sure to check your notes.

7. Start collecting headline ideas in your imaginary conversation. Think of ways to attract the attention of your one-person market, ways to hold this market's attention. (What would stop you and draw you in if you were this market?)

8. With every idea, every bit of dialogue that leads to your headlines, ask yourself "Will this make sense to the customer?" "What is my justification for saying this?" "Can I carry through on it?"

9. What if ideas don't come—nothing seems to jell? How can you jar the creative process and tickle the imagination? Two good ways:

> a. If your product or service has a good testing history, and you're lucky enough to have a collection of former direct mail packages and ratings on how well they pulled (your response index—remember *Research*!), see if you can figure out why one did well, why another didn't. For example: Let's say a women's service magazine calls on you to create a new subscription solicitation package. Among the research materials provided, is a full direct mail testing history that goes back several years. You are given fourteen different packages, each one indexed against the other, and marked to show the original control and those that subsequently replaced the control. All of the packages were professionally executed. Let us assume that all the offers were the same. Why did some succeed and others fail? What a delightful mystery!
> First, look for similarities among the winners—similarities in format, design, copy approach. Check for long copy versus short, drawings versus photography. Look closely at the ways in which the offer is stated.

What is promised on the outer envelope? How does each letter start? What is different about the losers? Compare, compare, compare, and gradually you'll be able to draw up your points, a list of the things the winners have in common. Once you're satisfied, you must decide how to capitalize on those points—the similarities—without copying the winners or doing a thinly modified version of the control.

Your job here is not to reinvent wheels, but to *take what works one step further.* Think of all the things you're learning about your market! What a great way to get started when you have the history to do it!

b. All good creative free-lancers or creative departments in direct marketing operations have what we call *swipe files.* These are extensive collections of other people's work. No one actually steals from them. But swipe files are great places for ideas. If you don't have a swipe file, start one! If you need one now, the Direct Marketing Association in New York City has one of the finest in the world. It's an extensive collection of hundreds of direct response campaigns submitted to the annual DMA Echo Awards competition. These awards cover all kinds of direct marketing and all media. (You can view this collection in their library, even if you are not a bona fide member of the association.[1])

WHAT DO YOU WRITE FIRST?

If you're holding back simply because you're not sure *what* to write first, let me dispose of the problem for you right now.

A few top professionals suggest you write your order card first. Ed Nash, President of BBD&O Direct, advises writers to do the ad coupon or the order card first because it is the one element of the promotion that is most often saved. He says "Later, when the time comes to write out the envelope and perhaps a check, the coupon itself is the only reminder of the reasons behind why they tore it out in the first place. The headline is gone. The pictures are gone. All that remains is the reply card or coupon."[2]

There's a lot to be said for coupon writers, but three of the best direct response writers I know start with the outer envelope! As all your prospects and customers will start there, too, surely it deserves your finest efforts and early attention. After all, if it doesn't get opened....

The majority of the writers I've tapped claim they generally start with the letter itself, and that has much to recommend it. Your letter is your true one-on-

---

[1]Direct Marketing Association, Inc., 6 East 43rd St., New York, N.Y. 10017, (212) 689-4977, or 173 K. Street NW, Washington, DC (202) 347-1222.

[2]Edward L. Nash, *Direct Marketing Strategy/Planning/Execution,* (New York, N.Y.: McGraw-Hill, Inc., 1982), p. 231, p. 258.

one address. It can help you feel closer to your prospect and it enables you to develop your sales dialogue. As you'll see in the next section, it facilitates your selection of an Approach.

Once you've started your letter, you may go right to the outer envelope with ideas for a copy promise that ties in to your letter.

You can also start moving from the letter to the brochure as bright insights for headlines and illustrations that work best outside the restraints of the letter come popping into your head.

Frankly, talk about where to start can be misleading. Neither you nor I nor anyone else can control the creative imagination once it gets going. It's entirely possible to come up with a great envelope line as you start your letter, or a headline for the brochure. And, it's equally possible for you—fired with inspiration—to charge through a first draft of the letter in an hour or so. The fact is wherever you start, before you know it, you'll be working all your components along together, moving back and forth from one format to the other.

CHOOSING AN APPROACH

As you sit down to write your letter—you the spokesperson, ready to start a dialogue with the one person who is the perfect embodiment of your prime market's characteristics—tell me how are you going to break the ice? What's your approach?

Think of your prospect as someone you'd like to know better. You want to arrange a date. How you approach this prospect will determine your success. ("Hey, Sweetheart, ya wanna dance?")

Ask yourself: How well do I know this prospect? (Is this a new prospect or a regular customer?) What's my proposition? How do I intend to get my prospect interested? What's my first sentence, my lead-in? *What's the "hook" that will capture my prospect's attention on the envelope? And carry it into the letter?*

First, review your copy strategy for a minute:

What's the hypothesis?

What's your big benefit?

Is the offer *the* big benefit?

Do you have a premium? Something FREE?

Is this a totally *new* product or service?

Who are you as actor?

Whom are you addressing? And what moves them?

Now choose a good *approach* to break the ice. Otherwise you'll stutter and stammer and drag your feet, and your prospect will go dancing off with someone else!

O.K. So I lied. You're not ready to start writing until you've decided on your approach. Actually, you and your artist could have picked an approach when you had your first meeting; if you didn't, now's the time. And yes—I owe you an explanation about "Approach," what it means, how it came to be.

Twenty years ago, professional copywriters used to discuss different approaches to their direct mail packages. They gave these approaches labels and the creative director or copy chief making the assignment would be sure that in a test each writer took a different approach—or led into the creative product from a different point of view or different angle, or with a different hook.

I don't hear much talk of approaches these days. It's possible that writers are not fully aware of the process or analytical enough about their own work to know how and where they employ the approach. Maybe they call it something else. Perhaps they just don't talk about it anymore. But approaches are there nonetheless—in every direct mail package ever produced. And, as with offers and structuring (see Chapter 3), these approaches can be analyzed; they can be modified and combined, one with another.

Your approach starts on the outer envelope, then moves right to the first paragraph of your letter. Your approach helps you decide whether or not to use a Johnson box or a headline at the top of your letter. It sets the tone for your package. You want it to grab your prospect by the eyelashes and lead that prospect through your letter to the point where it makes more sense to say "yes" than "no."

If you understand approaches, how and why you use one approach as opposed to another, you'll be in an excellent position to explain your finished copy and the direction or style of your package as a whole when you make your copy presentation.

There are twelve possible approaches in this chapter. There are others, no doubt, but with these (and combinations thereof), you're in a good position to get started. They are

1. The Generic Approach
2. The Invitational Approach
3. The Bartlett's Quotation Approach
4. The Testimonial Approach
5. The Identification Approach
6. The "If" or Assumptive Approach
7. The Question Approach
8. The Negative Problem/Solution Approach
9. The Fantasy Approach
10. The Analogy Approach
11. The Story Approach
12. The Be-a-Hero Approach

Most of the approaches are illustrated with examples taken from actual direct mail packages. These examples are representative of the finest direct mail writing by the best copywriters in the business. Some of the approaches require specific situations (like a new product introduction or a business product for a business market). Others are a question of pure creative choice—your choice. But first, review your hypothesis and make sure your selected approach enables you to move into the hypothesis quickly and easily and appealingly—up front.

YOUR TWELVE APPROACHES

1. *The Generic Approach:* This is the most widely used approach. It is basic and straightforward and starts right in with the major benefit and the offer. The Generic Approach is best (safest) when you're writing business-to-business mail, you're testing a brand-new product and have no control package, or you have a very exciting premium or unusually strong offer (offer-as-big-benefit).

The following are simple illustrations of the generic application:

a. Offer/Premium as lead

Dear Customer:
Here is a once-in-a-lifetime opportunity to purchase the Forbush Slip-Shod at 50% off its regular price. And—with every purchase, we'll send you absolutely FREE...

or

b. The Big Benefit as lead

Dear Friend:
Let me tell you about a remarkable new way to finance your children's education painlessly and risk free!

or

c. New product/first mailing lead

Dear Reader:
Now, for the first time—study the intimate life of the black snail—follow his daily patterns, his cycle changes and eating preferences—every month in a new magazine from the publishers of Zilch Havas:

Black Snail Review
Just $13 for 12 Monthly Issues

You'll find that a lot of direct mail packages are generic. It's a popular approach both for creative professionals and (ugh) for tacky technicians.

2. *The Invitational Approach:* This approach is best applied to a new product or service, or to a product that you're introducing to a totally new market. It is based on the assumption that everyone likes to be invited to things and that an invitation is always welcome mail.

When it's working best, the Invitational Approach is elegant in appearance—an announcement of importance (trumpets blare). It carries an exclusive, "limited" invitation (offer) with a few-are-chosen tone, "so please R.S.V.P." (reply) now.

The most effective Invitational Approaches have the style, tone and design—of a call to the royal court:

> Her Royal Highness and all the knights and ladies of the court, extend to you, John Sample, an exclusive invitation....

And they're full of R.S.V.P. in its many versions.

If you choose the Invitational Approach, try to make sure the graphics reflect the elegant invitational feeling from the outer envelope to the reply card. (For a top-notch *computerized* invitation, see the illustration on page 117, Chapter 5.)

3. *The Bartlett's Quotation Approach:* This one is a well-loved approach because it's pulled many a lost writer out of a blue funk and given direction, inspiration, and hope. The command, "Go to *Bartlett's!*" is not a panacea for writer's block in general, however. Some hypotheses will not lend themselves to this treatment. Some offers and products demand a more direct approach. Quotations go best with known products that carry an extensive testing history.

And when you go to *Bartlett's,* or any other accurate source, be sure

- that your quote is good enough to use on the outer envelope *and* at the start of the letter
- that it attracts attention (by being tantalizing, teasing, or impressive)
- that it's appropriate (without stretching a point)
- that it leads the reader directly into your big benefit (and/or hypothesis) gracefully and logically

Figure 6-2 illustrates another good example from *House & Garden* Magazine, this time by Linda Wells, a top free-lance copywriter. The outer envelope features the quote prominently without explanation, teasing the curious inside, while qualifying them with the magazine logotype ("Envelopes," Chapter 4). The first page of the letter hangs from the quotation and ties the product into it immediately. To go with the quote, the artist chose two soft, off-white colors for the outer envelope and the letter itself. The brochure, by contrast, was a crisp blaze of color.

4. *The Testimonial Approach:* Here is a powerful tool. Apply it at the right time and for the right reasons, and you'll walk away with a winner. Give it your serious consideration when you have a product or service that requires the kind of credibility that only customers can provide.

For example: Products that claim to improve health or fitness or personal appearance, products that promise to increase income, give the prospect new or improved skills—any products or services with intangible benefits (promises that can't be proved by product examination or demonstration and therefore create skepticism on the part of your prospects).

"OPTIMISM AND WHITE PAINT"

A Charter Invitation to preview the joyous new HOUSE & GARDEN. and to receive the current issue with the compliments of the publisher.

Bulk Rate
U.S. Postage
PAID
Permit No. 64
Jersey City, N.J.

HOUSE & GARDEN®

"I believe in plenty of optimism
and white paint"

—Elsie de Wolf

Dear Reader:

Down went the dusty, dark-red portieres!

Off came the dreary damask wallcoverings!

Out flew the crowded Victorian clutter!

She invented decorating as we know it today. She painted walls white. She let in the light. She tweaked antiques with the freshness of chintz. She loved comfort, she loved style, she loved life. Her joy in living showed in joyful decorating -- and it is to Elsie de Wolfe, Lady Mendl, that we dedicate our new HOUSE & GARDEN.

The new HOUSE & GARDEN is a celebration of what she called "optimistic decorating." And there's much to be optimistic about! For 80 years, we've published the best new interior design. But right now, there is such an extraordinary explosion of creativity in the applied arts, it is time for an extraordinary new magazine that reflects the vigor and vitality of these rich, rewarding and exciting times.

We still call it HOUSE & GARDEN, but otherwise, it's new all the way through. With a crisp, clean, contemporary new look. On newly luxurious stock of sybaritic weight, sheen, gloss and quality. With 100 new pages of superbly-reproduced, full-color photographs and brilliantly written articles that show you the very best

Courtesy of The Condé Nast Publications, Inc.

Figure 6-2

You'll also want to consider it when you have a product that generates a lot of unsolicited praise.

Caveat: Too many raving testimonials may create just the opposite of the desired effect. If your company is well known, you can dispel the problem with a modest disclaimer. (See the envelope flap in Figure 6-3.) If your company is unknown, temper your choice of testimonials and give as much data as possible about the contributors. (A testimonial from "a satisfied customer" is worth no testimonial at all.)

Figure 6-3 is an example of an all-time testimonial great.

This package for Rodale Press's *The Practical Encyclopedia of Natural Healing* sold *over* 1,000,000 copies of the book at $25.00 each. The package was written by Gene Schwartz, a master of the hard sell. Notice how he begins his testimonials right on the outer envelope and handles credibility beautifully by anticipating skepticism and dealing with it on the envelope flap!

As you can see, the testimonials cover the first page of the letter and continue right through the second page and into the third page!

5. *The Identification Approach:* After you look at this one carefully, you're liable to label it out-and-out flattery. But remember, flattery creates involvement (and that's just what you want). Besides that's only half the story.

Used properly, the Identification Approach starts on the outer envelope and immediately qualifies the prospect: It says, "I know who you are. You're someone special. That's why you're particularly going to like what I have to offer."

The approach first gained recognition over ten years ago when Ed McLean (another of our top creative free-lancers) found a new hook (and a new way to make his letters more personal) by examining all the mail order and magazine subscriber lists that were being used (rented) in his mailing.

He began his letter "If the list on which I found your name is any indication..." (instant involvement through curiosity and then flattery). The introduction to the offer is a form of "because you are discriminating and demanding, this product and products like it will have special appeal for you."

Today, you'll find Identification Approaches all over the lot from geographic: "For You—the Magazine That Makes Being a Texan More Fun!" or "How to Make It Big. Be a Californian." to hobby and sports: "Heads up, Gardeners. Here's a sharp trick that will get you..." or "Golfers—cut your score."

Figure 6-4 is a good example using nostalgia. It's done for *Bicycling* magazine by Jim Punkre, still another of direct mail's finest creators. He also uses a *faux* Johnson box to make sure that his lead attracts attention and draws the reader into the letter. And it certainly does!

The best of these Identification Approaches starts to qualify and involve the prospect right on the outer envelope, then begins the letter by enlarging on the identification linked to the benefits.

If your market is fairly clear-cut, the straightforward identification can work for you. (Gardeners, Bikers, Texans, Californians—what could be clearer.)

Thrilling news about
THE PRACTICAL ENCYCLOPEDIA OF
NATURAL HEALING

Its philosophy can be summed up in this one simple paragraph from the book, spoken by a nationally-known physician:

"You are more in charge of your life — and even the development and progress of a disease, such as cancer — than you may realize. You may actually, through a power within you, be able to decide whether you will live or die, and if you choose to live, you can be instrumental in choosing the quality of life that you want."

Read how, on the back of this envelope... and inside ...

Rodale Press, Inc.
Emmaus, PA 18049

IF THESE QUOTES CAME FROM A VOLUME PUBLISHED BY ANYONE OTHER THAN RODALE PRESS, INC. (WHICH ALSO PUBLISH PREVENTION® MAGAZINE) — YOU REALLY MIGHT NOT BELIEVE THEM. WHY? BECAUSE THEY MAY OFFER SUCH THRILLING HELP FOR AILMENTS ON WHICH YOU MAY HAVE GIVEN UP. LIKE THESE REPORTS IN THE BOOK.

"A 16-year old girl who had suffered with acne since she was 12 cleared up her face 'in one month' . . ."

"She has been treating migrain headaches with acupuncture for about a year and a half. Her success, she claimed, after treating between 350 and 400 patients, is 100 percent . . ."

" 'He had a herniated disk in his back and was ready to undergo surgery to correct it . . . I gave him a treatment that lasted about five minutes . . . The man got up and walked out of my office free from pain and without his cane . . . That was two years ago, and I haven't seen him since. He's still free from pain' . . ."

" 'Within 48 hours, the hemorrhoids disappeared, and not one bit of pain. I couldn't believe it . . . This has been like a miracle for me' . . ."

" 'I know three months do not make a cure. But I do not have pains, I can move about easily now, and I am off pain-killing drugs. I used to use about 200 . . . pills every five or six weeks, now I do not take any at all.' "

"At the end of the experiment, it was determined that every individual had experienced enlargement of the breasts, with increases ranging from one to 3½ inches."

"(She) lost 34 pounds in 20 weeks, and more importantly, she has kept it off."

" 'Up until 1971 I had so much pain with phlebitis that at one time I was in bed for three months. . . . now I walk for an hour or more every morning . . . my legs do not bother me now. I will be 70 years old soon.' "

And this is only a sample. There's more inside – Plus a FREE KITCHEN MEDICINE WALL CHART. Yours when you send the card!

Figure 6-3

If you want to know something of the power of natural healing, Dear Friend, then you have only to read this one startling paragraph:

"I immediately began taking nine to twelve tablets daily and in one week was without pain! I told my story to a friend, a nurse anesthetist, who has osteoarthritis. She had refused a total hip replacement three years ago and has been living on aspirin daily since that time. Within 10 days she was totally free of pain -- not one more aspirin!"

Interest in natural healing -- is perhaps greatest today among young physicians who have graduated from some of the nation's leading medical institutions!

Why? In our opinion for these vital reasons:

First, the record shows all too clearly that orthodox "medical progress" has in many cases spelled despair and even death for thousands of people who trusted their health to doctors and their "new, decisive answers" to just about everything.

Don't get the idea that the only good thing about natural healing is that it is relatively safe. It can also be surprisingly effective, sometimes much more so than drugs. In this book, you will read of many instances where something as simple as a slight change in diet or applications of an herb, succeeded in clearing up problems which had resisted the onslaught of drug after drug.

Want some specifics? Then just read case history after case history. And remember this when you read them: The same natural-healing techniques that produced these results can be yours to read, and perhaps use, without your risking a penny!

"A woman said that on the advice of a roommate 'my daughter began taking vitamin A, and in only two weeks had no more new eruptions on her face for the first time in five years! But her face had become so scarred it took several weeks to notice that the scars too were gradually disappearing' ... "

" ... he's treated 36 patients who came to him specifically for acupuncture treatment of psoriasis. He was able to effect 'some improvement' in all of them -- and to cure 60 percent. 'When I say 'cure',' the speaker emphasized, "I mean that these patients have been free from symptoms for at least five years."

(over, please)

Figure 6-3, *continued*

" ... Another reader with arthritic fingers started eating cherries and drinking cherry juice, and after two weeks said that there was less swelling, and the pain was entirely gone. "I hadn't been able to make a fist before, but now I can.'"

" ... brought about a significant reduction in blood pressure. Dr. Piotrowski believed that the herb lowered the patients' blood pressures by dilating the blood vessels, which relieved symptoms such as angina pain, dizziness, and headaches. He claimed that in 40 percent of his sample cases, relief was obtained within three to five days."

"Another patient, a 42-year-old graduate nurse, was so plagued by canker sores that she was unable to take proper nourishment. She was admitted to the hospital suffering from severe dehydration. 'Forty-eight hours after treatment with Lactobacillus therapy all ulcers had healed.'"

But this is only the beginning. Wait till you read these studies and examples ...

"In several carefully observed clinical trials, it has been found that on a bran-added diet, approximately 80 percent of patients are either completely relieved of their constipation or greatly improved ... "

"'The overweight diabetic who successfully peels off enough pounds to get his weight back to normal usually experiences a dramatic improvement in his condition. Indeed, the symptoms often virtually disappear,' ... 'Weight reduction and control can bring this incurable disease closer to complete remission than any medication.' In many cases, the newly slender patient can stop taking insulin."

" ... she developed a rash on her face that wouldn't go away. 'It made my face feel like sandpaper. I tried everything on it, even went to the skin doctor, but nothing I put on it would make it go away. Then I decided to try vitamin E on it ... Within three days the rash was gone. Now the skin on my face is as smooth as a rose petal.'"

"Some of the elderly people in the study who had heart disease and who could walk only a few hundred feet when first seen, were able to increase their walking distance to at least six miles and as much as ten miles a day at the conclusion of the six-month study."

And how about this thrilling possibility: "For the emphysema victim who really wants to be able to breathe again, there is considerable hope. And that hope depends not on any miracle drug or miracle vitamin but the patient's own determination."

Or how about these shortened quotes and comments:

"Is it truly the aphrodisiac it is reputed to be? 'Yes' ... Dr. Zofchak declared ... "

" ... painful varicose veins that had troubled her for 13 years, threatening to immobilize her. Where countless doctors and remedies had failed, the herb succeeded."

Figure 6-3, *continued*

155

I SEE YOU ON A BICYCLE

If I could gaze into the crystal ball of *your past*...

... chances are, I'd see a spritely youngster on a bicycle, pumping and pedaling and exploring your way through a fascinating new world. A world once off limits, but now virgin territory — opened to you, miraculously, by this simple invention.

I see a wide-eyed child: Absorbed in the detail of odd things and strange, new places. Smiling as you breeze through woodland and park. Exhilerated as you hurl downhill on some secluded back road. Healthy and happy and beaming in the fresh air and sunshine. And sitting "tall in the saddle," too — confident that these new legs would carry you anywhere you had a mind to go.

Remember that bike . . .?

Dear Reader:

Times have certainly changed. You with them.

And so has that bicycle.

But one thing obviously <u>hasn't</u> changed. That same freewheeling, freedom-loving free spirit still burns brightly deep within you.

Which is, no doubt, why you stay so active ... so on-the-go ... so fit, healthy and ruggedly self-reliant.

And which is why ...

... I want to introduce you to an exciting, yet practical, magazine that can help throw some more fuel on that blazing inner fire of yours. And help you rediscover the bicycle and the many important ways it can serve you once again. To keep your tummy flat and firm. Your heart strong. Your gasoline bills lower. And your family closer <u>and</u> healthier.

And if that interests <u>you</u>, just turn this page -- I want to tell you how you can get your hands on a copy of BICYCLING magazine for a special "trial run ... "

(over, please)

Courtesy of Rodale Press, Inc.

Figure 6-4

You can also use the "negative" identification ploy as a lead in. It comes out something like "Only serious photographers need apply" or "published only for a select group of people who are seriously interested in..."

If you know the demographics of your present customer market, you can do a playback identification. A sort of "Our customers are affluent, talented, well-traveled. We think you should be among them." This is similar to the identification/flattery from the original "If the list on which I found your name is any indication...."

Caveat: Don't go too far afield or your approach may indeed dissolve into meaningless flattery.

6. *The "If" or Assumptive Approach:* This approach, instead of identifying a gardener or a Texan or an upper middle-class affluent, uses "if/then." It identifies product or service benefits in terms of the goals and desires of its target market.

> 1. If you'd like your garden to flourish...If you'd like to know what's going on in Texas...If you'd like to shop in one of the world's most stylish stores...If you'd like to have a beautifully decorated home...

> 2. then surely you'll want to take this action (buy this gardening book...subscribe to this local magazine...order from this catalog) and realize your dreams and desires.

The letter in its most popular form is front-loaded with one benefit after another, ("If you...if you..."), culminating in a clash of cymbals as the offer is presented with the logical conclusion: "then have we got something for *you*...."

The If/Assumptive Approach enables a writer to fire off all benefits quickly and efficiently at the start of the letter, then move right in to the selling proposition on page one. It is often used in conjunction with the identification approach which acts as qualifier on the outer envelope.

Figure 6-5 is a perfect example of the approach done for *Darkroom Photography* magazine by William North (Bill) Jayme—one of the best-known, and just plain best, free-lance copywriters in the country. Notice how his Johnson box has been graphically modified (and modernized) here.

7. *The Question Approach:* A well-formulated Question Approach can be one of the most powerful ways to involve your prospects, as these all-time great advertising headlines attest:

> Do you make these mistakes in English?
> Does your child ever embarrass you?

Self-evaluation, quizzes, and seeking the prospect's opinion are also good examples of the Question Approach. ("Can you score over 90 on this personality Test?")

When do you use it? Look at your hypothesis and you major benefits. Can you come up with strong involvement questions that allow you to move right into your main benefits?

**SOME PEOPLE'S IDEA OF GREAT PICTURES
IS INSTANT FILM...OR LEAVING THE ROLL
OFF AT THE DRUGSTORE.
SERIOUS PHOTOGRAPHERS KNOW BETTER.
ANNOUNCING**

**THIS LETTER INVITES YOU TO SEND FOR
THE NEXT ISSUE.**

FREE

Dear Colleague:

If you take photography seriously ...

    If getting the shot is only the start of all the exciting things
you like to do with film -- developing, enlarging, cropping,
printing, mounting, exhibiting, selling ...

    If you look on your darkroom the same way an artist views the
studio -- a place for experimenting, for creating, for dreaming,
for letting your imagination run free ...

    If you're into pictures not only for pleasure but maybe also for
profit -- portrait work, magazine illustration, advertising,
fashion, posters, catalogues, annual reports, book and record
jacket design ...

... you're going to love DARKROOM PHOTOGRAPHY. With this letter I invite you
to send for the new issue -- no cost, no obligation, no strings. If you like
it, you can then subscribe at a special, low rate that saves you more than $3.

DARKROOM PHOTOGRAPHY is new and unique. It's the first magazine of its kind --
understandable, unbiased, authoritative. And it's the only one ever to cover
in depth not just the pleasures and possibilities of creating great pictures,
but also the considerable profits.

    You learn about new techniques, new procedures, new methods.
New ways to dramatize your black-and-white work -- toning,
brightening, adding contrast. New ways of bringing out color.
Tips on how to save time, work, money. Primers, refreshers and
checklists to make sure you're doing it all correctly.

    You learn about new products. New equipment -- enlargers,
lenses, processors, timers, baths, temperature controls, agi-
tators, accessories. New materials -- papers, chemicals, colors.
New kinds of film -- faster, more sensitive, more dramatic. New
gadgets, new timesavers, new troubleshooters.

                            (over, please)

Darkroom Photography, 5 Printmakers Alley, Marion, Ohio 43302

Figure 6-5

Figure 6-6 is a beautiful example of the Question Approach in action by Jim Punkre. It won the top prize from the Direct Marketing Creative Guild in 1982.

Hypothesis: Gardeners want more rewards/less work.

Big Benefit: A magazine that makes gardening easier, more rewarding for you.

Headline and Illustration: On outer envelope, "Can you spot the five mistakes here that make you work more and enjoy your garden less?"

Caveat: The Question Approach can also be tricky. When you plan your question make sure it involves your prospect by capitalizing on those human needs and desires reflected in your hypothesis and fulfilled in your benefits; otherwise a question can have negative effects, particularly those that try too hard to get the prospect to say yes. Just as we're all unconsciously compelled to finish the unfinished sentence, so we are also ornery enough to unconsciously say no when someone is trying too hard to make us say yes.

Wouldn't you rather have a Buick?
Aren't you sorry you're missing out on all the exciting things that are happening in...?
Are you ready to share one of the best kept secrets in the world of antiques?

8. *The Problem/Solution and the Negative Approach:* Somehow, no matter how bad things may be, advertisers always try to ignore the negative and latch onto the affirmative as an old song goes. And well they should. Negative selling can be very difficult—and dangerous.

This doesn't mean you can't use involving curiosity arousers like

Warning—this material is not for everyone.
Open this only if...."
Only the dedicated need apply...."
This may not be for you...."

No, no—it does *not* mean that.

The Negative Approach or Problem Solution in all its glory admits that there is trouble, serious trouble. It warns of gloom and disaster and it asks the prospect to participate in all this and help alleviate the problem.

Sure that's fund raising. And it's not dangerous. It's smart, you say.

Contribute to my campaign. If the opponent wins, up go your taxes.
Help this one child and you'll be helping all mankind—and feel the better for it. (The third child may starve if you don't.)
Help conserve our forests and make sure your children enjoy these trees.
Your contribution of $X can maintain one acre for a year.

Others are: "A clear and present danger." (A heart-tugging situation at most.) "Specific action needed." Often intangible, but strong, altruistic benefits for the reader.

How many of these common gardening mistakes are causing you to work harder than you really have to?

Dear Gardening Friend:

If you're working harder and enjoying your garden less ...

... could be, you're making a few common mistakes like our friend in the color photograph on our outside envelope -- mistakes that may be causing you extra work and added frustration.

Could be. Because one trait that the world's best gardeners have in common is how _little_ physical labor they actually do.

It's true.

After all, it's not how much you _do_ that leads to garden success, it's how much you _know_.

AFFIX STAMP
ON CARD
AND MAIL TODAY

And, right now, if you'd like to know more and work less ...

... we'd like to send you -- absolutely free -- a copy of THE BEST GARDENING IDEAS I KNOW, THE ORGANIC GARDENING HARVEST BOOK and BUILD-IT-YOURSELF HOMESTEAD ... these wonderful work-saving guides are yours just for taking a no-obligation look at ORGANIC GARDENING magazine.

To get your gifts ... just tear off the stamp on this page, affix it to the enclosed reply card and drop it in the mail. As soon as we hear from you, we'll send you the latest issue of our magazine and all three booklets ...

These FREE guides can save you work and mistakes.

... and you'll be on your way towards eliminating the common mistakes that could be taking the fun and pleasure out of your gardening. Mistakes that our friend in the photo is making like ...

weeding. You'll never have to do it

... again ...

(over, please)

Courtesy of Rodale Press, Inc.

Figure 6-6

This Negative Approach or Problem/Solution can also be used in consumer products and services and in business-to-business, although it is both difficult and dangerous unless the "you" predominates. Poorly executed, it will offend your prospects or encourage them to say, "Who cares?" Properly executed, it can be the strongest of direct response approaches, particularly in print advertising. The method here is: Set up the problem, then knock it down.

The danger is: If it's someone else's problem, you may get the "who cares?" If it's *the prospect's* potential problem (the "you")—you'll get a lot of good involvement.

Here's how you use it combined with the question approach: "Do you make these mistakes?" "Will you be able to support your family if you get ill?" "Is your job boring and unrewarding?" Strong stuff.

On the other hand, the consumer magazine subscription promotion in Figure 6-7 is a masterfully effective way of dealing with a serious non "you" problem. (How do you prospect for a magazine that's rumored to be discontinuing publication? Very carefully.) This is also a Negative/Bartlett's Approach—*a rare hybrid* and well worth your attention.

It took Frank Johnson, one of the all-time great direct response writers, to pull this off. The outer's copy is based on the famous Mark Twain quote, "The reports of my death are greatly exaggerated."

It states in simple typewriter type: "You've heard reports of our famous old magazine's impending death? (Greatly exaggerated) Now meet the people who rushed to our rescue...."

The letter is a lovely piece of construction. It starts with the negative, then builds up to an affirmative crescendo with strong reader testimonials starting right on the first page! (Frank, by the way, always does his outer envelope first.)

9. *The Fantasy Approach:* This approach is used primarily by sweepstakes writers and by top professionals when the hypothesis and benefits lend themselves to building dreams or building appealing imaginary situations.

There will be times—many, I hope, for your sake—when your product or service and its hypothesis cry out for the Fantasy Approach. It says, in effect, "Imagine this...imagine that...then imagine that you can...." Just as you get the reader with you, dreaming (or fantasizing right along), you pop up with the answer or solution: "Well, now you can...." No need to worry, here's your solution." There are some things you have to watch out for as you build the fantasy, however.

Most important: Don't cut the reader out by building *your* fantasy. This is a common mistake. At every step, you have to make sure your prospect can move into the fantasy easily and identify totally with the description you provide. Too much description and detail may lose you some prospects who will say, "Wait a minute. That's not *my* fantasy." Give your readers room to move *and imagine* within the fantasy framework you provide.

Figure 6-8 is an excellent example, written by Henry Burnett (another of *the* best of the direct response writers). Notice the fantasy in the Johnson box— it's the "island of *your* dreams." Hank describes it *conceptually, not physically.*

Harper's

TWO PARK AVENUE, NEW YORK, N.Y. 10016

Dear Reader:

You're invited here to subscribe to HARPER'S. Yes, HARPER'S — the famous 131-year-old magazine that's been having its lumps of late, as you've probably heard.

"Come on!", you say, "Why should I try a superannuated magazine that's been on the skids?"

Because we'll bet you — and back that bet with a free trial copy and a low trial subscription price — that you'll discover HARPER'S will provide much of the most invigorating, informative, entertaining, best written and insightful reading you'll enjoy all year.

"So?", you reply. "All editors make such claims." But I'm not quoting our editors. I'm quoting our readers, as you'll see in a moment.

But first, our problem. Early last summer, a widely carried item (and many rueful editorials) announced that HARPER'S, one of the oldest and most honored of U.S. magazines, had been losing money and would soon cease publishing.

Immediately, an amazing thing happened. Our mail box roared with letters of anguish and distress, from a great many of our 310,000 + subscribers. And not one asked for a refund. Instead —

"I was very happy to get to know Harper's as one magazine daring to speak the truth without any unwarranted bias.... I'm going to mail you as many gift subscriptions to people I know, as I can pay for...."

"With much sadness, I have learned that a magazine which was unafraid of telling it like it is...solid, literate...will soon be laid to rest."

"The extinction of Harper's magazine is unthinkable and unacceptable."

"Though I disagreed with much of what you printed, I never put down an issue without learning something of importance. You were a challenge and therefore, a friend ...."

"When I got serious about my reading, I went back to the classics — and I subscribed to HARPER's. Now, what a tragedy!"

"...extreme disappointment. I cannot say that I agreed with everything printed on its pages; but I can say that seldom was I not challenged to think."

(more--)

A publication of: The John D. and Catherine T. MacArthur Foundation
140 So. Dearborn, Chicago, IL 60603

Courtesy of Harper's Magazine

Figure 6-7

ISLANDS

AN INTERNATIONAL MAGAZINE, 123 WEST PADRE, SUITE A, SANTA BARBARA, CA 93105 (805) 682-7177

Somewhere out there, beyond the blue horizon,
lies the island of your dreams ... isolated by
oceans from trouble and strife, from concrete
and plastic, from politics and pollution ...
a place where geography grants immunity from
the impositions and incivilities of day-to-day
life in an over-civilized world.

Now you can find it, explore it, experience it
and enjoy it ... through the pages of a magnificent new magazine for the escapist in us all:

             I S L A N D S

This is your invitation to run away with us to
the most intriguing islands on earth ... to
become a Charter Subscriber at a special low rate
... and to get your copy of the Premier Issue.

Dear Fellow Romantic:

    Even the names conjure up magic and mystery.   Aldabra, Rarotonga,
Bougainville, Novaya Zemlya.   Tuamotu, Palawan, Corfu, Kodiak, Cozumel.
Ellesmere and Eleuthera, Kerguelen and Kermadec, Nicobar and Zanzibar,
the Isle of Wives and the Isle of Pines.

    There are more than half a million islands on earth.   Now, at
last, there's a magazine devoted to exploring them and learning about
them.   A magazine with the spirit of an adventurer, the soul of a poet,
the eye of a scientist and the insatiable curiosity of a social
anthropologist.

        It's called ISLANDS, and if you're as fascinated by
        islands as the rest of the human race has always
        been, you'll love it.   In a minute, I'll give you
        details on how to become a Charter Subscriber (at
        a low Charter rate) and get your copy of the beau-

                                        (over, please)

Figure 6-8

163

Bon Appétit

- You've decided to have a completely relaxing weekend. No pressure. No plans. But around midday on Saturday, you get itchy. So you get on the telephone. "Hey, why not come on over for dinner," you suggest to good friends who live nearby. "We'll have some drinks and I'll make a big casserole and we'll sit around the fire and just talk . . ."

- You meet some people who have just moved into your area. You like them. You'd like to know them better. You'd like them to meet your friends. You say, "Will you come over for dinner next Friday? I'll invite a few other couples. People I think you'll enjoy. . ."

- Today is his birthday. It's a big one. The party is on Saturday, but tonight, he says he'd like to spend the evening at home . . . just the two of you. You tell him, "I'm going to make something really special." You think, "Something romantic. Maybe exotic. A dinner that will put the best restaurant in town to shame . . ."

- You've decided—this year you're going to give a New Year's Eve dinner. You're excited. You're inspired. You're going to bring in the New Year in the most spectacular way. Maybe duplicate that James Beard New Year's Eve menu. Maybe do a complete Provencal buffet. But first, the guest list. You start calling. Before you know it, 10 couples have said (delightedly) "YES . . ."

Dear Friend:

You did it. You promised. You offered. You invited. Now what?

Do you panic? Do you worry? Do you roll your eyes and wonder why you ever started this? Do you fleetingly consider canceling? Claiming a sudden trip, a searing headache, a sick child, an unexpected visit from an aging, anti-social aunt?

Not anymore, you don't!

Now you turn calmly to The Bon Appétit Dinner Party Cookbook ...knowing that with this one book, you will get all the help you need to pull off a simply sensational dinner -- give a party so wonderfully original, so totally relaxed, so completely organized that you yourself will enjoy it just as much as your friends are bound to.

Figure 6-9

This allows "you" all the freedom in the world to visualize your own particular paradise.

Figure 6-9 is an award-winning letter by Emily Soell, President of Rapp & Collins, and a fine writer in her own right. It shows another effective use of fantasy. Each of her examples in the Johnson box really begins with "Imagine." And the solution to all of these common imaginary situations is right there on the front page of the letter. Of course.

Fantasy-come-true (in addition to the Negative Approach) can also be used in fund raising. "Imagine what you could do to help realize this dream" is an excellent approach to fund raising as long as the dream *is* realizable.

Some advice on sweepstakes. The entire sweepstakes concept is based on fantasy—the popular fantasy of "striking it rich" and the sweepstakes popularity fluctuates—up in difficult economic periods, down in stable or improved economic times.

If you have a hand in working with the sweepstakes professionals, keep in mind that you'll draw a better class of customer if the sweepstakes and its prizes are themed to complement or emphasize the product or service offered, rather than overshadow it. If you're called upon to do the sweepstakes writing, there are several basics to remember.

a. Go heavy on the hype. This is one place where it's clearly permissible. ("Imagine!" "Imagine!" "Imagine!")

b. Emphasize the Grand Prize and the smallest prize (the one that offers the best odds because so many are awarded). These are the two upon which most response is based—the fantasy of winning *the* grand prize; the reality that you just might win the smallest prize.

c. When the main prize is money (research shows that money is *the* most popular prize) fantasize about all the things that "you can do with it." Build dreams.

d. Use words like "imagine," "life of luxury," "dreams come true" "time of your life," "beyond belief," "high life."

e. Add involvement devices—peels, tucks, scratches, pastes, check-offs, initials. As opposed to all other direct mail, clutter and confusion (the experts claim) make sweepstakes *more* appealing.

f. Don't restrain the artist either. He or she may want a lot of illustrations, big seals, sunbursts, official-looking borders, and computerized forms.

g. As with strong premium offers, fight to maintain a position of prominence for your product or service—lest your prospect forget that an order is still the objective.

h. Learn from the real pros. Study sweepstakes mailings from the magazine business—*Reader's Digest*, Publisher's Clearing House, and American Family Publishers. They've been at it for years.

10. *The Analogy Approach:* Here's an approach that's recommended only if it comes to you in a blinding flash of inspiration, and it can happen—the perfect analogy—something so close and so much a part of the prospect's experience that he or she moves through it with you, right into the product or service benefits saying "yes, yes, yes" all along the way.

Even the perfect analogy is tough to execute effectively. You won't find many of these. Figure 6-10 shows the first page of one of the best I've ever come across. It's a combo analogy-cum-question approach, and it's loaded with involvement! (You'd be safe to guess that the hypothesis here is "Most people know less about their bodies than they do about their homes. Once they realize the absurdity of this situation, they'll want to change it.")

11. *The Story Approach:* People enjoy a good story and if you have a short, relevant one that pulls your prospect right into your benefits, don't be afraid to use it. If it's very good (and very pertinent) and your writing is especially keen, you might even consider starting on the envelope.

Figure 6-11 is the first of several excellent "story" beginnings. Notice that in most cases, the story in the telling demonstrates or acts out a big benefit. It is a vehicle for getting the big benefit across.

Figure 6-12 is a delightful Fund Raiser for the Nature Conservancy by Frank Johnson. It creates a crush of fan mail whenever the mailing is dropped. And it's mailed often—as nothing yet as been able to beat it!

It has gentle, *effective* humor. Who could resist this droll fellow on the outer envelope? Or the teaser copy? Or the salutation? Or the letter lead? Or the call to action in the third paragraph?

Frank Johnson is a pure wordsmith; his turn of phrase and choice description, his gentle commands and candid exposition can serve well as a lesson for all aspiring writers. Study every sentence. Understand and appreciate the craftsmanship until you come to the point where you can say, "I wish I had written that."

Caveat: Although the Story Approach allows you to use drama and all your descriptive talents—even humor—humorous writing is very hard to pull off. What tickles *your* funny bone may leave some of your market cold. Most of us do well to play it safe and not try humor or attempt to be clever.

One of the greatest mail order storytellers of all time was a real mail order entrepreneur. (And maybe that's why he was so great.) His name? Max Habernickel (or M. Habernickel, Jr., as he signed his letters). He was the cofounder of Haband, a mail order menswear operation that he started in 1925 with John Anderson. They expanded from selling ties by mail to selling shirts, trousers, belts—even suits. And from the beginning, Max was the spokesman for the company. That meant that all customers communications came from Max and they all had a small, family business flavor. Even after Haband had grown to a mail order business of $50 million in annual sales, Max kept that intimate family feeling in his letters.

He demonstrated that the letter itself is the true test of the professional. His letters demanded attention, aroused interest, gave direction, and called for

The Editors of TIME and LIFE
invite you to preview free
the Volume I, Number One issue of

our first new magazine since
SPORTS ILLUSTRATED
and the monthly publication designed
to help you and your family
lead healthier, happier, longer lives.

Dear Friend:

     May we have your permission, please, to conduct a simple
experiment on you? The experiment is this:

          AS SOON AS YOU COME TO THE END OF THIS
          SENTENCE, CLOSE YOUR EYES FOR A MOMENT,
          AND TRY TO VISUALIZE YOUR HOME.

          *   *   *   *   *

     Fairly easy, wasn't it? Most people know their homes
pretty well.

     You know more or less where everything is -- the furniture,
the pictures, what's in which cabinets and closets. You know,
too, how to keep things in running order -- dusting, washing,
changing the beds. And you know how to make minor repairs:

          How to replace a faucet, repair a
          screen, repaint a wall. Maybe even
          how to put in a new window pane, re-
          finish a table or chest.

     But now, compare the big home in which you live with the
smaller home you inhabit -- your body -- and how does your
knowledge stack up?

     You've heard all your life about your pancreas -- but do
you know where it is and all that it does? Have you any idea
what your duodenum is -- and how it connects up with your
stomach? And speaking of stomach, do you, like many people,
think of it as being round?

Figure 6-10

Courtesy of Time Inc.

SCIENCE 84

IT'S THE EXCITING
NEW MAGAZINE FROM
THE AMERICAN ASSOCIATION FOR
THE ADVANCEMENT OF SCIENCE.
MAIL THE ENCLOSED CARD PROMPTLY
AND GET A FREE COPY OF THE
NEXT EXCITING ISSUE.

Dear Reader:

She hoisted herself up noiselessly so as not to disturb the rattlesnakes snoozing there in the sun.

To her left, the high desert of New Mexico. Indian country. To her
right, the rock carvings she had photographed the day before. Stick
people. Primitive animals.

Up ahead, three sandstone slabs stood stacked against the face of
the cliff. In their shadow, another carving. A spiral consisting
of rings. Curious, the young woman drew closer. Instinctively,
she glanced at her watch. It was almost noon. Then just at that
moment, a most unusual thing happened.

> Suddenly, as if out of nowhere, an eerie dagger of light
> appeared to stab at the topmost ring of the spiral. It
> next began to plunge downwards -- shimmering, laser-like.
>
> It pierced the eighth ring. The seventh. The sixth. It
> punctured the innermost and last. Then just as suddenly
> as it had appeared, the dagger of light was gone. The
> young woman glanced at her watch again. Exactly twelve
> minutes had elapsed.

Coincidence? Accident? Fluke? No. What she may have stumbled
across that midsummer morning three years ago is an ancient solar
calendar. And in scientific circles, it's hotly debated as one
of the most intriguing archeological discoveries of recent years.

> It may change forever history's perceptions of America's
> early Indian peoples. And as an astronomical and
> geometrical marvel, it may rival Stonehenge.

If science whodunnits like this set your intellect a-jogging . . .
If you take pleasure and pride in keeping up with everything
significant that's being discovered, explored, invented,
postulated, verified . . .

Figure 6-11

Courtesy of Science 85 Magazine
Created by Jayme, Ratalahti, Inc.

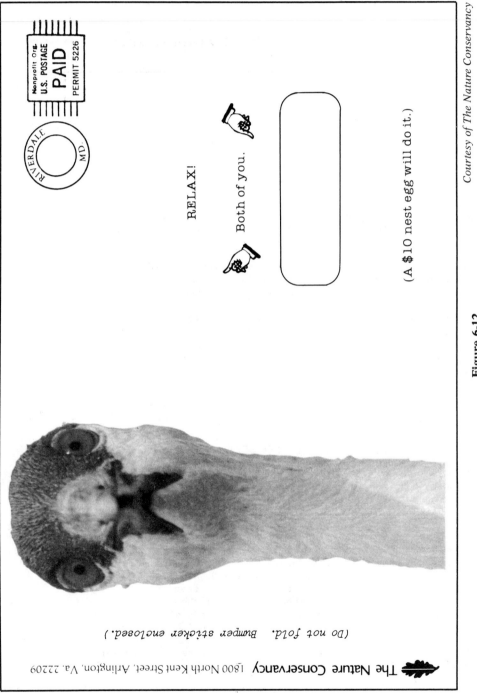

Figure 6-12

Courtesy of The Nature Conservancy

Nancy C. Mackinnon
Membership Director

**The
Nature
Conservancy**

1800 North Kent Street
Arlington, Virginia 22209

Dear Investor:

The bug-eyed bird on our envelope who's ogling you with such dis-
temper has a point. He's a native American sandhill crane and you may be
sitting on top of one of his nesting sites.

As he sees it, every time our human species has drained a marsh,
and plowed it or built a city on it, since 1492 or so -- there went the
neighborhood. It's enough to make you both a bit edgy.

So give us $10 for his nest egg and we'll see that a nice, soggy
spot -- just the kind he and his mate need to fashion a nest and put an
egg in it -- is reserved for the two of them, undisturbed, for keeps.
Only $10. (Watch those cranes come in to land, just once, and you're
paid back. Catches at your throat.) Then the cranes can relax, and so
can you. A bit.

How will we reserve that incubator with your $10?
Not by campaigning or picketing or suing.

<u>We'll just BUY the nesting ground.</u>

That's the unique and expensive and <u>effective</u> way The Nature Conservancy goes about its non-profit business. We're as dead serious about
hanging on to nature's precarious balance as the more visible and vocal
conservation groups. But our thing is to let money do our talking.

And we buy a whopping lot of land: starting with
60 acres of New York's Mianus River Gorge in 1951
(now 395 acres), we have protected 2,000,000 acres
-- about the area of Rhode Island and Delaware.
The plots are spotted coast to coast and from
Canada deep into the Caribbean, 3,157 of them
sized from a quarter of an acre to hundreds of
square miles.

All of it is prime real estate, if you're a crane or a bass or a
sweet pepperbush or a redwood. Or a toad or a turtle. And a lot of

Figure 6-12, *continued*

it's nice for people, too -- lovely deserts, mountains, prairies, islands.
(Islands! We own huge Santa Cruz, off the California shore, and tiny
Dome Island in Lake George, and most of the Virginia Barrier Islands,
and dozens more.)

So besides being after your $10, we invite you to see a sample of
our lands. We have 38 chapters in 32 states. Check your phone book. If
we're not there yet, call me at (703) 841-5388. We'll guide you and
yours to a nearby preserve where you're most welcome to walk along one of
our paths, sit on one of our log benches, look about, and say to the
youngster we hope will be with you, "This will be here, as is, for your
grandchildren." Nice feeling.

We do ask that you don't bother the natives. E.g., there's a sign
in one preserve that says "Rattlesnakes, Scorpions, Black Bear, Poison
Oak/ARE PROTECTED/DO NOT HARM OR DISTURB." For $10, you're privileged
not to disturb a bear or stroke a poison oak. Bargain.

> Bargains in diverse real estate are what we look
> for and find. Not just any real estate. We've
> been working for years to make and keep a huge
> ongoing inventory of the "natural elements" in
> each of the United States (so far, 32 are done).
> These "State Natural Heritage Programs" identify
> what's unique, what's threatened, what's rare or
> a rare natural sight to see in each state: ani-
> mals, birds, plants, bugs, lakes, river systems,
> swamps, waterfalls, woods ... and cranes' nests.

Then we try to acquire those places that desperately need protection
and preservation. We think big. Early last year, the Richard King Mellon
Foundation gave us the largest single grant ever for private conservation:
$25,000,000 -- if we can match that sum in other gifts within the next
five years. We will, believe us.

All that huge sum is earmarked to safeguard one of our nation's most
severely threatened resources -- aquatic and wetland ecosystems from the
Atlantic coast to Alaska. Among these are a desert wash system in southern
California's Coachella Valley, a key link in the New England coastal preserve system and critical habitat along North America's central flyway
reaching from Canada to the Gulf Coast.

But we don't just shovel cash at these projects. We buy some lands,
trade for others, get leases and easements, ask to be mentioned in wills.
Then we give or, preferably, sell up to 40 percent of what we buy to
states, cities, universities, other conservation groups -- any responsible organization which wants and loves the land so much that it doesn't

Figure 6-12, *continued*

mind our clever lawyers making it very difficult for anyone to "improve" any part of it, ever. Unless the someone can build nests or eat acorns.

That cash flow replenishes our revolving fund, every dime of which is plowed into the unpaved and as yet unplowed. All this activity generates a lot of fascinating true stories, and lovely photos. These we put into a small (32 pages) but elegant, sprightly and adless magazine, our report to our 215,000 members every other month: The Nature Conservancy News.

Here you may find that the land you and the rest of us have just bought is harboring a four-lined skink, or a spicebush, or boreal chickadees, or kame and kettle topography. You've a lot to learn and see that's most intriguing, as you'll discover.

The Nature Conservancy News also describes well-led tours of our various properties, tells you what we're doing in your state, and shows you how you can help and have some healthy fun at the same time.

You see, the millions of acres we own are mostly watched over by volunteer stewards -- wonderful men and women who are proud to show off their lovely charges. These likely include bats, salamanders, toadstools and such. Or cranes. You'll be invited to Nature Conservancy chapter meetings nearest you.

And if you paste the complimentary white-oak-leaf sticker we've enclosed with this letter on your bumper, backpack, boat, hang glider, pool, bicycle, wheelchair ... wherever, you'll attract grateful grins from your fellow cognoscenti.

> Now, you may think it's disproportionate to brag about how we're raising millions for our projects and then ask you for only $10. Who needs you?
>
> We need you, very much! Those hard-headed foundations and corporations and ranch owners and such who give us money or property must be convinced that our ranks include a lot of intelligent, concerned, articulate citizens: people who know we ought to let nature alone to tend to much of this finite earth and all its creatures ... if we're to be among the creatures.

Yes, we need you and your ear and your voice -- and your $10 ($10 times 215,000 members buys a lot of acres). Please join us today, like so: Get a pen. Check and initial the "membership application" form that your hand is touching. Tear off the Interim Membership stub, sign and pocket it, and wait six weeks or so for your first magazine and permanent

Figure 6-12, *continued*

card. Enclose a check for $10 in the return envelope (more, if you can spare it). NOTE that it's tax-deductible. Mail the form. Go.

Thank you, and welcome!, dear wise fellow investor in nest eggs. For your fanfare, listen for the wondrous stentorian call of that sandhill crane*.

Sincerely,

Nancy C Mackinnon

Nancy C. Mackinnon
Membership Director

* We borrowed his picture from Country Journal magazine where he illustrated an article about the International Crane Foundation of Baraboo, Wisconsin. The photo is by brave Cary Wolinsky. And we don't actually know if the crane is as upset as he looks. Maybe he's smiling? Certainly he will if, when he leaves the Foundation, his first motel stop has been reserved with your $10.

NCM/al

The most recent Nature Conservancy financial report filed with the Department of State may be obtained by writing to: New York State, Department of State, Office of Charities Registration, Albany, New York 12231, or The Nature Conservancy, 1800 North Kent Street, Arlington, Virginia 22209.

If you like to read financial statements, this one is a beauty. We're rather vain about it. Do ask.

Figure 6-12, *continued*

action. He used motivation, involvement, and incentive like a true pro. And Max didn't stop there. Each letter was a perfect melding of salesmanship and advertising from a master craftsman who could interweave humor and entertainment with good expository, hard sell mail order copy.

I doubt if there was ever a salesman who was on more familiar terms with the customers. He let them in on company secrets, regaled them with family anecdotes to reinforce his sales points. He cajoled them, gave them advice, and ultimately insisted that they act. Customers became part of the inner circle of the Haband Company, as they got to know Max, his family, his friends, and his employees. This added a delightful human dimension to doing business with Haband.

Max Habernickel died some years ago, but his friendly communications won't be forgotten. Max made sure of that. His son, Duke, now signs the letters.

Figure 6-13 shows an original, classic Max Habernickel letter. Notice that no matter what Max was talking about, he never failed to start the offer on page one.

12. *The Be-a-Hero Approach:* This approach, attributed to the late Paul Bringe, a well-known direct mail consultant, is the most popular and logical approach for business-to-business mail, or for any situation where your prospect is not buying directly for himself or herself.

Ostensibly, your business approach has an end goal of increasing corporate profits—doing something that will save the company time or money—but, altruistic motives asides, you are still talking to a weak human being. What might motivate your business prospect? One answer, said in different ways; "You will be a hero," which means

- Personal corporate recognition
- Rising success in the company
- A promotion

Your prospect, who may very well have to persuade the boss (and others) to agree to an action, needs your support and assurance that the action will be positive and innovative for the company. And you must provide this prospect with the tools to get the message across.

Figures 6-14 and 6-15 are the first pages of two good examples of this. The first is actually a business magazine solicitation, but it also employs the Be-a-Hero Approach. (The letter was written by Bill Jayme and designed by Heikki Ratalahti.)

The second is an executive mailing from Xerox Learning Systems, written by Robert Haydon Jones, another one of our top writers.

You started into this chapter expecting to come out of it with your creation firmly in hand, but look what's happened—you still haven't written a headline! You are, however, a lot further along than you think and this will become clear as you pull it all together in the next few pages. Chapter 7, as a matter of fact, is

Operating Through THE UNITED STATES MAILS Exclusively Since 1925

HABAND COMPANY

FAMOUS FOR TIES

M. HABERNICKEL, JR. *Men's Wear* PARCEL POST ASSN.

PATERSON, N.J.

Dear Haband Customer:

The other day, I met the smart-alec who runs a nationally famous pants factory. They have been written up in a couple of magazines, and he gives smug talks at various trade conventions. You know the type. He was saying that if you took a bunch of pennies and scattered them around the floor of the factory, with today's costs, you couldn't afford to have somebody pick them up!

Well, I was dumbfounded! Maybe you have to say things like that to become famous. But I'll tell you what would happen at Haband if somebody dumped pennies on the floor. I would pick them up. And probably crash heads with my son Duke and Miss Feeney and Don Schmidt and Eleanor and Bruce as we all dived to pick them up.

When I was a young man, I used to walk along the street actually searching the ground in front of me, hoping to maybe find a penny. And dreaming up good things I'd do if I found one. Now some whippersnapper industry genius says we couldn't afford to pick them up! No wonder his pants have to sell for $45 the pair! And no wonder more than two million penny-conscious American executives write to us in Paterson, New Jersey, for all their clothing needs! Such as our most deluxe Country Club executive dress slacks at 2 pair for $19.95!

In fact, last year the same slacks sold at 2 pair for $24.95. This year, the same slacks the subject of this important letter, with new colors and with several interesting new extra values added, are $5 less per order! Here's why:

Courtesy of the Haband Company

Figure 6-13

It is because I am more and more _horrified_ about Inflation. The prices of everything are running away, and my money just doesn't keep up with the Cost of Living Index! So there are more and more things that I wistfully decide I don't need any more "at those prices"!

And they talk so much about the "Quality of Life"! I do not claim that the quality of my life is much diminished by refusing to pay $5 for a seat in the movies. And I'll give up Foreign Travel, or Hollandaise Sauce, or Water Beds, without a whimper. BUT I WILL NOT ALLOW INFLATION TO ROB ME OF MY NATURAL BORN GOOD LOOKS!

"Hmpf!" says Miss Feeney, my secretary for 25 years. And I swear she winked at Duke. But it ain't no laughing matter! Especially in view of these very real bits of Hard Economic Fact:

*Today many Wholesale Textile Prices are setting _Record Lows!_

*Today some of the Biggest Names in the business are _Going Out of Business!_

*Today there are Plenty of Factories _Looking for Work!_

In view of such conditions, Haband went to market with a list of Consumer Demands we haven't dared ask for in over a decade. And we've come back with a package of Goodies that make us proud to be in business! We have loaded our Haband 1977 Country Club Executive Slacks with _Better Value_, and _Improved Long Wear_. And we offer it all at a real 20% PRICE REDUCTION on the newest, best, most stylish slacks in our Haband line! Here is what you get:

*100% polyester deluxe doubleKnit fabric. Still the most outstanding fabric I've ever seen for slacks! 2-way knit for two-way fit, and that means double value! Gentle two-way s-t-r-e-t-c-h that never binds, always feels good. (It gives and recovers as you bend, stretch or move.) No

Figure 6-13, _continued_

176

other fabric in the world packs and travels and shrugs off wrinkles like 100% polyester doubleKnit. And it is 100% NO IRON wash and wear permanent press! You save on the original price. And you continue to save on Cleaner's Bills and Pressing Bills (and Wear and Tear on your Wife) for the life of the pants!

*Haband's popular <u>INDELIBLE CREASE</u> that will not twist out, wash out, sag, bag or droop! I don't know why other people insist on chintzing on this feature. It is no trade secret how to do it, and it makes the most impeccable pair of executive double-Knit slacks ever! Even with the 1977 $5 price cut, we include this important feature.

*New <u>VALUE ADDED</u> "Polyastro" inner waistband canvas, for better waistband shape retention, through repeated cleaning and washing. "Polyastro" is fast-drying, non-fraying and longer wearing. A new improvement you will appreciate immensely.

*New <u>VALUE ADDED</u> "Non-Slip" <u>Shirt-Tail Gripper!</u> Keeps shirt tails tucked in, keeps slacks in place. A double track of a special rubbery gripper costs extra to put in, but pays off double in Better Looks and Better Comfort!

*New <u>VALUE ADDED</u> Modified <u>FLARE LEG!</u> Costs us more, but you look better! 'Nuf said. You've got it!

*New <u>VALUE ADDED</u> Resort Style FREE MATCHING BELT!! Here is the super-extra attraction that makes our already high-quality slacks something truly exceptional. Whether you choose the lighter pastel Country Club colors or the new more conservative Executive Club shades, the matching belt automatically gives you an extra $10 worth of good looks FREE! It's the kind of special attention to dressing correctly that makes people admire the way you look. And who else but Haband gives it to you?

Oh, I could go on and on! But the crux of the matter is in the personality of the House.

Figure 6-13, *continued*

Sure, we face rising costs in many areas, just like everybody else. Maybe our "20% off" price is too low! Maybe we shouldn't have cut our price at all! But Duke and I talked it over. We decided that after 52 years we are still working at building a nice, solid family business here, and we are going to do it by offering the best values we know how. Just as if it were your own family in the business! If we have been alert enough to pick up some impressive savings in the market, I want to pass them along to you. Duke is not quite sure I am right about the price cut, but he bows to the wisdom of my years and to my louder voice. So we invite you to take a look.

Remember, this is no "Sale"! This is no closeout! This is no Early Bird Special or come-on of any kind! Because we were able to make a very advantageous buy, what we have here is a <u>real 20% price reduction</u> on the newest, best, most stylish and well-made merchandise in our line! Haband's 1977 Country Club Executive Slacks, now TWO PAIR FOR $19.95! For the Office, for Vacation, for Weekends, and for Saturday Night!

The slacks are ready now, in your correct size, with five interesting colors to choose. (Miss Feeney suggests the new Medium Brown as the best for all occasions. I like the favorite Light Blue and Champagne Tan). Whichever you choose, send us your check for a couple of pairs right now. I guarantee you will see real improvement in your appearance and you will feel extra savings in your pocket!

Very truly yours,

HABAND OF PATERSON

M. Habernickel jr

M. HABERNICKEL, JR

MH/CV

Figure 6-13, *continued*

Business Week

By agreement, our magazine solicits subscriptions from men and women in middle and upper management positions.

With this letter, the Editors now invite you to join this exclusive and knowing circle...to save yourself or your company $29.50 on your subscription...and to receive free as a welcoming gift one of the most valuable business handbooks that's ever been privately printed.

With our compliments

Dear Colleague:

Hasn't it happened to you in business? It sure used to happen to me.

Let's say you go into a meeting. Everyone present has lots to say -- ideas, opinions, news. Finally you put in your own two cents' worth. You mention something you've just heard ...

    ... <u>only to discover that everybody else has known about it for days</u>. So you find yourself saying "Damn!"

Or let's say you're called upon to make a really important decision. You spend some restless nights mulling your options. You check out the available data. Finally, you make up your mind ...

    ... <u>only to learn too late that your data is incomplete or out-of-date</u>. So you find yourself saying "Damn!"

Or let's say you finally get the money together to make an investment for your family. The stock looks good. The time

                                           (Turn over, please)

Figure 6-14

Created by Jayme, Ratalahti, Inc.

Xerox Learning Systems
Depot Square
P.O. Box 810
Peterborough, NH 03458
603 924-9007

XEROX

Dear Executive:

Suppose you could arrange to give your secretary and/or administrative assistant an award that would confirm your appreciation of their contribution while it also helped them to become significantly better at their job.

My name is John J. Franco. I'm president of Xerox Learning Systems. Our business is helping people do a better job. Our clients include 357 of the Fortune 500.

Recently a number of our clients have asked us to help them with a fundamental issue that has troubled many executives.

It's the idea of encouraging your secretary and/or administrative assistant to grow. That's critical if they are going to help you as your responsibilities increase.

Secretaries are entitled to and need affirmation of the key role they play -- along with ongoing encouragement and systematic assistance in learning how to become more valuable on the job.

That's why we have created a learning system expressly for your secretary and/or administrative assistant. It's called BIZ. It's an in-service learning system delivered on an ongoing basis -- once every two months.

BIZ is mailed directly to your secretary. It is a large, distinctive looking portfolio that contains scientifically designed learning arranged in an attractive editorial format.

Here's a sample of the content:

Business Finance Made Easy
        (what every secretary and administrative assistant
          needs to know about the "language of business")

How to Get Something From Here to There
        (twenty-two ways to ship that package, and which to
          choose when)

Figure 6-15

Courtesy of Xerox Learning Systems

really an extension of this Chapter. I'm breaking it up just to give you a breather and a chance to order up a loaf of bread and a glass of wine.

CHAPTER 6 EXERCISES

Choosing an Approach

As a direct response professional, your keen, analytical eye is going to look at every piece of direct mail a little differently in the future; especially when you know the writer is employing an "approach." It's good practice to keep an eye out for such approaches in every piece of direct mail that you receive or can get your hands on, for that matter. See how effective they are in pulling you in. (Could you have improved on them?)

Some products and services cry for certain approaches, others almost seem to adapt to any approach. The hypothesis (Look for the words in parentheses below.) often gives the clue and points the way. Match each of the approaches in column A with the right product/benefit/hypothesis in B.

A. Approaches

Generic/Bargain Approach

Story Approach

Fantasy Approach

Testimonial Approach

Question Approach

Invitational Approach

B. Product/Benefit/Hypothesis

1. A travel magazine that brings you picture stories of cities and countries around the world. When you subscribe you are also entered in a big travel sweepstakes (the pleasure and cultural enrichment of reading about—and possibly visiting—faraway places).

2. A new limited editions club. Membership in this select collectors' group ensures that you will be offered quality objects with sound value that others cannot purchase (desire to belong to an exclusive group).

3. Correspondence course on conversational Spanish for business people. In Spain, without a working knowledge of the language, you cannot hold your own and maintain the respect of the native Spanish executives (desire to be successful).

4. A new video camera and video cassette recorder combination.

Every family can use and enjoy this. Now's the time to buy because the price is at an all-time low. (It enhances the quality of life. And increases enjoyment.)

5. An amazing new book that can change your life. The Smith book tells how John Smith amassed a fortune. Now you can do the same. (It offers security, freedom from money worries.)

6. A request for a clothing catalog. Order this catalog and enjoy fine clothing. And we will treat you royally. Our customers are fussy, tasteful people. And they stay with us. (People who are nervous about buying through the mail will look for assurance that they are using a quality company that doesn't make mistakes and readily accepts exchanges and returns.)

Answers

1 – Fantasy Approach
2 – Invitational Approach
3 – Question Approach
4 – Generic/Bargain Approach
5 – Story Approach
6 – Testimonial Approach

Got your answers? How did you come out? Don't agree? Don't worry, you don't *have* to agree. You may have come up with good creative solutions of your own and that's what it's all about. Shall we test?

chapter 7

Deathless Prose

You have just arrived at the portals of creativity with five suitcases, one large trunk, a pair of binoculars, and your Nikon camera around your neck, a tennis racquet under your arm, and golf clubs at your feet. (Oops, you dropped your raincoat!) What's this about creativity and inspiration? You can't get off the ground with the creative equipment I've been hanging on you...approaches, time frames, artist relationships, showers, shaving, and mothers-in-law?

Are you possibly suspecting that actual writing could become nothing more than a simple mathematical formula that you put into a computer—and out pops your copy, incorporating everything you've learned? That you'll never actually arrive at a point where you have to create? Doubting Thomas! For shame. You are there.

As your tour director thus far, I'm dismissing you with one sharp command to break ranks, go off and GET IT DOWN! No more procrastination. Ready or not—go! Write! Now. Don't come back until it's down. Check your baggage at the hotel, strip to your bathing suit or whatever, throw caution to the winds, and dive in. You'll never know where you are until you do. No excuses. You've eaten. (You had your bread and wine at the end of Chapter 6.) So get going. GET IT DOWN!

STAGE ONE—GET IT DOWN

This is not my idea of fun nor is it something I've invented just to torture you. GET IT DOWN *is* your first logical step to writing and whether or not you want to accept it—now is your hour! At the self-imposed command "Get it down" —and you must impose this command on yourself with every job, large or small—several things may happen.

1. You start right in, raring to go, full of ideas. You write for an hour or so—then you fizzle out.

2. You sit there struggling with your copy lead. You have ideas—even a possible approach—but you can't seem to eke out the first sentence.

3. You go back to Chapter 6 to see about getting started again—on the write foot.

4. You write on (and on for hours) despite your doubts. Then you read it

back and you hate it. (In extreme cases writers can even hate themselves and doubt their abilities at this stage.)

Question: Why am I telling you all this?

Answer: Because it's terribly important that you do not become discouraged. You must understand that *all* writers have these problems (although some don't like to admit it). Not even William Shakespeare, T.S. Eliot, or Gabriel García Márquez could roll off one deathless phrase after another.

Writing is hard work. It is a tough craft. No one would bother with this nasty business if there weren't some big emotional rewards. What's more, writers don't communicate constructively about their writing as Barbara Goldsmith attests in this excerpt from an article in *The New York Times Book Review:*

> Ultimately, although millions of words have been written on the subject, the public has been given little help in understanding the writing process. Few writers are adept at explaining exactly what they do, and, indeed, many do not seem to understand it themselves. William Faulkner thought of himself as a man "running along behind [his characters] with a pencil trying to put down what they say and do." Somerset Maugham wrote, "There are three rules for writing the novel. Unfortunately, no one knows what they are." And Marianne Moore warned the writer, "Be there when the writing is going on." The late Tommy Thompson, in urging writers to get over feelings of inferiority, offered only two words or advice on how to feel professional, "Get dressed."
>
> It is a truism that the more skillful the writing, the more invisible the act of creation. If the writer has done a competent job, his insights become so lucid and universal that they seem to belong to the reader himself. What follows, then, is the assumption that the reader could have produced them. This is, no doubt, in spite of all evidence to the contrary, why the fantasy endures that the writer merely extracts one's story as a dentist would pull out a loose tooth. One is reminded of how Michelangelo informed a man who admired one of his angel carvings that his job was not difficult, because the angel had been inside the stone all along. Michelangelo had simply set it free.[1]

A Word About Your Rewards

As a direct response writer you can take comfort in the techniques. You have formats and sequences to follow...rules that protect you...structures like AIDA to help you organize. In short, a lot is already done for you, but the fortune cookie says, "Direct response writer cannot thrive and prosper on technique alone."

If you don't already have a hundred ideas jumping around in your head, this is inspiration time—the time to visit the storehouse of your imagination. If

---

your curiosity has done its job, you'll have lots to work with. Start associating familiar experiences with your prospect and your product. Let your mind go. (And here's where "creative people" do enjoy themselves!) Imagine you are the prospect. Imagine your needs and desires as the prospect. Considering the major benefit, the hypothesis, and the offer, try to come up with the most appealing, compelling approach—letter starters, outer envelope copy, brochure heads; wander around. Review your notes. Have fun! Get involved! Be excited! Start your dialogue!

Caveat: You are not writing a novel or a story or an article of your choice here. Your product is selected for you; your market is established. How flexible is your mind? How elastic is your imagination? Can you empathize with people who are totally different from you? Can you get excited about a product or service that may not appeal to you? If you cannot (and indeed there may be times when you can't), you're not going to be very creative. You're even liable to be boring. And miserable. And hate the whole process.

You may not be able to write glowingly for the Republicans when you are a Democrat at heart (or vice versa). Or you may pull back from praising a product or service when you have serious reservations about its quality. These are moral issues and my advice is to steer clear. Don't tackle things you can't believe in.

However, if you plan to make a living as a direct response creative person, you must be prolific and you must *enjoy* being prolific. You must be able to imagine how it feels to be a young college student or a middle-aged business executive or an elderly senior citizen. As Bill Jayme puts it, "I can become a pregnant woman in nothing flat. A broke pregnant woman." You must empathize. You must identify your prospect's needs and desires, and link them to your product's benefits with flair and imagination and enthusiasm. You *must* enjoy doing this!!! Because (aside from the attendant satisfaction and the money) that *is* all there is.

Give yourself a fair chance. Test and try yourself on a variety of assignments. If this process continues to make you uncomfortable or miserable—or if you really believe you can't pull it off (try as you will)—you should not be writing copy for direct response advertising. Even if you manage to get by, you will be unhappy, and that's no way to live.

It's a bittersweet experience. The hard work of simply GETTING IT DOWN (followed by a lot more hard work) is balanced or offset primarily by the fun, the joy, the pure exhilaration of crafting words and spelling out ideas that will reach (and deeply affect) your prospect. These creative expressions and bright promotional ideas seldom come easily. You must gather insights and inspirations quickly as they come through, then work hard to enlarge on the best of them. Cull and discard as you go, replacing your first good idea with a bright new flash as it comes shooting out of the blue. Rework your words. Listen to them. Change them around. Imagine. Talk to your prospect. Then be your prospect. Now try it again.

If you can do this, if you can pick up this challenge *and* enjoy it, you will be special. You will be a craftsman, a dreamer, a magician, an actor, a salesperson!

You will be a writer who moves and affects others. You will be proud of yourself. And well you should be.

Enough of the rewards. On with the hard work.

I've divided your writing into three distinct stages or steps and GET IT DOWN is Stage One. This is not to say that everyone works carefully in three clear-cut stages like this, nor even that you have to do it this way. But consciously or unconsciously, professional direct response copywriters *all* go through an approximate version of this and it should be helpful to you to know you are not alone (and to have a little trail of crumbs to start you through the woods).

Once you're into Stage One, you may be wondering with all this GET IT DOWN business, just when you can stop. If you're going nicely, don't—for heaven's sake—stop simply because it's 5:00 P.M. or because the fire bell rings or you hear the phone or it's getting dark. Stop when you can do no more. When your resources are exhausted. When you're left without an idea in your head. When you're sick of the whole thing and are convinced you're writing drivel. (Actually, drivel's not so bad at this stage so don't let that stop you either!)

When you finally stop, you're likely to have

1. a half-finished letter
2. two-and-a-half finished letters
3. two headlines and one full brochure segment
4. an unacceptable copy line for your outer envelope (and a good visual concept)
5. reams of copy that ramble on and on without clear component definition or structure
6. all of the above or some of the above in different combinations

Leave it alone—but in a safe place; go out and take a shower, see a movie, have a drink, go to dinner. Do anything *but* think about your writing. (If new inspiration forces itself through, of course, take notes, then set them aside.)

Give yourself at least twelve hours of peace—more if you can. You have just emerged from the GET IT DOWN stage and you deserve a rest.

STAGE TWO—START ALL OVER

If Stage One is GET IT DOWN, why should Stage Two be START ALL OVER? You won't ask this question after several years in the business, but it's a fair question for now. Let me explain it this way (and I hope the analogy holds):

You are given $500,000 in a quiz show and told to furnish your house. If you fail to use up the funds in twenty-four hours, you will lose them. Thanks to speed and perseverance, you succeed. Now the mad rush is over and you have a little time, so you start to look at your house and what you've accomplished. It is a strange mixture of wonderful things and pure garbage. What a mess, but one worthy of careful salvage.

As you walk through it, you automatically discard some things (for the tag sale). How could you possibly have picked them up? Other things are inappropriately placed, so you move them around. Some articles have to change locations from one room to another, but they're worth keeping. Still other things are on the borderline, so you set them aside in a separate area in the basement.

You also find that you have two sofas and three coffee tables. You judge them carefully and keep only the best. Actually, with a little modification one of the coffee tables can be moved into the TV room. There's a problem with the bedrooms, however. You don't have nearly enough bedroom furniture to go around. You will need more.

The living room rug was the first thing you purchased—an Oriental, something you've always wanted, your prized possession. Your living room is decorated around it. Unfortunately, this means one of the easy chairs just doesn't work out. You can throw it away—or save it for later.

And so it goes. But need *I* go on? You can see where I'm heading. *And* where you'll be heading once you return to your copy. You may be lucky, of course. And everything will fall into place. You may not throw out one thing or rearrange even one paragraph (although nothing like that has ever happened to me or any writers I know).

Chances are, you'll feel like most good writers—somewhat discouraged, somewhat elated as you meander through the maze of words and phrases. You'll want to set things right first off. Look, here's a great headline for your brochure lying uselessly in the letter copy! (What a find!) And here—down here near the bottom of this page of letter copy—look at this gem! Why not *start* your letter with it? Try. See.

These three paragraphs have all the right data, but yuk—need a rewrite. Let's set them aside. By the way, if you're redoing your letter opening, how about this segment of it for the outer? Try. See. And while you're at it—need a Johnson box?

Does your spokesperson have clear and logical expressions—*in character?* If you can't hold the character, how about another character's point of view? Maybe a lift letter?

Now you're into the heavy stuff. You should be cutting, pasting, moving around, making margin notes, adding copy, killing copy, changing initial perceptions—even searching for a new approach.

Stage Two is your real, hard-core, make-or-break creative time. Here's where you can cop out and do it the easy, technician's way—or hang in and craft something beautiful—something that gives you a warm feeling of satisfaction (your reward).

Unfortunately, there's no way to begin Stage Two until you've done Stage One, and Stage Two generally takes off by blasting Stage One off the page—or literally picking it apart. Stage Two can take a long time, by the way. You may have to leave your work, then come back to it many times before you're finished. Even a simple double postcard takes time—if you care.

Everyone has a tendency to get discouraged at this stage, including top professionals. The secret to keeping it fresh and good is your determination, coupled with a schedule that *allows you time* to back out of the trees and look at your forest with perspective.

Now before we move on to Stage Three, here are some pointers to help pull through Stage Two.

1. You and The Written Word

To begin with, you must understand the language in which you are communicating. A basic grounding in elementary grammar, spelling, and punctuation may prove more important to you at this stage than a college degree in English literature. You need a knowledge of what's correct, combined with an understanding of (and an ear for) what's popular or common.

As a writer—and especially as a copywriter—you have an obligation and a position of power. Your obligation is to move people to action by *communication*. This is the power of the salesman. But you must go one step further; you must communicate by bending words and phrases to your purpose.

This is another power—a power that enables you to affect the way average people use words. You can alter the rules of proper English for dramatic effect and get away with it. You can adapt punctuation to serve your purposes. You can introduce new words or new ways of using old words and phrases and start new idioms and expressions. ("Where's the Beef?") And in so doing, you can begin to change usage. ("Winston Tastes Good like a Cigarette Should" is a classic example.)

This is heady stuff. But you will have *no* power to change words and phrases and punctuation if you do not understand what has gone before. You cannot break the rules of our idiom to move your market to action *if you do not know what those rules are.* You must know, for example

- how a sentence is structured (can you parse a sentence?)
- when to use commas, dashes, hyphens, quotations, apostrophes, exclamations, colons, semicolons, ellipses...
- the that/which quandary and all the who/whom/whose answers
- spelling and capitalization and split infinitives.

I will not insult you or bore you by offering a basic grammar course here, but if you are going to be a direct response writer, here are six books that are indispenable equipment:

- *Fowler's Modern English Usage* (Second Edition) © Oxford University Press, 1965. Paperback edition, reprinted 1983.

- *The Chicago Manual of Style* (Thirteenth Edition, Revised and Expanded) © The University of Chicago Press, 1969, 1982.
- *The Elements of Style*, William Strunk, Jr. and E.B. White © Macmillan Publishing Co. Inc., 1972
- *Roget's Thesaurus in Dictionary Form* © Berkeley Publishers, 1983
- *The American Heritage Dictionary of the English Language* © Houghton Mifflin Company, 1976.
- *Webster's Third New International Dictionary—Unabridged* © Merriam-Webster, Inc., 1981

2. What to Concentrate On

a. Your letter's tone (who are you?). Set it and stick with it.

b. Your letter's lead (Johnson box or no Johnson box).

c. Your envelope copy (if you decide to have copy).

d. Your brochure headlines (then the subheads).

e. A clean, clear statement of your offer for the order card.

f. Decision to lift or not to lift (letter).

3. Starting to Visualize

a. Envelope—white or kraft, large or small, black and white or lots of art and photography? *Justify it!*

b. Brochure—list exactly what you feel requires illustration. *Justify it!*

c. Your involvement devices and motivators—can you incorporate them easily? Do they make sense with your copy? With your visuals as you are planning them?

4. Developing Stronger Copy

Once you've got your leads and headlines in place, gather your specifics for stronger copy.

Weak	*Strong*
• It's big.	• It's big—a full 12″ × 60″
• It does all your chores for you.	• It washes your dishes, takes out the garbage, waxes the floor, and turns off the light.
• You'll have a truly enjoyable trip throughout the area…	• You'll see mountains 12,000 feet high, visit an old-fashioned country store, ride in a cable car with breath-taking valley views.

5. Working Toward Creative Unity

For example: If you're using the invitational approach, keep your tone elegant and use words like "invite," "preview," "exclusive," "invitation," "please reply" in all parts of the mailing. (And make sure your graphics reinforce this with every component.)

6. Making Sure Each Major Component Can Stand Alone

Since you can't be sure which piece will be read first, give your full story in the letter, your complete offer on the order card, and everything possible in the brochure. (And if it can't carry your offer, make sure the brochure at least refers to the offer on the enclosed order card.)

7. Giving Your Package More Credibility and Involvement

- You might add a picture of the plant, grounds, or offices
- a picture of "your customer service rep"
- a stronger guarantee
- testimonials with names (pictures)
- a list of specialists, directors, or advisors on the letterhead
- incentives and motivators (tokens, stamps, deadlines, limits and all kinds of premiums)

8. Remembering Your Objectives—Always

Review your hypothesis, copy strategy, and testing research. Precisely what will *your* package prove in its testing?

- That a new product or service itself will have appeal to a specific market?
- That an old product or service will have appeal to a specific new market?
- That X hypothesis is stronger than Y (or the control) hypothesis?
- That you can beat the existing control—all stops out—and the devil be damned!

Remember the inherent dangers in this last option. A laurel wreath if you win, the lions if you lose (see Chapter 5).

STAGE THREE—POLISH IT UP AND LAY IT OUT

Everyone likes to skimp at this stage. If you're working with an eager artist, he or she will jump from rough layouts to finished comps. If you're close to the final deadline, you may be tempted to give your work a read-through or two then commit it to the final typing or the word processor.

Stop! Don't let it happen this way—*not if you care for your copy!*

First, don't leave your rewrites and copy polishing until the last minute. Start the minute you GET IT DOWN and don't *stop* polishing till it's snatched from your hands at presentation time. But also leave time, though, between rewrites to reestablish your objectivity. (If you don't give yourself at least twelve hours—preferably twice that—you won't be able to distinguish between the smooth and the rough.) And remember, without polishing time, even your best copy concepts will fall to the curse of mediocre presentation.

Second, make sure you see layouts well before your deadline. No artist should keep you in the dark or present layouts that you haven't gone over together. When you do go over them, see that you and the artist have plenty of time for last minute changes.

Review Chapters 3 and 4. How do your components stack up? Does the outer envelope attract attention, qualify your prospect and make a promise? Does your brochure track? Does the order form look important? *It's not too late.* You can still change a headline or a word or even a concept and a layout *if* you've left enough time for polishing and revising comprehensive art work.

You'll find there is almost nothing worse than doing a good job but realizing at the last minute that the copy line on the outer envelope is all wrong or your letter's lead can be vastly improved by reversing one sentence. If this happens to you—and it can happen to the best writers—be sure you have the time to change it.

Procedures for Polishing and Fine-tuning Your Copy

As I said before, no good copy is ever really finished. You can always add a comma (or take one out), break up a long paragraph, or cut a word.

1. *Stick to the short of it.* If you are like most good writers, you have overwritten. Don't apologize. This is common practice in Stages One and Two. It's healthy and it's helpful to you.

You'll have a lot to work with when you go in to clean up and reorganize your house. Here's where you start cutting and culling, and you shouldn't stop until your copy's due.

- Look for places where one word can replace a phrase.
- Test a paragraph by leaving out a weak sentence or phrase. See if the idea comes through without the sentence. (Some entire paragraphs may prove dispensable.)
- Check to be sure you have no useless repetition.
- Test your adjectives and adverbs. Cut them out if they don't strengthen the copy.
- Bring in an outsider. Get a fresh, second opinion.

Be merciless. Wise cutting never fails to improve your copy. After a few passes even you, the author, will find you can do without some of your favorite, flowery phrases. And while you're cutting, remember the basic admonition to all direct response copywriters: Keep it simple. Use words of few syllables, short sentences, and short paragraphs. (Remember, this is a communication that must motivate!)

By Stage Three you want to produce what is called *tight copy*—where every word has at least one job to do, sometimes more. Tight copy is "fiddle-proof" too. Outsiders can't move in to change things around. The minute they try, it becomes clear that you've been there before, and anticipated, *and* chosen the best route.

2. *What else do you look for as you review your copy?* Each time you go back to your copy, read it to yourself. Then read it aloud. Does your eye have trouble moving through it, does your tongue stumble? How is it on the ear? Does it move smoothly or is it awkward?

Have you bridged? Good copy moves easily because someone has worked hard to help it along with bridges or transitions that carry the reader from one paragraph to another. Look at these bridges in the lead sentences here: "The construction wasn't always that simple. In 1962, the government built..." or "And that's just part of your gift. You'll also receive, absolutely free, this..."

Break up large bodies of copy. Four or five sentences can make two paragraphs, not one. Don't run details together or data of equal importance; break it out and line it up. Use columns or bullets. Use frequent subheads or "window" subheads in the middle of heavy brochure copy to pull the reader back into the text.

Emphasize your important words with underlines, italics, and ALL CAPS.

In your letter use margin notes to call attention to strong selling points, or use a second color, or emphasize the entire paragraph by indenting or boxing it.

Break punctuation rules for dramatic emphasis and style! Jump ahead with a dash in your letter copy—like that! Or run your thoughts together with ellipses...many writers do...and it's very effective *if* you don't overuse it!

Kill pet words. Edit your copy for repetition. Some words can pop up two or three times in the same paragraph. Unless you've planned it that way, weed them out and substitute. *Planned repetition: Go* out and check the prices at your local market; *go* to the shopping malls; *go* to convenience stores. *Go* and see for yourself! *Pet word syndrome:* It's a special chance to go over the summer stock. Next time you go to your local market, go to the special summer widget counter. You'll go crazy!

Eschew slang, jargon, dialect, or colloquialism unless you are very, very sure that it is *current* (and widely understood) and that your market will identify positively with it. If you must use it, do so carefully.

Don't be clever or cute. Somehow, most of us deep down inside are dying to be comedians, to make others laugh. Unfortunately, 99⁴⁴/₁₀₀ percent of us are not funny. I *must* assume that you (and I) fall into this majority. I *could* be wrong about you.

3. Read the additional guidelines. At the end of this chapter, you'll find these helpful suggestions: "A Creative Checklist for Your Components," Max Ross's "20 Questions," and Pat Farley's "Direct Mail Copy."

JUDGING THE LAYOUTS

You're into your fifth (or fifteenth) copy revision, major changes are made, things have come together nicely, and you've reviewed roughs and met with the artist on several occasions.

Now it's time to look over the completed layouts in conjunction with your final copy. (If you've been working closely with the artist, there will be no surprises at this stage.)

By the way, the word "judging" is used advisedly here as it's still not clear who's doing the judging and how. These are the choices:

1. The artist and the writer have met, but worked independently up to this point. Both feel strongly about the direction of the package and their own creative ideas. They judge each other.

2. The copywriter (a free-lancer) brought the assignment to the artist (a free-lancer) in the first place. In all meetings the copywriter directs and judges and the artist merely follows.

3. The reverse of 2.

4. The copywriter and the art director have worked closely together all down the line. They respect each other. They both contribute to each other's work. The client or their immediate supervisor will be the judge.

Obviously you'd do well to work for the fourth option. It is certainly the optimum way to achieve the best work from two talented people. Let us assume that is where you are. Now it's time for your final evaluation.

First, make sure all the visual concepts have been executed as you agreed, and that the readable copy is correct. (Some of the best artists can't spell or reproduce copy correctly on the layouts.) Check to see that every one of the components is there, life-size, in full color (or exact colors to be used), folded properly, and inserted correctly in the full-size envelope. (Make sure the artist protects the layouts so they will stand up after repeated openings. Reinforced fold areas, a clear spray on colored surfaces, and a clear plastic outer are all helpful.)

Here are some final checkpoints for you:

- Has the artist given enough specific graphic representation for nonvisual people?
- Has the artist provided a sample of envelope, brochure, or letter stock if it's something a little out of the ordinary?
- Has the artist shown how to nest and insert the components so that the

process can be handled by automatic inserters? (Most lettershop equipment cannot insert open edges into the envelope mouth.)

- Is the letter folded with the first page on the outside, not on the inside like ordinary correspondence? (Make it easy!)
- Are the layouts neat, clean, clear of finger marks and smudges?
- Do the art and format of the outer envelope contribute to its excitement? Do they imply value, help convey "open me" or "I'm important"?
- Is there art and copy on both sides? (If it's a strictly promotional outer envelope, many professionals use both sides. After all, who knows which side your prospect sees first?)
- Do the letterhead and letterhead design work with your copy to convey the feeling or impression you're seeking to convey from the speaker or letter writer?
- Has the artist "blocked in" or indicated typewritten letter copy that conforms to your letter configuration? (See Figure 7-3.)
- Does the order card look important? Valuable? Clean and uncluttered? Worthy of carrying back the dictates of your customer?
- Does it fit the tone of the offer (and the tone of the overall package)? A loud multifaceted sweepstakes offer deserves all the pizazz it can get: a business-to-business inquiry reply card (should you even decide to use a reply card) should be dignified and include a telephone number; a fund-raising or joining offer might include a membership card. (See Figure 7-1.)
- Can it be easily filled in—is there enough space? If the card is to be computer addressed or labeled, is it the proper size so that the address will show through the outer envelope's window without shifting around in the mail?
- If there is a BRE, is it large enough to carry your order form without folding it?
- Does the brochure give an exciting dramatization of your hypothesis? Does it show the benefits and features clearly (using charts, graphs, lists, photographs and illustrations, questions and answers)?
- Is there visual unity among the various components of the package?
- Has the artist maintained style throughout? (This means unity in the treatment of headlines, subheads, and captions. It means unity in selection of typefaces, the amounts of white space, and the general feeling.)

You and the artist may want to review all these poiints with your copy in hand. If you have any questions or doubts, now is the time to discuss them. Then as the artist retires to make some final revisions, you'll want to prepare *your* work for presentation as well.

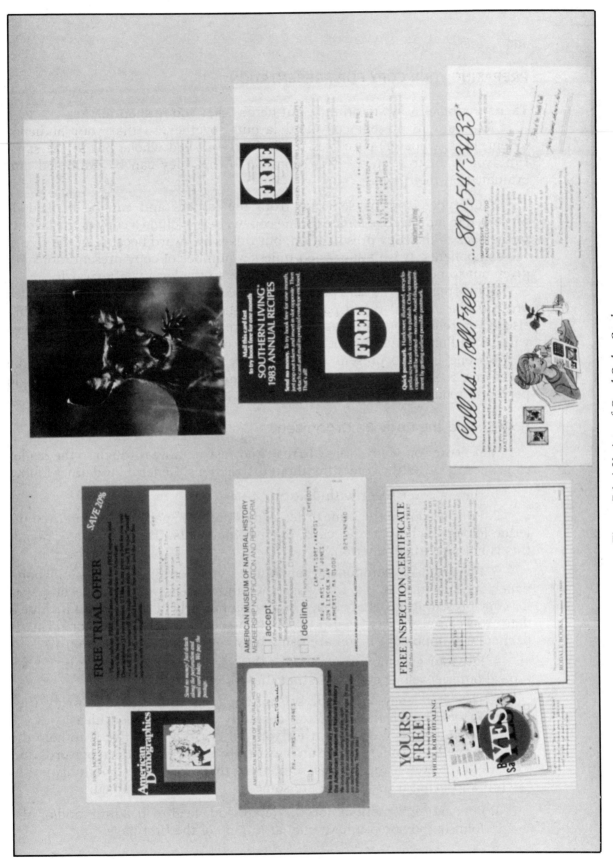

Figure 7-1 *A Variety of Good Order Cards*

PREPARING YOUR COPY FOR PRESENTATION

There are lots of ways to do this; but here's what you're shooting for:

You want to present copy and layouts together, so that your audience (client, boss, whoever) perceives the unified, finished whole, but at the same time you want to keep the two separate so that they can be examined and evaluated on their own.

Your typed copy is separate from the layouts and can be booked or presented in a protective folder. (Some copywriters include a copy of the layouts in the back of the copy presentation, but this is awkward because of the size of the components. It isn't suggested unless a number of copy presentations are given out to people who may not have access to the layouts afterwards.)

Some free-lance writers present only one set of copy, some two. One writer presents the original typed pages on extra-heavy quality stock. And nothing else. If you're working for an agency or a large company, your number of copies will depend on the number of people in the presentation.

No one likes to present to a committee, but in many cases it will be necessary. It should not be necessary for any committee or group or single person to read your copy on the spot. (More about this in a moment.)

How Should the Copy Be Organized?

Make sure your copy is easy to read and easy to move through so the reader can concentrate on the content without distractions. General guidelines follow.

1. Have a cover sheet with date and title.

2. Put the copy in the same order as the "dummy" package: outer envelope, letter, folder/brochure, order card, other components. (BRE copy is optional; this is not a creative function.)

3. Present each component separately, typed on 8½″ × 11″ plain bond paper, one side (unless, like many agencies and writers, you have special paper for copy presentations). Label each component clearly at the top and include a date. You can also give general production specifications at the top. (This is particularly important if you are using only copywriter's rough layouts.)

4. Put your graphic instructions at the side in parentheses. Figure 7-2 is a typical outer envelope copy page that illustrates this.

5. The letter copy should be set up *exactly* as you want it to print. (See Figure 7-3.) Although the artist can certainly contribute good ideas, you are primarily in charge of the layout for your letter. Your objective is to help the reader through...to offer the eye an irresistibly absorbing pattern of words and phrases. If the eye escapes for just a moment, there is always something new to catch it and bring it back. Here are some suggestions to help you:

   a. Put your instructions for the letterhead, lead-in headline and/or the Johnson box (if you have one) at the top of the first page.

Outer Envelope: Front (April 2, 1985)

Illustration: Montage of doers and professionals (mechanics,
                 carpenters, gardners, cooks, joggers, bikers, etc.
                 They should have brief captions, but need art work to
                 do this).

Corner Card: Rodale Press, Inc.
                 Emmaus, PA 18049

Outer Envelope: Back

Illustration: Montage continues

Copy for Flap: FREE LOOK...FREE BOOK (see inside)

Figure 7-2

AELS Letter: (Date)
Use Standard Executive Letterhead

"We've got to whip up some spirit here -- some teamwork.
"No one seems to care about the project."

"Enough of this talk -- here's what we're going to do."

"I never know what he's thinking. What's your guess
today? Is he in a good or bad mood?"

"She's criticized my reports for the last time. I'm asking for a transfer."

"Why discuss it? Your argument won't hold water without
a change in the budget."

"What do you mean I said I'd have the production figures
by Friday? How could I promise something like that?"

Dear Executive:

    Sound familiar? They should, because these comments re-
sult from management situations that most of us executives
face every day.

    They way you handle or avert such situations is the differ-
ence between managing and leading. And it's the difference in
how you move ahead in your company.

    Managers run things. They are more concerned with
    people's roles in a situation than with their needs.
    Managers' authority stems from their position. Con-
    flict is often the outcome.

    Leaders build and grow companies through people.
    They replace conflict with productive, harmonious
    dialogue, teamwork and long-term loyalty. They in-
    spire respect and admiration. Their authority
    comes from personal relationships.

    If you are not already actively working to enhance and de-
velop your valuable leadership skills, may I make a simple
suggestion:

    Spend one hour a day for a week with the Advanced
    Executive Leadership Skills (AELS is our Xerox self-
    administered program for executives like you). Spend
    it in the quiet of your home, before work or after --
    wherever it's most convenient. But after each hour's
    reading, listening and practicing, you must promise

Figure 7-3

198

to go to your office and apply what you have just
learned in three business situations.

If within a few weeks you don't agree that your newly
gained insights and abilities are already positively affecting the way you relate to the people around you, return the
program to me, and I will personally see to it that your
money is refunded.

Making this promise doesn't worry me one bit by the way.
You see, I believe you will accept. If you do, I know it
will work for you.

Why I'm betting you will elect to take AELS

We all have the basic qualities of leadership within us.
Sometimes it comes out more strongly in sports, social life,
college, the armed services. These qualities need only to
be developed and applied in business.

If it's that easy, you may wonder, why doesn't everyone
become a leader? Doesn't everyone want to be a leader?

Not necessarily. Many managers would like security,
recognition, and the rewards that go with it. Unfortunately,
they don't have the tools -- or know where to find them -- or
bother to apply them. They are not willing to work at it.

I have a theory. If the results of leadership are what you
want -- you will automatically self-select yourself to take
advantage of this opportunity because

> . you will be eager to learn the tested Xerox steps
>   to enhancing your skills, and willing to work at
>   perfecting them...
>
> . you will welcome the freedom and flexibility to
>   teach yourself at your own speed, imposing your
>   own disciplines...
>
> . you will want to start seeing results immediately --
>   right away -- in your office.

And because you have both the ability and the determination,
you will live a self-fulfilling prophecy. You will indeed increase your leadership performance.

As a result, I could promise you riches and power, but the
rewards of applied leadership skills go far beyond advancement.
While you work to develop your skills, you will find that there
are valuable intangible rewards, like the inner satisfaction of

Figure 7-3, *continued*

-3-

knowing you're doing more for your company -- and making good
business friends at all levels.

You may find that your fellow workers begin to treat
you with greater respect, that they listen more keenly
to your ideas and opinions; that your people will be
more enthusiastic and eager to tackle new projects for
you; that top management will take more notice of your
achievements.

This doesn't mean that you change your personality or
your style. Developing leadership abilities is primarily
recognizing and understanding four crucial aspects of leadership, then learning to incorporate these into your daily management pattern.

If you're as informed as I think you are, you may be
wondering what makes AELS different -- or better -- or more
effective than other leadership programs.

We do. Xerox Learning Systems. Our business is
helping business people become more effective.
We've been at it for 20 years. We have ten programs presently in use by thousands of top executives from major corporations around the country.
Scientifically developed, all of our self-admin-
istered programs have been field tested over and
over again.

As a matter of fact, I've taken Advanced Executive Leadership Skills myself. And I had some immediate, exciting changes
when I started applying the skills.

You may find right off, as I did, that you hadn't
really listened to some of your people in the past. I mean
listen hard. I do now. And it's made a difference.

I don't act impulsively anymore, regardless of business
pressures. I'm more sensitive to my fellow workers and their
problems. These are the kind of changes you can expect.

I think you'll appreciate the way the program's set up,
too. All it requires from you is a standard cassette player
and your full attention. There are two books that you'll
use along with the tapes. One's a workbook and the other's
your confidential business diary.

The diary leads to the most important part. Right off it asks
you to identify three problems you are presently facing on the job.
Then it works with you to solve these problems while you are actually

Figure 7-3, *continued*

200

self-administering the course.

This alone can be worth many times the price of the program. And, you get the benefits from day one!

I also found playback and review helpful in several areas. It was reassuring to have the ability right there at hand to practice, relearn, to strengthen by repetition.

It doesn't take much time to digest it all. It's the day to day applications that you'll find rewarding and long lasting:

how you conduct more productive meetings that give you the loyalty of the people around you...how you get others to support your ideas...how you improve individual performance without criticism...how you delegate to create enthusiasm...

how you prevent common misunderstandings that could lead to conflict...how you enlist the friendship and cooperation of your peers...how you make sure you are heard and recognized by top management.

You can take AELS in as little as six to eight hours, but you will use what you learn for the rest of your life.

So spend a week -- or longer -- with the course. Apply your new skills to those major on-the-job problems that you identified. Practice in every business situation. Slowly at first. Then increase, as you gain confidence. (AELS gives you the easier basics before it moves you up to the more complex applications.)

But by all means get started now, if you agree that leader- ship skills are indispensable to attaining your management goals. Simply complete the enclosed reply card and return it to me today.

Sincerely,

John J. Franco
President
Xerox Learning Systems

P.S. The cost of AELS is $79.95. Hardly a consideration when you think about the benefits. (In fact, your company might willingly pay for the course, as it certainly will improve your effectiveness and overall contribution.)

Figure 7-3, *continued*

b. Center your Johnson box or headline (unless you and the artist have other ideas) and estimate where your salutation should begin. Have it typed exactly this way.

c. Keep ample margins (at least 1½″ each side). Your job here is to help the eye move easily from one thought to another back and forth, up and down. (Don't make it fight its way across a wide page.)

d. Check your big (read "hot") break at the end of the page. Will everything fit comfortably between the salutation and the first break—with lots of air? (You may have to cut, shuffle, or rewrite, or change your page 1 break.)

e. Remember to keep all paragraphs short—especially your lead paragraph.

f. Indent each paragraph five spaces. It's easier to read than the block format.

g. For emphasis and pacing, indent or center an entire paragraph, or space off and center an important copy line.

h. If you have a row of examples or a list of features and benefits, stack them and set off each one with a bullet or a box. You can also indent these and double space between them.

i. Don't be shy about margin notes either. People notice them, so if they fit with the *feeling* of your letter (the President of the United States probably wouldn't have margin notes when writing the Queen of England), use your pen to call attention to important points in your letter copy.

j. Don't forget your dashes, ellipses, underlines, ALL CAPS, and exclamations! On the other hand, don't overuse them!

6. Lift letter copy, as your main letter, should be set up exactly as you want it to print. If you have copy for the outside (or back) of the lift, you can include this on a separate sheet with instructions.

7. Brochure, flyer, folder, or buck slip. These should be set up to follow the artist's layout. Your copy can be single-spaced or double-spaced (no one agrees on this) with double-spacing between paragraphs and at least four to five spaces to separate large blocks of copy or headlines. You should have two spaces between all secondary heads and subheads and your body copy. Set a style for headlines, subheads, and lead-ins throughout to make your order of importance clear to the artist or the type specifier as well as the client. *Be consistent.* For example:

Main heads: all caps

Secondary heads: upper and lower case, underlined

Subheads: upper and lower case

Lead-ins: underlined

Put your indications for art and photography in parentheses throughout so

Premium Flyer: Front (April 2, 1985)
(Large cover with big Red Cross)

Head: EMERGENCY FIRST AID
                    A Guide to 11 Critical Areas

                    (Sunburst)

                         FREE! This 50-page booklet, filled with
                         diagrams, charts and drawings

                    Do you know

                    -- the primary signs of internal bleeding?
                    -- where to look for a child's pulse?
                    -- how to recognize a third degree burn?
                    -- how to help a choking pregnant woman?
                    -- what CPR means and how to use it?
                    -- when to ignore advice in pamphlets, brochures
                         and even first aid manuals?
                    -- how to allow fluids to drain from the mouth?
                    -- how to put an unconscious person in the
                         recovery position?

                    If so, you might save a life. In not, you'll just stand there...

                    Emergency First Aid

                         Every adult should master these emergency aid techniques.
                    You owe it to yourself, your family and your friends to
                    familiarize yourself with each page of this valuable book.

                         It brings you full guidance, diagrams and drawings on
                    handling 11 of the most common emergencies plus a national
                    list of poison control centers, a Home Safety Checklist and a
                    section to help you start a Family Health Diary.

                         We'll rush you a FREE copy of Emergency First Aid as
                    soon as you send in your free examination request for
                    Rodale's Book of Hints, Tips, and Everyday Wisdom.

                         Keep it in a safe place. Be prepared. It could be
                    the most valuable book you own!

Figure 7-4

Premium Flyer: Back (April 2, 1985)

(Copy next to   Yours -- FREE -- When you order
head, boxed)

                          RODALE'S BOOK OF HINTS, TIPS, AND
                                  EVERYDAY WISDOM

Head: Emergency First Aid
                 A Guide to 11 Critical Areas

                 Sometimes, no matter how careful we are, things go
                 wrong -- very wrong. When this happens, don't be
                 a distraught, frustrated bystander. Act quickly,
                 cooly and with confidence. You could be the
                 difference between life and death.

Lead: Learn to administer first aid effectively in 11
                 situations:

                                  Bleeding
                                  Bone and Muscle Injuries
                                  Breathing Crises
(Illus. 3 to   Burns
4 spreads   Chocking
from book-   Electric Shock
let)   Foreign Objects
                                  Heart Attacks
                                  Poisoning
                                  Seizures
                                  Unconsciousness

                 Identify the crisis, execute treatment procedures,
                 apply preventive measures, learn how to improvise,
                 how to help yourself, what not to do (complete with
                 diagrams and drawings).

Lead: Safety-Proof Your Home -- A checklist of over 40 ways
                 to prevent home accidents.

Lead: Set up a Family Health Diary -- a quick reference in
                 case of illness at home or when you travel. Good
                 records are the first step in prventive self-care.

                 Emergency First Aid -- to make sure you can think fast,
                 keep a cool head and a hopeful attitude. It's yours FREE
                 when you send for Rodale's Book of Hints, Tips, and Everyday
                 Wisdom.

Bottom band: No home should be without this first aid book!

Figure 7-4, *continued*

Order Card: Tips & Hints (April 2, 1985)

Head for both sides: Two Free Offers for You -- Put Them Together

Left-hand side:

Left head: FREE BOOK (illus. Emergency First Aid token)

Move this token to your Free Examination Card at the right

We'll send you a FREE copy of Emergency First Aid --
just for looking at Rodale's Book of Hints, Tips, and Everyday
Wisdom.

Right-hand side:

Right head: FREE LOOK

[ ] Yes -- I'll take a free look at Rodale's Book of Hints,
Tips, and Everyday Wisdom. If I like what I see, I'll pay
$6.65 for each of three easy monthly installments (plus postage
and handling). If I'm not satisfied, I may return the book in
15 days and owe absolutely nothing. In any case Emergency First
Aid is mine to keep, free of charge.

[ ] Save cash by sending $19.95 now. We'll pay postage and
handling costs. If not completely satisfied, just return your
book in 15 days and we'll send you a full refund. Again -- you'll
keep your Emergency First Aid, whatever you do.

Rodale Books
Emmaus, PA 18049

Figure 7-4, *continued*

that it is easy to see where your copy goes in the artist's layout (Figure 7-4 gives you a good idea of how all this goes together.)

8. Your order card may present a typing problem as it often has a right and left side as well as a front and back. Keep your instructions clear and set up your copy so that it makes sense to a naive reader coming upon it for the first time.

In all cases, your objective is to make a professional presentation that gives your copy the best possible reception. Now let's talk about that reception.

PREPARING FOR THE PRESENTATION

To begin, all work must be presented by its creators. Your baby should not be allowed out in the callous world without you the first time around. Whether it's one-on-one with your boss or a client, or a full-court press with the marketing team, you can make your baby's presentation into another rewarding aspect of your work.

In the process you've just been through, note that nothing has been left to chance. You've had rules and guidelines, research findings, creative strategy development, hypothesis development, approach strategies and clear objectives. To present (or "sell") your creative solution, you simply retrace your steps to explain *why* you've done what you've done—before you show copy or layouts or hand out anything.

Begin with a restatement of the objectives. Then review your creative strategy. (If you worked totally alone at this stage, of course, you'll have to go through it step by step, including the research findings.)

Once your client or team starts moving along with you through these points (and assuming that there is consensus in reviewing the basic strategies and assumptions), you are ready to discuss your creative decisions.

Glad You Asked That Question...

In each case you will have a reason for your choices and decisions. Nothing you've done was "intuitive" or "instinctive." In the same way, you can explain every component of your package.

There is a reason for your approach. There is a reason for your outer envelope copy line. There is a reason for your choice of spokesperson. There is a reason for your lead-in paragraph. There is a reason for the Johnson box. And so on. You should *welcome* questions, as they allow you to reinforce your creative position.

As you field all questions intelligently, you carry your listeners along with your own story of creative development that can convey to them some of the enthusiasm you felt in doing your package. If you are doing a formal presentation of a major new package, I suggest you consider doing a brief written rationale to leave behind with your copy. (People don't always listen and they most certainly do forget.)

The same reasoning approach applies to the artist's presentation if he or she joins you. Everything in the layouts is done for a reason—the format, colors, artwork for each component have a rationale. If you are going on with the artist, by the way, it's a good idea to have an informal run-through or rehearsal.

You're On

There you stand with the artist, "booked" copy, rationale, and layouts in hand.

What's the best or most productive agenda? How do you proceed? If you can pull it off, here's the optimum sequence.

1. First, don't let *anyone* see your copy or layouts before you're ready. It will be distracting and raise many unnecessary questions.
2. Get everyone's attention. Be dramatic. And enthusiastic. On your feet if it's a group meeting.
3. Review the objectives, go over your conclusions from the test history and other research. Make sure everyone is following your reasoning; make sure they are with you.
4. Review the creative strategy development, the hypothesis and big benefit. Make sure they are following; make sure they are with you.
5. Pause for questions. Wait. Listen.
6. Discuss your approach.
7. Bring out the layouts. Show how the layouts reflect the approach. (The artist, if you have one, will probably want to do this part of the presentation.)
8. Go over tokens, deadlines, other motivators and incentives. Discuss the envelope. (Again, your artist may be contributing here.)
9. Let the artist describe the brochure.
10. Once this is over, pause for questions.
11. In some cases, although it's not necessary, you may want to read your outer copy and also your letter's lead-in as you present the layouts.
12. Now pass out your copy books (and rationale, if you have one), deliver the layout to the proper person, and
13. Break for the door!

The best creative presentation ends *before* any one person starts reading copy. Copy must be read in peace and quiet, thoughtfully. Comments on the copy should be presented at your next meeting, *after* all those concerned have discussed their thoughts on changes. You cannot do creative writing and designing by committee.

For your sake, I hope all presentations turn out as easy as 1 through 13. Chances are, a few of your presentations will not go according to the list alone. We've all gotten trapped by the client who insists on reading the copy right now. Then, as the client reads, he or she starts to ask questions. The next person then picks it up—and so on around the group. You want to kill. To die. To do anything to get out.

Take heart. All writers hvae been there once or twice. What's more, you *do* have a reason for everything you've written. If someone wants you to change copy, you can defend your points logically. In many cases, you can even explain how and why the promotion will be weakened if it's changed, as long as they agree with your rationale.

A professional enjoys presenting his or her baby to the public as much as does any proud parent. The professional also wants to protect that baby from mistreatment. You will, too. Wait and see.

GETTING BABY READY FOR ITS NEXT BIG PUBLIC APPEARANCE

Your presentation is over! It was well received because you were well prepared. Take a well-deserved bow.

Now, however, you're in for some copy revisions. Don't let this bother you. I've never met a writer—good, mediocre, or superlative—who hasn't had to put up with a moderate number of revisions. Often these are purely technical, sometimes new product or pricing data have been introduced while you've been working away. Occasionally, there will be questions of phrasing or clarity or emphasis.

How to Get Through This with Your Spirits Up and Your Baby Intact

Even the most experienced creative people can get burned or wounded or just plain angry at this stage. If you've worked hard and honestly and had a successful presentation (no misunderstandings, no major misconceptions from the start, no lag in communications) then you deserve to have your rights read (and I'm going to read them here).

First, Get Yourself a Mouthpiece. You'll need one central contact who represents the client, or one who speaks for your company (usually your boss), or—if you are a free-lancer—get the individual who signed you on for the project. All suggestions (or dictates) for copy changes must flow through this *one* individual. You cannot—must not—deal with a committee on copy revisions, or you may certainly be driven to kill—understandably.

Your mouthpiece should mull and consider changes thoughtfully and pass them to you with clear explanation, constructively—and not one at a time, but all together, at a designated time.

Next, Evaluate the Criticism.

1. *Legal criticism:* This really isn't criticism at all, of course. This is what happens to your copy when (and if) your mouthpiece has to submit it to the corporate lawyers. There's just one point for you to remember here. Lawyers are out to make doubly sure that nothing rocks the boat. For this, they are extremely cautious and conservative.

When you are told of legal's changes, if some of these present enormous problems (like, "We don't want to use the word 'free'"), try to fight back. Or ask your mouthpiece to reason with them. Remember, their decisions are not cast in stone (well, not always). In many cases, you *can* persuade them to compromise or come up with reasonable alternatives. Give it a try before you give up.

2. *Constructive criticism:* Come on, now—you *know* some suggested changes will be good for your baby. You're not the only one who knows how to care for it. Be honest. Compliment the giver and show him or her how smart you are in recognizing good thinking. After all, everyone has an interest in seeing your baby become a healthy adult!

3. *Destructive criticism:* Here's where you get "I don't know. This just doesn't sound right…" or "It's not what I expected…" or "Maybe we shouldn't push so hard here…" or "Why does the envelope look so promotional?"

If this sort of thing gets past your mouthpiece you have two choices: reason it out; draw the line.

Most of us humans, working with others and striving to get along, will opt first for reasoning it out. But it's also important to know when it's right and proper to draw the line.

Often, all you have to do is refer back to the strategy statement and show how the copy reinforces the points. Sometimes people forget or lose sight of what you'd agreed to in the first place. Then again, you'll find many people just can't express themselves clearly. A little calm probing on your part can turn a threatening mountain into a molehill. Here's an example of this in action. It happens all the time in one form or another to all creative people:

Client "I dunno. I just don't like this."

Writer "The *letter* you mean?"

Client "Well, no—but look here on the first page. This is all wrong."

Writer "What exactly bothers you?"

Client "Well, the positioning…the approach…the feeling, I guess."

Writer "O.K. But I thought we'd all agreed on this in the beginning. What exactly is wrong?"

Client "Ah—first off, the widget isn't 'attractive.' It's 'beautiful.' And then, you call it 'strong,' here. That's no good."

Writer "What would you rather call it?"

Client "Ah, sturdy. That's the word. Sturdy."

> *Writer* "Now let me read it to you. You'll find the widget is beautiful and surprisingly sturdy. How's that?"
>
> *Client* "That's good. Nice. Nice letter, too."

Unfortunately, it's not always this easy. At some point you may have to cut or shoot. Here's a guideline that can help you: Listen carefully for little changes—a favorite word here or there. A personal preference. Be honest with yourself. Does this little change hurt the big concept? Jar the rhythm? Ruin the feeling? Create pet word syndrome through overuse? Will it hurt response?

If none of the above, be gracious. Give in here and pick up your points in a more important area.

Sad to say, nonprofessionals can't tell the difference between a harmless little change and one that absolutely pulls the keystone out of good tight writing ("Can't you just move this paragraph down to here?"). Or one that blasts a basic concept right out of the water.

But *you* know the difference because *you're* the master builder. And here, *you* have to hold the line. If you've got your strategy statement, blasting a concept (or destroying a hypothesis) is easier to fend off than destroying smooth-flowing, well-paced copy construction.

If someone is set on destroying the concept, however, you must defend yourself and make it clear that the copy can no longer do the job it set out to do. Go on record. Be firm. Try to come up with a satisfactory alternative.

Although this really should not happen to you if you've moved through your presentation with a mutually agreed-to creative strategy, cruel reality forces me to admit that some copy changes that seem blatantly unfair (and unprofessional) may be foisted upon you from time to time. And you will have to make these changes (or lose the job). If you can't hold the line, try to explain how and why you believe the copy has been seriously weakened. Then try to make the best of it. At some point in your career, you may even have a few samples of your work that you're ashamed to show. Join the group. It's happened to *all* good creative people.

There is an emotionally satisfying alternative that some have tried. But it doesn't make any friends. Or help get more work or a better position. You can snatch your copy away, stride from the room, slam the door and refuse to capitulate. I suggest you file this under "soothing fantasies" instead.

HOW LONG SHOULD YOU HANG AROUND WITH THE KID?

I'm always surprised at the number of free-lancers who abandon their babies at the door of the art department. Once final copy is approved, they turn and run without a backward look at their creations.

On the other hand, many ad agencies and in-house promotion departments insist that the writer stick with the baby right to the printer and through the proofing. If you have a choice, opt for the latter, whoever your client may be.

– It proves that you care. And if that's not directly important to *you* at the time, you'll find it is important to your client or your boss (and your future).

– It enables you to take part in the many small (and often significant) changes and decisions that arise as the original layout concept is transformed into camera-ready art.

– It allows you to participate in actual picture selection and photography sessions—so that the illustrations will be as you envisioned them.

– It lets you participate in solving unforeseen crises should such arise.

– And—let us hope it never happens, but—it assures that if copy needs cutting you are the one to cut it.

There are too many writers who dropped the baby and ran, and couldn't even recognize the adult package when they saw it.

Enough said.

EVALUATING YOUR WORK

Once it's in the mail and your job is truly done—aside from a pat on the head, a big fat check, a raise or a promotion—two things are owed you: (1) samples, and (2) test results. This sounds like a simple, obvious assumption. It's common courtesy to give you three to five (or more) finished samples, and a report on the relative success of your brainchild once the test results are in. Everyone who's worked with you on the job will agree with this, but you may—just may—have to work hard to get either.

Free-lance writer, agency, or in-house, samples are usually mysteriously hard to come by. Often "the overruns are short" (they didn't print enough)...sometimes there are so many people on the distribution list that it's hard to scrape up enough for the writer; more often, people just forget. Keep at them. Don't you give up. *Samples are owed you.* You need them for your sample book if nothing else.

As for test results—that's a different story. If you are working in-house or as an agency, results shouldn't be hard to obtain. Free-lancers may have a tougher time. Believe it or not some clients don't tell free-lancers when they have a winner; maybe they forget(?). Some clients even hesitate to come clean and tell them if they have a big *loser.* The best clients, of course, are as open as they can be about the details.

This is important, because the more you can learn about the test results (overall response, backend response, specific response from various lists, comparative response to control/other tests) the better for you *and* the client. Remember, a good test is one in which you *learn.* The best test, of course, is one in which you *win* and *learn.*

We hope you'll be able to participate in a debriefing session on the test, its objectives and achievements and next steps. (This is good procedure for agencies and in-house operations, but if you're a free-lancer, don't count on it.)

Too many good writers lose interest once they've finished creating their babies. They forget to push for samples or ask about test results, or they aren't aware that they are entitled to push for these things. Time goes by. Then all of a sudden, it's too late. They end up without samples or a clear knowledge of what happened. After all that work. Can you believe it?

Believe it. But don't let it happen to you!

CHAPTER 7 EXERCISES

I. Test Yourself on Editing and Polishing

Each of the following excerpts can be improved by cutting, "pet" word weeding, bridging and breaking out ideas, dramatic punctuation, and graphic emphasis (indents, caps, underlines). Each is followed by a number in parenthesis, representing a minimal number of potential improvements. See how well you can do. See if you can do even better than the minimum. It's not easy.

1. Dear Stove-Watcher, Batter Mixer, Sauce-Stirrer,

If you're like most homemakers you probably spend a lot of time in the kitchen. For example, if you don't eat out at all over the next 12 months, you will have to cook 1,095 meals.

With that many meals—plus all the other things you're busy with—who has time to fuss at every meal? (7 possibilities)

2. So, after having spoken these cold, hard truths, what do I have that I can offer you? Simply this. I can offer a monthly source of plans and strategies to help you make your work work for you, instead of the other way around. The name of this source is MOVING UP! and it talks about the working life like no other magazine ever has. (6 possibilities)

3. In these superb figurines I have something from my most loved dances to look at and to remember, to hold on to, to cherish, to make those living moments come alive over and over again. It is extremely gratifying to see the classic moment from each ballet captured in perfect elegance, plucked out of time by a true artist's sensitive touch. (6 possibilities)

4. Dear Reader:

If you don't mind being trampled and having your money taken, read no further. But, on the other hand, if you're sick to death of being short-changed on every dollar you spend, if you are mad at the prices you pay for phony quality and rip-off repairs, and if you are wary of what you're told and wary of the advertising that supports it and want to know how to fight back and protect yourself then welcome to Publication X, the first and only publication that tells you where you're getting short-changed, how your family's well-being may be endangered, and how to spot it and what to do about it. (12 possibilities)

II. A Creative Checklist for Your Components

1. *Outer envelope:* Everything begins—or ends—here. Review Chapter 4. Then ask

- Does my envelope copy make a strong promise?
- Does it offer my prospect an irresistible tease?
- If the product or service is not for everyone, does it play fair and qualify the prospect market?
- Does the copy tie in to the letter lead?
- Will the envelope look important enough to get through the mailroom and/or past the secretary?
- Will it stand out in the mailbox?

2. *Letter*

- Is my lead strong and compelling (instant involvement plus big benefit)?
- Does it reflect the hypothesis?
- Is my approach the most effective approach, considering the hypothesis?
- Have I framed my letter with the lead, returning to it at the close, using logical references to it where possible in the body copy?
- Is my offer properly set off on page one (using a Johnson box if appropriate)?
- Do I carry sentences over from one page to the next and try to make the sentence break on page one irresistible?
- Am I putting the P.S. to the best possible use?
- Does my nuts 'n' bolts sum up the full offer with clarity and a pace or tone that implies action?
- Do I give my prospect a reason to act now?

3. *Order card (or form)*

- Do I state *what* is being ordered, what the form itself represents (to order the Deluxe Widget Holder, Subscription Form for *Black Snail* Magazine)?
- Do I start with a prospect commitment (Yes, please send me…Enter my subscription…I accept the invitation…O.K., I'll give it a try…)?
- Do I clearly restate all terms of the offer?
- Has the guarantee been spelled out dramatically?
- If there's an *800* number, is it a prominent choice?
- Have I limited the decisions to prevent inertia?

– Will a near-illiterate, or a well-trained dog, find the form equally clear and easy-to-use?

4. *The Brochure (or flyer or folder)*

– Does your *copy* track, drawing your prospect in with a strong headline, leading your prospect through your word and picture story with good subheads and lead-in lines?
– Are all the features and benefits of your product or service clearly set down and, where possible, dramatized visually?
– Does your brochure story flow in an orderly pattern and build or develop as your prospect moves along?
– Have you added a brochure coupon (or order form) if you're not price testing?

5. *Other Components*

– If you've decided to include a lift letter, does it offer a clear, new point of view that underlines a major benefit?
– Have you taken advantage of the "buck slip"? If you have an unusual product feature, a brand-new feature or benefit, an important deadline, a premium in your offer—all of these can be emphasized with a buck slip (a small, 5″ × 7″, 3″ × 4″, or 3″ × 8″ miniflyer).

III. More Guidelines

The following writer's guidelines are some of the best I've come across. Apply them at all stages of your copy development.

Direct Mail Copy—The Marketing and Creative Process[2]
by Pat Farley, Copy Consultant

1. Keep words, sentences, and grammar at an easy reading level. Use short, "Hemingway-like" sentences as much as possible.
2. Avoid semicolons—they slow the reader down. Dashes and ellipses can separate complex or long thoughts...yet carry the reader onward.
3. Keep copy in the active tense—complex sentence structures make copy boring and hard to follow.
4. Generally avoid humor or being too cute. Both can backfire.
5. Avoid too much involvement such as puzzles or riddles. They can occupy the reader to the detriment of the copywriter's offer.
6. Start with a strong opening headline and lead paragraph, immediately stressing benefits to the reader.

---

[2]Pat Farley, "Direct Mail Copy—The Marketing and Creative Process," in *DMA Manual*, Release #3103, (New York, N.Y., Direct Marketing Association, Inc., May 1979).

7. Appeal to the emotions and self-interest.

8. Describe products or services adequately. Take nothing for granted. Repeat key features.

9. State the price and offer on all interior package elements unless they are being tested.

10. If available, include testimonials. They are unbeatable assurance. Names are better than initials; specific comments on specific aspects of the product are better than general praise; results are more powerful than opinions.

11. Specifics are always more effective than generalities. Concentrate on examples, titles, names, even quotes. Position product benefits as reader benefits—tell the reader what's in it for him or her.

12. Follow the "rule of three" —a series of three has more rhythm and balance than two or four examples or adjectives.

13. Odd numbers ("seven reasons why," "21 basic rules") are more effective than even numbers.

14. Always seek a rhythm in copy—it should "sing." Read your copy out loud or have someone read it to you to be sure it reads the way you hear it in your mind.

15. Whenever someone has to reread a sentence or ask for clarification, change the copy—it will bother a substantial portion of the audience as well.

16. Suit imagery and vocabulary to the market and the product. If you are selling a magazine, for instance, the copy should reflect the style of the magazine.

17. The headlines, subheads, boxes, photograph captions, and sunbursts in a brochure should be a full sales presentation for non-readers.

18. Underlines, indents, and a second color in the letter should be used for pacing (to break up the copy) and to make all the key sales points stand out clearly to the prospect who only skims.

19. Never ask a reader a question in a key headline or on the outer envelope that can be answered, "No, I don't want this" or "I don't care."

20. The letters in a package should be personal and look like letters, with typewriter type, a salutation, and signature. Use "I" and "you," with more of the latter.

21. The first paragraph of a letter should be no more than one or two lines, three at most, to make it easy to begin reading.

22. At least the first page of the letter should "break" to the next page in midsentence, preferably at a point that pulls the reader onward. For example, "The small child ran directly in front of the speeding car and…"

23. Mention the product on page one of the letter; include price and offer if either is a key selling point. If the letter has a "story" opening, consider a "preface" above the salutation to state the offer.

24. Present an ironclad and absolute guarantee of satisfaction.

25. In concluding the letter, return to the theme that began it.

26. Ask for the order.

27. A postscript is one of the most read portions of a letter. Use it to reinforce the sales pitch and stress the incentive for immediate response.

28. Components of a direct mail package do not all have to be "themed" together, but there should be a sense of continuity throughout.

Here is another excellent exercise in polishing and editing your copy.

How to Play 20 Questions—And Improve Your Own Copy![3]
by Max Ross

1. Does the lead sentence get in step with the reader at once?

2. Is your lead sentence no more than two or three lines long?

3. Do your opening paragraphs promise a benefit to the reader?

4. Have you fired your biggest gun first?

5. Is there a big idea behind your proposition?

6. Are your thoughts arranged in logical order?

7. Is what you say believable?

8. Is it clear what you want the reader to do, and did you ask him to do it?

9. If there is an order form involved, does the copy tie in with it, and have you directed attention to the order form in the letter?

10. Does the letter have "You Attitude" all the way through?

11. Does the letter have a conversational tone?

12. Have you formed a bucket brigade through your copy?

13. Does your copy score between 70 and 80 words of five letters or fewer for each 100 words you write?

14. Are there any sentences where you could have avoided beginning with an article— "A," "An," or "The"?

15. Are there any places where you have strung together too many prepositional phrases?

16. Have you kept out "wandering verbs"?

17. Have you used action verbs instead of noun construction?

---

[3]Bob Stone, *Successful Direct Marketing Methods* (Lincolnwood, Illinois: Crain Books, an imprint of National Textbook Company, © 1984), pp. 195-6.

18. Are there any "that's" you don't need?

19. How does the copy rate on such letter-craftsmanship points as: (a) using active voice instead of passive, (b) periodic sentences instead of loose, (c) too many participles, (d) too many split infinitives, (e) repeating company name too often?

20. Does your letter look the way you want it to insofar as these items are concerned? (a) placement on page, (b) no paragraphs over six lines, (c) indentation and numbered paragraphs for emphasis, (d) underscoring and capitalization used sparingly, (e) punctuation for reading ease.

chapter 8

An Evening with the Good Stuff

> The best letters seem to me the most delightful of all written things, and those that are not the best the most negligible. If a correspondence, in other words, has not the real charm, I wouldn't have it published even privately; if it has, on the other hand, I would give it all the glory of the greatest literature.
>
> *Henry James to*
> *Charles Eliot Norton in 1899*[1]

That's just what we're going to do here—spread a little glory over some outstanding examples of fine letter writing. Sit back and relax while I treat you to an evening of top armchair entertainment. Bring over what's left of the bread and wine from Chapter 6, and let's have some fun.

Before we start, however, two things need clarification. First, if you're a little suspicious or wary as to the objectives of this tour, let me explain what it can do for you (besides entertain, of course).

In a world of Jim-Jam letters—a business where it's even possible to purchase computer software to generate "customized" letters—we all need a little inspirational reinforcement. Something to remind us that direct mail can—and indeed frequently does—soar above the commonplace mailbox stuffing.

I also want to surround you with quality here and throughout this book in the hope that you'll osmose and come to expect that same quality from yourself and from others. A home that's filled with beautiful music or works of art, whether or not it puts forth musicians and artists, does certainly develop individuals with a keen appreciation and sensitivity to music and art. Well, perhaps this book can provide you with quality experience in direct marketing. Surround yourself with excellence, learn to recognize the good stuff, and it will be easier for you to appreciate it and work toward it in everything you do.

Second, as you move through the good stuff—examining it critically, learning, understanding why it's good—you might wonder why so many

---

[1]The letters of Henry James, Vol. IV, 1895–1916, Leon Edel, ed. (Cambridge, Mass.: The Belknap Press of Harvard University Press, 1985).

examples throughout this book come from publications, from magazines and book clubs. There's an answer for this. As Aaron Montgomery Ward was a pioneer in mail order, so book clubs and magazines have been pioneers in the use of direct mail to acquire members and subscribers. Many of them have been at it for half a century and even longer.

They generally promote to a highly literate market—an audience whose attention span has not been eroded by the video medium—and they use top creative people to execute their direct mail. Some of the best free-lancers in America vie for the control position with certain publications. Those publications afford them a true creative showcase for their best work and a place to measure themselves against their peers.

Enough explaining. Let's get on with the examples. We'll start off at the top with two Direct Marketing Association Gold Mailbox winners. (The Gold Mailbox is the highest award given by the DMA.)

The first was written by Ed McLean, president of his own company today, but in 1965 when he wrote this famous Mercedes-Benz letter he was working for Ogilvy and Mather advertising.

The letter (Figure 8-1), which played a major role in introducing the Mercedes-Benz Diesel, is reprinted here (complete with Ed's own margin notes) from "The Basics of Copy, A Monograph on Direct Marketing" by Ed McLean.[2]

This second Gold Mailbox winner is commonly referred to as the "Admiral Byrd" package. Written by Henry Burnett in 1968, the letter was sent to 13,600 top U.S. business executives to enlist their participation in a $10,000, 26-day round-the-world trip. (A difficult *offer* at best for busy executives.) The objective was to get only 50 participants. Seven hundred responded. Against a budget of $5,230, some $600,000 income was generated.

The inspiration for the lead in the letter came from a famous ad by polar explorer Ernest Shackleton in a London paper in 1902:

> Men wanted for hazardous journey. Small wages, bitter cold, long months of complete darkness, constant danger, safe return doubtful, honor and recognition in case of success.

This package broke two major rules. (Remember, you can break the rules after you've been playing around with them for a while—*if* you're an accomplished creative type!)

1. It did not use a color brochure to dramatize the benefits.

2. It did not carry a reply card. (Nor did it enclose a telephone number.) Prospects were "qualified" by writing a letter, using their letterhead or personalized stationery, accompanied by their deposit of $2,500!

The outer envelope, although computer-personalized like the letter, carries only this simple corner card:

---

[2]Reprinted by permission of Ed McLean.

MERCEDES-BENZ OF NORTH AMERICA, INC.

158 LINWOOD PLAZA
P O BOX 318
FORT LEE NEW JERSEY 07024

HEINZ C. HOPPE
CHIEF EXECUTIVE OFFICER

CABLE MERCEBENZ FORT LEE
TWX FORT LEE 201 947-5922
OVERSEAS TELEX 23 01 2351
DOMESTIC TELEX 01 2351

*Basics of copy reader:
Note my comments in margins.
— E. McL.*

July 12, 1965

Dear Sir:

"Forget it, Heinz," the experts told me. "It just won't sell here."

They were talking about the Mercedes-Benz 190 Diesel -- a car that is owned and driven daily by over 500,000 people overseas.

"Americans won't buy it," said the experts. "Why pay $4,068 for a German car with a noisy engine when for $891.37 more they can get a Cadillac?"

]"Positioning" of product with "negative sell" approach

I had reason to believe the experts were wrong.

Some Americans have paid $4,068 for this German car with the "noisy engine."

As a matter of fact, if it wasn't for the "noisy engine" many of these Americans wouldn't have found out about the car. While in Europe, they saw Mercedes-Benz Diesel cars and noticed the noise made by the engine. Fascinated, they asked questions.

And what they learned from European drivers up and down the high-speed Autobahns convinced them the Mercedes-Benz Diesel is a great car.

As for the noise, they found it does sound different from a gasoline engine. In fact, a few people may give the car a second look as you idle at a traffic light. But you won't be bothered by the sound above 25 miles per hour. Some 190D drivers report they actually enjoy the unique

/Note mid-sentence break

Figure 8-1

sound of the Diesel. Many owners tell me, "If it didn't make a little noise, people wouldn't know it's a Diesel!"

Mr. John J. Gray of Albany, Oregon is one of these owners.

He travels all over the western U.S. for his firm, Kashfinder, Inc. In the past 7 years, he has driven his Mercedes-Benz Diesel car 652,000 miles.

TESTIMONIAL REASSURANCE

> "652,000 miles is a long ways to drive one car," writes Mr. Gray. "It has taken me 7 years -- during which my faithful Mercedes-Benz Diesel has run more efficiently and far more cheaply than any car I have ever owned. And the car still doesn't rattle..."

Recently, we asked other Mercedes-Benz Diesel car owners in America:

> "If you had it to do all over again, would you buy another of these automobiles?"

Before I tell you their answers, I'd like to reveal what I learned from the U.S. Automobile Manufacturers Association. I asked them how many Americans buy the same make and model of car they owned previously. They told me that fewer than four out of ten do.

RESEARCH REASSURANCE

> Yet, when we asked our Mercedes-Benz Diesel car owners in America if they would buy another Mercedes-Benz Diesel, better than nine out of ten said YES.

The experts were wrong about these Americans. But one question remains unanswered for me.

How many other Americans want a great motorcar?

I'll soon know the answer.

You -- and a small number of others -- have been selected to receive the most unusual offer ever made by a car manufacturer.

INTRODUCTION OF OFFER

> I will pay for all fuel, all motor oil, all oil filters, and all lubrications on the

NOTE MID-SENTENCE BREAK

Figure 8-1, *continued*

new Mercedes-Benz 190 Diesel for the
first 15,000 miles you drive it.

This offer is from Mercedes-Benz of North America. ← *BIG-COMPANY REASSURANCE*
It is <u>not</u> from your Mercedes-Benz dealer. It will
not affect your trade-in or terms in any way. I
feel certain you will like this car and will help me
spread the word about it.

That's why I can offer you all fuel free. ← *OFFER REPEATED*
All motor oil free. All oil filters
free. All lubrications free. All are
yours free for the first 15,000 miles
you own and drive your new Mercedes-Benz
190 Diesel.

No other manufacturer of a full-size 4-door sedan in
the entire world could afford to make this offer.

I can make it because the Mercedes-Benz 190 Diesel ← *READER BENEFIT*
averages over 30 miles per gallon of diesel fuel --
and diesel fuel costs 1/3 less than gasoline in many
states.

<u>In fact, the 190 Diesel regularly saves its owners</u> ← *READER BENEFIT*
<u>more than 50 per cent on fuel costs alone.</u>

And, like all Mercedes-Benz cars, the 190 Diesel is ← *READER BENEFIT*
so finely machined it uses scarcely any motor oil.

That's not all.

The 190 Diesel never needs a tune-up. It has no ← *READER BENEFIT*
carburetor to adjust or replace. No spark plugs, no
points, no condensers, no distributor.

Mechanics will tell you that many cars need a new set
of rings after 75,000 miles.

John Gray -- the Diesel owner in Oregon -- reports his ← *TESTIMONIAL REASSURANCE*
car didn't need a ring job until after it had gone
275,000 miles!

Even crack mechanics are surprised by <u>that</u>.

We build the Mercedes-Benz 190 Diesel so that, with ← *PRODUCT FEATURE*
normal care, it will last for hundreds of thousands of

Figure 8-1, *continued*

miles -- long after most of today's cars are chopped
up for scrap!

We give it 7 coats of paint, <u>inside</u> and out. ← *PRODUCT FEATURE*

We install special safety locks on all doors -- the
same locks used on the Grand Mercedes 600 that sells
for $20,291. ← *PRODUCT FEATURE*

We equip it with two separate braking systems. If
something happens to one system, you can stop with
the other. ← *READER BENEFIT*

> Most new cars are not built for high-speed
> panic stops. The car's wheels will pull to
> one side or the other. The back end swerves.

> <u>The disc brakes on the Mercedes-Benz 190
> Diesel bring it to an emergency stop from
> 80 mph -- in a straight line. There's no
> swerve. No fade. You are in control every
> foot of the way.</u> ← *PRODUCT FEATURE* ← *READER BENEFIT*

Other car makers bolt the body on. We weld it. Welding
guarantees a tighter, firmer body structure -- with less
chance of annoying rattles. ← *PRODUCT FEATURE*

We also give the 190 Diesel the same suspension system
with independent rear axles that we use on the famous
Mercedes-Benz 230SL sports car. (The 230SL sells for
$6,239.) ← *PRODUCT FEATURE*

All in all, we spend hundreds of dollars extra to make
the Mercedes-Benz 190 Diesel a great motorcar. That's
why we must place a price tag of $4,068 on it.

I personally believe that when you try it, you will
agree: it's well worth the price.

Why not let me put one at your disposal?

Drive it as you would your own car. Put it through the
paces of city and highway traffic. Try it on hills.
See how it takes curves. Test its disc brakes, its 4
forward speeds -- or the optional 4-speed automatic
transmission. (The only one of its kind in the world.) ← *OFFER RESTATED IN ANOTHER WAY*

I'm so confident you will want one of these remarkable
automobiles, I will pay you for <u>all</u> fuel, <u>all</u> motor oil, ← *OFFER REPEATED*

Figure 8-1, *continued*

all oil filters, and all lubrications for the first
15,000 miles you drive your new Mercedes-Benz 190
Diesel.

So please accept my invitation to drive a 190D and
reach your own personal, private judgment. Simply
return the enclosed card in the postage-free envelope.
I will also send you a special brochure called "The
Amazing 190D."

← CALL FOR ACTION + HOW TO DO IT

My offer expires Monday, August 16, 1965, and is limited
to the first 1,000 people who respond. I hope you take
advantage of it. Thank you.

← ASK FOR ORDER AGAIN

                         Yours truly,

                         Heinz C. Hoppe

                         Heinz C. Hoppe
                         Chief Executive Officer

HCH/a

Figure 8-1, *continued*

Edward C. Bursk
Admiral Richard E. Byrd Polar Center
18 Tremont Street
Boston, Massachusetts 02108

Now read through the letter (Figure 8-2), then we'll talk some more.

What a promise. Immortality! Adventure! Danger! All for a greater good. Talk about moral imperatives!

I hope it's absolutely clear to you by now why no brochure was included. How much better for the good writer to use prose and let the reader use imagination! Sure, one picture is often worth a thousand words, but one stimulated imagination is often worth 10,000 pictures!

And how about the P.S.? It's delivered like a virtual throwaway line—but what impact and persuasion! A video record for your children and grand-children. You couldn't have a stronger clincher.

Notice the difference in style and tone between this letter and Ed McLean's. Both were right for their offers. Both were tremendously effective. Credible. Involving. Motivating. McLean's approach was "Story" with a touch of Negative, Burnett's "Generic," but Generic of heroic proportions.

Now here's another rule breaker with a totally new tone and style (Figure 8-3). The approach here is strong Story—so strong that the first two paragraphs are featured on the outer as an envelope opener. Read. And appreciate. And see if you can tell me what's the rule breaker here.

You guessed it! Can you imagine putting the offer (and the product) on the *second* page in a two-page letter? Just isn't done—*unless* it's done this well.

The charming, nostalgic—almost naive—approach touched a nerve and far out-pulled all other approaches tested by Omaha Steaks. It deserves to be called "Romance."

Not all good direct mail *breaks* rules, but Figure 8-4 broke some traditions and helped establish new ones for Rodale Press in terms of the credible spokesperson. This example uses the If/Assumptive Approach combined with strong editorial credibility to establish close rapport with the reader.

Since Rodale's editors and staff actually *do* practice what they preach, why let the reader imagine them in suits and ties in a stuffy office? What could be more logical than to show them in their natural habitats as spokespersons?

This "family support network" approach was carried out and incorporated in all components of the package, from the outer envelope to the letter, the guarantee, and the order form—for a winning promotion.

Figures 8-5 and 8-6 represent the work of two fine writers for *Vanity Fair* magazine. The first package is the original control, a winning Identification/ Invitational Approach by Emily Soell, President of Rapp & Collins. It ruled the roost, unassailed, for over two years. The outer, a monarch on cream stock, was computer-addressed and carried a corner card and simple R.S.V.P. in the lower right-hand corner of the envelope face.

Study the approach carefully and you'll see why its success was well

EDWARD C. BURSK
SOLDIERS FIELD
BOSTON, MASSACHUSETTS 02163

EDITOR
HARVARD BUSINESS REVIEW

Please reply to me in care of:
Transpolar Expedition
Admiral Richard E. Byrd Polar Center
18 Tremont Street
Boston, Massachusetts 02108

September 3, 1968

Mr. Richard M. Archer
141 Corinne Ave.
Pelham, N.Y. 10803

Dear Mr. Archer:

As Chairman of the Admiral Richard E. Byrd Polar Center, it is my privilege to invite you to become a member of an expedition which is destined to make both news and history.

It will cost you $10,000 and about 26 days of your time. Frankly, you will endure some discomfort, and may even face some danger.

On the other hand, you will have the rare privilege of taking part in a mission of great significance for the United States and the entire world. A mission, incidentally, which has never before been attempted by man.

You will personally have the chance to help enrich mankind's fund of knowledge about two of the last earthly frontiers, the polar regions.

I am inviting you to join a distinguished group of 50 people who will fly around the world longitudinally, over both poles, on an expedition which will commemorate Admiral Richard E. Byrd's first Antarctic flight in 1929.

Among the highlights of this transpolar flight - the first commercial flight ever to cross both poles and touch down on all continents - will be stopovers at the American military/scientific bases at Thule, Greenland, and McMurdo Sound, Antarctica.

Because this expedition has the interest and support of much of the Free World, you and your fellow members will be honored guests (in many cases, even celebrities) at state and diplomatic receptions throughout the itinerary. You will have the opportunity to meet and talk with some of the world's important national leaders and public figures, such as Pope Paul VI, the Emperor of Japan, General Carlos Romulo, and many others who are already a part of history.

By agreeing to join this expedition, you will, in a sense, establish yourself in history too. For you will become a Founding Trustee of the new Admiral Richard E. Byrd Polar Center, sponsor of the expedition.

Your biography will be recorded in the Center's archives, available to future historians. The log, photographs and memorabilia of the expedition will be permanently displayed in the Center. And your name will be inscribed, with those of the other expedition members, on a bronze memorial tablet.

Figure 8-2

Before I continue with the details of the expedition, let me tell you more about the Byrd Polar Center and the reasoning which led to its establishment this summer.

Located in Boston, home of the late Admiral and point of origin for each of his seven expeditions, this nonprofit institution will house, catalog and preserve the papers and records of both Admiral Byrd and other Arctic and Antarctic explorers.

But the Center will have a more dynamic function than merely to enshrine the past. It will be a vital, viable organization devoted to furthering peaceful development of the polar regions, particularly Antarctica.

It will become, in effect, this country's headquarters for investigation and research into the scientific and commercial development of the poles. The Center will sponsor, support, initiate and conduct studies and expeditions. It will furnish comprehensive data or technical assistance to the United States, or to any university, institution, foundation, business organization or private individual legitimately interested in polar development.

In other words, the Center has set for itself a course which the Admiral before his death endorsed wholeheartedly. He foresaw that mankind would one day benefit enormously from development of Antarctica's vast potential. And he perceived that Antarctica's unique and diverse advantages and resources might best be developed by private capital in a free enterprise context.

The Byrd Polar Center is dedicated to these objectives. And the essential purpose of this commemorative expedition is to dramatize the role that private enterprise - and private citizens - can play in the opening of these last frontiers.

At the same time, the expedition should help prove a few other important points. It should demonstrate the feasibility of shrinking the world through longitudinal navigation. It should also help blaze a trail for commercial air travel over the South Pole. Presently, to fly from Chile to Australia, you must go by way of Los Angeles, even though a straight line trans-Antarctic route would be far shorter.

There is another factor I should mention, one which I think lends a certain urgency to the work of the Center. Development of the polar regions enjoys a high official priority in the Soviet Union - higher, some believe, than in the United States.

The Center's activities can provide a tangible, effective complement to those of our own government, and over the long term, contribute meaningfully to preservation of the Arctic and Antarctic regions for peaceful purposes.

These objectives, I think you will agree, are entirely valid. And important, for the future of humanity. It is for this reason that the inaugural activity of the Byrd Polar Center will be an expedition of such scope and magnitude.

The expedition will be led by Commander Fred G. Dustin, veteran of six polar expeditions, advisor to Admiral Byrd and one of the intrepid group which

Figure 8-2, *continued*

spent the winter of 1934 in Little America on Byrd's Antarctic Expedition II. Commander Dustin is a member of the U.S. Antarctica Committee and President of the Byrd Polar Center.

Considered the ranking American authority on the polar regions, Fred Dustin is probably better qualified to lead this expedition - and brief members on virtually every aspect of the polar regions - than any man on earth. The Center and the expedition are fortunate to have Commander Dustin, as you will discover should you decide to participate.

The flight will be made in a specially outfitted, four-engine commercial jet with lounge-chair-and-table cabin configuration. A full flight crew of six will be headed by Captain Hal Neff, former pilot of Air Force One, the Presidential plane. Special clothing and equipment, such as Arctic survival gear, will be provided by the expedition and carried aboard the plane.

The expedition members will meet in Boston on the evening of November 7, 1968, for briefing and a reception and send-off party with the Governor of Massachusetts, Mayor of Boston, local officials and directors of the Byrd Polar Center. Next day, we will take off, head due north from Boston's Logan International Airport and follow this itinerary (as I have not yet visited all these places myself, I have drawn on the descriptions submitted to me by Commander Dustin and the other experienced people who have planned the expedition):

Thule, Greenland

Far above the Arctic Circle, past the chill reaches of Baffin Bay, lies desolate Thule, the northernmost U.S. air base. Almost 400 miles further north than the northern tip of Alaska, Thule was originally surveyed as a possible military site by Admiral Byrd and Commander Dustin. Here, in the deepening Arctic winter, you will get your first taste of the rigors of polar existence. You will have the chance to inspect the installations and meet the men for whom Arctic survival is a way of life.

North Pole

According to those who have crossed the North Pole, you will completely lose your day-night orientation. Sunrise and sunset can occur within minutes of each other, a strange and unforgettable phenomenon. After Thule, you will cross the geographic North Pole, just as Admiral Byrd did in his pioneering trans-Arctic flight with Floyd Bennett in 1926. A memorial flag will be dropped.

Anchorage, Alaska

After crossing the pole, the plane will bank into a 90° left turn and head south, over the Arctic Ocean and Beaufort Sea, past Mt. McKinley, North America's highest peak, and on to Anchorage. There, you will meet the Governor and key officials.

Tokyo, Japan

The highlight of your stopover in Japan will be an opportunity to meet the Emperor and Premier. (Fishing; excursion to Hakone and Atami by bullet train; tea ceremony at private homes.)

Figure 8-2, *continued*

Manila, Philippines

General Carlos Romulo, the legendary patriot and statesman, an old friend of Admiral Byrd, will give the expedition a warm welcome in Manila. (Folklore performance; hunting for duck, deer, wild boar and a special species of water buffalo; fishing for tuna and marlin.)

You will note that here and elsewhere we have prearranged a considerable amount of hunting, fishing, and so on. These activities are optional. (Members of the expedition will be asked to indicate their preferences 30 days before the flight.) For those who do not want to participate in any of these events, there will be sight-seeing, golf and many other things to do.

Darwin, Australia

Hard by the Timor Sea, tropical Darwin offers some of the world's most superb beaches. You will have time not only to sample the sand and water sports, but to see Australia's great outback. With its spectacular chasms, canyons and gorges, the rarely visited outback is a scenic match for our own West.

Sydney, Australia

You can look forward to an enthusiastic reception in Sydney by the Prime Minister and government officials. For one thing, Australia is on particularly good terms with the United States. For another, Australia has traditionally been in the vanguard of nations involved in Antarctic exploration and development. (Hunting for kangaroo, crocodile, buffalo, wild boar, duck, and geese; or off-shore fishing for rifle fish, salmon, and giant grouper.)

Christchurch, New Zealand

This is our staging point for the flight to Antarctica, and it couldn't be more appropriate. Most of the early expeditions departed from New Zealand, and Admiral Byrd is still considered a national hero there. New Zealand is Antarctic-conscious and its people take almost a proprietary interest in the frozen continent. You will be something of a celebrity in New Zealand, and can expect a thoroughly enjoyable visit while the expedition awaits favorable weather reports from McMurdo Sound. (Deer hunting - where deer are so plentiful that they pay a bounty; fishing for all of the great species of marlin - in an area known for the greatest marlin fishing in the world - also Mako shark.)

McMurdo Sound, Antarctica

I am told that only a total eclipse of the sun is comparable, in emotional impact, to the first sight of Antarctica. Once experienced, neither can be forgotten. If you prove to be like most who have seen Antarctica, you will need somehow, someday, to return. And when you do, the emotional impact will be just as profound. That is what the Antarctic veterans say.

For Antarctica exists well beyond the boundaries of the world you know. You will see there a sun you have never before seen, breathe air you have never before breathed. You will see menacing white mountains towering for thousands

Figure 8-2, *continued*

229

of feet over a black ocean in which, with luck, you might survive for 45 seconds. You will see the awesome Ross Ice Shelf, as large as France, with its 50 to 200 foot ice cliffs cleaving the sea for 400 miles. You will see the active volcano, Mt. Erebus, 13,000 feet of fire and ice.

And you will see the huts, so well preserved they seem to have been inhabited only yesterday, which Shackleton used in 1908 and the ill-fated Scott in 1911. Antarctica, apparently, is not subject to the passage of time as we know it.

At McMurdo Base, you will meet the military men and scientists who inhabit this strange, alien territory. And you will inhabit it for a while too - long enough to feel its bone-chilling cold, to hear its timeless silence, to perceive, at the very edge of your composure, the terror of its mindless hostility to human beings.

While you are there, you will learn, as few men have ever had the opportunity to learn, about Antarctica. You will learn about survival, but more important, about what men must accomplish to truly open this formidable frontier.

South Pole

Admiral Byrd was the first man to fly over the South Pole. In all of history, probably fewer than 200 men have crossed the pole, by air or otherwise. As a member of this expedition, you will join that select group.

Punta Arenas, Chile

From the South Pole, you will fly to Punta Arenas, on the tortuous Strait of Magellan which separates continental South America from bleak Tierra del Fuego. The visit here will be brief, but you should get some idea of the flavor of this nearly forgotten outpost.

Rio de Janeiro, Brazil

This memorable stopover will include a diplomatic reception You will also have a chance to relax and sample the sights and sounds of fabulous Rio. (Special plane to Belo Horizonte for hunting boar, duck, jaguar, panther, water buffalo, crocodile and deer.)

Dakar, Senegal

You may never have expected to see Dakar, but you will on this expedition. (Tribal dancing; safari.)

Rome, Italy

No trip would be complete without a stop in Rome, where we will be received enthusiastically. During our stay there we will have a private audience with the Pope.

Figure 8-2, *continued*

<u>London, England</u>

From London, the expedition will fly back across the Atlantic and terminate with a debriefing, critique and farewell dinner in Boston, on December 3.

As mementos of the expedition, you will receive a leather-bound, personalized copy of the log book and a piece of the fabric from Admiral Byrd's original plane, mounted in crystal.

You will also be presented with a framed certificate from the Admiral Richard E. Byrd Polar Center, affirming your appointment as a Founding Trustee and expressing appreciation for your interest in, contributions to and efforts on behalf of the Center and its objectives. In the future, you will be kept fully advised of the plans and activities of the Center, and be invited to participate to whatever extent you wish. And of course, you will have life-long access to the Center's archives and services.

Most important, you will take back with you a once-in-a-lifetime experience. The day may come when journeys to and over the poles are commonplace. But today, the privilege is available to very few.

It is true, I think, that this privilege does carry responsibility with it. By the time you return, you will have received a comprehensive indoctrination course in the polar regions by the world's leading authorities. Your responsibility will be to make the most of the knowledge you will gain, to become an active advocate - perhaps even a disciple - of polar research and development.

It is a responsibility which, I trust, will weigh easily upon you. For once the polar air has been absorbed into your bloodstream, there is no cure. Like others who have been stricken, you will probably find yourself reading every word you can find on the North and South Poles. And, most likely, thinking about your next trip.

But first of all, you must decide about this trip. If you have a sense of adventure, a certain pioneering spirit, and if the prospect of taking part in a mission of worldwide significance and historical importance appeals to you, perhaps you should consider joining the expedition. It is doubtful that you will ever have another chance like this.

Obviously, you can't make a decision of this magnitude instantly. But a word of caution: reservations will be accepted in the order received - a total of only 60, including ten standbys. The departure date, remember, is November 8, 1968, so there is little time to waste.

The price of $10,000 includes food and beverages, all accommodations (the best available under all circumstances), transportation, special clothing, insurance, side excursions - virtually everything except your travel to and from Boston.

Money received will go into escrow at the United States Trust Company in Boston until the time of the flight. To the extent that revenues from the

Figure 8-2, *continued*

trip will exceed costs, the activities of the Polar Center will be accelerated.

To reserve your place in the expedition, just drop me a note on your letterhead or personal stationery, with your deposit check for $2,500, made out to the United States Trust Company. Incidentally, if anything prevents your leaving as planned, you can send another in your place; otherwise, cancellations cannot be accepted later than 30 days before departure.

If you have further questions, please write to me in care of the Transpolar Expedition, Admiral Richard E. Byrd Polar Center, 18 Tremont Street, Boston, Massachusetts 02108.

I hope we may hear from you soon - and that we will welcome you to the expedition.

Sincerely yours,

Edward C. Bursk

Edward C. Bursk

ECB:EHK

P.S.: We have just made arrangements for a professional camera crew to accompany the flight, and as a result we will be able to provide you with a short film clip and sound tape of your experiences.

Figure 8-2, *continued*

" I awoke before dawn. In the stillness, I could hear my wife's gentle breathing as she lay sleeping. How I adored her!

"Yet I wondered if she were dreaming of a different life than the one she found with me. I couldn't blame her if she were, because...

". . .I hadn't spent much time with her lately. I couldn't even remember the last time I told her I loved her. It must have been weeks, even months, ago.

"You see, my job had kept me on the go constantly for the past several months. To be sure, it was an exciting time. I had a chance to really advance my career. But, as I now realized, my personal life was suffering.

"That morning, I decided to do something about it. . ."

Dear Customer,

What you've just read is part of a letter I received from one of you. In a moment, I'll tell you how the story ended.

But first, let me tell you why I've reproduced this letter here. I think it shows the kind of time problems most of us have today. And too often it's our loved ones who suffer neglect when we get too busy.

Especially that <u>one special person</u> in life -- with whom we share a deep love, priceless memories, and a lasting friendship.

I'm writing to you today with a suggestion that can bring you and that special person closer together -- and enrich your lives. It starts with setting aside <u>time</u> -- perhaps an entire day -- to spend together, and rekindle the glow of your love.

> Your day can begin quietly, with a leisurely breakfast.
> Then choose simple, relaxing things to do. Things you
> both enjoy.

A walk through the woods on a snowy afternoon. . .jogging along the beach. . .shopping for antiques. . .a tennis match. . .or maybe just snuggling in front of your fireplace.

The perfect ending to such a day would be an intimate dinner for just the two of you -- right in your own dining room. Candlelight. . .roses. . . soft music. . .your best china and silver. . .plus foods with an aura of elegance, and romance.

Then -- when the mood is just right -- remind your mate how much your life together means to you.

To make this meal as special as the occasion deserves -- you'll want to choose something distinctly out of the ordinary.

May I suggest. . .

Courtesy of Omaha Steaks International

Figure 8-3

. . .tender, juicy Omaha Steaks. Our luscious steaks would add so much
enjoyment to your special time together.

You'll both thrill to the superb taste and tenderness of our gourmet
meats. Whether you choose Filet Mignon. . .Chateaubriand. . .or any of the
fine foods shown in the enclosed booklet.

And here's something just as important. Omaha Steaks products are planned
for easy preparation by the cook in your household. So your romantic mood won't
be ruined by long, tiring hours spent in the kitchen.

> That's why using our foods means enjoying life more.
> You can savor meals of the highest quality, without
> losing precious hours in food preparation -- hours
> you can put to far better use.

Shopping for our meats is easy, too. All you do is browse through the
enclosed booklet and make your choices. Then just pick up the phone and call.
It's free. Or use the enclosed, easy-to-use order form and postpaid envelope.

If your romantic meal together isn't as easy and enjoyable as I've promised,
just let me know. I'll send you a replacement shipment, or a full refund,
whichever _you_ prefer. You have nothing to lose.

So place your order now, while you have everything in front of you. If
you act promptly, you can plan your special time together around St. Valentine's
Day. This year, February 14 falls on Thursday.

In addition, we'll enclose a ¼ lb. box of Godiva Chocolates _free_ with
your order. Plus. . .several popular packages are available at special prices
(for a limited time only). One of these could be perfect for your romantic
evening together.

Now here's what happened to the man whose letter I quoted on page one.
He did just what I've suggested to you. And the time he took to spend with his
wife -- truly brought them closer together. They were lucky enough to rediscover
all the joy they'd once known.

> And it was so simple. Just a few hours together,
> quietly sharing thoughts and feelings -- while
> enjoying pleasant activities and good food.

This could well be just what you and _your_ special person need. May I
hear from you today?

Best Wishes,
OMAHA STEAKS INTERNATIONAL

Frederick J. Simon

P.S. Remember -- Omaha Steaks products really _can_ help you and someone
special enjoy life more.

Figure-8-3, _continued_

FROM ALL OF US AT RODALE PRESS:
YOUR INVITATION TO CHOOSE 3 VALUABLE BOOKS FOR $1.00
(plus delivery)
when you join the first book club for people who care about the quality of their lives. (And are willing to do something about it!)

Dear Friend:

You're alive!

And better yet, you're aware of it!

That puts you in a small but growing minority of very special people in this world -- people who want to make the most of being alive.

This is me, Terri, checking the tomatoes in my greenhouse. I get a lot of help from *The Solar Greenhouse Book.*

Terri Lepley, Book Division Artist

People who want to get back to basics and put human values ahead of material ones...to live in closer harmony with their environment...to be healthy and fit...to wisely use the natural resources the world gives us for rich, full and peaceful lives...

That's our goal too (all of us at Rodale Press) -- to build the best lives we possibly can for ourselves and our families. Healthy, active, doing lives -- with the emphasis on quality, not quantity.

You know, we feel a special fellowship with others who share our interests. That's why we've designed a new club for people who want to live like we want to live.

A book club, in a way -- but something more.

The SELF-SUFFICIENCY BOOK CLUB is a lifestyle "support

Figure 8-4   *Courtesy of Rodale Press, Inc.*

network" too. Because through our books, we hope to
share ideas, inspiration and practical information with
people who share our -- and your -- way of life.

As you may know, Rodale Press was incorporated over a quarter of a
century ago for the purpose of seeking and publishing just this kind of
information. Rodale is the publisher of NEW SHELTER, ORGANIC GARDENING,
PREVENTION, and BICYCLING magazines and countless books on energy,
gardening, cooking, do-it-yourself, fitness.... And we practice what we
publish. A lot of the information that eventually goes into the magazines
and Rodale books is learned right here in the Rodale gardens and experimental kitchens in Emmaus, Pennsylvania, and in our own homes and farms
nearby.

For instance,

BEST IDEAS FOR ORGANIC VEGETABLE GROWING
and
RODALE'S NATURALLY GREAT FOODS COOKBOOK

are two of our most popular books. They're _useful_, you see.
They show how _anyone_ can have a bountiful vegetable harvest
in a home garden -- _and_ follow up with the most exciting,
delicious and nutritious meals ever.

I guess our policy's kind of unique. Our editors and publishers favor books which answer specific needs with timely,
practical information. And when there's no existing book,
and we don't have the answers ourselves, we literally search
the world to find the experts who can prepare the authoritative -- yes, _definitive_ -- works we want on the subjects in
question. Expert authors...

I'm Bill – sawing the boards for
a tool shed I'm building. I got
the idea and guidance from a
great book, *Working Wood.*
*Bill Hylton, Managing
Editor/Book Division*

...like the well-known architect, Alex Wade, who, with
photographer Neal Ewenstein, brings you 30 ENERGY
EFFICIENT HOUSES...YOU CAN BUILD. They
tell you how you can build your own solar-
heated home -- the low-cost way -- with
complete details on insulation heating,
ventilation and natural lighting.

...and Mike and Nancy Bubel. They share
their secrets of how to find and use old
but serviceable materials to make some
very useful things in WORKING WOOD: A
GUIDE TO THE COUNTRY CARPENTER.

And have you ever wondered...

...what it would be like to "live off the land"?
John Vivian tells how you can in THE MANUAL
OF PRACTICAL HOMESTEADING.

I'm proud of my energy-efficient
home. I found *30 Energy-
Efficient Houses...You Can
Build* invaluable in planning
and building it.
Carol Stoner, Editorial Director

Figure 8-4, *continued*

...or whether you could be successfully -- and happily --
  self-employed? You'll want to read WORKING FOR YOURSELF
  by Geof Hewitt.

The books available through the SELF-SUFFICIENCY BOOK CLUB span a
whole lifestyle -- from WOOD HEAT to PRODUCING YOUR OWN POWER to THE
SOLAR GREENHOUSE BOOK. From RAISING SMALL LIVESTOCK to UNUSUAL
VEGETABLES to MANAGING YOUR PERSONAL FOOD SUPPLY. From NATURAL
BEAUTY to USING PLANTS FOR HEALING to GET FIT WITH BICYCLING.

I don't know how you feel about it but I suspect you'd agree that it's
pretty hard to find quality woodwork at a decent price these days.
Often enough it saves dollars (and makes sense) if you do it yourself.
We'll show you how.

You see, we bring you books that help you <u>do</u> things...

                ...simpler, safer, cheaper and better.

Now you can have these hard-to-find books delivered to your
front door! (We know that busy, active people value their
time -- which is another reason we formed the SELF-
SUFFICIENCY BOOK CLUB.)

We'd sincerely like you to become a part of the Rodale
family and to share our way of life through the SELF-
SUFFICIENCY BOOK CLUB. And we're making it easy for you
to start your "better living" library with any three of
the 24 fine quality books shown in the enclosed holder
for just $1.00, plus shipping and handling. (New members
also receive our brief primer, "The Basics of Self-
Sufficiency," <u>free</u> on joining.)

We're not asking you to risk anything at all. Feel free
to inspect the books you receive for 15 days, and if
you're not pleased with them, you certainly may return

Here I am at my favorite spot of
all — the dining room at Rodale's
Fitness House! I love the food here,
especially since I know it's all
natural and healthy. (My favorite
dishes are all in *Rodale's Naturally
Great Foods Cookbook.*)
  Roger Yepsen, Book Editor

them at no cost to you, and we'll
cancel your membership. (The "Basics
of Self-Sufficiency" is yours to keep,
whatever you decide.)

But we're pretty sure you'll stay with us
when you see your first books. And once
you're a member, we'll continue to offer you
the newest and best books like these at prices
averaging 20% off bookstore prices.

We do ask that you take at least two books within
the first year; and, of course, if you wish, you may
always cancel membership after this two-book
commitment is fulfilled.

We think you'll find the books an amazing value though --

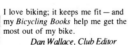

I love biking; it keeps me fit — and
my *Bicycling Books* help me get the
most out of my bike.
  Dan Wallace, Club Editor

Figure 8-4, *continued*

237

-- and jam-packed with the kind of useful information you've been looking for to help you keep growing and building -- and truly enhancing
the quality of your life.

We hope to hear from you soon!

Sincerely,

Dan Wallace
Club Director

Please join us!

Carol Stoner
Editorial Director

Bill Hylton
Managing Editor Book Division

**The Rodale
SELF-SUFFICIENCY BOOK CLUB**T.M. Reg.
P.O. Box 4514
1716 Locust Street
Des Moines, Iowa 50336

Take care,

Roger Yepsen
Book Editor

Let us know soon, won't you?

These are the *ORGANIC
GARDENING* gardens – our pride
and joy – and the source of the
valuable information that went
into *Best Ideas for Organic
Vegetable Growing*.

Terri Lepley
Book Division Artist

SS187

Figure 8-4, *continued*

The Condé Nast Publications Inc.
350 Madison Avenue
New York, NY 10017

David O'Brasky
Publisher, *Vanity Fair*

Mr. Sheldon Satin
1175 York Ave. 10j
New York, NY 10021

Dear Mr. Satin:

You may just be the solution.

Here is the problem: How do you find the right
subscribers for an extraordinary magazine -- BUT, a
magazine that isn't for everyone? A magazine that is,
in fact, for only a handful of bright, literate people
who still, in this world of instant communication, love
to sit down with a good book.

In an age where television and home video games
give easy access to simpleminded entertainment, where
canned music is supposed to soothe and uplift, and where
people wear their philosophy of life on the front of
their T-shirts or on the bumpers of their cars, we're
looking for people who still enjoy a beautifully written
work of literature. Still make the effort to go to the
theater and important films, live concerts, art and
photography exhibits. To whom 10 minutes of stimulating
conversation means more than 10 hours of game shows and
situation comedies. And who, while they watch
television, long for more quality in what they see.

If I am correct in my intuition, you are one of
these people.

Of course, my "intuition" comes from a very
specific source -- a list from which I got your name.
The list includes people who buy good books and
subscribe to important publications. Consequently, I
know that the quality of your reading is high. And that
suggests to me that you may well be interested in the
arts, politics, and popular culture. That you are

Continued

Courtesy of The Condé Nast Publications Inc.

Figure 8-5

239

intrigued by ideas, images, graphics, and photography. That you are excited by our life and times and would welcome a new magazine that speaks to your intelligence, education, and taste.

On the chance that I'm right, I'm writing to you with exciting news and an equally exciting offer.

In March of 1983, Condé Nast Publications launched a magazine that is in line with your tastes. _Vanity Fair_. This letter is your invitation to accept a complimentary issue and enroll as a subscriber at a saving of $16.03.

If the name _Vanity Fair_ means something to you, perhaps you are familiar with its legendary predecessor -- a publication of the 1920s and '30s which introduced the American public to an array of writers and artists whose names are household words today.

Writers such as Robert Benchley, Thomas Wolfe, e.e. cummings, Dorothy Parker, Noël Coward, Aldous Huxley, James Joyce, Edmund Wilson, Edna St. Vincent Millay, Walter Lippmann, W. Somerset Maugham. Artists such as Picasso, Gauguin, Monet, Renoir. Photographers such as Steichen and Beaton. Performers such as Yehudi Menuhin, Helen Hayes, Katharine Hepburn, Gary Cooper, and Cary Grant.

Today's _Vanity Fair_ can't be like the old one. We can no more bring back the original than we could bring back the '20s. _Vanity Fair_ was a mirror of its time. And times have changed.

But the _need_ has not changed. The need for a magazine that captures the sparkle and excitement of our culture. That provides a showcase for talents of our day. That critiques and celebrates our time with dash, allure, intelligence, and a sense of fun.

Vanity Fair is such a magazine.

For those who relish good reading, _Vanity Fair_ is a literary feast -- with exciting new works of fiction and nonfiction appearing in every issue. Pieces by Arthur Miller, Philip Roth, Susan Sontag, Dick Cavett, Italo Calvino, Paul Theroux, Joseph Brodsky, to name but a few. This is only the beginning of a parade of literary lights whose work you will find in future issues of _Vanity Fair_.

Continued

2.

Figure 8-5, *continued*

We bring you the excitement of reading -- before
book publication -- excerpts of new works such as Philip
Roth's brilliant novel The Anatomy Lesson, Luis Buñuel's
fascinating autobiography, My Last Sigh, and Dick
Cavett and Christopher Porterfield's Eye on Cavett.

We discuss popular new books and bring to light
literary discoveries from the past. Two recent coups:
Thomas Wolfe's unpublished last poem -- and four
unexpected stories by Colette, never before published in
English.

And each issue of Vanity Fair is a feast for the
eye -- presenting, in dazzling color portfolios, such
varied delights as the paintings of Susan Rothenberg and
Dali, classic masterpieces by Manet, and photographs by
Annie Leibovitz, Irving Penn, Snowdon, Helmut Newton, and
Man Ray.

The performing arts receive focused attention.
From Lucinda Childs's hypnotic choreography to Julia
Child's new 13-part television series. From opera's
Jessye Norman to jazzman David Murray. From Edward Duke's
uproarious Wodehouse monologue, Jeeves Takes Charge, to
Jeanne Moreau's splendid documentary on Lillian Gish.

We turn thumbs up/thumbs down each month on the
liveliest arts with reviews, previews, and overviews as
varied as Susan Sontag's critical study of Fassbinder's
15-hour film, Berlin Alexanderplatz, and our own succinct
critique of the movie Purple Haze: "It's more '60s
schlock. And hell no, we won't go."

We probe with political commentary and reporting --
inviting such top writers as Carlos Fuentes, Ronald
Steel, Simon Hoggart, and Paul Berman to explore
international trouble spots, to unravel the mysteries, to
bring some perspective to the complexities of our world.

We provoke thinking men and women with criticism
and reports on everything worth doing, seeing, knowing
about in theater, film, music, dance, television, books,
art.

You will not find a more handsome, readable magazine
in America today -- that I can assure you. Everything
about Vanity Fair is of the finest quality. Right down to
the magnificently designed format, the heavy paper stock,
the incomparable printing.

Continued

3.

Figure 8-5, *continued*

If you are intrigued by the magazine I've described to you, you owe it to yourself to at least sample an issue. Just tell me so by returning the enclosed RSVP form and I'll arrange to send you a copy.

The price of Vanity Fair is $3 on the newsstand (less than most quality paperbacks) or $36 for a year of 12 issues bought separately. But as a new subscriber, you pay only $19.97 -- a saving of $16.03.

But that's entirely up to you. After you've enjoyed the complimentary issue, you can pay the invoice we will send you, and get 11 more issues. Or you can simply write "cancel" across the face of the bill and the matter will be closed. You won't pay or owe anything at all.

Frankly, I will be very surprised if you are not delighted with your complimentary issue. But all you need do now is decide if you want to take a look at Vanity Fair without cost or obligation of any kind. To accomplish this, simply return the enclosed form in the postage-paid envelope provided.

Sincerely yours,

David O'Brasky
Publisher

Figure 8-5, *continued*

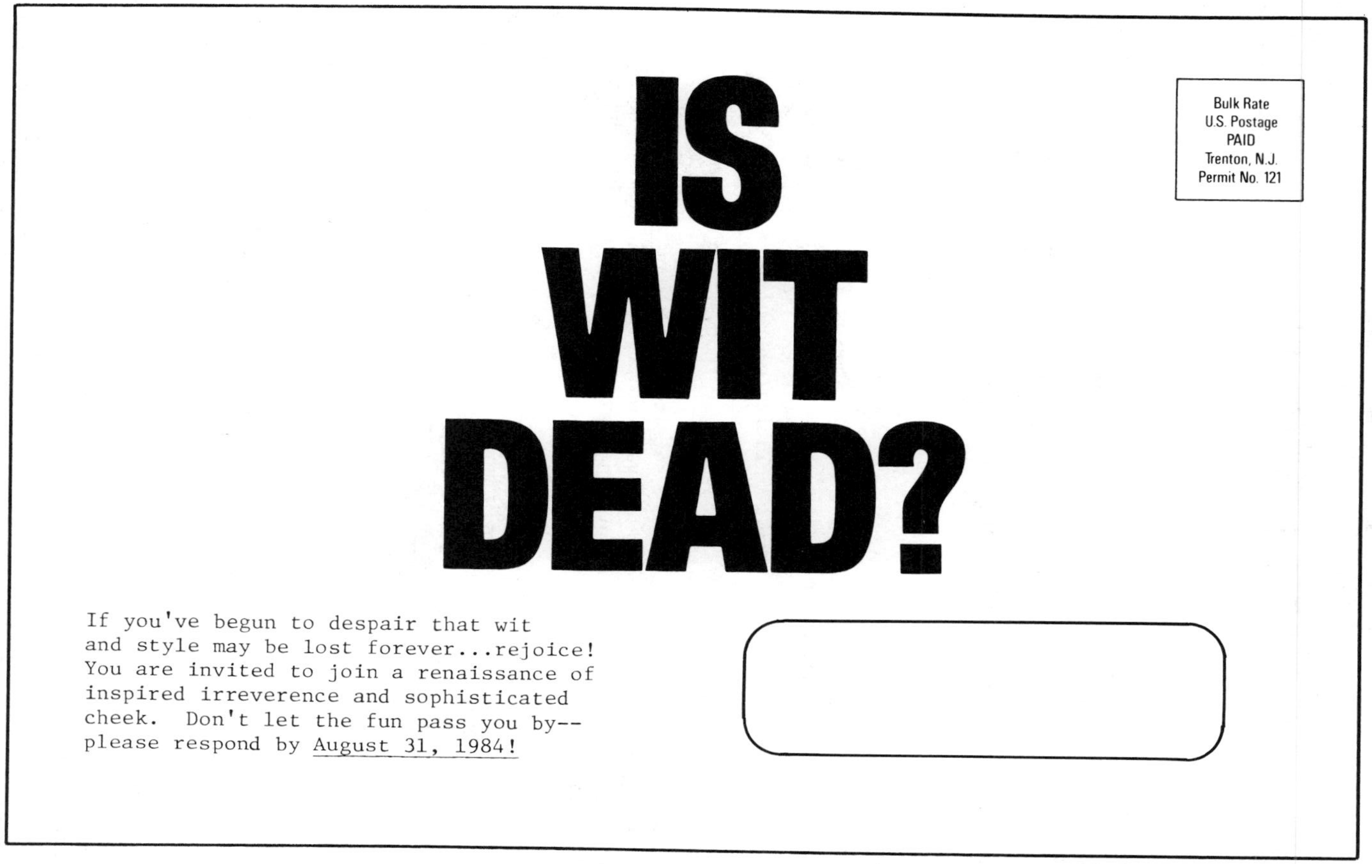

IS WIT DEAD?

Bulk Rate
U.S. Postage
PAID
Trenton, N.J.
Permit No. 121

If you've begun to despair that wit and style may be lost forever...rejoice! You are invited to join a renaissance of inspired irreverence and sophisticated cheek. Don't let the fun pass you by-- please respond by <u>August 31, 1984!</u>

Courtesy of The Condé Nast Publications Inc.

Figure 8-6

They say a good, wicked laugh is beneficial
to the spirit. . .and may even keep the
arteries free of cholesterol.

We heartily agree!

In fact, that's why our staff of literary
iconoclasts invites you to join the fun--
and become a part of publishing history!

Dear Friend:

I'm writing you today because I have reason to believe that you belong
to a perpetually endangered minority.

You see, it's been said that a relative handful of individuals in
every generation are born with a rare "inner ear" which unerringly picks
up the pretense, the sham, and the hypocrisy that surround them.

Such individuals are especially sensitive to the unintentional humor
and absurdity of conventions and behavior which the rest of society invari-
ably regards with deadly, unrelenting seriousness. Hence, their permanent
minority status!

> Now, I'm sure it comes as no surprise that the men
> and women of whom I speak are nearly always the
> brightest and wittiest of their generation. They tend,
> also, to possess the uncommon courage to explore the
> bold, the new, and even the controversial in the arts,
> politics, and culture.

As I said, I have every reason to believe you fit the profile I've
just described. If I'm correct, I have excellent news for you. . . and a
remarkable invitation to be a part of publishing history. . .

> With this letter, you are invited to participate in
> the renaissance of an American literary tradition.
> The enclosed card entitles you to subscribe to the
> new VANITY FAIR at our attractive half-price rate.
> You will enjoy substantial savings amounting to $12!

But why have we chosen NOW to launch such a historic and legendary
publication as VANITY FAIR?

Very briefly, we believe that the times demand a voice that speaks for
wit, for style, for intelligence. Many years ago, a similar, equally criti-

(over please)

Figure 8-6, *continued*

cal need existed. . . and it was answered by an unprecedented publication that went on to shape the tastes, the perceptions, and the attitudes of an entire generation of thoughtful, literate Americans. . .

In the America of our grandparents' youth, a band of singularly gifted men and women cast their delightfully jaundiced eyes on the personalities and goings-on around them--an amazing scenario that included Calvin Coolidge, Prohibition, Teapot Dome, Krazy Kat, Sacco and Vanzetti, bathtub gin, Theodore Bilbo, Warren Harding, Al Capone, Father Charles Coughlin, Polly Adler, Babbitt, and a nationally acclaimed, best-selling novel which portrayed Jesus Christ as the greatest salesman in all of history.

Needless to say, this circle of intelligent critics found much to amuse them--and much that genuinely outraged them.

And so, armed only with their talent, their taste, and, most important, their wit, they punctured the pomposity and pretentiousness that surrounded them and, in the process, defined forever the tone, the spirit, and the folly of their generation.

And they did it all in the pages of VANITY FAIR.

Looking back at the "old" VANITY FAIR and the extraordinary individuals who made it a publishing legend, one can be forgiven for wishfully thinking, Where are they now that we need them?

Indeed, one can only speculate on how a Dorothy Parker would demolish the modern-day phenomenon of slickly packaged "literature" sold by the carton at supermarket checkout counters. . .how a Robert Benchley would deal with pre-recorded messages that urge one to "have a nice day!". . . how a Walter Lippmann would skewer the likes of a Jerry Falwell or an Edwin Meese III.

Sadly, we cannot bring back the VANITY FAIR of yesterday. But we've done the next best thing. Condé Nast Publications has gathered the brightest, the wittiest, the most keen-eyed observers of our time and given them this challenge: Capture the mind and soul of America in the Eighties as no other publication today does.

VANITY FAIR brings you a revealing mirror of our times. It catches the sparkle, the excitement, and--yes--the lunacy of our day with style, wit, and a sense of fun!

It has been truly said that to discover where a nation and its people are headed, you must look to those who shape its popular culture. And that, in a nutshell, is why the new VANITY FAIR is so much more than just a review of contemporary art and literature.

You see, at VANITY FAIR we're fascinated by the growing interaction-- the almost symbiotic relationship--between modern-day culture and important social issues. Indeed, a whole generation of artists, writers, photographers, poets, and filmmakers is not only addressing the critical events of our era--they are shaping them to an astonishing degree!

Figure 8-6, *continued*

And so, every month, VANITY FAIR takes you on a fascinating tour of the American cultural scene. . .

You'll sample the most stimulating new works of fiction and nonfiction. You'll see the work of artists and photographers who are breaking new ground in their respective fields. You'll focus on what's new and exciting in the performing arts--theater, dance, opera, jazz, even the big blue tube itself, television.

Through the eyes of some of the most perceptive minds of today--Arthur Miller, Philip Roth, James Wolcott, Joan Didion, Norman Mailer, Susan Sontag, Judith Martin, Anthony Burgess, Garry Wills, to name only a few-- you'll be able to see the frenetic energy of our whole generation.

We might also add that, in an age of X-rated video games, televised church services, drive-in croissant stands, nuclear missiles dubbed "peace-keepers," execution by lethal injection, and (perhaps most alarming of all) professional football in June, VANITY FAIR can make a substantial contribution to your mental health and well-being.

Or, to put it another way, VANITY FAIR, with its biting commentary and scathing satire, will help you discern the method in this age's apparent madness--as well as the madness in its apparent method.

> Reports of the death of wit are certainly premature. The proof is alive--and wickedly thriving--in the pages of VANITY FAIR!

Alice Roosevelt Longworth once remarked, "If you don't have anything nice to say about anyone, come sit beside me." We like to think that Mrs. Longworth, if she were with us today, would celebrate the return of VANITY FAIR.

Please don't misunderstand us. We're the first to applaud genuine talent and quality. And you'll find plenty of both in our pages.

Ah, but we must admit a helpless attraction to those superbly inspired examples of hype, sensationalism, and bad taste that transcend mere trash and tawdriness. Indeed, such phenomena spur us to produce much of our finest and most socially significant work, as you'll discover for yourself in articles such as these:

> TRULY BADLY WRITTEN SEX (Sex scenes you'll be glad you didn't write--much less live through)

> MICHAEL JACKSON'S GLOVE (Does it keep him warm--or hide a hideous skin affliction?)

> BLONDE AMBITION (Our intrepid Hollywood reporter checks out the bland and the beautiful)

> THE NEW VOICE OF "COOL" (If lizards could talk, they'd sound just like this)

Yes, there's a lot of good, wicked fun in VANITY FAIR--but there's

Figure 8-6, *continued*

a wealth of beauty too. In fact, each issue is a veritable portfolio of visual delights--the paintings of Susan Rothenberg and Salvador Dali, classic masterpieces by Edouard Manet and Thomas Gainsborough, the stunning photography of Annie Leibovitz, Irving Penn and Helmut Newton. We know many collectors who have kept their copies of VANITY FAIR dating from the Twenties and Thirties. We suspect that, after seeing your first few issues of the new VANITY FAIR, you'll be tempted to do the same.

The enclosed card is all you need. Just detach it along the perforation, then mail it in the postpaid envelope provided. The new VANITY FAIR will be sent to you at our attractive half-price rate of only $12.00. That's a saving of <u>$12 OFF</u> the price you'd pay for 12 monthly issues at the single-copy price.

I believe you will quickly see that there is no other American publication remotely like VANITY FAIR--that it is that rarity of rarities, a true <u>classic</u> in every sense of the word.

Of course, it is entirely possible that you may disagree.
In that case, simply cancel your subscription and I'll
see to it that you receive a prompt, full refund on all
unmailed copies.

Come join our renaissance of wit, style, and taste. Try the new VANITY FAIR by returning the enclosed card to me. Thank you!

Cordially,

David O'Brasky
Publisher

P.S. No need to send your payment now. We'll bill you later. To ensure that you receive your first issue without delay, just detach the card along the perforation and mail by <u>August 31, 1984</u>. Postage is on us!

VANITY FAIR
A Condé Nast Publication
350 Madison Avenue/New York, NY 10017

FW

Figure 8-6, *continued*

247

The year, 1930. The place, Berlin. You are a practicing psychoanalyst confronting an interesting new patient. His name is Adolph Hitler. He is a professional politician regarded as one of the country's rising young men. Now he has come to you because (continued inside)

(continued from outer envelope)

he is troubled by persistent anxieties. He speaks confidently about his plans for Germany, yet he admits to fear of failure and therefore punishment by "lesser" beings. Lately, however, when he considers some of the harsh deeds demanded by his grandiose plans, he has been bothered by feelings of guilt. Nevertheless, he is convinced that the ends justify the means. He is bothered only because his increasing anxieties and guilt feelings may impede him in the execution of his designs. Hitler asks you to put an end to these disturbing feelings. Can you help him?

from Psychology Today's
"Morality in Psychotherapy"
by Marvin Frankel

Dear Reader:

  You don't have to be a professional to be interested in --
even fascinated by -- this hypothetical problem. Not a professional
doctor, psychologist or minister. All it takes is a normal amount
of curiosity and interest in how and why people act as they do.

  Because I believe that description embraces you, you see here
an invitation and a tempting offer. It is to . . .

    become a subscriber to the magazine that bridges
    the gap between laboratory and living room . . .
      PSYCHOLOGY TODAY

  The benefits of subscribing are more rewarding than they are
tangible . . . but nonetheless real.

  Psychology Today is not abstract, disconnected, academic theory,
but, rather, an assessment of fascinating, logical, senseless, con-

A PUBLICATION OF THE AMERICAN PSYCHOLOGICAL ASSOCIATION

Figure 8-7

deserved as it harks back to Ed McLean's famous identification line "If the list upon which I found your name is any indication..."

Not content with one winner, however, *Vanity Fair* set out to develop a control-beater to follow in the footsteps of this approach with Figure 8-6.

Both mailings carried colorful brochures, but this mailing by free-lancer Ken Scheck (another of our finest), added a lift letter and an extraordinarily dramatic outer envelope that "enticed" with the Question Approach. It was done in stark black and white on 6″ × 9″ outer.

Notice that Ken Scheck's approach after the question on the outer moves right into *another* Identification Approach, flattering, creating agreement ("yes, that's me!") all through the first page of the letter. Notice, too, his use of the lift letter to bring in a second voice. Nice job.

Without perusing more than the materials reproduced here, can you guess what enabled the second package to win out over the first? Was it the outer? The letter? The lift? All of this? None of this?

I'm not going to tell you the answer—because I don't know. But I do know that the exercise is a good one, as it encourages you to be analytical as you appreciate. Say, for example, you were asked to do a package to beat *Vanity Fair's* current control. Make a list of all the things you'd include and the elements you'd avoid. See what you can learn from these fine letters.

If you weren't convinced by now, Figure 8-7, an example of quality letter writing should leave no question in your mind as to the value of a compelling outer envelope. This is a relatively recent mailing but the original was done over a decade ago. The letter is attributed to a fine free-lance professional, Jack Walsh. Hank Burnett, however, moved a copy block from the letter to the outer envelope.

In that form, the mailing became a control for *Psychology Today* some fifteen years ago. The magazine has changed owners several times since and recently this old (very old) control was resurrected.

The letter combines the Story and Identification Approaches with a top-notch involvement device that starts on the outer and continues to the first page of the letter.

How are you doing? Want to stop and stretch a minute? Wash your hands? If so, this is a good time to do it. If not, back to the show! And what better star to start you off on the last leg than *Interview*, a magazine with real celebrity glitter! (Figure 8-8.) This direct mail winner was written by Bill Jayme and designed by Heikki Ratalahti.

Strong grahics on the outer envelope catch your attention, and the copy draws you in with the question, "When they seat you next to Bette Midler should you pretend she's not there or what?" The main letter uses a modified Johnson Box and the Question Approach tempered by the If/Assumptive *and* a strong dose of Fantasy.

Check out the verbal austerity. Although the letter is rife with action words, it's lean pickings for the flowery phrases or strings of juicy adjectives. This is

Figure 8-8

We've been damned by *Mother Jones*, plugged by Liz Smith and Suzy, insulted by *Esquire*, syndicated by *The New York Times*, parodied by the *Village Voice*, quoted by the *London Daily Mirror*, spoofed by the *National Lampoon*, praised by *House & Garden*, and given the eye by *Forbes*. You're invited to find out what all the excitement is about by sending for our next issue

Free.

Dear Reader:

When you find yourself seated at dinner next to someone unusual like Bette Midler, you've got two choices.

You can ask what her brother Danny is up to, why she worships Bobby Darin, whether they really paid her in gold for her recent round-the-world tour, why she thinks that Paloma Picasso should design clothes, where her favorite hot dog stand is in L.A., and how she feels about Barbra Streisand.

Or...you can say, "Excuse me. Could you please pass the salt?"

If you have an open and honest curiosity about men and women who are larger than life—creators, achievers, dreamers...If you get a kick out of good conversation—the little-known fact, the amusing anecdote, the detail that reveals and illuminates...

If you thrive on keeping up with what's being designed, filmed, written, composed, sculpted, choreographed, painted, modeled, raced, erected, bought, collected, revived, applauded, thought, said and whispered these days...

...then welcome to INTERVIEW, the magazine where people tell all. The magazine about success. And the magazine that can show you too the ropes by revealing how others have done it.

This letter invites you to get to know INTERVIEW, if you don't already, by sending for our next issue free. If you find it fun, relevant, helpful, you can then continue your subscription and save a full $8. More about this in a minute.

In international creative circles, INTERVIEW is probably the most talked-about new magazine of the past decade. It was invented by Andy Warhol. It comes to you each month tabloid big, printed like a newspaper. And as you might guess from the name, it's filled with interviews with people. But what interviews! What people!

No other magazine so nakedly reveals what today's newsmakers are really like. Our method? We just let them talk. And no magazine gives you more intimate insights into what makes the creative world tick. Fashion. Communications. Entertainment. The arts. Advertising. Retailing. Sport.

INTERVIEW gives you the inside story on everyone you've ever wanted to know. What's their background? What are they like? Who put up the money? How much is truth, and how much is hype? How long before the bubble bursts? What happens then? Where are they investing it? How do they live? What did they have to do to get there?

INTERVIEW shows you how others have done it. Horatio Alger, move over. Our magazine chronicles a new success story on virtually every page. And by osmosis, you too learn the ropes. The preparation you need. The contacts. The breaks. The places where it's now happening. Who can help. Who might stand in the way. How the system works.

(over, please)

Figure 8-8, *continued*

INTERVIEW makes soaking in the tub more profitable. Unplug the phones. Turn on both taps. Make a pillow out of your towel. Then climb in, magazine in hand. For the next hour or two, you're alone with your fantasies. With your ambitions. With your dreams.

That new rock star—should you get tickets? That new playwright—should you invest? That new author—should you put him on your list? That new designer, artist, architect, photographer, athlete, diplomat, collector, entrepreneur, millionaire—is there some way you might do a little business?

Supermarket and subway newsstands don't carry INTERVIEW—too sophisticated, too little volume. Where and when you do find a copy, the magazine is $2 an issue, or $24 a year. But when you send in the enclosed card promptly, you'll get our next issue free. No cost. No obligation. No strings.

Send no money. If it's not for you, just mail back the subscription bill within two weeks marked "cancel," and that's that. You've spent nothing. You owe nothing. The first issue is yours to keep free.

Save $8. But if you love INTERVIEW, your price for a full year's subscription of all eleven additional issues is only $16. Not the $24 others pay. Your price is just $16. You save a full $8.

Early postmark. INTERVIEW chases news right up to deadline, then prints only as many copies as are needed—no overruns. First come, first served. Avoid disappointment by mailing the card back quickly so as to get the earliest possible postmark. Thank you!

Cordially yours,

Lucy Lustig-Curtis

Lucy Lustig-Curtis
Circulation Director

Interview®

19 East 32nd Street New York, N.Y. 10016

Figure 8-8, *continued*

spare action writing for the video generation—the generation raised on television, the upwardly mobile young set—a group that doesn't slow down for anyone. Serve it up, then move out.

The brochure (which is not included here) is a stunner done in a format that replicates the interview Q & A technique. The package won a Gold Award in the 1984 *Folio* magazine Circulation Direct Mail Awards Competition.

Let's move from consumer show business to show business at the office with a five-part BOAC Cargo mailing done by the Yeck Brothers Group in Dayton, Ohio. (Figure 8-9.) It's Generic in approach, but it's a lot more, too. Starring Dave Schneider, the Cargo Manager of BOAC, U.S.A., this group of five letters illustrates the use of humor with hard-hitting competitive copy from a highly credible (and photogenic) source, to create a strong, favorable image. The BOAC service story is made more credible because the manager is willing to put his name and reputation on the line (and to discuss past problems candidly). The letters are short, to the point and designed to influence busy doers, not readers. (You might almost compare them to print ads.)

Did you spot the rule breaker in the BOAC series? O.K., what was it? If you said "salutation," or lack of one, you're awake and thinking. The Yeck Brothers Group business mailings frequently replace the salutation with a highly involving copy lead. It breaks a big rule, but you can rest assured they know what they're doing (and can back it up with test results). Note also the close that pulls you right into the signature, and the telephone number. A logical and appropriate response device for business mailings. (These letters were so successful, by the way, that Dave Schneider got a well-deserved promotion!)

This last letter (Figure 8-10) is a membership acknowledgement mailing or "Welcome" mailing to new Quality Paperback Book Club members. Like the BOAC business image builders, this requires no customer response but serves largely to acquaint the new member with club procedures and help develop customer rapport.

The letter accomplishes this deftly while reselling the club itself. It also dispatches several housekeeping chores without creating a negative or restrictive image. The copy flows smoothly and logically. It is, quite frankly, one of the best welcome letters I've ever read.

Well, that's the show for now. No more talk about letter writing and direct mail in the Chapters that follow.

But please don't forget these great examples by Bill Jayme, Hank Burnett, Ed McLean, and Ken Scheck—and the others that preceded them, in Chapter 6 (the Frank Johnson letters, the Jim Punkre, Gene Schwartz, Linda Wells, Bob Jones, and Max Habernickel examples). Go back to them all when you need inspiration or challenge. Reread them. Enjoy them. Understand what makes them good.

And if, by chance, you say to yourself "Anyone can write like this..." then take Frank Johnson's sandhill crane letter for *The Nature Conservancy* and rewrite it. A humbling exercise, I guarantee you.

IF ANYONE CAN GET YOUR CARGO THROUGH

LONDON QUICKER THAN I CAN, I'LL BUY YOU

THE BEST STEAK DINNER IN TOWN

Let's be very clear about why I'm writing. First because I

believe you may be concerned about BOAC's ability to get your

245 Park Avenue • New York, N. Y. 10017

Figure 8-9 A

cargo through London quickly and right.

And I know exactly why.

In an effort to make our London Terminal the best in the world, we've had some problems. Not monumental ... but problems none the less.

Today those problems are over.

As BOAC's Cargo Manager, U.S.A., I'll match our facilities in London and our computerized customs clearance against any airline that you do business with.

We'll either match or beat them.

Fact is, I'm so confident of this ability that if you try us, and it doesn't work out exactly as I promise, I'll arrange to come to your office personally and buy you the best steak dinner in town.

All you have to do is write or call me, and give me the facts.

A big promise? Maybe. But with so much behind me, I don't plan

to lose.

DS/ybc

Dave Schneider

Cargo Manager, USA

(212)-983-3657

Figure 8-9 A, *continued*

245 Park Avenue • New York, N. Y. 10017

February, 1973

GIVE YOUR NEXT SHIPMENT
ANYWHERE A LITTLE BOOST
OF "SCHNEIDER POWER."

Here at BOAC, we have a secret advantage that other air-
lines can't offer you...at least when it comes to shipping
cargo.

You've guessed it. We call it "Schneider Power."

Where does it come from?

Well, frankly, "Schneider Power" comes from me...and the
responsibility I've been given to see that you (and every

Figure 8-9 B

agent and consolidator) get the best service possible in
sending cargo to any major spot in the world.

This includes service on the ground, of course, as well
as in the air...quick attention to every question you ask
and every problem you encounter...747 capacity wherever
possible, compatible container service...everything that
can make your job easier and more profitable.

Fact is, if you call BOAC and don't get exactly what
you're looking for every time you need it, I hope you'll
call me and let me go to work on it.

You'll find a little "Schneider Power" can take you...
clear across the world

and back,

Dave Schneider
Cargo Manager, U.S.A.
212/983-3657

DS/ybc

Figure 8-9 B, *continued*

BOAC
British Airways
CARGO 245 Park Avenue • New York, N.Y. 10017

July, 1973

THIS IS MY FRIEND, JERRY HILL.
HE'LL FLY YOUR CARGO TO SINGAPORE,
HONG KONG AND TOKYO ABOUT
ANY TIME YOU SAY.

It's only natural, I suppose, when you think of BOAC to think
of London and Manchester and Prestwick as most of our cargo
world.

But the truth is BOAC flies regularly scheduled flights to
every major spot in the world -- 25 times a week to the Orient,
22 times a week to the Middle East. With full capacity and
every possible service to assure your cargo arrives intact,
on time, in places like Singapore, Hong Kong, Tokyo, Bahrain
and Teheran (to name a few).

Figure 8-9 C

Besides this, as you may know, we have daily flights to Johannesburg, six flights a week to Sydney and Darwin, as well as a regular schedule of flights to Melbourne.

And nearly all have 747 capacity.

I'm sure you know what I'm driving at. I believe that BOAC offers you everything you want from an airline every time you ship cargo. Full capacity. Regular flights. Compatible containers that let your cargo arrive in the same containers they leave in. Fast, sure service on the ground. And people who <u>care</u> that everything goes smoothly and right.

Do yourself a real favor.

Next time you have a shipment headed for any place in the world, take a minute to call us first and get the facts in full detail. I guarantee we'll answer your questions promptly, give you every possible attention, and meet or beat any other airline you've ever done business with.

As a matter of fact, if it doesn't work out that way, I suggest you call me at 212/983-3657 and I'll move the world to make it right.

Sincerely,

Dave Schneider
Cargo Manager, U.S.A.

DS/ybc

Figure 8-9 C, *continued*

259

245 Park Avenue • New York, N.Y. 10017

April, 1973

WHEN IT COMES TO SHIPPING CARGO,
I'LL MATCH THIS NAME
AGAINST ANY AIRLINE
IN THE WORLD.

It's me again. Dave Schneider.

For a few months now, I've been writing to you about BOAC
and a little of the spirit behind our name. Our hope, as
I'm sure you've gathered, is to offer you more service,
more attention and more understanding than any other airline you can do business with.

What do I mean by service?

Well, to begin with, I mean such things as compatible containers that let your cargo <u>arrive</u> in the same containers

Figure 8-9 D

they _leave_ in ... 747 capacity to nearly every major spot in the world, and frequent long-haul flights to such destinations as South Africa and Australia.

Fact is, we have daily flights to Johannesburg and six times each week to Sydney and Darwin (not to mention a regular schedule of flights to Melbourne) ... so any day is a good day to call us.

Attention and understanding?

Let me say first that everyone here and in every BOAC office is dedicated to seeing that you call BOAC _first_ when you have cargo to ship. This means that every one of us will do everything possible to meet everything you ask of us ... including me.

My phone number is 212/983-3657, and my door is always open.

In other words, I'll match BOAC and our "Dave Schneider" family against any airline in the world for shipping cargo ... benefit for benefit, flight for flight, and dollar for dollar.

Call us and see,

Dave Schneider
Cargo Manager, U.S.A.

DS/ybc

Figure 8-9 D, _continued_

May, 1973

THERE'S A LITTLE
DAVE SCHNEIDER IN
EVERY CONTAINER THAT
LEAVES OUR TERMINALS.

I hope you've gathered by now that BOAC looks at cargo
shipments a little differently than most people do.

As a matter of fact, we think it's a great deal <u>more</u>
than simply offering frequent flights to hard-to-reach
places like Dubai and Bahrain, and big capacity, and
even such important advantages as our compatible containers.

We believe that superior service lies in offering you
the help, spirit and enthusiasm of people who are just

Figure 8-9 E

262

as "hard to please" as you are ... who try as hard, who expect as much.

In other words, we want to show you that no one can do a better job for you than BOAC ... on the ground or in the air.

And we take it sort of personally.

That's why I say there's a little Dave Schneider in every container that leaves our terminals ... a little Arnold Zinn, a little Frank Puleio, a little John Catcher, a little of everyone at BOAC who want you to keep coming back.

Do this: next time you have a shipment that's headed for anyplace in the world, take the time to put it in the hands of people who know the difference that people can make.

In fact, anyone at BOAC, where ...

                                        a little means a lot,

                                        Dave Schneider
                                        Cargo Manager, U.S.A.

DS/ybc

Figure 8-9 E, *continued*

Quality Paperback
Book Club, Inc.
Middletown, Pennsylvania 17057

Dear QPB Member:

Some club you've joined. No dues, no swimming pool, no secret
handshake and no obligation to buy anything.

Since we're so different (most other book clubs require new
members to buy three or four books), we thought we should not
only welcome you but describe how the Club operates.

The main thing we have to offer you is our harvest of the best
softcover books published in this country. We screen and read
about 50 books for every one we offer. Not only are these
titles, in our opinion, the best books available, they are also
in many cases unique editions -- manufactured exclusively for
QPB and not sold anywhere else.

> And all our editions are manufactured with high
> quality paper and bindings. After all, just
> because books are made from trees is no excuse
> for their leaves to turn yellow and fall to the
> ground.

Some people are amused that we call ourselves a "club" at all.
It sounds a little too cozy for our operational center in
Pennsylvania, where we make sure that your books are shipped
properly, that you are billed correctly and that any complaints
are noted and answered -- all with the aid of our friendly
computer and other clever little machines.

But computers don't read books; people do. And because we
share the same devotion to books that our members do, we have
a very personal sense of responsibility to our members. We've
invested a great deal of time, talent and money in the assumption that if the Club works for you, it's going to work for a
lot of other people too.

QPB 300:02   (OVER)

Please include your account number in any communication to us.

Figure 8-10

The proof of our efforts will rest with our success or failure with <u>you</u>. And we know we can only count on your loyalty as long as you're getting real values and straight talk from us.

What can you do to help us? Two suggestions. The first concerns invoices and the payment thereof. We expect our members to pay their bills with reasonable promptness because every unpaid invoice, every bad debt hurts -- not just us but authors, publishers and that very small community in America that constitutes what we optimistically refer to as "the reading public."

Secondly, the biggest favor we could ask of you is this: if you are happy with QPB, please tell your friends about the books we offer and the service we provide. In our business "word-of-mouth" is the only form of advertising that really counts. So spread the word...not only for our sake but also for the sake of the books and their authors.

One last thought. It's my immodest belief that this is the book club of tomorrow. It has to be. The prices of hardcover books are going right through the ceiling, and there's no end in sight. Quality softcovers -- not mass-market paperbacks that immediately self-destruct, but reasonable priced, durable, permanent, large-format softcovers -- are clearly the wave of the future. We're riding that wave and so are you.

Quality Paperback Book Club occasionally makes the names of its current and past subscribers available to other mail order companies on a very selective basis. These companies are carefully screened for the value and quality of their products. We feel the decision on whether to receive these offers should be yours. If you do not wish to receive other offers in the mail, please notify us.

Again, welcome to our Club and write to us whenever you feel like it.

                              Sincerely yours,

                              Lorraine Shanley

                              Lorraine Shanley
                              Director

Figure 8-10, *continued*

There is one thing all these fine writers and others like them share. We talked about it briefly in Chapter 7 when I brought up the intrinsic rewards of writing and all the hard work that goes into it. Good writers actually enjoy writing; they love words and word crafting, despite the hard work. Furthermore, when it comes to polishing and improving, most professional writers quite literally never finish. They can't help themselves. Right up to the last second of the final deadline they'll be working away, putting finishing touches on "the baby" —not because the copy's late or unfinished, but simply because the writer, never quite satisfied, feels compelled to make just one more tiny change or alteration—much like the great chef finishing a piece de résistance, the composer as the final chord is written, the painter as the canvas is finished.

Poor or mediocre writers will not understand this; they will be easily satisfied with far less, handing in their work while the professional writer continues to struggle, reword and rewrite.

THE JOY FACTOR DIFFERENCE

Several years ago when I had my own agency, my copy supervisor was reporting to me on the progress of a junior writer. The supervisor was a very sensitive writer with great talent, and she was troubled by the junior writer's attitude. She said, "He takes no joy in his writing. He never feels compelled to polish or rework for the sake of his craft. For him, it's just pure punishment."

I've always remembered her comment because for me this Joy Factor so clearly distinguishes between the true creative professional and the hack. Those who work quickly and resist reworking their copy and perfecting their art are almost always lacking in the Joy Factor. They'll never be good direct response advertising creators. They can't take the hard work, because writing gives them no satisfaction, no pleasure.

So look for the Joy Factor in yourself, and in those creative people who work for you and with you. Without the Joy Factor, fame, recognition, and wealth are unattainable. Where the Joy Factor exists, *you have a writer!* And that in itself is a big reward.

How to Create Winning Print Ads (A Space Program for You)

O.K., the party's over. Back to business.

Up to now we've given short shrift to all forms of direct response advertising except direct mail. Now it's time for you to move out—into space! Before we blast off, however, if you haven't been there before, you'll want a little briefing on some of the technicalities and terms of space, or print, as it's most commonly called. We'll start with a basic question: "How is print advertising used in direct marketing?"

In business-to-business direct response print is used primarily to generate inquiries (for more information or a sales call) and to acquire prospect names. In consumer direct response it's used (1) to generate inquiries on large ticket products and services, (2) to make a sale, to get a "member" or subscriber, (3) to acquire names of qualified prospects (catalog requests), and (4) to test a new product or service.

Print is used much like direct mail, except for the name gathering. Direct mail is too costly for this activity. (Print is often positioned as "cheaper than direct mail with better quality prospects than broadcast." Since broadcast prospects are at the bottom of the quality scale, you can see where print takes you.)

How about all those *800* ads for reservations or the ads with redeemable coupons? Frankly, *any* print ad that asks for a response (be it inquiry or order) can be called "response advertising." It only becomes *direct* response and/or *direct marketing* when the prospect or customer record, a name and address, is captured by the company computer for tracking, evaluation, and cultivation.

What constitutes a print ad? (As if you didn't know. But can you name three or four different *types* of direct response print ads?) Try this.

1. Large space (one page—or a spread even—in a magazine) with coupon
2. Small space (half or third of a magazine page, one column or less) with coupon

3. One page or a spread with bind-in reply card (for easy response)

4. *800* ad (large or small space with only an *800* toll-free response device)

5. One-page insert (a preprinted page bound into a publication)

6. Two- or three- or four-page magazine bind-in with perforated reply card (or an entire catalog bound into the magazine!)

7. Advertising supplement, preprinted newspaper insert or freestanding insert

8. Even a full spread with coupon and *800* toll-free option with tipped-on plastic card!

Rules of thumb:

– Best quality response usually comes from the good old-fashioned coupon ad, because it takes some effort (just fill out below, clip, then address an envelope, get a stamp, etc.).

– A bind-in or perforated reply card offers slightly less qualified respondents (no stamp, no cut out, no envelope to address).

– An *800* number respondent is also less qualified than the coupon clipper (easy, easy).

– The use of a separate bind-in card in a magazine should *more than double* response (it generally doubles cost).

– The price *and value* of magazine inserts is all over the lot and hard to evaluate (best to start your testing in simple one-page ads before expanding to these).

DEFINING THE BOUNDS OF "SPACE"

If you're sensitive to direct response ads, you may feel that they run everywhere, all the time in all sorts of media. The fact is, certain media have better reputations for bringing in good customers—or for just bringing in customers—than others.

As with direct mail (all direct response, for that matter), direct marketers put a lot of emphasis on the "quality" of the respondent or the *backend* performance. (How well does the prospect or customer *perform* over the months ahead? Does the prospect purchase? What? How often? Does the customer pay his or her bills? Or is this just a looker or a freeloader?) That's how you learn that some print and some print formats perform better than others—quantity *and* quality response. Good media people work hard to recognize and track this.

They also work to match your customer profile to the right publication in business and consumer print advertising, just as you do with lists in direct mail.

Basically, although the consumer market covers women's publications, men's publications, youth publications, dual-audience or general publications, and special-interest publications, some publications in each of these groups have a natural affinity for mail order and direct response; others don't. Just to give you an idea, here are a few of the more popular ones right now (but remember, things are always changing):

TV Guide
Parade (newspaper supplement)
The National Enquirer (tabloid)
Good Housekeeping
GQ
Cosmopolitan
Self
Esquire
Redbook
Vogue
Woman's Day
Smithsonian

While the special-interest magazines enable you to reach defined markets that share one specific interest (fitness, hunting, tennis, fast cars), most mass magazines are now segmented to allow advertisers to reach special groups of subscribers within their circulation, like educators or doctors or students or blue-chip business executives.

In business there are such general publications as the *Wall Street Journal*, *Business Week*, *Forbes*, and *Fortune*, plus specific trade or special-interest publications for just about every industry or field of endeavor.

SPACE AS A TEST MEDIUM

Aside from a variety of formats, most print also offers cost-effective opportunities for testing.

1. New product or concept testing has long been carried out in *small space* by some astute practitioners. One mail order professional tested every potential new product in small space first (one column by only a few inches), using newspapers like the *Christian Science Monitor* or the *Wall Street Journal* or national tabloids like the *Star* or the *Enquirer*. If response hit certain levels in this space, he could reliably project he had a winner that would pull significantly in large print ads in magazines and newspapers across the country.

2. A/B split testing means simply that the magazine publisher allows advertisers (for a premium) to alternate two different ads—one in every other copy of a particular issue. It literally "splits" the magazine run

equally so that every other copy carries ad B, while the remaining copies carry ad A. This is big testing and particularly good for major creative and offer tests.

3. In regional testing, many publications with broad national readership offer advertisers "regional editions." Although this is an expensive media purchase (because of the costs of segmentation), regionals give excellent opportunities to test more than one creative concept or aspect of a direct response ad in the same medium. Most important, they allow you broad hypothesis testing (more about this in a few pages).

WHY USE SPACE AT ALL WHEN YOU HAVE DIRECT MAIL?

Good question. And, as with so many questions, the answer is largely based on economics. Print makes sense

- when you're starting out with a new product or service and have a market that is not clearly targeted. (For example, with minimum investment, you want to know how your product or service will appeal to business executives as a whole. You need a show of hands to determine if you have a market, where you have a market, what your market's potential is.)
- when you have a market that isn't reachable by direct mail lists. (You want a specific level of executive but no lists offer you a clean break-out with names, titles, and addresses.)
- when you want to generate as many inquiries as possible, efficiently *and* inexpensively.
- when you've used all productive direct mail lists and you need ideas for new lists—more prospect names—names you can get at a reasonable CPM (cost per thousand, remember?). So you scout around in print.

There is an important interrelation between some print and some lists (I touched on this in Chapter 2, on research). Lists that work (mail order buyer lists and publication subscriber lists) can indicate publications that will work. (If *Business Week's* lists work for you, *Business Week* should work for your ad—and *maybe* even the *Wall Street Journal* or *Forbes* or *Fortune* will, too.)

If you know the product or publication's source of customers (to whom did it mail *its* solicitations?) this can offer you even more print and list opportunities. For example: If *X* product's customer lists work well for your direct mail promotions, and they advertise for customers in *Y* magazine, *Y* magazine may work for you, too. So may similar magazines.

You may (I hope) be shaking your head at this point, saying that I haven't answered the question fully. Good for you. You're right. How do you know which to use—direct mail or space? "Economics," I repeat. After all, what's the difference between testing 5,000 and 10,000 names from a subscriber list, or running an ad in the subscriber magazine? Economics. Sounds like my record's stuck. Right? Wrong. The answer is different for every product or service. Only testing gives you the *economics* (read "answer") for your product or service. For example:

- Some prospects may respond better to print or space advertising than to direct mail (and vice versa).
- Some products and services require the expansive formats of direct mail.
- Some products want the privacy of direct mail—others want the publicity of space (and its secondary rub-off benefits, like broader product recognition, corporate image building).
- Some space ads produce a poorer quality prospect than does direct mail.
- Some lists or groups of lists are too expensive (read inefficient) for your product, so you substitute space in publications whose market demograhics are the same as or similar to the lists.

Clearer? If your R.Q. is still high, read Chapters 3 and 4 in Bob Stone's *Successful Direct Marketing Methods* or Chapter 6 in Ed Nash's *Direct Marketing/Strategy, Planning, Execution.*

Ultimately, space is the best way to find out. It is not only an inexpensive way to uncover new prospects (and new list opportunities) it is also a good creative test medium. Use it to test which hypothesis is best in your creative strategy—which approach, which graphics. (I'll show you how to do this in a minute.) Enough of the background; now on to the fun.

APPLYING WHAT YOU'VE ALREADY LEARNED

At some point as a creative person, you'll probably be asked to do an ad, or a series of ads (a campaign) for a product or service. When this happens, you have every reason to apply your normal (by now, I hope) procedures:

- Research
- Proposition testing
- Feature listing and benefit extraction
- Hypothesis development
- Creative strategy outline

Some Questions to Ask First (or How to Get into the Marketing Planning)

Before you start, protect yourself and make sure you have answers to the obvious big picture questions: "Why is print chosen as opposed to other media (direct mail, broadcast)?" "What kinds of ads?" "What is their purpose?"

"What's the media plan? Is print being used alone or in conjunction with other media?"

You can't carry out your research or test your proposition without these answers. You must be comfortable with the market *and the media for reaching the market* as well as the product and offer. This harks back to your format planning—the use of one-step versus two-step direct response in Chapter 5. It involves basic *objectives and budget* and all the discussions between the marketers, product managers, and powers that be that occurred before you came on the scene. How many ads are planned? How large can they be? Are these ads planned to test several hypotheses? To test format (size, bind-in versus no bind-in)? To test a series of ads or a single ad? To generate inquiries or sell right off the page?

All space ads are *not* alike, nor do they attempt to accomplish the same thing. I've divided them into three simple categories here.

The Workhorse Ad: Any ad that must sell off the page and take an order (firm commitment) on its coupon, card, or *800* number, has a tremendous job to do. It toils. Every inch of it strategizes and strains to set the information down, to hold the prospect, to involve, to motivate, and to answer all questions.

In most cases, unless the product or service or sponsor is universally known, your illustrations will be very important. Workhorse ads do especially well for book clubs, magazines, and educational services (in situations where cash with order is not essential).

Size or format is also crucial to you. You can't sell many major products and services on less than one page of a magazine; two is better still. If you get less, it may be the time you want to push for format testing.

Testing for workhorse ads often involves hypothesis testing as well. When your copy strategy gets going, try to develop three to four good hypotheses to see if it's worth a test.

The Thoroughbred Ad: This ad, which generates an inquiry (request for more information, request for someone to call, etc.) is called the thoroughbred ad because, by comparison to the workhorse, it has the time and space to be elegant; it can move in a leisurely fashion. Its job is to involve and motivate, but also *to qualify* or screen prospects.

Thoroughbred ads are predominantly ads for business and large-ticket consumer products or services. You may need less space for thoroughbreds as their requirements are lighter; they like to travel in groups, too, so you might also want to consider a series or group of ads.

The Thoroughbred Workhorse: There are print ads today that do double duty by both selling (charging for a trial or sample) and obtaining a request for more information (a catalog). The sale or up-front charge may be simply a qualifier (which is credited against future purchases), or it may be a bona fide product. In some cases the ad may offer an either/or situation (purchase and/or request a catalog).

These offers are used predominately by catalog companies looking for new customers.

Three Handy Habits to Develop in Formulating Your Creative Strategy

1. *Balance the "media buy" (and format) with objectives.* You asked the right questions. You understand the big picture. You've tested your proposition and you're comfortable. Your objective tells you whether it's a workhorse or a thoroughbred. Now—*what do you need and what can you have?* What are the reasonable assumptions you can make based on the maximum allowable cost per order? Can you have full magazine spreads? Bind-ins? Single page? How about color? Can you test three to four hypotheses? Should you consider a series of two to three ads? What makes financial *and* creative sense?

2. *Use teamwork for mutual agreement on hypothesis development.* Creative strategy, as you know, can be a solo thing or a team effort. Hypothesis development, as part of this, makes up the very heart and soul of your ad, be it workhorse or thoroughbred. Your headlines and leads, combined with your approach and the graphics, will make or break your ads. But your hypotheses are the bases for this and they form the foundation that determines your success or failure. Your planning will be much easier with print ads if you have accord and cooperation on this from the start.

3. *Introduce graphic considerations up front.* Your artist was important in direct mail. Your artist is even more important now. Don't go it alone. You'll need all the visual reinforcement you can get for hypothesis exposition, approach, benefit dramatization, and credibility. Work as a team from the start.

Your Rules and Formulas

When it comes to space there will be considerable creative baggage that you'll want to bring along. Some you can check at the gate, but keep the *big* four: credibility, involvement, offer, and motivation.

AIDA as a formula or superstructure works particularly well with print ads.

A – Attention
I – Interest
D – Desire
A – Action

What you *won't* have are a lot of stamps, tokens, and peel-offs. You won't have to worry about computerization and package components. And you lose your letters and your spokesperson or specific point of view (unless, of course, you do an ad from the credible spokesperson direct to the prospect: "How I developed this fitness course for you" ...or ... "What my new book can do for you...").

How You Create

An ad is the direct mail outer, letter, brochure, and reply card *all in one.*

You could say that the headline is the outer envelope and the letter lead, the body copy is the brochure, and the coupon is the reply card. Back in Chapters 4 and 7 we talked about each of these components, which you write first, the purpose of each one. Now it's combined, often on one magazine page or less, and sometimes in space that hardly allows more than a headline, an offer, and a response address. But there *is* an organization—a creative procedure.

1. *From Hypothesis to Hook:* Just as in direct mail, you have the all-important hypothesis. But there's no outer envelope to start it, no brochure to support it, no letter's lead to introduce it. So? *Put it into deathless terms in your headline,* and follow it through in your lead sentence. Here's where you hook your prospect! *The headline is 75–80 percent of the ad.*

2. *Approach:* In presenting your hypothesis, will you approach your prospect with a story? An invitation? A question or questions? A problem/solution? A fantasy? Or a straightforward generic announcement of the big benefit?

3. *Graphics:* What graphics best illustrate the hypothesis? *And* the approach? How many benefits can it show? How much space does it require?

4. *Body copy:* organize your benefits and features. Keep it tight and theme their presentation off your approach.

Your first job is to *attract attention.* Your next job is to *qualify* your prospect (and it's best to do both at the same time). You may not be fighting a group of envelopes in a mailbox, but you have pages of print—editorial and advertising—to compete with.

Your big headline (often with the help of graphics) does this. It is your outer envelope and letter wrapped in one. It introduces your hypothesis. It puts it in glowing, compelling terms. But it won't put it in glowing terms until you decide on the approach.

Many workhorse ads use the Generic Approach with the big benefit. (Save $150…Never worry about money again…Be Your Own Boss, etc.) But you'll find that the Question and Story Approaches have been almost as popular. Many also combine these with the Negative Problem/Solution Approach. This recognizes a problem or sets up a problem based on wants, needs, and aspirations, then moves quickly to solve it. Let's take a famous oldie as an example.

a. *Hypothesis:* Many people fear that they will lose business and social standing because of their poor command of conversational English.
Headline: Do You Make These Mistakes in English?
Approach: The Question Approach with Problem/Solution.
Try this headline with the Generic or Story Approach. Is it as strong?

Here are other classic workhorse examples.

b. *Hypothesis:* During certain periods of physical development, young people have complexion problems that embarrass them and make them feel socially inferior.
Headline: Now—get rid of ugly skin blemishes fast!
Approach: The Generic Approach with Problem/Solution.

c. *Hypothesis:* Many people feel that they are not well-read, but new books are often expensive and difficult to obtain.
Headline: Enjoy current bestsellers. Choose any three for just $4 (with membership).
Approach: The Generic Approach with Problem/Solution.

d. *Hypothesis:* Most people worry about money and want the security that wealth brings. This book on finance can help people build and maintain their fortune.
Headlines: Never Worry About Money Again (Generic Approach)
Money Worries Got You Down? (Question Approach)
How I Made a Million in Six Months (Story or Testimonial Approach)

Then, of course, there are the problem/solution headlines that go with self-improvement correspondence courses—the Story Approach with the old (and still valid) before-and-after examples. A classic muscle development and fitness course used a series of cartoon frames showing a "97-pound weakling" before and after the Charles Atlas course. To paraphrase the ad, it claimed "They won't insult you and take your girl away if you take this course." You also have the famous John Caples ad that began "They Laughed When I Sat Down At the Piano. But When I Started to Play!—" and the ever-popular before/after testimonial diet ads, "How I lost 75 pounds…"

These headlines are all over 40 years old, but you can see how compelling they were and are—even today! Your greatest challenge will be developing compelling, qualifying headlines like them. Your creative methodology should follow along these lines: (1) Determine what specific hypothesis embodies the most appealing or strongest benefit(s); (2) decide which headline and approach give it the most strength; and (3) see how your graphics can help. (Notice that when the hypothesis recognizes a problem, the primary approach becomes problem/solution. Too loosely applied, it becomes the basis for all hypotheses and all headlines.)

The Multilevel Role of Graphics

A few great ads have been successful without illustrations. (Figure 9-1.) In most cases, however, you'll need graphics along with your headline. Good graphics can be used to attract attention and qualify. Graphics support your hypothesis and approach and can even supplant some copy. (Figure 9-2.) Graphics also provide quick credibility (a picture of "the founder") and product

See companies naked.

Xerox Learning Systems has created an exciting, innovative approach to learning for people who need to quickly and surely evaluate financial reading matter.

Called "Reading and Evaluating Financial Reports" this remarkable learning system has only recently been offered to individuals. It can help you learn the ins and outs of high finance in a way you'll never forget.

The material is easy and *fun* to take. Xerox Learning Systems believes that learning is a pleasurable experience. Our idea is to offer you the chance to enjoy yourself as you obtain information you really need.

"Reading and Evaluating Financial Reports" is designed so that when you do read a financial report you will, in effect, see the company naked. You'll know what there is to know (including vital information you might otherwise have overlooked).

Every investor, stockbroker, indeed any conscientious executive who must evaluate companies and their financial statements will benefit from learning how to cut through the special vocabulary of high finance.

You take "Reading and Evaluating Financial Reports" on your own—at home or in the office. The materials are mailed to you complete. You teach yourself; you test yourself. So you will probably find that you are getting far more out of each minute of study than you ever have before. You go at your own speed—and in just a few hours you will have acquired a significant new expertise at quickly and surely reading and evaluating financial reports.

It should be obvious that such knowledge could very well save or earn you or your company considerable sums.

This exciting breakthrough in learning has been proved out by thousands. Investors, brokers, chief financial officers and managers report it fills a real need. Further, Xerox Learning Systems guarantees your complete satisfaction or your money back.

To order "Reading and Evaluating Financial Reports", simply call us, toll free, at:

1-800-453-4002

Major credit cards accepted or send check for $49.95 plus $4.75 shipping and handling to Xerox Learning Systems, 6 Commercial St., P.O. Box 944, Department REFR-R9JWE, Hicksville, N.Y. 11802. In many cases this learning system may be tax deductible.

XEROX

Xerox Learning Systems

Teach yourself speed reading in 10 hours or your money back!

1-800-453-4808

Most executives must read a million words each week if they are to do their job.

1,000,000 words! And that's reading related to immediate business. It does not include other business related reading—you know the reading that helps you stay ahead of the game.

That's why most executives spend almost half of every work day reading. About 3 hours a day is average.

The good news is that now you can cut this load in half—at the very least.

You can use Speed Reading Self-Taught (SRST) to teach yourself speed reading. In just 10 hours or so you can double or triple your reading speed and increase your comprehension. Xerox Learning Systems guarantees this or your money back.

Speed Reading Self-Taught was originally created especially for our clients. (We help thousands of companies help their people do a better job, including 357 of the Fortune 500).

Thousands of executives in sales, data processing, engineering, marketing and management have proved out the SRST learning system, reporting significant gains in reading speed as well as impressive lifts in comprehension. SRST works for slow readers . . . for fast readers. It will work for you. The materials are mailed to you complete. All you need is a cassette recorder and a watch with a second hand.

SRST costs $95. Your organization will probably pay or reimburse you. We guarantee SRST will teach you lasting speed reading skills or your money back.

Most executives read at a seventh grade pace. Isn't it time you broke out of that pack?

You can teach yourself speed-reading in 10 hours with SRST. You can double or triple your reading speed and increase your comprehension. Xerox Learning Systems guarantees this or your money back.

To order Speed Reading Self-Taught, simply call us, toll free, at 1-800-453-4808. Major credit cards accepted or send check for $95.00 plus $4.95 shipping and handling to Xerox Learning Systems, 6 Commercial Street, P.O. Box 944, Department SRST-S9QWE, Hicksville, N.Y. 11802.

XEROX

Xerox Learning Systems

Figure 9-1 *These three ads for Xerox Learning Systems appear regularly in the* Wall Street Journal—*firm evidence of their compelling qualities without the use of illustrations. In some print media a strong headline stands out best without pictures.*

Figure 9-1, *continued*

Figure 9-2 *The haunted house here is used (with the headline) to attract attention and qualify prospects. Through the years it continues to do this more successfully than any other illustration—and many have tested against it!*

recognition. In small space (see Figure 9-3), you can almost get by with a two-word headline if you have good product pictures: "Only $9.99!" Think of all the things the illustration does!

In the case of the finance book, let's say you decided on the generic headline, "Never Worry About Money Again." How can graphics be used to attract attention, qualify, *and* enlarge benefits? If it shows benefits, which

Figure 9-3 *Nothing can replace the effective use of pictures in this small ad. Just imagine it without them!*

benefits illustrations will most people relate to? Or with a headline that promises so much, should you perhaps concentrate on establishing credibility instead with illustrated testimonials? Here you might institute a three-way graphics-cum-approach test:

1. Combine the Generic with the Testimonial Approach for credibility (testimonials with pictures of the people themselves).
2. Combine Generic with Fantasy visuals for broad benefit appeal (illustrations of the wealthy life—symbols of money: furs, limousines, jewels, mansions, airplanes).
3. Combine the Generic with Identification visuals to show intrinsic benefits of wealth—happy, confident families enjoying the good things.

Let's take another example, a genuine pearl necklace.

Hypothesis: Women will want this product for social confidence, for the security of an investment, for enhanced self-esteem, for pure enjoyment, and because it is a bargain. Which of these needs or wants is most important? (And wouldn't it be nice to emphasize all of them?) Here's where basic hypothesis/approach testing is important; graphics are important as well.

Say you decide on a Generic "value/bargain" Approach because it covers all bases—safely. (Everyone wants a bargain, everyone who wants a pearl necklace wants to buy one at a bargain price. Some of these people want the necklace for pure enjoyment. Others want it as an investment, or to impress friends.)

Headline: Own the Pearl Necklace of Your Dreams and Save $150!

Now with your graphics show an attractive, pleased woman surrounded by friends. She is showing her new necklace to friends. She is proud of the necklace. Friends admire it. All of this implies value and peer approval. (This also introduces the idea of gift giving.)

Your picture has attracted attention, qualified the prospect, introduced the main and secondary benefits. (Properly used, graphics solve problems this way.) And your headline has set down the big benefit (and reason to act).

O.K. You've got offer, involvement, and motivation going for you. Next? I hope you said *credibility.* What qualifies you to make this offer? How do you justify the price? Need to add a close-up inset picture of the pearls? Got a guarantee? You're on your way now.

SOME RULE BREAKERS

You understand by now that a print headline, like a letter lead or outer envelope copy, should offer the big benefit-cum-moral imperative. You know it must attract attention, and qualify and involve the prospect as well—just like the old outer.

And just like the outer envelope, headlines must promise something *or arouse curiosity.* Headlines can be short (one word) or long, two lines or even three lines. As John Caples claims, in *Tested Advertising Methods,* "Long headlines that say something are more effective than short headlines that say nothing."[1]

When it comes down to the act of writing headlines, leads, and broad appeals, no one can give you better advice than the dean of direct response advertising, John Caples. His advice is based on hard data and testing—facts, not opinion. However, it is good to remember that our markets are always changing and as they change, tested appeals may change with them. The strongest, most powerful appeals of 1950 may be less appealing, less attractive, to the markets of the 1980s.

What About the "Teasers" and Those Ads That Don't Have "You" in the Headline?

If you've been following these guidelines closely, you may be a little puzzled. I have *not* been describing a lot of the direct response ads you see today.

- How many ads have you noticed with teasing headlines—headlines that certainly don't set forth any hypothesis, but merely hint at one to come?

- How about the softer-selling workhorses that don't put "you" in the headline?

- How about the ones with big pictures and little copy—not even a list of benefits?

- How about the ads with *no* coupon at all—only an 800 number?

There are two reasons for these rule-breaking ads.

First, up to now, I've been describing primarily the solid, old-fashioned workhorse ad; the classic on which the mail order business was started. (And some of these early ads were pretty cluttered and pretty tacky. *And* pretty effective.)

There's a lot to be learned from them. And chances are good that if you do any print for book clubs, book programs, magazines and correspondence courses, you'll need to use this classic format, a format where "you" is always stated up front or clearly understood.

This doesn't mean there is no room for good teasing workhorses or workhorses that talk product and product benefit without the "you" up front. (See Figures 9-4 and 9-5.) Remember, a major rule to get the envelope opened is *"arouse significant curiosity."* If you have a teaser or a big benefit headline that really does this, well—go for it.

Thoroughbred ads (and thoroughbred workhorses, Figure 9-6) don't *have* to sell off the page and therefore allow you more leverage. They want to qualify

---

[1] John Caples, *Tested Advertising Methods,* 4th ed. (Englewood Cliffs, N.J.: Prentice-Hall, Inc., 1977), p. 19.

Nautilus bring
fastest way to a trim

Now, maintaining a lean waistline doesn't have to be a full-time occupation. Spartan diets aren't fun.

And ordinary exercises like running and tennis don't do much either. Because no matter how hard they work your arms, legs and lungs they just don't challenge the abdominal muscles.

A trim waist without sacrifice.

Finally, there's a quick, efficient way to have the lean, flat stomach you want—thanks to an extraordinary invention from Nautilus: the new home Abdominal Machine. An engineering triumph so powerful it tones and tightens your mid-section *in less than 10 minutes a day.* Applying the same advanced principles to abdominal exercise that have made all Nautilus body conditioning equipment legendary—*variable resistance.*

Variable resistance. The key to fast progress.

Fixed weights, like barbells, are limited in their ability to exercise muscles. Why? Because the structure of every muscle is unique, and each one has different capacities at different points in contraction. (For example, the biceps can lift more weight near full contraction than when extended.) In practice, this means that the amount of fixed weight you can lift is limited by the muscles' weakest point. So barbells light enough to lift with reasonable

effort aren't heavy enough to work the strongest parts of your muscles.

Nautilus overcomes this limitation with a simple, brilliant invention: the cam. The cam's genius is that it automatically varies the amount of weight (or resistance) you work against, challenging a muscle at every point in its contraction. The harder one part of a muscle can work, the more resistance a Nautilus cam gives it—through its *entire range of movement.* And without the danger of strain or injury.

The new Nautilus Abdominal Machine uses the same principle to tighten your stomach. And does so with such efficiency you'll start to feel results in only one or two workouts.

You literally see results in a few short weeks. No other form of exercise even comes close.

Five minutes of Nautilus versus an hour of situps.

Everyone considers doing situps or leg-lifts. If you've ever tried doing them regularly, you already know what a grueling exercise in futility they are. Worse yet, increasing the number of repetitions is wasting even more of

The Nautilus cam (resembling a deep sea nautilus shell) works your muscles in a way normal exercise can't.

your time. And the reason is not readily apparent: situps and leg-lifts never work your abdominals to capacity because it's actually the hip flexor muscles that are doing most of the work. And since resistance is limited to the weight of the upper body alone—it would take a torturous number of repetitions to noticeably increase your abdominal strength.

Nautilus exercise is totally different. The Abdominal Machine is precisely engineered to completely isolate and work your abdominals. This is exercise that leaves you elated instead of exhausted.

Sitting on the comfortable, padded seat, you begin your workout by pushing the movement arm forward and down, as far as possible. As your abdominals contract you feel an invigorating warmth; pause a moment and slowly raise back up (releasing yet still pressing against the machine's resistance). You get *twice* the workout, strengthening your muscles on both the forward and back strokes. This positive/negative resistance is essential to balanced muscle development.

As your strength grows, nine tension settings from mild to strenuous let you gradually increase the resistance. A muscle needs constant challenging to remain vigorous.

Exercising on Nautilus five

Figure 9-4 *This Nautilus ad for The Sharper Image Catalog illustrates several new Workhorse features:*
—It eliminates the coupon and encourages 800 toll-free ordering;
—It has a strong headline without "you";

home the tight stomach.

minutes a day, three times a week is all it takes to turn a flabby tummy into a tight, strong stomach.

A strong stomach–a friend to your back.

Shaped-up abdominal muscles do a lot more good for you than you think. Besides a trim appearance, they're essential for good posture, proper breathing and even a healthy back. Because without full, firm abdominal support your lower back is forced to take on more and more of the job supporting the upper body. This continual strain can lead to tension and tightness, greatly increasing the risk of serious, painful back injuries.

But stomach exercise can fight this imbalance. With the Nautilus Abdominal Machine, the benefits to your back, in fact, start with the first day of exercise. Before long, posture will improve, you'll stand taller, tension will be lessened. And you'll have more stamina.

A toned abdomen is literally your back's best ally.

Famous Nautilus construction.

Nautilus is known to build their machines like battleships. And this compact home unit is no exception. The husky tubular steel frame will stand up to a lifetime of energetic exercise. All contact surfaces are cushioned with high density foam and covered with tough, double gauge Naugahyde. Measures $48 \times 38 \times 35\frac{1}{2}$". Weighs 150 lbs.

Minimal assembly is required and takes less than 5 minutes. Comes with full instructions, exercise program and 90 day warranty. And you don't have to move a muscle to own it.

The Nautilus Abdominal Machine is available to you by mail with a free phone call to The Sharper Image.

Home test Nautilus risk-free for 30 days.

In the past 12 years Nautilus has changed the way the world exercises. Today, over $3\frac{1}{2}$ million men and women stay in shape on Nautilus equipment— including professional football players, olympic skiers and marathon runners. And now this legendary company brings that wealth of experience into your home.

Best of all, you have 30 days to try your Abdominal Machine, absolutely risk-free. You must be fully satisfied with the results or simply return it for a full refund. (Please allow 3 to 4 weeks for delivery).

Call toll-free or write today to order the remarkable Nautilus Abdominal Machine. And in only minutes, do for your stomach what diet, weights and hours of sweat can't.

ORDER TOLL FREE

For fastest delivery, credit card holders please call toll free. Order product #MNT200 for the Nautilus Abdominal Machine. Or send a check for $485 plus 55.00 delivery. CA residents add 6% tax.

ORDER TOLL FREE 24 HRS. EVERY DAY.
800-344-4444
Overseas/Canada (415) 344-4444

THE SHARPER IMAGE ® 680 Davis Street, Dept. 8452
San Francisco, CA 94111
©1984 The Sharper Image

Call toll free for our catalog of innovative products.

Figure 9-4, *continued*
–It asks for an unusually high ticket sale right from the page (without prequalifying the prospect via inquiry response and follow up); and
–Its illustrations have a prominent role.

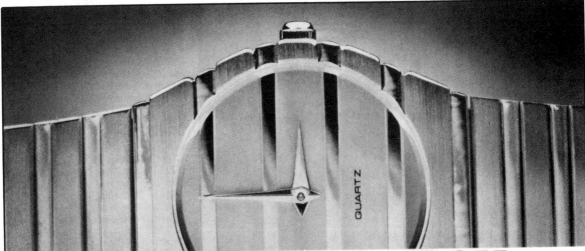

THE DESIGNER LOOK
WITHOUT THE DESIGNER PRICE

The classic look, solid feel and quality crystal accuracy convince you this is an expensive Swiss designer watch. But unlike the $12,000 solid gold version, this $99 replica has a generous 5 micron coating of 18K gold. So you save—without sacrificing accuracy or looks.

We wish you had this watch in your hands right now. You'd see and feel the quality that has made this one of our best selling products recently. Each band link (100% solid stainless steel) is double stamped to produce the exact size and taper required. Each link is then individually ground, polished, and plated with 5 microns of real gold—to keep its luster for many years. (We defy anyone to find workmanship like this, elsewhere at this price.)

ACCURACY PLUS

Not content to just look like its famous prototype, this authentic replica performs like it too. Its accuracy is ±5 seconds a month—exceeding even the highly regarded Swiss Chronometer standards. The quartz crystal coupled to a computer-engineered electronic movement gives absolute accuracy at a very low cost.

GREAT EXPECTATIONS

You expect a lot from Exeters. The products we've introduced recently are among the most talked about in America.

And we expect just as much from this watch. In addition to exceptional beauty, it reveals the kind of dedicated detail found only in the most patiently engineered timepieces. The fully adjustable, gold coated bracelet, for example. And the scratch-resistant, tempered mineral glass crystal. Most other watches in this price range give you nothing better than plastic. And nothing picks up scratches faster than plastic.

In fact, we're so confident you'll share our enthusiasm over this new watch that we're backing it up with an unusual triple guarantee.

First, the included factory warranty: limited one year parts and labor (in the rare event that repair is needed, you'll find this service-by-mail feature extremely convenient).

You'll also have the opportunity to decide if this watch is right for you. If not delighted, return it within two weeks (in new condition, please) for a prompt and courteous refund, including delivery charge. You must be satisfied.

Lastly, a third guarantee to introduce you to this watch—and give your investment even more protection. If this timepiece should fail for any reason (other than deliberate abuse), return it to us for a new replacement. Without charge. And without delay.

Watch battery (included) lasts a full year, and is easily replaced by any jeweler. Includes full instructions and a gift box. Silver version made of 100% polished stainless steel, with a liberal 3 microns of 14K gold applied to the band links available for $89.

PLEASE ORDER NOW

You'll be surprised how many of your friends will mistake this for a much more expensive watch. But please order soon as this most popular watch is in limited quantities, and in high demand at this price.

ORDER TOLL FREE

Diners Club/Credit Card holders may use our toll-free lines. Or send a check for $99 for Gold/$89 for stainless plus $3.50 delivery. CA residents add 6% sales tax. Ask for product #MG68(Mans Gold), #LG70(Ladies Gold), #MS69(Mans Stainless), or #LS71(Ladies Stainless).

800 443-0100 EXT. 244

Canadian/Overseas (714) 551-1733

EXETERS®

7 Westport, Dept. 15S • Irvine, CA 92714

Call toll free for our catalog of unique products

© EXETERS 1984

Figure 9-5 *This ad from Exeters also sells with a strong headline and graphics, replacing the coupon with a toll-free telephone number.*

Figure 9-6 *A Classic Thoroughbred Workhorse used to get new customers for the Norm Thompson catalog.*

prospects, primarily. They also work to create an image. To do this, they attempt to impress you with their company and their products in general, *their* qualifications, their credibility. A good tease is particularly O.K. here.

All of this doesn't mean such thoroughbreds can win their races if they remove the "you" completely. Ads that forget you, you, you will receive weak response compared to the more compelling "you" copy of the old workhorse. (Figure 9-7.) What's more—*"clever" headlines can flop.* (A lot of those you see— once—may be flops.)

You can afford to play around a little if you're in friendly, familiar (tested) media, or talking to your own customers. Don't take chances in unfamiliar territory, or with strangers. And always test.

The *second* reason that you see a lot of so-called nonconforming direct response ads is that, simply, there *are* a lot of rule-breaking ads that are tried, tested, *and* successful these days, particularly in the areas of mail order soft goods and business lead-getting. (And we'll get to these in a minute.)

NEW OR TRADITIONAL—YOUR CREATIVE REASONING MAKES THE DIFFERENCE

It's important for you to understand *what* the headline must do as well as *how* to do it. Understand why the headline and the graphics work together. If you've got the rules down, you can experiment. For example: Let your graphics attract attention and qualify. Use your headline as a teaser that leads into the copy. Or play with your approach; make a question out of your headline and an answer with your graphics—or vice versa. If you understand *why* you do what you do, you're safe. If you do it because it sounds tricky or looks flashy, forget it.

You already know how to check research, test your proposition, set up the format, execute the creative strategy and pull a hot hypothesis or two (Chapter 5). You know how to use your hypothesis, your approach, and graphics to set up your headline. You're *equipped* to experiment. Work at it. Be confident! And test.

Notice how quickly you can move through AIDA with a good headline and strong approach...how you can attract attention *and* qualify your prospect with the right visuals...how you state your hypothesis and create involvement *with* major benefits—all through headline, copy approach, and graphics.

A piece of cake? No way. The simpler the result, the harder it is to achieve. And this first step is 75 to 80 percent of your ad, so it had better be good—it had better work hard. So will you before you get to the small print.

How to Handle Your Features and Benefits

How about the poor body copy? With small space ads or one-pagers in magazines, there's hardly any room for it. Book club advertising is a classic example of this. Graphics are prominent (the more book choices, the better the ad) and offer terms are relatively long and complex. This frequently leaves only

An IBM 4361 computer system is an ideal vehicle for moving data quickly.

To improve inventory control, Schwinn linked its IBM System/36 computers at four distribution centers with an IBM 4361 computer system. Better control has helped reduce inventory investment and improve customer service.

The 4361 is just one of a number of easy-to-use Business Computer Systems from IBM.

Whatever size your business, they'll help you do what you do, better.

They can be used as stand-alone computers or as part of a network.

You see, there are as many ways to use IBM Business Computer Systems as there are businesses.

For a free brochure, call IBM Direct at **1 800 IBM-2468, ext. 42.** Or send in the coupon below.

Write to IBM, DRM, Dept. KK/42, 400 Parson's Pond Drive, Franklin Lakes, New Jersey 07417

☐ Please send me a free brochure on IBM Business Computer Systems.
☐ Please have an IBM marketing representative contact me.

Name

Company

Address

City

State   Zip

Business Phone

IBM®

Schwinn Bicycle Company's IBM 4361 computer system is the hub of its nationwide distribution network. So you see, no matter what business you're in, an IBM Business Computer System can help take you where you want to go.

IBM®

Figure 9-7 *This IBM Thoroughbred has fun-and-games with a bicycle wheel that makes it an eye catcher. The wheel does have a logical relationship, however. And, after all, we must assume IBM is looking for highly qualified business prospects only.*

a sentence or two for the lead-in paragraph. The rest is headline/graphics/offer.

At the other end of the spectrum, of course, you have the newspaper advertising supplement of four to eight pages (copy-cum-illustrations) and all the variations in between.

How do you treat this "body of information"? Let me make a suggestion: In establishing your hypothesis, you had to set up a hierarchy of benefits. And before you could do this, you had to list all the features. Take all of this *and organize it a little like a brochure* (Chapter 4).

In ordering and organizing you may want to apply one of several methods. A lot will depend on your overall approach. For example: If you're telling a story, your benefits may unfold sequentially as your story progresses.

In the Question Approach, you can present benefits and features in the form of questions and answers. ("What kind of books can you expect to receive every month?") If you use a Fantasy Approach, you may want to build all the benefits into the dream. ("Imagine that you're...then picture your...") With a straight Generic Approach you could employ the old countdown, listing the benefits and features in descending order, biggest first, smallest last. ("First, you'll have...then...next...")

In many cases, when your space is limited, you might consider the *Cluster* effect, where you take each benefit separately (usually in descending order) and surround it with the features that produce the benefit. ("You'll enjoy the sheer beauty of your necklace. Each individual pearl is matched perfectly to the next. The color of the pearls together gives a pure, soft white glow." or "Be conversant in all areas of current thought. Every month you'll choose from a wide variety of new nonfiction books on subjects like conversation, politics, history, scientific advances...")

Then, of course, in severely restricted space, there's always the *Clothesline* or the *Stew* presentation. With the *clothesline* treatment, benefits and features are strung out and hung (again, in descending order) from the lead, looping back and forth across the page until they dribble off and get tacked down just before your final wrap-up and call to action. The *stew* is similar except it just indiscriminately shoves a jumble of benefits and features into a cramped pot of type lying between the lead and the close, often running benefits or features back to back with no sentence structure. (Such techniques surely need no illustration here.)

Magic Words—Don't Forget Them!

We've talked a lot about the value of "you" (the second best word) and "FREE" (the most magic word we have). If you can justify it, use both liberally. John Caples also points out that "new" or giving news is important.

We have a lot of action words (like Now, Here, Hurry, Today) that convey a sense of newness, importance, and urgency—fast. (Now for the first time...Do it now!) You'll need these particularly in small space. The action words are also right for...

Your Exit Lines and Offers

It's probably superfluous to tell you at this point that you'll want to wrap up your copy with the traditional call to action and ordering instructions. Make it easy to order, give the options, set out a coupon with the same care as you do your direct mail order form. Where you have a coupon or order form, make sure it states the offer in full (so that it can stand alone if it gets clipped and set aside).

When space is very tight, you don't have to repeat the offer in your wrap-up *if* you have a coupon that clearly states the offer. But coupon ads, once clipped, are no good to you or anyone else unless the full offer remains behind (with an address for additional ordering).

Old proverb says: Interdependent coupon separated from interdependent ad produces two worthless pieces of paper!

All of this takes time. But in terms of budgeting your schedule, not as much time as direct mail planning and execution, unless you're doing a series. By the time you have your creative strategies down, you should be more than halfway finished.

John Caples says "Now, I spend hours on headlines—days if necessary. And when I get a good headline, I know that my task is nearly finished. Writing the copy can usually be done in a short time if necessary."[2]

WINNING ADS AND WHAT YOU CAN LEARN FROM THEM

In many ways, direct marketers are gradually capitalizing on what standard advertisers have always worked for: good, strong advertising that can build a company's image and make prospects aware of the company and its products. Direct marketers have carried this one step further. They intend that good, strong advertising can build a company's image and create awareness while it is also gathering prospects and/or garnering sales. (And I say, "God Bless Direct Marketers for It!")

They have an ear for the tempo of the times, as well. Just as direct marketers are bringing out new products and services for today's markets, so they are accompanying these with new graphics, strong visuals, *and* sound copy (without the hoopla of the circus barker). They understand that the big new markets of the eighties and nineties take plastic or credit cards and the telephone for granted. They know the power of pictures. And they are finding that often a greater space investment up front pays off with quality prospects in the long run. (You'll find some prime examples of this in Figures 9-8 through 9-13.)

As the costs of direct mail (and postage!) continue to rise, space or print advertising offers exciting alternatives. Learn to use space well. Make it work for you. You'll be a hero!

---

[2]John Caples, *Tested Advertising Methods,* 4th ed. (Englewood Cliffs, N.J: Prentice-Hall, Inc., 1977), p. 19.

Figure 9-8 *Royal Silk broke a lot of rules (and changed mail order history) when it ran these four-color, full-page ads.*
Its high fashion, moderately priced products sold right off the page—and they sold well enough to make such expensive ads profitable.

Figure 9-8, *continued*
The ads broke from the traditional rectangular coupon to the triangular coupon and now it's become a distinctive Royal Silk "trademark."

Figure 9-8, *continued*

Figure 9-9 *When American Express went after the young working woman, it did so by identifying the American Express Card with exciting, interesting females.*
The picture did the job. All American Express had to say was, "The American Express Card. It's part of a lot of interesting lives. What are you waiting for? Apply now."

Figure 9-9, *continued*

Figure 9-9, *continued*

295

"ONLY THREE PEOPLE CAN FIT INTO MY SCHIZO SCHEDULE:
LIZ CLAIBORNE, CALVIN KLEIN AND WHAT'S-HIS-NAME."

"Moving in. Going to school. Working an eight-hour day. No wonder my
one-and-only is calling himself ol' what's-his-name.

Actually, I think I may have found a way to save *all* of my favorite
relationships: Spiegel.

Because, with Spiegel, I can call (free) and order anytime. So I can get
Liz Claiborne jeans and Calvin Klein skirts when *my* schedule permits—
even if it's 2 AM. What's more, they come to *me* for free pickups on returns.

Which saves me precious time. So now, I can spend more of it on
Accounting 101 and playing with Max…and, oh yes…a guy who happens
to be named James."

ALL STYLE. ALL SERVICE. AL
To get your copy of the new Spiegel Spring Catalog, mail $3 with the attach

Figure 9-10 *In the late 1970s Spiegels
changed direction completely, moving from
an older, low-income market to a young,
affluent market. It used a continuing
space campaign to announce this. Here are
a few of a highly successful series of
dramatic, four-color ads designed to
reposition the company and its catalog—*
and *to get new prospects to order a
catalog.*

Moisten here and seal.

SEND $6 FOR YOUR SPIEGEL SPRING CATALOG TODAY
AND GET THIS $20 PIERRE CARDIN TOTE BAG PLUS
A $3 CERTIFICATE AT NO EXTRA CHARGE.

A wonderful deal, wonderfully simple.
Just fold this card and drop it in the mail with $6.
Or call 1 800 345 4500, Dept. 222 and charge it.
In return, you'll get this Pierre Cardin tote bag (a $20
value) plus a $3 certificate good toward your first Spiegel
purchase.
The new Spring Catalog has over 500 pages of fashion
and home furnishings from over 200 top names.
Plus toll-free, 24-hour ordering. UPS delivery. Free
pickups for returns. And a complete satisfaction guarantee.
YES! SEND ME THE NEW SPIEGEL SPRING CATALOG!
☐ Enclosed is my check to Spiegel for $6.
☐ Charge $6 to my   ☐ VISA   ☐ AMERICAN EXPRESS   ☐ MASTERCARD

Credit Card Number   Exp. Date

Signature

Name (please print)

Address

City   State   Zip
Requests received after March 15, 1985 will receive our next major catalog. Offer not
good outside U.S.A.

Working Woman
1G2SZB3

Moisten here and seal.

**"HOW I EARNED MY CALVIN KLEIN MERIT STRIPES
ON THE 8:19 LOCAL."**

"Just settled down to some exciting commuter reading *(Statistical Analyses of Demographic Trends)* when Pack 253 piled on and proceeded to tell every one of the world's worst knock-knock jokes.

This called for evasive action. I stashed statistics, pulled out the Spiegel Catalog, and went shopping.

Somewhere between Montauk and the 67th knock-knock, I settled on a Calvin Klein jacket and skirt for myself, an Oscar de la Renta shirt for Mr. Right. (If he doesn't like it, they'll pick it up—free.)

Then I just called from the office (toll-free) and ordered everything.

Which made shopping quick, painless, and in the final analysis, highly rewarding. Now that's *my* idea of a good deed."

Spiegel

ALL STYLE. ALL SERVICE. A̶L̶L̶ ̶
To get your copy of the new Spiegel Spring Catalog, mail $3 with the attach̶

Figure 9-10, *continued*

**"HOW I FOUND ALEXANDER JULIAN,
NORMA KAMALI AND LIZ CLAIBORNE
AT 40,000 FEET."**

"I've successfully managed one aviation company, two children and three languages. But managing to find time for ordinary tasks—like shopping—was another story.

Then, on a rare flight to NYC (rare because I was the passenger, not the pilot) I opened a Spiegel Catalog. There I found Alexander Julian. Ralph Lauren. Liz Claiborne. Hundreds of designers.

I filled out an order form on the plane—mailed it from La Guardia. A week later they delivered everything right to my office. What's more, they even offered to pick up any returns. Free.

So at 40,000 feet over New York, I finally managed to shop the world's top designers.

Now that's what I cal

ALL STYLE. ALL SERVICE
To get your copy of the new Spiegel Fall Catalog, mail $3 with the a

Figure 9-10, *continued*

SEND $3 FOR YOUR SPIEGEL FALL CATALOG TODAY AND GET $3 OFF YOUR FIRST SPIEGEL PURCHASE.

It's really simple.

You just drop this card in the mail with $3. Or, simpler yet, call 1 800 345 4500, ask for Dept. 107 and charge it.

In return, you'll get a certificate worth $3 on your first Spiegel purchase.

The new fall catalog has over 600 pages of fashion and home furnishings from Liz Claiborne, Norma Kamali, Laura Ashley—over 200 top designers in all.

Plus it brings you the special services that are uniquely Spiegel: Toll-Free, 24-hour ordering. Quick UPS delivery. Free UPS pickups for returns. And a complete satisfaction guarantee.

Yes! Send me the new Spiegel Fall Catalog!
☐ Enclosed is my check to Spiegel for $3, applicable to my first Spiegel purchase.
☐ Charge my $3 to ☐ VISA ☐ American Express ☐ MasterCard

Credit Card Number _____ Expiration Date _____

First Name (please print) ___ Initial ___ Last Name _____

Address _____

City ___ State ___ Zip ___
Requests received after September 30, 1984 will receive our next major catalog. Offer not good outside U.S.A.

1CXJLA8

Glamour

A

Moisten here and seal.

298

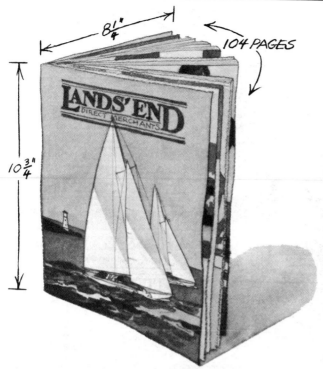

The Store We Mind

Our store is 10¾ inches tall, 8¼ inches wide, and 104 pages deep.** It has no crowded parking lots, clogged elevators, or hidden rest rooms.

It displays over 600 pieces of merchandise. And by the time you count colors and sizes and shapes and variations, you are up to 8,300 items you can shop from—assembled under one "roof" from the four corners of the earth, wherever quality calls.

Most of these items are shown on or with models so much like you they could live in your neighborhood. Every item is unconditionally guaranteed by the world's shortest guarantee. In two words: GUARANTEED. PERIOD.

We mind our store 24 hours a day, 7 days a week. You can buy from us in the comfort of your own home. But first, remember, we're only a phone call away— wherever you live. The toll-free telephone number: 800-356-4444. Or fill in the coupon below.

Oh, yes—we accept AX, MC, or VISA. And we deliver by United Parcel Service or U.S. Mail. You name it.

LANDS' END
DIRECT MERCHANTS

of fine wool and cotton sweaters, Oxford button-down shirts, traditional dress clothing, snow wear, deck wear, original Lands' End soft luggage and a multitude of other quality goods from around the world.

**This describes our "store" for the Spring of 84. The dimensions may vary by season, but you can always count on the quality, price, and service.*

☐ **Please send free catalog.**
Lands' End Dept. D-24
Dodgeville, WI 53595

Name_____

Address_____

City_____

State_____Zip_____

Or call Toll-free:
800-356-4444
(Except Alaska and Hawaii call 608-935-2788)

THE NEW YORK TIMES MAGAZINE / JANUARY 15, 1984   45

Figure 9-11 *For several years Lands' End has been running a delightful campaign to reassure or convince mail order* and *non–mail order buyers that Lands' End is a fine and responsible company to do business with. Here, again, the ads serve two purposes—to set forth a strong Lands' End image and to get new mail order customers.*
These ads are an education in Lands' End policies and products. They've broken the rules that say direct marketers cannot afford to spend an advertising budget prospecting without an array of product and offers.

At Lands' End we want to do more than make a sale to you.

We're out to build a relationship.
Through service.
Therefore:
1. We select or develop a quality product.
2. We price it fairly.
3. We ship it immediately.
4. We guarantee it. Period.

LANDS' END
DIRECT MERCHANTS
of fine wool and cotton sweaters, Oxford button-down shirts, traditional dress clothing, snow wear, deck wear, original Lands' End soft luggage and a multitude of other quality goods from around the world.

☐ **Please send free catalog.**
Lands' End   Dept. J-31
Dodgeville, WI 53595

Name_____
Address_____
City_____
State_____Zip_____

Or call Toll-free:
800-356-4444

Figure 9-11, *continued*

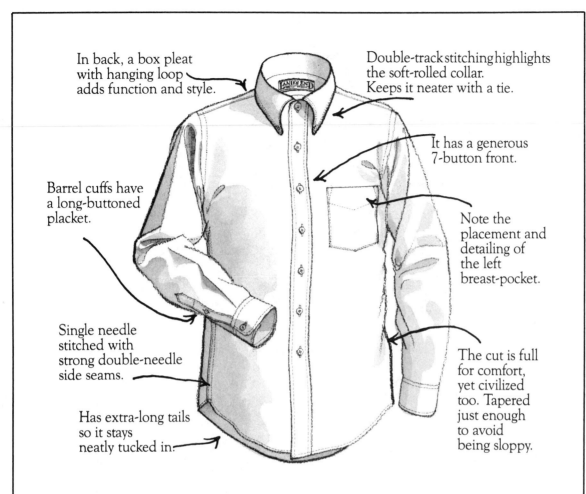

In back, a box pleat with hanging loop adds function and style.

Double-track stitching highlights the soft-rolled collar. Keeps it neater with a tie.

It has a generous 7-button front.

Barrel cuffs have a long-buttoned placket.

Note the placement and detailing of the left breast-pocket.

Single needle stitched with strong double-needle side seams.

Has extra-long tails so it stays neatly tucked in.

The cut is full for comfort, yet civilized too. Tapered just enough to avoid being sloppy.

We set out to make the world's best buttondown. This one comes close. At $25.

This is the Hyde Park—the latest addition to our impressive Oxford Collection, featuring both shirts of 100% cotton and our Lands' End reverse cotton blends.

Check it out feature for feature, beginning with the knowledge that it's made of imported 100% cotton Oxford. Heavier. More densely woven for a nicer drape. It launders better, resists wrinkles; best of all, it wears longer than normal.

For those of you interested in more specifics, we've provided this step-by-step "tour" of the shirt—available in pink, ecru, blue, maize, helio and white solids, as well as stripes and tattersalls, too.

Why make so much of a single shirt? We may have told you more than you ever wanted to know about a shirt. But only to make a point about the Lands' End philosophy of doing business.

It is a simple philosophy really:

First, *quality*. Then, *price*. And always, always *service*.

A quality item at a reasonable price represents a Lands' End value. Anything less is someone else's ballgame—not ours. What's more, every item we offer you— from soft luggage to sweaters to snow wear to shoes—is unconditionally guaranteed.

Figure 9-11, *continued*

Why this New York ad man leaves his $300 attaché case in the closet and carries our $37.50 Square Rigger.

Dick Anderson, an Executive Vice President of Needham, Harper and Steers, explains it this way:

"I'm always trying to jam more things into an attaché than it was ever meant to hold. That plays hell with stiff-backed cases. So I find myself leaving my $300 leather case in the closet, and carrying my canvas Square Rigger. It swallows overloads without complaint, has inside pockets for my calculator and appointment book, even a snap hook for keys."

And more.

That's not even the whole story of our Square Rigger. It's made of tough yet soft 18 oz. Square Rigger cotton canvas. Has comfortable padded handles. Smooth-operating YKK zippers. Comes in six businesslike colors.

Pretty impressive for $37.50. And we'll add your monogram for just $5 more.

We make the Square Rigger and over a hundred other Lands' End items at our duffle works in Boscobel, Wisconsin. That way we can guarantee the best possible materials and workmanship. And sell our soft luggage to you without middleman mark-ups.

First quality, then price.

What we have to offer goes beyond soft luggage, even beyond our great sportswear and accessories. The Lands' End tradition affects everything we offer you.

First, *quality*. Then, *price*. And always, always *service*.

That's why we offer a guarantee that would put lesser merchants out of business. Simply: "If you are not completely satisfied with any item you buy from us, at any time during your use of it, return it and we will refund your full purchase price."

If we're new to you, we don't ask that you trust us. Just try us. By phone, you can reach us toll-free 24 hours a day at 800-356-4444 (except Alaska and Hawaii call 608-935-2788). Or fill in the coupon. Order a Square Rigger or not, as you like. But let us send you a free copy of our Lands' End catalog.

☐ **Please send free catalog.**

Lands' End   Dept. G-02
Dodgeville, WI 53595

Ship_____ Attachés. $37.50 ea.
plus $2.80 shpg. ☐ Tan ☐ Navy ☐ Green
☐ Brown ☐ Gray ☐ Burgundy

$5.00 to monogram 3 initials: ☐ ☐ ☐

☐ Check enclosed   ☐ American Express
☐ Visa   ☐ Master Card

Card No._____

Expiration Date_____

Name_____

Address_____

City_____

State_____Zip_____

Or call Toll-free:
800-356-4444
(Except Alaska and Hawaii call 608-935-2788)

of fine wool and cotton sweaters, Oxford buttondown shirts, traditional dress clothing, snow wear, deck wear, original Lands' End soft luggage and a multitude of other quality goods from around the world.

Figure 9-11, *continued*

Why this New York ad woman leaves her $300 attaché case in the closet and carries our $37⁵⁰ Square Rigger.

Ms. Patrice Dermody, a media executive at Needham Harper Worldwide, explains it this way:

"I constantly find myself trying to jam more things into an attaché than it was ever meant to hold. That kind of treatment would break the back of my beautiful stiff-backed case, so I find myself leaving it at home, and taking my canvas Square Rigger to work. It swallows overloads without complaint, and has inside pockets for my calculator, even a snap hook for keys."

And more.

That's not the whole story. The Square Rigger is made of tough yet soft 18 oz. Square Rigger cotton canvas. It has comfortable padded handles. Smooth-operating plastic zippers. Comes in six businesslike (and ladylike) colors. Pretty impressive for $37.50. And we'll add your monogram for just $5 more.

We make the Square Rigger attaché and over a hundred other Lands' End items at our duffle works in West Union, Iowa. That way we can guarantee the best possible workmanship. And sell our soft luggage to you without middle-man mark-ups.

First quality, then price.

What we have to offer goes beyond soft luggage. Even beyond our great sportswear and accessories. The Lands' End tradition affects everything we offer you.

First, *quality*. Then, *price*. And always, always *service*.

That's why we offer a guarantee that would put lesser merchants out of business. It is unconditional, without limitations of any kind, and consequently, we can express it in two words:

GUARANTEED. PERIOD.

If we're new to you, we don't ask that you trust us. Just try us. By phone, you can reach us toll-free 24 hours a day at 800-356-4444.

Or fill in the coupon. Order a Square Rigger or not, as you like. But let us send you a free copy of our latest Lands' End catalog.

Figure 9-11, *continued*

WELCOME TO THE END OF LIFE AS WE KNOW IT.

If you've been an insurance agent for any length of time, chances are you've built a good part of your business selling whole life policies. But that could change.

Investment-conscious consumers, not content with the marginal yields offered by whole life, are switching over to investment-oriented products offering substantially higher returns.

And they're doing it rapidly.

So rapidly, in fact, that a 1981 article in *Institutional Investor* estimated that half of today's life insurers will merge or go out of business by 1990.

Where does this leave you?

That depends. If you continue to offer your customers only whole life policies, chances are that you will not only find it increasingly difficult to sell new policies, but also harder to keep the whole life business you now have.

On the other hand, if you can give customers an alternative to whole life — a profitable one — you may still do well. Perhaps very well.

"Today, an adult male in his mid-thirties, in good health, can purchase the same amount of coverage that he did ten years ago for nearly the same premium, despite the fact that he is ten years older. Now, more than ever before, replacement can represent a 'good buy' for the consumer."

That quote came from a joint study by the American Council of Life Insurance, the Million Dollar Roundtable and the Life Insurance

Marketing and Research Association — all traditional defenders of whole life.

As of January first, 1981, ITT Life has stopped selling whole life insurance in favor of more desirable term policies. Since that time, we have made a complete commitment to the replacement market.

And it's paid off.

In just one year, ITT Life has doubled the rate of new sales. As well as the number of our representatives. At the present rate, we should double the number of our representatives again in 1983.

As an agent, ITT Life can offer you the following: a national organization with the resources to back up any commitment. A product with indisputable consumer advantages. Consumer initiated leads. Very competitive commissions *paid weekly.* Annualization. Production bonuses. Extremely competitive rates including special products for non-smokers.

We also offer specialized repositioning underwriting, computer software and extensive consumer advertising.

If you're a marketing professional and need an aggressive marketing company to help you, call **612-545-2100.** Ask for the sales department.

The insurance world still has a future. Go with ITT Life and you will, too.

ITT ITT Life Insurance Corporation

Figure 9-12 *Here (and Figure 13) are two series of Thoroughbred inquiry ads that demonstrate the growing power of illustration (and humor) in direct response business ads. They represent close teamwork between copywriter and artist.*
The ITT Ad "Hong Kong" won a first in a general advertising competition. The three Control Data ads have won numerous awards, including a Gold from the Direct Marketing Creative Guild in 1984. Both campaigns were created by Fallon McElligot Rice, Minneapolis, MN.

WHEN THEY FIRST CONTACTED US, SOME OF OUR MOST SUCCESSFUL AGENTS PLAYED A LITTLE HARD-TO-GET.

Dear Benedict Arnold MacDonald,

I sell whole life insurance. My father sold whole life. My grandfather sold whole life. It's been good enough for us and it should damn well be good enough for you.

But no. Here comes ITT Life trying to screw up the whole system. What do you want to rock the boat for, Benedict? Don't you understand that there's no future in being a lousy traitor? Say what you want about the changing market, there's no good reason to

---

Rbt. MacDonald Pres. ITT Life

How can you sleep at night, knowing that every agent you sign up to sell your fancy "new wave" insurance is headed right smack for the poor house? I hope you rot in

---

...a trouble-maker and you always were... good men and I still heart the whole life you sold us fifteen years ago... Sure it's a different economy now. Some our investment is way behind inflation. But the MacDonald family has always stood behind whole life and not always...

DEAR ITT LIFE:

You BOZOS! IT WILL BE WITH GREAT SATISFACTION THAT I SEE YOUR HAIRBRAINED OUTFIT STANDING IN THE UNEMPLOYMENT LINE. A...

Listen, MacDonald, don't bite the hand that feeds you. I happen to know that you pounded the pavement for five years. All that pounding must have gone straight to your head. Any agent with a double-digit IQ knows you can't make a living by admitting that whole life is going kaput.

Seriously, MacDonald, you're going to be very, very sorry. Oh you'll make a big splash, all right, but in the long run you'll

---

OUR CLASS, THE PROFESSOR REFERRED TO ITT LIFE AS A "SCAM". I'VE DONE SOME RESEARCH ON MY OWN, AND IF YOU'RE RUNNING A SCAM IT CERTAINLY SEEMS TO BE A POPULAR ONE WITH THE BUYING PUBLIC. NEVERTHELESS, WHEN

---

night I add, on behalf of the agents I represent, that we join our voices as one in vilifying the opprobrious manner in which your sacrilegious philosophy of insurance has diverted much-needed revenues from the sale of traditional whole life.

See you at the club Saturday,
Phil

Maybe strombouug whole life is the best thing for the consumer, but it's going to be suicide for you, I predict that by 1984 you won't even be able to afford advertising...

---

of appointments.

From the moment ITT Life quit offering whole life in 1982, some agents were a bit shy about signing on with us.

For that matter, some were even too shy to sign their letters.

Oh, did they let us have it. ITT Life was accused of being everything from anti-agent to suicidal.

Any insurance company foolish enough to take a stand against whole life was taking the high road to ruin.

THE DIRE PREDICTIONS BACKFIRED.

But despite the doomsayers, ITT Life's 1982 term sales volume jumped 223% in a year when the rest of the industry crept up about 12%.

And in 1983 we're *doubling* that rate.

Not surprisingly, many of our most vigorous opponents started to reconsider. Maybe ITT Life was an idea whose time had come.

So before long, more than 10,000 new agents decided to stop selling ITT Life short. And start selling ITT Life fast.

THE SCANDALOUS TRUTH.

With some of the outrageous things in the trade press, you might think ITT Life was in the business of foisting bizarre products on an unsuspecting public.

Actually, we offer an intelligently designed selection of economical term plans combined with flexible, high-yield annuities.

And bonuses of up to 100% for those of your clients who stay fit and don't smoke.

If none of this sounds particularly shocking, it shouldn't. The only thing scandalous about our insurance is the demand.

WE'RE NOT OUT TO SPOIL THE AGENCY SYSTEM. JUST OUR AGENTS.

Some critics claim that ITT Life doesn't really believe in the agency system. If that were true, we wouldn't bother providing our agents with such lavish support.

Such as ITT Life's state-of-the-art telemarketing program. We made 120,000 cold calls for our agents in the first half of 1983. And set up thousands of appointments.

Or ITT Life's high commissions, bonuses, specialized replacement underwriting, computerized policy comparisons and powerful consumer advertising campaigns.

SIT DOWN WITH OUR PRESIDENT.

There are a lot of misconceptions about ITT Life. And Robert W. MacDonald—the man behind our recent notoriety and success—wants to clear them up for you.

So he's recorded a cassette that tells the whole, unvarnished truth about where the insurance business is headed. It could earn us a few new enemies.

And, very likely, a few thousand new agents.

Call ITT Life collect at **(612) 545-2100**, extension 32—and we'll send you a free copy of The MacDonald Tape.

Once you've heard it, you too may feel like sending us a letter. With a resume enclosed.

ITT *ITT Life Insurance Corporation*

Figure 9-12, *continued*

IN 1986, WE'LL HAVE MORE AGENTS IN HONG KONG THAN THE C.I.A. AND THE K.G.B. COMBINED.

For a long time our agents knew there was a very special mission in the offing.

But its exact nature was veiled in secrecy.

Now the story can be told. ITT Life's top-producing salespeople will be rewarded with a trip to our 1986 convention.

In Hong Kong. For six nights. Along with their spouses Transportaton included.

That shouldn't be any trouble. After all, this is Hong Kong we're talking about.

And if you have a really good couple years, we could also be talking about Athens, Bali, Cairo, Honolulu, Melbourne, London and Paris. Just for starters.

Now, if you can't imagine sitting around an insurance convention for nearly a week, neither can we. So you'll undoubtedly be left with quite a bit of time to kill on your own.

Because after the ITT Life convention, you could qualify for our additional travel bonuses—ranging from two nights in Honolulu to a fifteen-night trip around the world.

By the way, our Hong Kong incentive isn't some unattainable golden carrot.

Any reasonably good agent has an excellent chance.

That is, any agent who's signed up with us.

Which brings us to the point of this ad. For all the details about our current sales opportunities—and about our mission to the Orient—call ITT Life at **(612) 545-2100.**

We may not be the only organization that sends its agents to Hong Kong.

But we're the only one that can promise to bring them back.

ITT *ITT Life Insurance Corporation*

Figure 9-12, *continued*

Figure 9-13

Figure 9-13, *continued*

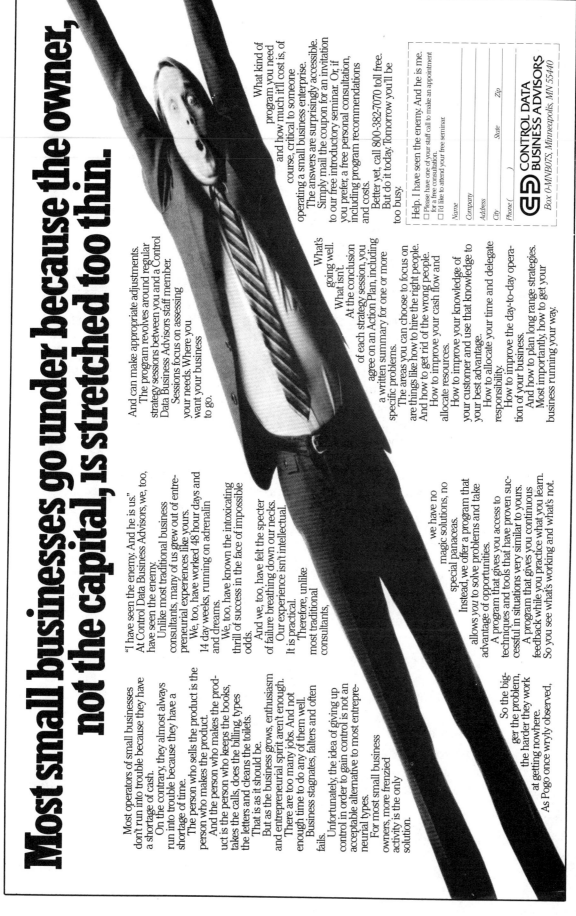

Most small businesses go under because the owner, not the capital, is stretched too thin.

Most operators of small businesses don't run into trouble because they have a shortage of cash.

On the contrary, they almost always run into trouble because they have a shortage of time.

The person who sells the product is the person who makes the product.

And the person who makes the product is the person who keeps the books, takes the calls, does the billing, types the letters and cleans the toilets.

That is as it should be.

But as the business grows, enthusiasm and entrepreneurial spirit aren't enough. There are too many jobs. And not enough time to do any of them well. Business stagnates, falters and often fails.

Unfortunately, the idea of giving up control in order to gain control is not an acceptable alternative to most entrepreneurial types.

For most small business owners, more frenzied activity is the only solution.

So the bigger the problem, the harder they work at getting nowhere.

As Pogo once wryly observed,

"I have seen the enemy. And he is us."

At Control Data Business Advisors, we, too, have seen the enemy.

Unlike most traditional business consultants, many of us grew out of entrepreneurial experiences like yours.

We, too, have worked 48 hour days and 14 day weeks, running on adrenalin and dreams.

We, too, have known the intoxicating thrill of success in the face of impossible odds.

And we, too, have felt the specter of failure breathing down our necks.

Our experience isn't intellectual. It is practical.

Therefore, unlike most traditional consultants, we have no magic solutions, no special panaceas.

Instead, we offer a program that allows *you* to solve problems and take advantage of opportunities.

A program that gives you access to techniques and tools that have proven successful in situations very similar to yours.

A program that gives you continuous feedback while you practice what you learn. So you see what's working and what's not.

And can make appropriate adjustments.

The program revolves around regular strategy sessions between you and a Control Data Business Advisors staff member.

Sessions focus on assessing your needs. Where you want your business to go.

What's going well. What isn't.

At the conclusion of each strategy session, you agree on an Action Plan, including a written summary for one or more specific problems.

The areas you can choose to focus on are things like how to hire the right people. And how to get rid of the wrong people.

How to improve your cash flow and allocate resources.

How to improve your knowledge of your customer and use that knowledge to your best advantage.

How to allocate your time and delegate responsibility.

How to improve the day-to-day operation of your business.

And how to plan long range strategies. Most importantly, how to get your business running your way.

What kind of program you need and how much it'll cost is, of course, critical to someone operating a small business enterprise.

The answers are surprisingly accessible.

Simply mail the coupon for an invitation to our free introductory seminar. Or, if you prefer, a free personal consultation, including program recommendations and costs.

Better yet, call 800-382-7070 toll free. But do it today. Tomorrow you'll be too busy.

Figure 9-13, *continued*

CHAPTER 9 EXERCISES

Testing the Hypotheses in Space

Figures 9-14 through 9-18 illustrate five ads developed for *Prevention* magazine in 1985 and tested in *Reader's Digest, TV Guide, Parade,* and *Saturday Evening Post.*

They are all *exceptionally good ads,* and each has a strong, very clear hypothesis of its own. But one of them beats the others hands down.

Study them closely. Identify the hypotheses. Appreciate. Now rank them. (You'll find the rankings at the end of the chapter, but *don't peek* until you've ranked them all!)

14 Points from David Ogilvy[3]

[In this article you'll find some valid suggestions from an advertising legend on increasing readership of long body copy in print ads. This can help you as you block out your body copy. It can also help your art director.]

Magazine editors have discovered that people read the explanatory captions under photographs more than they read the text of articles; and the same thing is true of advertisements. When we analyzed Starch data on advertisements in *Life,* we found that on the average *twice* as many people read the captions as read the body copy. Thus captions offer you twice the audience you get for body copy. It follows that you should never use a photograph without putting a caption under it, and each caption should be a miniature advertisement, complete with brand name and promise.

If you can keep your body copy down to 170 words, you should set it in the form of a caption under your photograph, as we have done in our magazine advertisements for Tetley Tea.

If you need very long copy, there are several devices which are known to increase its readership:

1) A display subhead of two or three lines, between your headline and your body copy, will heighten the reader's appetite for the feast to come.

2) If you start your body copy with a large initial letter, you will increase readership by an average of 13 percent.

3) Keep your opening paragraph down to a maximum of eleven words. A long first paragraph frightens readers away. All your paragraphs should be as short as possible; long paragraphs are fatiguing.

4) After two or three inches of copy, insert your first cross-head, and thereafter pepper cross-heads throughout. They keep the reader marching forward. Make some of them interrogative, to excite curiosity in the

---

[3]David Ogilvy, excerpted from *Confessions of an Advertising Man.* Copyright © 1963 David Ogilvy. Reprinted with the permission of the author.

next run of copy. An ingenious sequence of boldly displayed cross-heads can deliver the substance of your entire pitch to glancers who are too lazy to wade through the text.

5) Set your copy in columns not more than forty characters wide. Most people acquire their reading habits from newspapers, which use columns of about twenty-six characters. The wider the measure, the fewer the readers.

6) Type smaller than 9-point is difficult for most people to read...

7) Serif type...is easier to read than sans serif type...The Bauhaus brigade is not aware of this fact.

8) When I was a boy it was fashionable to make copywriters square up every paragraph. Since then it has been discovered that "widows" increase readership, except at the bottom of a column, where they make it too easy for the reader to quit.

9) Break up the monotony of long copy by setting key paragraphs in boldface or italic.

10) Insert illustrations from time to time.

11) Help the reader into your paragraphs with arrow-heads, bullets, asterisks, and marginal marks.

12) If you have a lot of unrelated facts to recite, don't try to relate them with cumbersome connectives; simply *number* them, as I am doing here.

13) Never set your copy in reverse (white type on a black background), and never set it over a gray or colored tint. The old school of art directors believed that these devices forced people to read the copy; we now know that they make reading physically impossible.

14) If you use leading between paragraphs, you increase readership by an average of 12 percent.

Answers to Your Hypotheses Quiz Prevention Rankings

5. Subscribe to a health magazine.

4. 20 steps.

3. Life extenders.

2. Medical myths.

1. Illness isn't natural (almost twice as effective as 2!).

Subscribe to a health magazine. Even if it isn't ours.

We're not philanthropists. And we're not crazy.

Why, then, are we urging you to subscribe to any one of the many health and fitness magazines flooding the nation's newsstands and mailboxes these days?

Because we believe health magazines — many of them, not just ours — have made important contributions to the tremendously reassuring events on the American health scene today.

Cardiovascular-disease deaths have dropped dramatically in the past 15 years. ...A USDA survey indicates that more than 60% of American households are switching to healthier eating habits ... And infants born today can expect to live about 30 years longer than 1900's newborn!

Does credit for all these remarkable gains belong to the health magazines? Of course not.

But it does belong, in many cases, to the people who *read* these magazines.

They were among the first to realize that achieving good health is often up to the individual.

They made the decision to take control of their own lives; to *help themselves* to feel better.

And so they were the ones who went looking for information about the basic sources of health— authoritative guidance, clearly and interestingly written, about tested techniques and new discoveries they could use.

They found it in health magazines. And, for many of them, it made a big difference in their lives.

It could do the same for you — and that's why we hope you'll start reading a health magazine regularly.

Naturally, we'd like it to be *Prevention* magazine. Moreover, we think there's a very good reason why it should be:

Of all the health and fitness magazines, *Prevention* has by far the largest number of readers. And we don't think it could continue to be the largest if it hadn't helped so many people over the years.

Indeed, we're so sure that you'll like *Prevention* — and benefit from it — that we're ready to offer this special "try us" opportunity.

Take a free examination copy *and* three free booklets— we'll take the risk.

We'll send you the current issue of *Prevention* to examine, as well as your personal copies of the three booklets described in the box. If you decide *Prevention's* not for you, just cancel...keep the booklets without obligation...and owe nothing.

That's our promise. So, subscribe to ours — or subscribe to theirs. But we urge you to find out, now, how millions of people are adding new dimensions of vitality, productivity, and enjoyment to their lives: With a health magazine.

> **In every issue of *Prevention*, you'll find helpful articles like these...**
> - A consumer's guide to over-the-counter drugs
> - Health rating America's favorite new foods
> - Nutrition vs. Cancer — more good news
> - 12 ways to feel better without doing anything
> - Best and worst occupations for good health
> - B vitamins can chase a lady's blues away
> - Foods that keep cholesterol honest
> - A simple way to fall asleep faster
> - Sex and nutrition — a perfect marriage
> - The best exercises for your back
> - The Top 25 "Superfoods"
> - And many others

THESE THREE BOOKLETS YOURS <u>FREE</u> WHEN YOU TRY *PREVENTION*

21 Surefire Stress Releasers —This 55-page guide is packed with sound ideas for transforming stress from a killer into a health motivator.

How to Live It Up and Live Longer— Tells about nutrients that help increase your functional lifespan by 5 to 10 extra years... and much more in its 40 pages.

Herbs for Health—This 46-page report explains the uses of 70 healing plants and herbs — many available at little or no cost.

Figure 9-14

THE 20 MOST IMPORTANT STEPS YOU CAN TAKE TO LIVE LONGER.

66Comply with only *one*...and your chances of living longer and avoiding illness or injury go up.99
—R. Barker Bausell, Ph.D., University of Maryland*

Your hopes for reaching a ripe old age—and then some—do not necessarily depend on luck.

Nor even on your genes.

But your longevity may well depend on whether or not you know such vital facts as these:

• *What is the single factor experts consider most significant in affecting health?*

• *Is it more important to get lots of sleep or to eat breakfast daily?*

• *Do you fit into one of the categories of people most likely to engage in good preventive health behavior?*

• *What do 81% of all Americans fail to do, even though experts call it the third most crucial health-promoting behavior?*

Most important...and most encouraging...you only have to take one of the twenty steps cited by the experts—*any one!*—to increase your chances of enjoying a longer life. Less illness-prone, more injury-free.

Now available—a breakthrough guide to better health.

All of these important insights—and much, much more—are presented for the first time in a special report recently released by Louis Harris and Associates, world-famous researchers. Based on a study conducted for the Prevention Research Center, the report is called, "20 Important Steps to Better Health."

In their innovative probe, Harris researchers interviewed 103 recognized health experts. They also interviewed more than 1,254 private citizens in a scientifically selected random sampling of the U.S. population.

The result: a fascinating, first-time overview of what highly respected authorities think you should be doing to help yourself to better health...insights

into your fellow Americans' health habits...and an opportunity to determine how you measure up to the general standards.

The report can be yours—free— with a low-cost, no-risk subscription to America's largest health magazine.

To receive a copy of this unprecedented and revealing report, *free*, you need only try a money-saving subscription to *Prevention* magazine at the introductory rate of $12.97 for twelve monthly issues.

And with the magazine comes our promise that it will cost you nothing if you're not completely satisfied. Simply cancel your subscription and you keep the special report, with our compliments.

For it *is* a report you will want to keep.

Like *Prevention* itself, "20 Important Steps to Better Health" aims to give you information that can make a big difference in your life—*if you know about it.*

Every month, *Prevention*—the largest health magazine in America—gives over 7 million readers a wide range of stimulating health ideas on nutrition, insomnia, backaches, allergies, fitness, depression, stress, beauty hints, and much more.

You, too, are likely to find each issue of *Prevention* a rewarding, enriching experience. So, mail the coupon today—and find out how much healthier and more productive your life can be!

FREE.

20 IMPORTANT STEPS TO BETTER HEALTH

Read the startlingly innovative research by Louis Harris and Associates revealing what experts think you should be doing to help yourself live longer ...how well you measure up to these standards...and how you compare with other Americans. *20 Important Steps To Better Health* is yours—without charge —just for trying *Prevention* at a low, introductory rate.

*Affiliation noted for identification only.

Figure 9-15

Figure 9-16

How many of these medical myths do you still subscribe to?

If you still believe in any of these medical myths, PREVENTION—America's most popular better health magazine—would like to offer you a second opinion. Because an ounce of information now, could save you a ton of trouble later.

Illness is a natural part of growing older.

NOT SO. Sure, sickness *does* occur, but that doesn't mean it *has* to. In fact, the latest scientific thinking indicates that *we* create most of our health problems. By eating and doing what we shouldn't. And by ignoring things that could help. Research clearly shows that *the majority of illness can be prevented or can be avoided altogether.*

How?

For over 40 years, the pages of PREVENTION have been filled with medical reports that show people how to keep their health longer. These days, PREVENTION is reporting on the very newest health discoveries. Like what you can do to prevent stroke. How you can bring down high blood pressure without drugs. Plus a way of eating that offers the best-known protection against cancer. So if you're missing PREVENTION, you're missing a lot.

If I eat well enough, I won't need vitamins.

SORRY. Researchers have found that the foods we eat today are so processed that many won't even support laboratory life. In fact, experts *blame* our poor diet for many of today's serious health problems. This, they report, plus our extra stress, requires that we strengthen ourselves with vitamins to be optimally healthy.

But which vitamins do what? And how much do you need? And what are the best sources?

In PREVENTION magazine, you'll read about vitamins that give extra energy. The vitamin that banishes depression and perks up memory, according to a medical study. The vitamin shown to build a stronger heart. Plus ten ways to heal with vitamin C, many of them new. When it comes to vitamins, PREVENTION is the most reliable source of information in print today.

The doctor knows best.

NOT ANYMORE. As helpful as doctors are, they don't have all the answers. And the good ones will be the first to admit it. Nearly 20% of all hospital patients *get sick as a result of their medical treatment.* As high as 25% of all surgery may be unnecessary, it is estimated.

Who knows best?

You should. Because you just can't afford to depend on your doctor for health, no matter how good he or she may be.

That's why PREVENTION magazine brings you news of how to take better care of your health yourself, so you can have it longer. You'll see how to rate your physician—and important questions to ask. Plus a list of the most addictive and sickening prescription drugs. And how to tell if

your x-rays, tests, and surgery are really necessary.

These days, it's easy to make a medical mistake. Or *become* one.

Take better care of yourself.

MAIL THE COUPON BELOW TODAY for *a free examination* of the latest issue of PREVENTION and see why nearly three million health-loving Americans subscribe to its natural advice.

FREE BOOK BONUS! Mail the coupon today and receive a free copy of "How to Live It Up and Live Longer." In it you will discover little known ways to add perhaps 5 to 10 extra years to your life . . . find more energy . . . relieve stress . . . plus so much more. Send for your free copy right away.

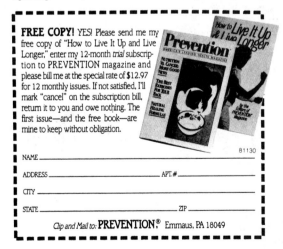

FREE COPY! YES! Please send me my free copy of "How to Live It Up and Live Longer," enter my 12-month *trial* subscription to PREVENTION magazine and please bill me at the special rate of $12.97 for 12 monthly issues. If not satisfied, I'll mark "cancel" on the subscription bill, return it to you and owe nothing. The first issue—and the free book—are mine to keep without obligation.

81130

NAME _____

ADDRESS _____ APT.# _____

CITY _____

STATE _____ ZIP _____

Clip and Mail to: **PREVENTION.®** Emmaus, PA 18049

Figure 9-17

315

Illness isn't natural.

It isn't even inevitable.

And if you find it hard to believe, mail the coupon below and we'll send you a *free copy* of a book that may change your mind. And perhaps your life.

Sickness may *seem* like a natural part of life . . . until you consider just how much sickness we actually *create for ourselves.* By not taking good care. By doing things we shouldn't. Or avoiding things that could help.

Take cancer and heart disease, today's leading killers. Nature didn't create them, *we* did. And medical experts have already linked them to how we eat. To the extra stress and pounds we carry around. And to our habits.

In fact, many doctors now agree that *many illnesses may be preventable.* The serious stuff *and* the minor ailments.

What's more, the really modern physicians now say it's *easy* to look better, feel younger, and live longer, just by making some simple (and, we think, pleasant) adjustments in your . lifestyle.

People want to know "Which ones? Is it going to hurt? Will these changes help my arthritis? Can I eat

healthier and still love food? How much exercise do I *really* need? Is there truly a way to be rid of this heavy, half-sick feeling once and for all?"

And PREVENTION, America's best-kept health secret, says: in many cases, *yes!* For the past 40 years we've been helping millions to discover the path *beyond mere relief.* To a state of more positively robust and radiant health.

We take readers beyond the commonplace "low salt/high fiber" topics. (Good advice, but many PREVENTION readers have enjoyed those health benefits since the 1950s when we first reported on them.)

These days the pages of PREVENTION are filled with today's really exciting health discoveries. Like how to prevent a stroke, the nation's third biggest crippler. Ten ways, researchers say, you can now heal with vitamin C—not just colds and flu, but now wounds, nerves, periodontal disease, even high cholesterol. Plus reports on simple, natural ways to relieve arthritis pain.

PREVENTION is buzzing with news of the vitamin that banishes depression and

perks-up memory, according to a medical study. And meals that help bring high blood pressure down. Plus the foods so totally health-building, they're being called " the 25 best superfoods."

And there's much more, too, but you get the picture.

The bottom line is: all this illness just isn't necessary. Or natural. And there's plenty you can do to keep much of it off your doorstep.

Want proof? Mail the coupon below for a free copy of our book, "How To Live It Up and Live Longer," and see for yourself.

And while we're mailing your book, we'll also include a *free inspection* copy of the latest issue of PREVENTION with a money-saving opportunity to try our magazine on a "don't like it, don't buy it" subscription offer.

Naturally, you've got nothing to lose, subscribe

or not. (Except some of your *un-natural* ills, pills, and doctors bills.)

FREE BOOK BONUS!

Mail the coupon today and receive a free copy of "How. To Live It Up and Live Longer." In it you will discover little known ways to add perhaps 5 to 10 extra years to your life . . . find more energy . . . relieve stress . . . plus so much more. Send for your free copy right away.

free copy!

Figure 9-18

Lights, Camera, Action! On Stage —You with the Pencil!

You may have been wondering when we were going to get down to something really glamorous, like TV (or even radio). Well now's the time and, although I don't want to deglamorize it for you, I suspect you'll find broadcast surprisingly similar to print.

With TV you may get to take part in casting, go "on location," visit a studio, or sit in a darkened editing room, but you'll find the thrill wears off pretty fast. It's hard work—and hard waiting. You'll get pretty bored standing around the set or location all day between takes (see terms at the end of this chapter). You'll also understand why everyone working on location seems to carry a book or magazine.

Before we get into the creative part, let me give you a little background. National television is undisputedly the largest, most far-reaching medium that direct marketers use. It works fast. And it can generate a lot of heat in the form of orders, inquiries, and awareness. On the downside, however, it doesn't deliver the quality that print—and especially direct mail—can. And it will prove totally inefficient for some highly specialized markets.

Of course there are other forms of video. As early as 1970, everyone was very excited about the more specialized capabilities of cable TV and satellite communications, and about the possibility of interactive video. The Direct Marketing Association even themed its annual conference around the video future that year. Many prophets were certain that in a decade or so, mail and print would bow to the video medium. It hasn't happened that way.

Cable TV finally arrived in the eighties (it "arrived" when it reached a circulation of over 30 million homes). This opened special-interest channels to direct marketers—sports channels, music channels, ethnic channels, financial and news channels. It also opened opportunities to test new commercial forms (like infomercials or five- and fifteen-minute commercials).

Interactive video services, linking home computers and telephones with the TV screen have been in a testing mode for nearly ten years, and every year, we get a little closer. Some people are already using it, but the numbers here are too small to count.

There is always a big story in direct response trade publications about the success of some form of video for one product or another, but most of us are still milling about the starting gate, waiting for the race to begin. Occasionally, someone darts forward for a short sprint. But ultimately, most direct marketers merely continue to test and learn. Ask any big video user how his or her program is going six months to a year later and you're likely to hear something like, "Oh, it's O.K. We're still testing. Naturally, we don't rely on it for the bulk of our business."

WHAT YOU SHOULD KNOW ABOUT BROADCAST TODAY FOR TOMORROW

Let me be candid with you for a moment regarding this glamorous broadcast medium and your place in it. Although most far-seeing professionals acknowledge that we are certainly moving into exciting video technologies, it will be a long time before pure electronic interaction arrives. O.K. Technologically, right this minute it's possible for you to view a video sales message, respond within minutes, have your order processed within twenty-four hours. But it still takes days to ship it, if you have to rely on Parcel Post and UPS. And are you ready to cough up $400, $200, or even $100 for a piece of the new equipment? Mass-priced technology isn't ready, but it will come, as did the video player. (Remember when no one knew what *that* was?)

Good direct marketers believe in a bright video future and that's why they've spent and are spending money experimenting and learning. But even commercial television is still just one small element in the media mix. It has not yet proven a viable alternative medium for most products and services. Even simple 60- and 120-second commercials (one- or two-minute commercials) have failed to meet profit projections for many direct marketers.

Caveat: If you want to move into direct response *just* to do TV commercials and video productions—don't. There's not enough out there to keep you going—yet. If, on the other hand, you want a creative grounding in broadcast—expecting (as you have every right to) that someday it will be an important part of your work—then we're moving ahead together "in synch" (as they say in TV lingo).

Wherever you start in direct marketing, it's highly unlikely that you'll be doing much broadcast, at least not at first. But if and when you do, let me tell you what to expect. First, guidelines are called for. And there are two kinds of guidelines.

1. Those that grow from what you've been learning all along here. They'll give you the basic understanding and feeling for the medium, the confidence to use it properly for direct response.
2. Those new rules and formulas indigenous to broadcast.

Even though it is still heavily experimental, television already has its rules and guidelines, and you can tie radio right on to its coattails.

I'm going to cover only the creative aspects here. Read John Witek's book, *Response Television: Combat Advertising of the 1980's,* for a good overview. Then talk to a video producer and an editor and learn all you can about basic television production and editing capabilities before you start creating commercials.

Some of John Witek's formulas, or structures, are set forth here to help you understand the creative process—and that's what you and I are going to concentrate on now. A little broad-brush economics to start with: TV commercials are expensive. The cheapest ones (practically home movies) start at $10,000 and they go up from there to $30,000–$50,000 for a respectable production, then on up for the more impressive jobs with large casts and expensive locations.

Once a commercial is produced (monies spent), you spend still more for testing on air. If it works—hallelujah! If it doesn't, you're out a bundle. Point: This is no place for amateurs.

Next (please keep this in mind at all times as we move through the chapter): *All broadcast is linear.* You *start at a given point and move straight through to the end. No going back to reread, check a fact, get a phone number, or examine a drawing. Your promotion makes it on the first pass or it doesn't make it at all!*

There are three kinds of direct response broadcast commercials (in radio and TV).

1. *Support:* This is the announcement that tells you to "watch your mail" or to look for something in print that's about to come your way. It can be used much as the announcement postcard is used, or even in conjunction with it. It can be used with local billboards, too, or newspapers, or any other medium. It's used with direct mail as a segment of a multimedia program.

This national television support, however, is limited to mass-appeal products such as Time-Life Books or *Reader's Digest* or big magazine subscription agents like Publisher's Clearing House and American Family Publishers. For anything less, it is costly and inefficient. (Radio is more flexible and can be employed on both a local and national basis.)

Television support can increase response from 10 to 50 percent or more. That's respectable. So it's certainly worth testing if you qualify as a big mailer with a mass-appeal product.

2. *Lead generation:* This is a pet medium for such broad lead gatherers as the Armed Services, public services, financial services, tourist boards of many countries, and job training schools.

You can compare this to your thoroughbred print ad in terms of objectives, but the quality of the broadcast leads (particularly TV) will seldom measure up to those you get from print. That means your marketing chiefs will give special consideration here to stringent qualification, extra follow-up conversion steps, and careful testing and tracking.

3. *Selling:* The commercials that make an offer and actually call for orders are the workhorses of broadcast and you probably visualize lots of hit records, Ginsu knives, and vegetable juicers when you think about them. Tabletop demonstrations and "talking heads" in front of blue curtains—that's the way it

used to be. And just like our hard sell print ads, these talking heads and tabletop demonstrations got orders. Lots of them.

You and I both know that's not the case anymore. Thanks to Time-Life Books, *U.S. News & World Report,* The Franklin Mint, Colonial Penn and National Liberty, CBS Video, Margrace, and many others, we have commercials that look great, sound good, and get orders—the kind you wish you could say *you* did while your friends are watching.

These commercials (or *commercial spots*—or just *spots*) come in three sizes: 30 seconds, 60 seconds, and 120 seconds. The 60s are generally relegated to selling products—especially products that are good TV actors. This means lots of moving parts and demonstrable benefits.

Television sells the dream, too. And it's known to do a good job on some magazines and single records, club programs, and continuity series. (Remember the joining offers with premiums from Chapter 3? Those are the kinds of offers that work best.)

Magazine subscriptions and continuity programs use the 120 commercial successfully. But all workhorse commercials should test at both 60 and 120.

John Witek has given a basic structure to each of these commercial categories along with the recommended—or, dare we say, traditional—length. (The numbers below all represent time ranges in terms of seconds.)

Classic 60—Second Support Commercial[1]

A.	B
10-30	30-50

The elements of the support commercial are:
1. Dramatization of proposition (10 to 30 seconds)
2. Facts about the primary medium (30 to 50 seconds)

Classic 30-Second Lead-Gathering Commercial[1]

A	B	C
5-10	10-20	10-15

The elements of the lead-gathering commercial are:
1. Statement of benefit or a problem (5 to 10 seconds)
2. Dramatization (10 to 20 seconds)
3. Telephone number and/or address (10 to 15 seconds)

Classic 60-Second Direct Response Commercial[1]

A	B	C	D
5	10-15	30	15

The elements of the direct response commercial are:
1. Attention-getting opening (about 5 seconds)
2. Premise and/or mention of premium (up to 15 seconds)
3. Product display, possibly with premium (30 seconds)
4. Ordering information and telephone number (15 seconds)

---

[1]John Witek, *Response Television: Combat Advertising of the 1980's* (Lincolnwood, Illinois: Crain Books, an imprint of National Textbook Company, 1981), pp. 24-37.

Classic 120-Second Continuity Commercial[2]

A	B	C	D	E	F
5-10	15	40	20	10	20

The elements of the continuity commercial are:
1. Opening and premise (5 to 10 seconds)
2. Introduction of series (15 seconds)
3. Dramatization of series (40 seconds)
4. First installment display (20 seconds)
5. Premiums, if any (position variable—10 seconds)
6. Terms of offer, ordering instructions, telephone number (20 seconds)

Although such structures can be very helpful to you for starters, please remember that our video medium as a whole is still in the testing stage. Direct marketers are still learning and trying *and* changing. Smart marketers challenge and test such things as

- Do I really need 60 seconds on my support…let's test 30 seconds against this (or—are ten 30-second supports better/worse than five 60-second ones)?
- Can I get my product message across in 60 seconds? Will I need 120 seconds instead?
- How about lead generation—isn't 60 more effective than 30? Can we afford it?

When such questions of length arise, you'll find that marketers may ask you to do the longer commercial in such a way that they can merely lift out or pull out the shorter version. The shorter commercial is, in effect, an edited or cut version of the longer one. (This way, you get two commercials for the price of one—almost.)

Study the four commercial structures or formulas for a while; I think (I hope) you'll find several familiar refrains in terms of technique.

The two "selling" commercials or video workhorses, incorporate AIDA. They have to work very fast, but their first job is to attract attention (opening); their last job is to call to action (ordering instructions). The lead-gathering commercial usually starts with a big benefit or a Problem/Solution approach, followed by a dramatization and a call to action. This could be easily compared to your thoroughbred print ad.

The Underlying Law (Does this make sense?) applies *at all times*. How do the commercial structures relate to the big four from Chapter 3—Involvement, Offer, Credibility and Motivation?

Involvement: All the good commercials use the "you" just like your print ads and direct mail.

Offer: Without a strong offer, no TV spot can make it today. This usually means a premium of one kind or another and a 100 percent guarantee. If your offer doesn't have both, find out why.

---

[2]Ibid.

Figure 10-1 *Here are two kinds of storyboard treatments for TV spots. The first board is an early effort for initial client presentation. The second one is a more advanced presentation with detailed video instructions. This can be used for production costing and bidding.*

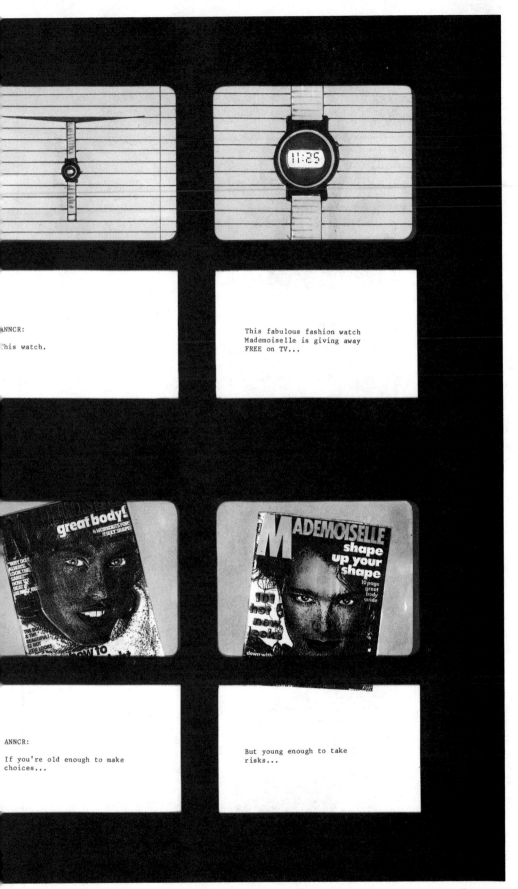

ANNCR:

This watch.

This fabulous fashion watch
Mademoiselle is giving away
FREE on TV...

ANNCR:

If you're old enough to make
choices...

But young enough to take
risks...

Client: The Condé Nast Publications Inc. Agency: Rapp & Collins Inc.

RAPP&COLLINS INC.
475 Park Avenue So., NY 10016

Client MADEMOISELLE

Title "Watch Out" -- :120

Job 2163   Date 3/13/85

Video

Audio

1. FADE UP.

   MS STYLIZED APARTMENT INTERIOR. BACKGROUND IS A SWEEP OF PINK. SLAT BLINDS THROW SHADOWS ON THE WALL. A WOMAN STANDS WRAPPING A TOWEL AROUND HERSELF. HER BACK IS TO CAMERA.

   ADD SUPER I: ©1985 The Conde Nast Publications.

   LOSE SUPER I.

ANNCR:

Watch out mademoiselle!

2. ZOOM IN TO CU AS WOMAN SWINGS AROUND RESPONDING TO V.O.

GIRL:

Which watch?

3. CUT TO MS OF SLAT BLINDS AS WATCH SLIPS INTO VIEW BETWEEN THE SLATS.

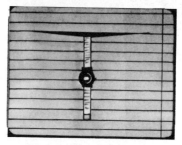

ANNCR:

This watch.

4. ZOOM IN TO CU OF WATCH.

This fabulous fashion watch Mademoiselle magazine is giving away FREE on TV...

5. SLATS ARE REVERSED TO REVEAL THE WORD "FREE" WRITTEN ON BACK.

   ADD SUPER II: FREE WITH YOUR PAID SUBSCRIPTION.

   LOSE WITH CUT.

To any woman who's ready for the time of her life.

Figure 10-2

RAPP&COLLINS INC.
475 Park Avenue So., NY 10016

Client __MADEMOISELLE -- PAGE 2__
Title __"Watch Out" -- :120__
Job __2163__ Date __3/13/85__

Video

Audio

6. CUT TO CU OF WOMAN.

GIRL:

That's me!

7. CUT TO ANIMATION OF AUG. '84 COVER.

ANNCR:

If you're old enough to make choices...

8. CUT TO ANIMATION OF OCT. '84 COVER.

But young enough to take chances...

9. CUT TO ANIMATION OF APRIL '85 COVER.

Try new things...better ways to express yourself...

10. WIPE ON ANIMATION OF COVERS WHICH WIPES OFF REVEALING...

MARCH '85   JUN '84
NOV '83   FEB '84
OCT '83

Now's the time to subscribe to Mademoiselle magazine...

Figure 10-2, *continued*

Motivation: Thanks to a strong offer, and heavy emphasis on ordering instructions, good television utilizes the same kind of motivators and motivating language that you'll find in good workhorse and thoroughbred ads. And it promises almost instant gratification with its *800* response number.

Credibility: I've saved this one for last. Although the basics of credibility don't change (Who are you? Why are you qualified to make this offer?), two factors are unique to television. Let's look at them.

1. Most products and services using television do so because of broad appeal and/or broad recognition. There is less need (and less time) to establish the "who" and "why."

2. Credibility is most often established for a company (particularly a service company in a competitive situation), *by the choice of spokesperson.*
   Some products and services do this by

   – Celebrity presenters (like Art Linkletter, Ed McMahon, Willard Scott, Jack Nicklaus, Kenny Rogers, Joe Montana)
   – Real-life testimonials (with real people)
   – Dramatizations that demonstrate effective, reliable services
   – Actors, cast as presenters to convey a sense of solid reliability and honesty.

In addition to AIDA and the big four, your creative concept development and all that goes into it—your research, your hypothesis, big benefits and the approach—will also work for you with commercials. It *must* work to enable you to develop a sound foundation for your creative work, the actual planning and writing of the commercial.

Try this analogy: In your commercial, your opening is like the direct mail outer envelop (or headline/graphics in a print ad). The spokesperson and approach from your letter become the audio dialogue of your commercial. The brochure becomes your audiovisual story with dramatization of benefits and exposition of features. Your nuts 'n' bolts, the order card or coupon becomes your ordering information at the end.

Magic words and action words (FREE, you, here, now, new, act today) are just as important as ever. Repetition is also important—even more important in the case of ordering instructions. (Response commercials not only show the *800* number, but they repeat it several times.) As with small space, you have to get it all across fast and efficiently.

Got it down? Fine. Feel comfortable with the analogy? Good. Because now I want to underline the differences for you. And they are big—so big from a creative point of view that some competent direct response writers will just never do good commercials (*not you*, I hope—but some).

HOW TO DETERMINE IF YOU HAVE THE RIGHT STUFF

In addition to all the basics we've talked about, there are really two major creative qualities that you need to pass muster. These are directly related to those wonderful abilities that you honed and developed in Chapter 1 (your curiosity and your imagination). At least, I sure hope you did—or can—and will. First is the ability to visualize—*well*. Second is the ability to write good dialogue. They go together but I'm going to take them on one at a time.

1. Your Ability to Visualize Well

This requirement should come as no shock to *you*. You've been encouraged to do this with every print ad, every direct mail package, alone *and* in conjunction with the art director.

Do I hear you crying "Foul" out there? *Not* the same thing, you say? Stay with me a minute. We're doing a logical progression.

In a direct mail package your brochure's job is to dramatize your benefits *and* show all the features. Your print ad's graphics carry a heavy visual burden because they have a lot to accomplish (attract attention, qualify prospect, introduce a benefit or two). Now what do the visuals in a commercial have to accomplish?

Attract attention

Qualify the prospect

Dramatize benefits

Show the features

However, and this is a big HOWEVER, *to do it well* you need a well-fed *creative imagination combined with a technical (or production) knowledge of what makes up good (creative, compelling, and cost-conscious) visualization within a tight time frame.* Some mouthful. But a very important mouthful.

You also need to apply the Underlying Law—will this make sense? Even in a video fantasy, it can make sense if the viewer actively suspends disbelief. (Translation: You make viewers want to believe, even though they know it's not real.)

Let me give you an example: Say your product is a magazine for car lovers. Your offer is a one-year subscription with a "car evaluation" premium. Your creative strategy meetings have kicked out a hypothesis that says, "People who appreciate new cars, fast cars, sports cars will identify with this publication and be motivated to subscribe when they learn about the premium."

Now you're sitting down with the artist for the first time. And since we're doing a commercial, let's even put this example in a script form to get you used to it.

Scenario 1

VIDEO	**AUDIO**

SCENARIO

A CONFERENCE ROOM WITH TWO CREATIVE INDIVIDUALS. ONE HAS A BEARD AND WEARS A RUMPLED SHIRT AND DUNGAREES—THIS IS THE ARTIST. THE OTHER, WITH NO BEARD IS THE CONSERVATIVELY DRESSED WRITER. THE WRITER IS *YOU*!

BOTH ARE SITTING AT A CONFERENCE TABLE SURROUNDED BY PAPERS. THERE ARE TWO HALF-EMPTY COFFEE CUPS. THE ARTIST HAS A STORYBOARD PAD IN FRONT OF HIM.

STORYBOARDS ARE A SERIES OF PICTURES THAT FOLLOW THE SCRIPT, GIVING ILLUSTRATION TO EVERY CHANGING VISUAL AND CAMERA MOVE. THESE PICTURES SHOW SCENES (INDOOR AND OUTDOOR), DETAILS OF THE SCENES, PEOPLE, THEIR DRESS, FACIAL EXPRESSIONS, HANDS. THE STORYBOARD FRAMES SERVE AS A GUIDE FOR THE DIRECTOR, CAMERAMAN, PRODUCER, SET DESIGNER, EDITOR—EVERYONE WHO WILL BE INVOLVED IN PRODUCING THE COMMERCIAL. STORYBOARDS ARE THE LAYOUTS OR FINAL COMPREHENSIVES OF VIDEO ADVERTISING. (SEE FIGURES 10-1 AND 10-2.) THE SCRIPT IS YOUR COPY. IT RECORDS EVERY WORD, *SOUND*, ACTION, AND SETTING IN YOUR COMMERCIAL.

VIDEO	AUDIO
THE ARTIST SITS OPPOSITE THE WRITER. BOTH SEEM SOMEWHAT RIGID, UPTIGHT.	*ARTIST* (TONE, SELF-ASSURED AND SLIGHTLY OVERBEARING): Here's how I see it. We'll need a race track. A lot of really classy sports cars parked next to the track. Then, if
THE WRITER FROWNS.	we can get this guy that won the Indy 500, shoot him racing..then he
THE WRITER SHIFTS NERVOUSLY.	drives right up to the camera and holds up a copy of the magazine. We CU on it, then dissolve to someone like Howard Cosell telling the viewer..
FINALLY THE WRITER CAN'T HOLD BACK. WRITER STANDS UP AND INTERRUPTS.	*WRITER* (VOICE HIGH-PITCHED AND AGITATED): I don't see it that way, Harry. I think we ought to theme the whole thing as a dream sequence. All the new cars featured on the premium should sort of float across the screen with
ARTIST SQUIRMS AND STARES OUT THE NEAREST WINDOW, ALL BUT IGNORING THE WRITER.	these elegant models standing around. At the back we'll have a symphony orchestra with Burt Reynolds conducting and…

CUT!

Scenario 2
(Same as Scenario 1)

ARTIST AND WRITER ARE HUNCHED OVER A PILE OF PAPERS AT THE END OF A LONG CONFERENCE TABLE. THEY ARE FRIENDS AND YOU GET A SENSE OF REAL COLLABORATION.	*ARTIST* (WARM VOICE BUT CONCERNED): I think this is going to be tough. We only have $28,000. That sort of zaps out the celebrity spokesman.
	WRITER (THOUGHTFUL, INTELLIGENT): Yup. And if we have to shoot in December, we can't afford to do location.
	ARTIST (ENERGETIC AND OPTIMISTIC): California would have been nice. Well, much as I hate stock footage, here's a list of what's around.

VIDEO	AUDIO

	(READS SLOWLY FROM LIST)
	   race track and race...
	   classic car show...
	   antique car race...

	WRITER (INTERRUPTING THOUGHTFULLY): You know, if we could do something *nice* with stock footage, we'd have the budget for a real race driver!
ARTIST BEGINS TO SKETCH. CAMERA MOVES IN TO CU OF PAPER	*ARTIST* (SPEAKS WITH SLIGHT HUMOR): I take it you're not planning on a cast of characters?
	WRITER (THOUGHTFUL AS ALWAYS): One really good actor should do it—unless we can find a real live race star. Willing and cheap....
AS THE TWO OF THEM WORK YOU CAN SEE THE EXCITEMENT BUILD.	*ARTIST* (WITH ENTHUSIASM): We've also got all those beautiful spreads from the magazine!
	WRITER (NODDING HEAD AND LOOKING THOUGHTFULLY AT PAPERS): Yes—and the premium. Wow! I'm running short on time already.
FIRST THE ARTIST JUMPS UP, THEN THE WRITER. THE TWO WALK TOWARD THE DOOR TOGETHER, COMPLETELY ABSORBED IN THEIR CONVERSATION.	*ARTIST* (JUMPING UP WITH ENTHUSIASM): I'll check out the stock footage. And see what the chances are on a big star....
	WRITER (WITH DETERMINATION): Good. Meanwhile, I'm going to play with a couple of approaches.
	ARTIST (HOPEFULLY): Will you have something by next week?
	WRITER (RESIGNEDLY): Sure. I guess so. Damn—I wish this was shooting in June!

CUT!

Now which is the right scenario? And who said this is a glamorous business?

You haven't even begun to draw on your creative imagination and already you're dramatically limited. What's more, you desperately want this commercial to win. A tough assignment. But it's not unusual. And it gives you a good idea of the many production elements to be considered long before you get *your* good idea.

Start with budget and production requirements; gain a firm knowledge of what things cost before you start spinning your creative wheels. Otherwise, you'll walk in with a perfectly great visual idea that's either totally unproducible or way out of the bounds of your budget. To do this, you need some technical grounding in

- the cost of location work
- studio and set costs
- costs of talent (and residuals)
- ballparks on big names
- abilities of editing equipment and costs of editing
- advantages and disadvantages of tape versus film

Once you have it, let your creative imagination go for a strong visual image that can dramatize your benefits within the bounds of the budget and the restrictions of time.

2. Your Ability to Write Good Dialogue

This is a second essential and you won't even get past your creative supervisor if you can't handle this one well. All along we've been discussing dialogue marketing, one-on-one, and "talking" to your market as you talk to one individual. By now you know every direct mail letter needs a logical spokesperson. And, as the writer, you should perceive your many-sided role also as actor and salesperson. You take on these roles primarily to establish a dialogue with the prospect out there. Some part of your commercial will talk directly to this prospect. Right?

But *this*, this is the real thing, you may say. It's—well—*audio*. Right again! How it *sounds* is every bit as important as how it reads. When you write, you write in the sound of tinkling glass, a footstep...a deep, authoritative tone...a hesitant, weak reply...the clock ticks, the door slams, the announcer talks on. And you must *hear* it all. Then record it, on paper.

How inadequate. Paper and pencil. To record something so alive, so vibrant. But someone, many people (director, actors, actresses) will need a map to follow and that's what your copy—your script—will give them.

Imagine this for a moment. You've started visualizing, digging around for a really keen idea that can work within your budget and your time frame. Now who are your actors? Who is your logical spokesperson? Is this a simple one-on-one (one announcer to one viewer)? Or are you doing a dramatization *for* the viewer? Or both? Do you want to hear and see your announcer? Or just a voice? And how do you get started?

This may be the toughest part for you. But think for a minute. How've we been starting all along? Your approach. Remember? What's your approach?

1. Put down your hypothesis.

2. Choose your spokesperson (don't forget credibility!).
 – disembodied (but credible) voiceover
 – dialogue between two people
 – a presenter (on camera)
 – a celebrity presenter

3. Now go for your approach. *What works best with your big visual?*

Many television spots just drop the viewer right into a dramatization for starters. You can do this, too. Viewers are used to it...thirty seconds in someone's bathroom...fifteen seconds in a strange kitchen or a speeding car. (Think how many commercials do this to you every time you watch TV.)

O.K. Back to first base. How do you get a strong fast start?

Answers:

1. Lead with a hot dramatization and voiceover—or a dramatization in which the primary figure becomes the spokesperson.

2. Lead with a standard presenter on camera and a simple "Hello." Then move right into your headline—your strong lead that attracts attention and qualifies the prospect ("Hello. How'd you like to win a million dollars? You can. Listen carefully.")

3. Lead with a celebrity presenter on camera. Go for instant identification, then move right into the lead. ("Hi, I'm Thistle Braithwaite. Have you ever seen the pain in a hungry child's smile?")

Close your eyes and go over your big visual. Now choose your approach or approaches:

Negative/Problem/Solution: ("Make sure your white shirts never look gray and dingy.")

Big question: "How many times have you made this same mistake?"

Testimonial: "Boy, I never thought *I'd* be a winner."

Story: "There we were, 100 miles from nowhere with a flat."

Fantasy: "How'd *you* like to be Queen for a Day!"

If/Assumptive: "If you're tired of coming home to dirty dishes...."

Generic: "Now, for the first time, enjoy exercising at home...."

And so on.

"GET IT DOWN" TIME

Listen to the dialogue in your head. Follow your big visual. Use your approach. Remember your structure. Write it all down! Then go back and fix it up.

Suggestion: Block out the action. Overlay your rough timing: your opener—five seconds, your offer—fifteen seconds, your dramatization—twenty-five seconds, your wrap-up and order information—fifteen seconds.

Then make sure your dialogue builds on the visuals and moves you logically into the sales message, through the visuals and out at the end to your call to action. Your TV spot is a stage and every segment of your drama must flow into the next with continuity. Don't worry about the details (like sound effects) *until* you organize that dialogue. And *don't* step out of character. Hear your characters speak as you write. Keep the spoken words short, clear, direct.

"Christmas...Crisp, cool mornings and warm memories...."

"Designed by skilled Florentine craftsmen...."

"What a lovely gift idea!"

"This amazing little knife even grates cheese...."

"The lion—if it's hungry, it will eat you."

"Enjoy it all, every month, in the pages of...."

"...and it's all yours for only $19.98!"

"Here's how to order...."

Caveat: Here's one of the biggest mistakes you may make as you start out. Don't use dialogue to repeat the visual. Let the camera do a lot of your talking. See it. Then use words to *complete* and *expand* the visual. For example: A dirty, tired man sitting on a kitchen stoop.

No: "Boy, am I dirty and tired...."

Yes: "Boy—I'm going to think twice before I try to clean the cellar again."

Next, what kind of sounds will you have? And how about your stage instruction? Listen. Listen to your dialogue. Voice sounds, room sounds, outdoor sounds. *Hear* the footsteps, hear the floor creak while you see the door opening. Hear the sounds of a cup connecting gently with its saucer as the woman moves it aside.

• Now *listen* to her. You know *what* you want her to say. But you must also make her warm and credible and authoritative and clear *and* convincing. In twenty seconds. Every word counts.

• You want a couple discussing the pros of the product. O.K. How do you get them on? How do you position them and make them real?

• You want the gentle touch of a child—a brief comment from a small boy. Justify him. Can you get him on and off in fifteen seconds? What editing techniques might you apply?

• You plan to have a man and a woman presenter. Who should they be? Why are they qualified? Orchestrate the sound and pitch of their voices mentally. Who's the heavy? Does it work?

• What's the dialogue structure between the two actors—question and answer? A countdown list? Point and counterpoint? Any humor? You have forty seconds.

• You're going to tell a story with only an announcer's voiceover to carry it along. How do you finish? Should the announcer come on camera? You have only twenty seconds for the order information.

• How about background music? Ouch!

Once you've gone through "Get it down!" and "Do it over," and put in all your sound instructions and staging, get yourself a stopwatch and start timing and cutting. It's time to polish it up.

And remember, budget enough time for this. (You probably recognize this as the same set of guidelines you've had all along. But now you also have to see and hear and orchestrate it all together in your script within your allotted time.)

The best way to cut and polish—the *only* way I can see doing it—is out loud with your stopwatch. (People will think you're going crazy after a while, so close your door.) Visualize, read out loud, act, change, improve. Time it. Visualize, act out with emphasis, change, improve. Time it. And on. And on.

By the way, when you get those technically correct Jim-Jam writers doing commercials, you're liable to hear what I call a lot of "audio hype." And it really does sound like a circus barker. This goes hand in hand with those old-fashioned talking heads. There was a place for this once in the early days of direct response commercials. But not anymore. Avoid audio hype. Use your creative imagination along with your acting abilities to create warm, friendly, *credible* dialogue. Play it straight. Keep it simple. (Remember small space ads!)

HOW OTHERS FIGURE IN WITH YOU

1. *The Artist or Art Director:* By now you've probably guessed what I'm going to say. Yes, call in your art director early—especially if you have worked as a team through the creative strategy development. (Remember, artists have a reputation for thinking visually.) Keep it going right through your creative presentation (you with the script, the art director with the storyboards). P.S. Artists working on commercials are almost always called "art directors."

2. *The Casting Director or Supervisor:* After all the approvals are in and the script is finalized, a production house is chosen and the casting begins. If you can stay with it (if they'll let you), don't abandon your baby! Try to sit in on the casting, make your opinions known. After all, you heard that voice when you wrote the script. You saw that face. Now shouldn't you have a say in making the selection? I think you should.

3. *The Director:* Once your final script is approved, the director takes over. I hope you can go along. There's only one caveat. At some point, *your baby also becomes the director's baby.* You can't be a tyrant or fight to protect *your* baby here. Work closely with the director. (He or she is in charge). Watch and listen.

4. *The Editor:* If you felt you could help with casting, imagine what you can add to editing. Here they'll be cutting and combining footage, adding sound (SFX) and special effects (DISS, RIP, FREEZE, SLOMO, FADE, WIPE, S.S., SUPER). Be there if you can! You saw it and heard it first. It was your concept. See it through. (This goes for the artist or art director, too.)

Your contribution to production and editing will depend a lot on the director's relation to you and on the rest of the production and postproduction group. If it's a loose operation and you know your film business, you may be part of the filming or taping and work directly with the editors. In some (rare) cases the director may not want you on the premises. I hope this doesn't happen. You'll learn more about creating good commercials when you know all the magic things a director and an editor can do. By the way, you'll grow to love good editors. They're the miracle workers, the problem solvers, the sharp edge smoothers who will give your commercial a professional shine.

BET YOU THOUGHT I FORGOT RADIO

I might have ignored it but I didn't forget it, and I hope you don't either. First, it's a thoroughly delightful place to learn, practice, and apply dialogue principles without having to worry about visuals. It's easier to script, it's easier to cast, no artist is needed, and in a pinch, you can even double as the director (unless, of course, it's one of those big productions with personality talent teams and tailor-made jingles).

Radio experience can also give you an entree to TV. It comes in about the same sizes and shapes as TV; it's used the same way. But the budgets are miles apart. You write it, bid it out (to a sound studio), cast it, rehearse it, tape it, and edit it. And often you can come in under $1,000 (and get more than one commercial). Of course, where original music or top personalities are involved, costs can go much higher. But on the simpler commercials, *your* cost (the cost of creating the script) is probably the biggest number in the budget.

Does radio work? I don't think anyone knows the big answer to this. Some people use it regularly because it works for them—*on a small scale.* It pops up frequently as part of one media mix or another. But no one has done any heavy research on radio. Consequently it languishes.

You won't find much support radio in our business, either. On a national basis, the big support users prefer television, and when radio is used on a local basis, nobody seems to bother to test such a low-budget investment. With no measurements you have no success story—and no big popularity.

Radio ranks well below television as a selling medium as it lacks visual credibility. Overall, radio has a pretty tough time attracting and holding attention and getting someone to pick up a pencil, unless the product is already known to the audience and the spot is run frequently.

Magazines have done well with 60-second spots for subscription sales *(Smithsonian, Working Woman)*, but this can be directly attributable to good media buys where the market already knows the product. I'm not aware of many—or any—other products that sell by pure radio. It can work for lead getting with a premium. But this is part of a mix. Radio just is *not* a primary medium.

From your point of view, however, radio could be good news. If you do get a radio assignment (I have my fingers crossed), try to avoid radio's equivalent of the talking head. Think about it. It's bad on TV, but doubly bad (boring) on radio! There are two alternatives to a blaring monologue floating without root or reason on the airwaves.

1. Get the local announcer to do it (and take your chances) or
2. Do a peppy dialogue between two people.

Either alternative can be effective. Both offer easy on-stage/off-stage possibilities. The dialogue can be a lot of fun for you, and fun for the listener, especially if you're out for pure support. It's one place where there's room for levity—a little, anyway. But make sure it's ho-ho-ho, not ho-hum. Do your timing and your reading out loud just like TV. Give yourself enough time, too—just like TV.

The big difference: With radio you don't augment the video. You've got dialogue, but no one can see, so your dialogue builds the picture. No lines like, "What are you doing here?" Instead, "What are you doing in the basement?" For the man on the stoop, back to, "I've never felt so dirty and tired...." Your words build the visual.

I'd like to be able to tell you that radio is making a big comeback today. It deserves to. Perhaps it is. Watch for it. And write for it when you can. It's a delightful experience. Every time.

YOUR MEDIA MIX

You've heard me refer to most broadcast as part of a media mix or part of an advertising campaign rather than a primary medium all on its own.

Because of this, your work in broadcast, be it television or radio, must also tie in with *the* campaign, reinforce its offers, incorporate its themes. Your big visual may come directly from the print ads...your radio may reproduce (reinforce) the TV spot's audio (same jingle, same slogans)...your support spot may tell the viewer not only to watch for the mail, but also how to respond to the mail to get an extra premium. ("Check the empty box on the reply card for an additional free gift.") This sort of thing gives you a solid measure of the effectiveness of your support TV. All such media planning is usually done at one time up front, well-coordinated and timed, part of the big picture.

You may run into the mix often these days as Direct Marketers are becoming more and more involved with multimedia programs. They are learning to make the media work together for image building and awareness as well as selling (just like the new print campaigns). Even though true measurements on the value of each medium have been nearly impossible to achieve, the overall impact, both immediate and long-range, can often more than justify the expense (as with the Spiegel's and Lands' End campaigns in Chapter 9).

SOMETHING TO COME AWAY WITH

Film biz is funny biz and fun, too. When you're on the outside, you want to be a star. But once on the inside you'll find all the insiders (stars included) want to be directors.

After you've scripted a few commercials, I'm betting you'll want to direct, too. It's a normal longing, especially if you care about your baby.

The job of this chapter on broadcast is to pass on to you what I call *creative perspective.* With it comes confidence, gained through understanding. If you understand why you do what you do, there's no mystery, no mystique to put you down. It frees you to do your best work. It gives you the ability to analyze and judge your own work and that of others, because you understand what makes good work tick.

Understand, too, that *the creative process really changes very little from one medium to another.* Once you're secure with this, you can tackle just about anything, and do it well. That's my wish for you. I also hope you turn out to be a stellar visualizer and dialogue writer. And get some good chances to prove it! (Keep eavesdropping and exploring! Keep that imagination going!)

CHAPTER 10 EXERCISES

I. Here are some film terms and lingo that will help you communicate as you visualize and write your script.

Shoot: What a camera does when it films or tapes.

Shooting or the Shoot: Filming or taping, the filming or the taping.

Point of view (Abbr. POV): Exactly what the camera should see at the precise angle from which you want it seen.

Voiceover (Abbr. VO): A voice without a visual on the screen. Usually the announcer.

In synch (Abbr. for In Synchronization): Sound effects or dialogue that coincide with the proper or correct action. It's also used to signify lip synchronization—the movements of the lips matching the words spoken on the sound track. It also means in the same mode with someone; to agree with someone is to be "in synch" with that person.

The location: The site for a film or taping outside of a studio. (You are "on location" while you work there.) Location is chosen for greater realism—and when the cost of reproducing the setting in the studio is impractical.

Studio: Where you go when you don't shoot on location. Studio shooting is usually done for better control and efficiency.

The Set: The setting, usually indoors. It is set up, actually, for the shoot.

A set-up: The arrangement of lights and camera to make an individual shot.

Tabletop: A term used to describe a demonstration commercial where most of the action is limited to a flat, tablelike surface.

Slice of life: A commercial dramatization usually involving a common, or popular, situation (family meal, two women shopping, wife doing laundry, car and mechanic).

Limbo: A shot in which the product appears to be floating in air without any spatial relations.

Talking head: The good old head and shoulders, face-on stationary presenter. Usually shot only from one POV.

A Take: The director breaks the script into scenes or takes, then shoots only one scene (or take) at a time.

Close Up (Abbr. CU): A shot in which a subject is very large, filling the screen.

Zoom: What a Zoom lens does—moves out and back easily and allows you to bring an image closer or move it farther away without moving the camera.

Pan: The camera's eye moves from one side to the other and up and down just like your eyes when you move your head from side to side or up and down.

Dolly: The camera itself changes position (back or forth, from one side to the other), as you move your body.

In the can: This is the equivalent of "the shoot's over." It implies that the film has been used and is in the can ready for development.

II. *Now, try your hand at planning a few TV commercials* (and, this time, don't worry about your budget!).

1. The first product is a broad-appeal health and fitness magazine. Let's just call it *Gym*. The offer is one year for $15 plus a large exercise and diet chart as a premium.

The hypothesis you've chosen is: People generally want to be more fit today, but lack of discipline and motivation causes them to neglect exercise or slack off. (A major benefit is the promise that the magazine can motivate the reader to plan and act and keep him or her enthusiastic.) You have 60 seconds.

What's your approach? (Question? Story? Testimonial? Fantasy? Problem/Solution? A combination?)

Who's your spokesperson? (A voiceover with dramatization? A fitness training instructor? A celebrity athlete? An average guy?)

What's your strong visual? (A fitness center in action? A runner? A before-and-after drama? Color pictures from the magazine? A dramatization of organizing and planning your own fitness program with the help of the magazine?)

Block it out on the time frame: 5 seconds for openers to attract attention (big benefit), 10 seconds for the premise and offer, 30 seconds for product and premium display, 15 seconds for ordering information.

2. The next product is a continuity book plan with instructions, recipes, and illustrations for gourmet cooking. It's called *Secrets of the Gourmet Chef.* There are twelve volumes. The lead (or first book sent) is *French Cuisine.* A new book will follow automatically every month thereafter until the customer cancels. (Each book costs $18.00, and each is shipped with its own invoice.)

When the customer signs on, he or she will be sent volume 1, *French Cuisine,* plus a special premium book on growing, buying, and using herbs and spices, *Herbs and Spices.*

The hypothesis you've chosen states that although women spend less time cooking for the family in general today, more time is spent planning and cooking elaborate, sophisticated meals for special occasions, parties, and holidays. (The major benefit of the series is its promise to make readers gourmet cooks—to impress their guests and gain the rewards of self-expression through entertaining.) You have 120 seconds.

What's your approach?

Who's your spokesperson?

What's your strong visual?

Block it out on the time frame.

3. The Smith Credit Corporation is looking for homeowners who might consider a second mortgage. They would like interested homeowners to write or call and they'll send out further information and application forms. (Lead-getting, right?)

The hypothesis is: Many people need extra cash for good reasons. If they qualify, they can take a second mortgage on their home and get that cash. (The big benefit here is one of security and enjoyment—you can send your kids to college or put an addition on your home this way.) You have 60 seconds.

What's your approach?

Who's your spokesperson?

What's your strong visual?

Block it out on the time frame.

III. *How about some dialogue practice?* Try your hand at this 60-second *radio* support. (Remember, your prospects can only *hear.*)

Marcia and John are out to alert the radio audience to an exciting direct mail package that arrives next week. The package announces a sweepstakes with a $1,000,000 grand prize and 7,000 additional prizes of rainbow umbrellas. The mailing consists of a bright red outer envelope, sweepstakes entry certificate, and opportunities to subscribe to 60 top magazines all at cut-rate prices.

Who's your spokesperson? Who are John and Marcia anyway? Nameless voices in limbo? Mail deliverers? Husband and wife?

What's your approach? How are they going to start—with a problem/ solution? A question? A generic statement? A testimonial? A Story? A Fantasy? How will you play them off to give your dialogue cadence and variety? (Balance your speakers. Don't give one more time than the other.)

Block it out on the time frame. Then fill in with dialogue—and have fun. (If you enjoy this exercise, chances are you'll do well with dialogue.)

chapter 11

Other Creative Areas in Direct Response and How You Figure In

While you've been out generating all those prospects, subscribers, and customers through direct mail, print ads, and broadcast, perhaps you wondered who was going to pick up the ball and continue the dialogue—promote those inquiries, renew the subscribers, sell to all the customers.

THE BACKEND—A MUCH-NEGLECTED, CRITICALLY IMPORTANT CREATIVE AREA

The glamour creative jobs bring in the prospects and customers through our national media, whether it's mail, print or broadcast. This is where the recognition lies and the awards are made. The Stars work here. The agencies fight to get this business.

But who continues the dialogue? You just paid six dollars in promotional costs to get a customer on television or fifteen dollars in the mail. Who's going to make that customer pay off? And how?

Sure—good product and good service are critical to this, but along with them, who continues the dialogue?

- Who encourages the club member to purchase and purchase more? With every member mailing?

- Who convinces the catalog recipient that everything in the catalog store is wonderfully appealing? Each time?

- Who reminds the magazine subscriber to renew the subscription? Annually?

- When the prospect inquires, who tells him or her all about the product or service? Then goes on from there?

Most direct marketing creative people get their initial training right here. It's a wonderful place to begin, because it teaches the basic workings of dialogue, its value and its importance. It's not a bad place to work in any event, wherever you are now. So you'll want to have this chapter around, just in case.

IF YOU HAVE A CHANCE TO BE CREATIVE WITH A CATALOG

What an opportunity! Don't let it get by you. Grab it! (Catalog specialists, by the way, may complain about classifying catalogs as backend. Technically, they're correct. Catalogs are both backend and frontend. They are, in fact, ongoing vehicles. However, for our purposes, they are backend here in that their primary job is to continue the dialogue.)

Don't be fooled. Catalogs are a lot more than product pictures and descriptions; at least, *good* catalogs are. Let me give you a little background first.

Catalogs are "in," hot, *the* thing. A busy mail order buyer can receive as many as 100 or *more* catalogs in September, October, and November. And around 50 or more in January! That's a lot of merchandise. And it keeps coming all year long. Experts have been worried about this so-called glut of catalogs. There are far more than even a serious mail order buyer can use. Many duplicate each other or offer similar products.

Some catalog owners are concerned that this may affect existing mail order operations as the mail order-buyer pie is being sliced too thin to support all the catalogs coming out. The pie itself, however, is growing, because more and more buyers are entering the mail order market every year as direct marketing booms. The end result? Some new catalogs are indeed bound to fail. So may some of the weak, older catalogs. Many more will succeed. And thrive.

Why will one catalog fail and another one flower? Not because of any mail orderer's pie. There are three basic areas that are important to a catalog's success.

First, the merchandise selection. The best catalog people are just natural-born merchants. Lillian Vernon, founder of Lillian Vernon, is one of these. She'll select an article out of dozens of possible products and say, "This is good. I'll take it." She knows what her customers want. She finds it for them. She is phenomenally successful. Roger Horchow is another superlative buyer. Like Lillian, he has a nose for his market's tastes.

Smart new merchandisers select their products to fulfill certain needs and desires that are not being filled for a substantial market segment. They look for a niche, an exclusive area to carve out for themselves.

The second area that's critical to success is fulfillment and customer service. Poor order processing, poor record keeping, slow delivery, and difficult returns and exchanges lose customers rapidly. It takes trust and confidence to become a mail order customer. Betray that trust once, and you lose your customers forever. Smart mail order companies today are doing everything possible to create a strong feeling of bona fide personal customer service.

The third area (and most important from your creative point of view) is the catalog image—identity—personality. With today's catalog glut, many catalogs tend to look and sound alike. Bad sign. Even more important, they go out uninvited to the prospects' homes without explaining *who* they are or *why* they are qualified to offer the enclosed products. They lack credibility. What *right* do they have to go into a strange home and sell? Why should a prospect use them?

How can you, the creative person, contribute? Let's hope your catalog has carved out a market niche, has good merchandising and fulfillment, and is working to establish an image. (If any of these brings a resounding "No!" be prepared for a short-lived relationship.) Assuming all systems are "go" —what is your creative role? How do you know to what extent the catalog is sound? Or where and how creative comes in? Or how much you will be able to help?

Taking the Creative Measure of Your Catalog

Here's where you go back to your basics and apply the Underlying Law. Look at your proposition. Based on the objectives and the market definition does this product (this catalog) make sense? Ultimately, the catalog's job is to establish and maintain a dialogue. Is it going to do this?

Work your benefits to develop a hypothesis. "This catalog was planned for X market in the belief that this market would be receptive to Y products because…"

Next take your four sales guidelines (Involvement, Credibility, Motivation, Offer) and a formula like AIDA (*A*ttention, *I*nterest, *D*esire, *A*ction) and *overlay them on your catalog*, then ask these questions:

1. What makes this catalog look distinctive, different from other catalogs, easily identifiable? Does it have its own tone or sound? Just like people, catalogs should look and sound (or read) distinctive. (Both Eddie Bauer and L.L. Bean are nationally famous outdoor and sports gear catalogs. You could never confuse one with the other, however. Aside from the format and the layouts, the copy tone and copy treatment are totally distinct in each.)

2. As you consider the graphics and tone, ask who's speaking. From whom is your catalog coming? Where did the tone come from and is it sustained throughout? In other words, who's the logical spokesperson?

A good catalog comes *from someone credible* (owner, president, manager, or a team—Harry and David—or a family, even) who speaks out, usually up front or on the order form, to explain why the catalog is there (if it's new) and why and how the spokesperson is qualified to do the speaking. Generally these are statements of commitment or newsy, friendly communications that directly or indirectly reinforce credibility and qualifications to do business with the customer. They also help to establish a dialogue. (This is the catalog's answer to the letter.) (Note: Many, if not most, department store catalogs neglect the up-front note or letter from the logical spokesperson. This could be an outgrowth of the old traffic-building catalog concept. All of these *started* as retailers not direct marketers. Since people came *to them*, they probably just never picked up the habit, or the logic, of credibility.)

Figures 11-1 through 11-7 offer you good examples of successful catalog spokepersons.

800 SPIRITS INC.
TWO UNIVERSITY PLAZA
HACKENSACK, N.J. 07601

Dear Executive:

When you need to send corporate or business gifts—whether it's one gift or a hundred, whether it's year round or for the holiday season—800 SPIRITS® is the service to rely upon.

800 SPIRITS® is a worldwide gift delivery service for champagnes, wines, spirits and a wide assortment of quality foods. With our toll free 800 number (1-800-BE THERE,™ 1-800-238-4373) convenience of gift delivery is as near as your telephone. Or if you prefer, your order can be placed by mail simply by completing the order form found in this catalog.

Whether you are sending gifts to the homes of your office colleagues, to clients in other cities or to key business contacts clear across the country, 800 SPIRITS® will see to it that each and every gift is delivered with as much care as you would take in presenting it yourself. Every gift will be attractively wrapped and accompanied by a handsome gift card with your personal message.

Gift giving need not be limited to just the holiday season. A gift of champagne, wine, spirits and food is a thoughtful personal message that can be used in many ways:

       —To set a tone prior to an important meeting and to say thank you afterward.
       —To acknowledge key accounts.
       —To congratulate a birthday, promotion, retirement, your secretary on her special day, etc.

Further, with our expertise 800 SPIRITS® can assist you in setting up incentive marketing programs. It is also possible through our services and advice to send reports, catalogs, books, press releases or whatever message you wish to convey along with an 800 SPIRITS® gift selection. 800 SPIRITS® can assist you to develop that perfect and special promotional!

Should you need assistance in gift selection or have a question please call us collect at (201) 342-6330 and ask for our 800 corporate representative, who will be happy to help you.

Over the year you may charge your gift purchases to the corporate account which will be opened in your name. Our special corporate catalog has been developed for you, the business executive, and affords you savings of between 10 percent and 30 percent off the prices of our consumer catalog. As terms of payment, we have a system of revolving billing with payment due thirty (30) days from the date of billing; excepting on orders of $1,000. or more where half payment must accompany your order.

Our aim is to serve and please you in a most convenient and professional manner.

Very truly yours,

Arnold G. Dowalsky

800 SPIRITS® INC.

Figure 11-1

For me, Lands' End is a dream that came true. I always wanted to create a company of my own, and here it is.

It began in 1963, with two of us filling orders out of a basement on Elston Avenue in Chicago's tannery district. Now there are about 1,000 of us at various locations in Chicago, Wisconsin, and Iowa.

I started with a stake of 10,000 borrowed dollars, a few ideas, and some good friends. I have had a lot of help along the way from some very talented people. Without them, and without "a little bit of luck", as the song goes, we could not have done it.

Because I was able to do it, I know that it can still be done in America today, and I encourage all of you who have the burning desire to start your own business, to try it. Start with an idea, and a niche, and I wish you "the little bit of luck" you'll need.

It is ironic that several of the large corporations with whom we compete, and who have the financial resources to create any kind of business they want to, have elected to make imitations of the Lands' End Catalog. Apparently they don't have the imagination or the pride to come up with an idea of their own.

The reason there is an interest in what Lands' End does, is that we sell more pieces of some kinds of merchandise today than the biggest stores in America. We buy a lot of piece goods. We tie up a lot of production. It has not all gone unnoticed.

What *has* gone unnoticed is that it is not pretty pictures and colorful patterns that have made my company successful; but a philosophy of doing business that began in the Elston basement 21 years ago. Much of it is counter to the prevailing retail practices of today, some of which intelligent customers object to.

On the cover and throughout the catalog are the Lands' End principles of doing busines. Our competitors (and maybe you) should copy them. If they did, retailing in America could be better for all of us.

President

3

Figure 11-2

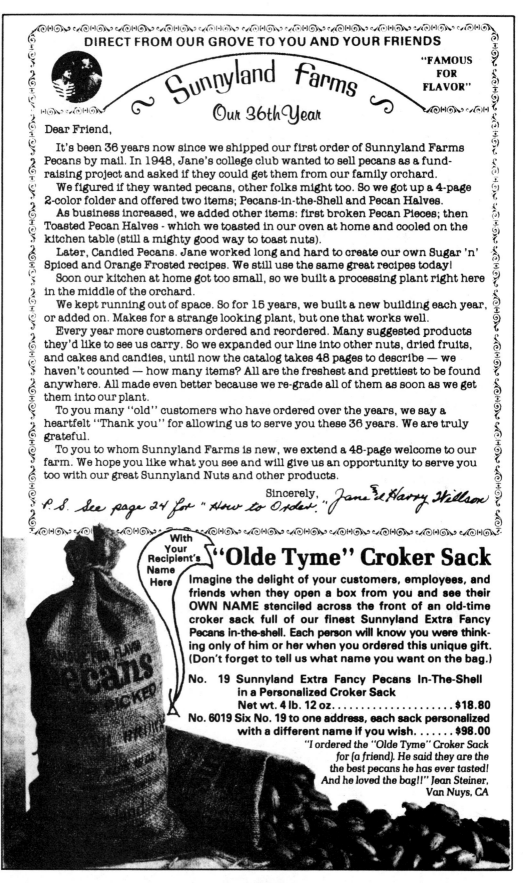

DIRECT FROM OUR GROVE TO YOU AND YOUR FRIENDS

Sunnyland Farms
Our 36th Year

"FAMOUS FOR FLAVOR"

Dear Friend,

It's been 36 years now since we shipped our first order of Sunnyland Farms Pecans by mail. In 1948, Jane's college club wanted to sell pecans as a fund-raising project and asked if they could get them from our family orchard.

We figured if they wanted pecans, other folks might too. So we got up a 4-page 2-color folder and offered two items; Pecans-in-the-Shell and Pecan Halves.

As business increased, we added other items: first broken Pecan Pieces; then Toasted Pecan Halves - which we toasted in our oven at home and cooled on the kitchen table (still a mighty good way to toast nuts).

Later, Candied Pecans. Jane worked long and hard to create our own Sugar 'n' Spiced and Orange Frosted recipes. We still use the same great recipes today!

Soon our kitchen at home got too small, so we built a processing plant right here in the middle of the orchard.

We kept running out of space. So for 15 years, we built a new building each year, or added on. Makes for a strange looking plant, but one that works well.

Every year more customers ordered and reordered. Many suggested products they'd like to see us carry. So we expanded our line into other nuts, dried fruits, and cakes and candies, until now the catalog takes 48 pages to describe — we haven't counted — how many items? All are the freshest and prettiest to be found anywhere. All made even better because we re-grade all of them as soon as we get them into our plant.

To you many "old" customers who have ordered over the years, we say a heartfelt "Thank you" for allowing us to serve you these 36 years. We are truly grateful.

To you to whom Sunnyland Farms is new, we extend a 48-page welcome to our farm. We hope you like what you see and will give us an opportunity to serve you too with our great Sunnyland Nuts and other products.

Sincerely, *Jane & Harry Willson*

P.S. See page 24 for "How to Order".

With Your Recipient's Name Here

"Olde Tyme" Croker Sack

Imagine the delight of your customers, employees, and friends when they open a box from you and see their OWN NAME stenciled across the front of an old-time croker sack full of our finest Sunnyland Extra Fancy Pecans in-the-shell. Each person will know you were thinking only of him or her when you ordered this unique gift. (Don't forget to tell us what name you want on the bag.)

No. 19 Sunnyland Extra Fancy Pecans In-The-Shell in a Personalized Croker Sack
Net wt. 4 lb. 12 oz. $18.80
No. 6019 Six No. 19 to one address, each sack personalized with a different name if you wish. $98.00

"I ordered the "Olde Tyme" Croker Sack for (a friend). He said they are the the best pecans he has ever tasted! And he loved the bag!!" Jean Steiner, Van Nuys, CA

Figure 11-3

346

Why They Come Back to the Same Old Stand

Dear Friend,

Hammacher Schlemmer has been around for a long time—136 years—longer than most any other store in America. Yet people keep coming back to the same old store, I think, because we've never changed.

That is, we've never changed the search for innovative, functional, unique and unusual products that has kept us in the forefront even though the values that guide our search are as old as the store itself.

When you consider such innovations as The Infinity Recumbant Bicycle (page 3) and the Instant Wine Chiller (page 38), you may wish to consider that years ago, the original steam iron, the pop-up toaster, the portable radio, the pressure cooker, the kitchen blender, the microwave oven and countless other products that are now common were first seen in America on the shelves of our store on 57th Street and, in the pages of our catalog.

Today I think we are probably better equipped than ever to live up to the unchanging standard for innovation at the same old store. A newly established Hammacher Schlemmer Institute, an associated but independent not-for-profit research facility, is beginning to conduct tests and comparisons, without commercial prejudice, to determine which products are truly best or unique. Some of its findings are included in this supplement.

And, as always, there is our unconditional guarantee of your satisfaction, the essential bond of confidence between our customers and our store.

Why do they keep coming back to the same old stand? I really think it is because they always know what they can expect to find at Hammacher Schlemmer: the best products, unique products, products that work, and a guarantee of service and satisfaction second to none.

Very sincerely,

J. Roderick MacArthur,
Chairman

P.S. If you have any questions regarding an item, please call our Mr. Ernie Hovland or one of his technical advisors at 312-664-7745. They have the Institute's testing and research data at their fingertips and should be able to give you a quick answer.

OSHIBORI TOWEL HOT BASKET. Continuing the tradition observed in Japanese households for over two centuries, this steamer basket heats up to fifteen small towels at a time for use by guests at your dinner table. The basket preheats to 150°F in 3-5 minutes and produces hot, moistened towels within 15 minutes more. Automatic thermostat maintains basket temperature between 120° and 150°F. Comes with rack for steaming foods such as pastries, breads, dinner rolls, cookies and cake. Plugs into household outlet. One dozen 12x12-inch blended cotton towels included. Height: 7½ inches. Length: 12½ inches.
21421R...............$49.50 Postpaid and Unconditionally Guaranteed

THE ARIA LIGHT SOCKET FAN. Imported from Italy exclusively by Hammacher Schlemmer this unique fan fits into any light socket in place of a bulb, and circulates cool or hot air gently and noiselessly as its blade spins at 800 RPM. It is useful in corners, over desks, work or cooking areas, or in small spaces where a large, noisy fan is not desirable. Used in a ceiling fixture, it circulates air throughout the room. The Aria Light Socket Fan consumes only 18 watts. Maintenance-free, and made of durable ABS plastic.
22617R $39.50
Postpaid and Unconditionally Guaranteed

© 1984 Hammacher Schlemmer

ON THE COVER

The Classic College Scoreboard can be used to time and score swimming meets, debates and other leisure time events; p. 71. **The Infinity Recumbent Ten-Speed Bicycle** allows you greater pedaling efficiency and a relaxed position for viewing scenery; p. 3. **The Heated Car Seat Pad** quickly warms up the entire seat of your car for driving comfort in cold weather; p. 4.

SHIPPING INFORMATION

All prices include the cost of shipping, insurance and handling except those items marked "Freight Collect" which are shipped via overland motor because of size and weight. Rather than include general freight charges on these items, we send them collect so that you pay only what it costs to transport them directly from the manufacturer to your doorstep. When such items are sent as gifts, we will ship them prepaid and bill you separately. Please allow four to six weeks for delivery of "Freight Collect" items.

PLEASE VISIT OUR STORES:

147 EAST 57th STREET NEW YORK CITY

618 NORTH MICHIGAN CHICAGO

Figure 11-4

Figure 11-5

"ALL GOODS WORTH PRICE CHARGED"
LYNCHBURG, TENNESSEE 37352

Herb Fanning   Eddie Swing

Dear Friend,

    I am just going to have to learn to keep my big mouth shut, I guess. Specially around my hotshot young partner, Eddie Swing. Three years ago, I happened to mention that maybe I ought to take on a partner in the old Hardware & General.

    First thing you know, we've shook hands and we're painting Eddie's name on the front door.

    Here after Christmas, Eddie and I were sitting quiet over a cup of coffee, letting our nerves unjangle some after the holiday rush and all. And I commented, casual like, on how nice it was in the old days when our business was smaller and our catalog was skinny enough so's you could remember everything in it without having to look it up and all.

    Bigmouthed me!

    This morning here comes Eddie as proud and smiley as a mama cat with a new batch of kittens.

    "Here you go Herbie," he crows. "A skinny little catalog full of Fanning's Favorites!"

    I tell you, with Eddie's energy and my good sense, we may make something of this old store yet.

    Seriously though, everything in here carries our personal guarantee of satisfaction, as always. And we do our best to pack up your order within a few days after we get it. So let us hear from you. We'll be pleased to do business with you.

Sincerely,

Herb Fanning

Herb Fanning

P.S. Our prices include delivery and handling, as always.

Figure 11-6

Behind Our Catalog —

When we first set up shop five years ago, we did so determined to offer the most extensive selection of natural fabric safari (translate: functional, intelligently-designed khakis and whites) clothing on earth. Nobody else was even attempting to do this. There were shops that blew in the flimsy winds of fashion; there were sanctimonious, hardcore backpacker-style outdoor stores, there were sporting goods retailers selling athletic wear, mostly of the unmentionable substance called polyester.

So we had our unique idea, but where to find the clothing? It took some digging. Journalists by trade, we set out. First we located old-world manufacturers who did not play the fashion game, and put them to work producing nowhere-to-be-found classics that had always been favored by journalists, writers, photographers, musicians, artists, film and theater people. But as we soon found out, nobody anywhere did authentic safari styles as well as the military. The finest garments, in terms of styling, workmanship, and functional authenticity had already been designed for one army or another. That's where we went looking, and thus, in a moment of whimsy, we named ourselves Banana Republic. We traveled (and still do) to the steamy jungles of South America, to the icy wastes of the arctic, to the dusty plains of Africa, to the furthest corner of Her Majesty's crumbled empire. We've scouted up many a dark alley in many a damp country, with one purpose always in mind: To find and buy up stockpiles of sartorial gems tossed out by the new regime whose generals wouldn't dream of wearing a shirt that had been designed for the old regime.

When we find a particularly enduring classic that we cannot get any more of, we produce it ourselves, thread for thread, zipper for zipper, as authentic as the original. Most of our customers wear our clothing to travel in, to relax in, and where it's appropriate, to work in. We know, of course, that trends, like regimes, come and go. That's why we at Banana Republic Travel and Safari Clothing find and favor the classics, determined never to be toppled as the pre-eminent clothier of honest-to-God value, inventive, unique, authentic, natural fabric safari and travel wear on earth.

Mel Ziegler
Patricia Ziegler

OUR STORES

The clothing featured on these pages is sold by mail and in our stores. Our stores (there are five in California) also stock some very unusual and rare authentic international surplus we've found in our travels. Our sales personnel are well-versed on the clothing and can assist you in putting together a wardrobe for any destination, any time of the year. Each store is open seven days, and a few have evening schedules as well. We welcome you as a customer. You'll find our staff happy to serve you, and likely to remember you when you return again and again, as we hope you will.

For those customers outside the San Francisco and Los Angeles areas, our catalog staff is on hand seven days a week to serve you with the same personal care and attention.

Copyright 1983 by BANANA REPUBLIC, Inc.

the locations:

SAN FRANCISCO: 2253 Polk St. (at Green),
  415 777-4665
PALO ALTO: Stanford Shopping Center,
  415 322-0200
SAN MATEO: Hillsdale Shopping Center,
  415 345-9300
MILL VALLEY: 76 E. Blithedale,
  415 383-4900
BEVERLY HILLS: 9669 Santa Monica Blvd.,
  213 858-7900
MAIL ORDERS:
Box 77133, San Francisco, CA 94107

ORDER TOLL-FREE
② **800-527-5200**

Figure 11-7

3. Does your catalog offer extra, editorial commentary? Catalogs with unusual products or product lines that have interesting stories can give the reader educational and anecdotal information in addition to straight product copy. Informative and entertaining, these stories increase involvement. Used extensively throughout the catalog, they create what some people call a magalog or catamag (a hybrid catalog cum magazine).

Smith & Hawken's Garden catalog (which is practically a magalog anyway) takes the cake for involvement with this customer request. (Figure 11-8.)

To the Gardener:

With your help, we would like to change our catalog. Up to now, most of the photographs in the catalog were taken by ourselves, in and around the gardens of friends or at our homes. Starting with our summer catalog, we would like to show the tools in *your* garden. And we would like to see you too.

We would like to receive photographs—color transparencies are ideal—of a Smith & Hawken tool with its user in a garden or work setting. Smith & Hawken will give $50 in tools for each photograph used in the catalog. Serious, humorous, active or wild, we would like to see them. There are some beautiful gardens out there, and the catalog is a perfect place to show them.

When sending in photographs, address them to Paul's mom, Margaret Hawken. She will send you an acknowledgment that we have received them and take good care of them while they are in our possession. Before we go to press on a catalog, we will notify the people whose photographs are used and send them a credit for tools. Thank you in advance for your help.

In the meantime, there are a bunch of new tools in this edition. Some of the most fascinating are the new Japanese tools made in Kochi Prefecture. Japanese design, both in fashion and housewares, has become very big in the past few years. These tools are designs that have endured for decades, even centuries.

Have a wonderful spring.

Paul Hawken & Dave Smith

A Gift Certificate

FOR MERCHANDISE
IN THE AMOUNT OF

SMITH & HAWKEN
25 Corte Madera, Mill Valley California 94941

Figure 11-8

The White Flower Farm catalog is famous for such copy. It is a pleasure to read and certainly greatly increases involvement. It regales the reader with current anecdotes and friendly news from the neighborhood. It has even been known to include a first rate "fish" story. (Figure 11-9.)

Community Kitchens starts, "We are the Saurages of South Louisiana. Nearly every day of our lives we've known and shared some unforgettable moments of dining...." (Figure 11-10.)

Banana Republic advises "Yell like hell when you encounter a crocodile (you will) while rafting down Ethiopia's Omo River and he'll dive under water."

Sunnyland Farms, Inc. tells the farm's history and the family story in pictures and text in the margins of the catalog pages. They even show the family cat.

Sir Thomas Lipton's Trading Company makes tea time an art and offers tall tales about teas of all kinds. (Figure 11-11.)

have been shipped and there have been expressions of discontent from new customers about this practice. If it seems unreasonable, we are sorry. It is one of the burdens of doing business with a nursery that grows everything it sells. There are, we believe, offsetting benefits.

Another Hydro Project

For the same reasons that the pond was expanded, we also planned to dig a new well last summer. Since there are few good wells in the area, it was clear that a simple hole in the ground wouldn't do the job. To improve the odds, we secured the services of Mr. Whitey Phelps, a local dowser of some reputation. His visit to the nursery on a bright Saturday afternoon (see photo) drew the kind of crowd you expect around a sidewalk game of 3-card monte. With a freshly cut wand held firmly in the heavily calloused hands of a professional logger, he criss-crossed the back fields looking for the sharp downward tug of a "vein" of water. The tug, he explained, is caused by electricity attending the moving water below, but sensitivity to it seems to vary with the individual. This he confirmed by passing a pair of straightened coathangers among his audience and asking each of us to walk the same path with the wires extended straight ahead, supported by a handle formed by turning the ends at 90 degrees. In some hands, the parallel wires parted to form a straight line, always over the same spot, but others got no movement. Having seen the same procedure used by the power company to find buried lines, we were not surprised. But when a length of red maple jerked his hands down hard enough to tear the skin, we paid attention though no one could duplicate his experience. Via a process of dead reckoning, he identified another vein that crossed this one. At the intersection, we drove a heavy pipe into the ground, then thanked Whitey and handed over a check.

Being cautious folks, we also retained a firm which locates wells by using a sensitive device that measures magnetic fields. With no clues, and for a good deal larger fee, they made their own search and placed the preferred site within 50 feet of Whitey's choice. There followed a good deal of discussion about their experiences with dowsers (inconsistent except for a couple of exceptional individuals), drillers (some have a better sense for water than do dowsers), and plantsmen (never saw so many tractors for a small farm). The im-

plicit consensus, which never managed to become explicit, was that we'd find 30 to 40 gallons per minute between 200 and 300 feet down. A call to Whitey confirmed that this sounded sensible. Would we drill? Indeed we would.

We've had some time now to reflect on the marvelous coincidence of two technologies, apparently quite separate in their levels of precision, arriving at the same conclusion. It seems to bode well for the survival of some elements of the past that appear too fragile to compete in the space age. Since we're in somewhat the same category, the prospect is encouraging.... The well? Oh, yes. Three tries, two to 400 feet, one to 500. No water to speak of.

The End of an Era

Our collection of rare and unusual Dwarf Evergreens was begun almost 20 years ago. At that time, these marvelous plants were little known and we struggled to secure stock—ultimately setting on a list that ran, at one time, to more than 60 varieties. That was back before the emergence of huge southern nurseries producing millions of container-grown shrubs and trucking them all over the country. They started with the basic items such as Rhododendrons and Hollies, but it wasn't long until they discovered our little friends. Between their climatic advantage and the rise in UPS costs, they shortly established that they could deliver a beautifully grown plant in a large size at a price we couldn't begin to match. Yes, you have to find a garden center that stocks a full line, but that's what telephones are for. After several years of looking like either fools or villains, we are throwing in the sponge. We will offer our remaining stocks over the next two years, but have already stopped propagating. If you've been postponing a purchase, it's time to move.

Miscellany

Let's start with our annual invitation. Litchfield Open House will be held Saturday, July 14th, and visitors are encouraged to join us for tea and cucumber sandwiches on the lawn by our house. Several years back, we added cookies to the menu and observed an increase in the number of little people. We like that.... In a bow to Bruce Kellas, our head gardener, we have had manufactured a left-handed version of the Dutchook, the standby weeding tool which we cadged from Holland. Bruce maintains more than ten acres of display gardens here and is probably the only person alive who can honestly say he has worn out a Dutchook. Now he has one designed just for him.... Mrs. Elizabeth MacDougall of Washington wrote a delightful letter in which she reported inadvertently storing a shipment of our Peonies and Iris in a refrigerator for a year-and-a-half. All survived and, after a season or two to recover their composure, took to blooming as if nothing had happened. It's not recommended procedure, but is comforting to consider when delays in planting crop up.... Due to a recent change in Connecticut tax laws, those of you who have orders shipped to Connecticut addresses will now be charged 7½% sales tax on shipping and handling as well as on the goods themselves. We regret the development but really have no choice in the matter.... The front cover of this edition is a photo of the Moon Garden in front of our house. It was re-

6

SOUTH LOUISIANA'S COMMUNITY KITCHENS

We are the Saurages of South Louisiana. Nearly every day of our lives we've known and shared some unforgettable moments of dining. Our family is typical of this region's special tastes and traditions. Baton Rouge is the soul of South Louisiana's reputation as the nation's coffee capital. Many thousands of gourmets have sampled our Community Coffee, first blended by our grandfather over sixty-five years ago. Now we combine our coffees with other uniquely American flavors—a collection of gourmet foods and accessories selected by a family with an appreciation of fine taste.

Imagine yourself as a guest in our homeland—for only in this book will you discover the extraordinary tastes of South Louisiana's Community Kitchens, beginning with the history, flavor and freshness of Community Coffee.

Community Coffee

There is no routine human beings adore more than a simple morning's coffee. It gives an added pleasure to rising. It freshens our thought. And, as the day grows more involved, coffee continues to offer its unique relief and refreshment.

There may be some exception taken to this point of view, as the average cup of coffee is an unpredictable thing; you are often left disappointed. But, for us, all doubts and reservations are resolved by quality. We have our philosophy about the way things should be, and we pursue the ways in which those things are done well.

Here is a taste that makes the routine extraordinary.

A History

South Louisiana has a typically independent French heritage: our lives are different than yours, as is our taste in coffee. Because, since

the early years, we've roasted and brewed our own blends, we have developed a sensitivity to especially good, fresh coffee, both pure coffee and coffee and chicory blends. It's not that we've reserved the best things in life for ourselves. The truth is, very few Americans will have known what they are missing until we make a proper introduction.

Please meet Cap Saurage.

Our Community Coffee label began with Mr. Henry Norman Saurage, Sr., whose own life started simply enough—with no intention of intertwining his family's roots with those of coffee history. Nonetheless, history was insistent.

By the early 1900's, Baton Rouge had several groceries. One was Cap Saurage's. Just as this was the Henry Ford era, Cap Saurage was a singular spirit of the time. When he opened a second store, it was thoughtfully named The Full Weight Grocery, a principle that both he and his customers treated as a creed.

Talent is what shapes history for the better. Cap Saurage had a rare sense of coffee, a loving and incorruptible devotion. He knew that quality and economy when combined could better the lives of his customers.

To do this, he combined his own loves, coffee and family. Brother-in-law Albert Dupuy became salesman for the roasted coffee beans which Cap bought, ground, and packed for the local grocers; his wit and Cap's coffee gave the Community label a flavor that was (in all ways) personally satisfying. It was the basic attraction of good coffee for good people.

Their business grew, but not by chance: its quality improved directly as Cap established the Baton Rouge Coffee Mill in a converted barn behind his house. This wasn't meant to be an industry—only one tabletop grinder, pre-made bags, a hand scoop and a scale. The excellence of the

2

Figure 11-10

Tea Tales

2737 B.C. The Discovery of Tea—
Legend tells us that tea was discovered in 2737 B.C. by the Chinese Emperor Shen-Nung, "The Divine Healer." Observing that people who drank boiled water enjoyed better health, the wise Emperor insisted on this precaution. When tea leaves accidentally fell into boiling water, Shen-Nung first approved the pleasing aroma, and then the delightful flavor. The taste for tea was born, and from China it spread to Japan and other Far Eastern lands.

1800 A.D. Origins of Afternoon Tea—
In the early nineteenth century, Anna, the Duchess of Bedford, originated afternoon tea as a social custom to combat, in her words, "that sinking feeling." Time proved she was right, and the soothing lift of an afternoon cup of tea swept the country and maintains its prestige to this day.

Double Duty Tea—
William Gladstone, the grand old man of British politics, was an ingenious tea drinker. It was his custom to take a glazed pottery "hot water bottle" filled with piping hot tea to Parliament, as well as to bed. This served him well two ways; to keep his feet warm, and to provide a drink of soothing tea.

Samuel Johnson in Praise of Tea—
Johnson described himself "a hardened and shameless tea drinker who for many years diluted his meals only with the infusion of this fascinating plant; whose kettle has scarcely time to cool; who with tea amuses the evening, with tea solaces the midnight, and with tea welcomes the morning."

⭐ **U.S. Presidents
...and Tea—**
George Washington, Thomas Jefferson, Abraham Lincoln were great tea enthusiasts. Of our more modern day Presidents, Roosevelt, Eisenhower, and Kennedy were known to enjoy tea at various times of the day.

Top of the Morning to You!

A. GOOD MORNING MARMALADE. Only the most natural marmalade should start your English day—16-oz. of Sarabeth Orange-Apricot Marmalade, golden in color, rich in aroma and ever so delicious. And to cheer your day, a white ceramic jam jar, with spoon, decorated with colorful oranges. *A good morning gift!*
#5530S Good Morning Set **$16.50**

B. COZY COTTAGES. Made in England, naturally! The endearing 5-cup handpainted teapot with its thatched roof lid is an enchanting way to serve tea. And when you add the charming covered sugar bowl and creamer, you'll have a cozy set.
#4524P Cottage Teapot **$28.00**
#8547R Sugar/Creamer **$28.00**
#8548R Cottage Set **$50.00**
(Save over 10%)

C. TOAST OF THE TOWN. The perfect way to start your day. This silver-plated reproduction of a classic English toast rack holds six slices. 6½" x 4¼", made in England. Comes with 12-oz. of all natural Vintage Orange Marmalade, made in Elsenham, England. And add 5-oz. of our English Breakfast leaf tea for a perfect English Day!
#7034L Toast of Town Set **$26.00**

16

It's involvement, credibility, and the basis for a stellar new kind of catalog all in one!

4. Does your catalog present its products dramatically, clearly, and with compelling copy? Just giving a list of product features and a price is not enough. Each product should be treated like the subject of a small space workhorse. The product picture is your valuable graphic that works with your headline. (Remember?)

Many catalogs rely only on this illustration and a flat-out single line product description (like "Miniature Garden Seat" … "Doorman's Giant Umbrella" … "The Deli Meat Slicer" … "Cashmere Cardigan" … "Cotton Camp Shirt" … "Solid Maple Display Table" … "Luggage Rack") for the headline. When the descriptive copy that follows is filled with promises (benefits to you) and features, they seem to get on fine.

But how much *stronger*, in a competitive market, to use such headlines as

File of rich oak. A friendly alternative to cold steel.

Flexible fins. A new power source for swimmers.

From beans to brew while you sleep *(The Sharper Image)*.

A silken touch of bedtime luxury.

You'll love how you look in a Felt Crusher!

The last watch you'll ever need to buy *(Early Winters)*

Little silver salt spoons are hard to find these days….

Our quiet little box fan moves heat from room to room….

Bring the tang of Vermont Pine and Balsam woods into your home….
  (Vermont Country Store)

How many times have you reached for your flashlight and found it useless
  because of dead batteries?

Someone finally realized that the step you use most often on a stepstool is
  the second one.

This is the greatest mirror we've ever seen. *(Comfortably Yours)*

Or even longer ones likes these:

Lands' End "Ultimate" sweats. Not flimsy or fashiony but heavy-duty like
  the kind college teams work out in. More expensive than imitations, but
  worth it for long wear and superior performance in action.

Some think we sell more pinpoint oxfords than anyone else because of our
  lower price—$29.50. Maybe. Lands' End Quality Specialists, who com-
  pare our pinpoints to others, tell us we sell more because it's the best
  pinpoint on the market. *(Lands' End Direct Merchants)*

Fine headlines, all. And in all cases, they're followed by equally fine copy. Notice, too, that each group from each catalog has a consistent and distinctly different tone (or approach), suited to its image.

5. Does your catalog have a strong offer? Is there a carefully worked 100 percent guarantee? Does it use deadlines, discounts, or bonus coupons? Are instructions clear? Does it have a competitive credit policy? Is the order form easy to use? Are there assurances of active customer service, fast delivery (specific times), and a good return policy? Do you use testimonials from satisfied customers? Is the *800* number in clear view? Do you ask for referrals?

You can learn a lot from our top catalog companies in this area. Copy heavily from the best of them, if you can. For example:

- L.L. Bean instituted Federal Express delivery for Christmas orders, while Early Winters has an Instant Gratifier service *and* next day delivery (all at extra charge).
- Sunnyland Farms offers free recipes next to the order form.
- Sturbridge Yankee Workshop, Orvis, and Wigs from Paula Young all feature their service staff and fulfillment operation.
- Some catalogs offer small, impulse items on their order forms for add-on sales.
- Every one of them provides a prominent airtight guarantee, and most have toll-free telephone service. (See Figures 11-12 through 11-16.)

Study the order forms of Sharper Image, Orvis, L.L. Bean, Smith & Hawken and White Flower Farm; they all have an excellent reputation with their customers. And this is where it starts. Remember, lack of clarity in ordering creates inertia!

Now Go For It!

Once you've asked your questions and made your comparisons, make your contribution by being sure the overall catalog image or personality gets through to the customer loud and clear. Strengthen the image with

- a logical spokesperson with commitment and credibility
- an explanation *and* demonstration of how and why the owners and the company are particularly well-qualified to bring the products to the customer
- stories, examples, history of how this was achieved
- a look at the operation today, the people who serve the customers now
- quotations from real customers in praise of the catalog
- invitations to visit the store(s)
- lots of good pictures to build credibility

Reinforce that image with merchandise presentations in a tone and a format that support the image, while doing the job of small workhorse space ads (with strong involving headlines). Extend the image right onto the order form and make sure your company is a paragon of customer service virtues.

Some Good Illustrations of Customer Service

BEHIND THESE SMILING FACES*-- A SERIOUS PURPOSE ...

... To provide our customers with the *very best service possible*. We were not surprised to be recently named on a national T.V. show as "one of the best catalog companies in the country." These are some of the people who make it happen. There are many more as well, all standing ready to serve you with total commitment to your absolute satisfaction. We all look forward to it!

LOOK FOR OUR COMPANY SYMBOL -- IT HIGHLIGHTS ITEMS OF EXCEPTIONAL VALUE!

Through hard bargaining with our vendors, we have managed to maintain many of last year's low prices, and some items have been reduced even further! For your benefit, products that we feel are outstanding values have been flagged with our company symbol. Also -- please don't miss our *special sale section* in the center of the catalog.

Happy shopping!

John I. Riddle
President

*Front Row: Connie Lamper - Customer Service Rep.; Celeste Chabot - Payroll Clerk; Sue Plummer - Accounting Clerk; Norma Tuell - Packer; Ginny Norton - Stocker.
Middle Row: Steve Beaulieu - Stocker; Donna Plourde - Customer Service Rep.; Becky Moran - Graphic Artist; Eugene Smith - Shipper; Mary Jane Andrews - Receiver
Back Row: Dana Haupt - Assistant Buyer; Sarah Colton - Receptionist; Ellen Kornetsky - Copywriter; David Valyou - Buyer.

GENUINE ROSES IN CRYSTAL VASE
Natural red roses preserved in all their brilliance, artfully arranged in a shapely hurri-cane-style crystal vase. A rare, eye-catching accent sure to be a conversation piece. 8"h. x 3¼" diam. 1-21-4021 $16.95

BONE CHINA SWAN FLOWER RING
This unusual three sectioned ring of fine bone china swans holds fresh blossoms or candy. Your candle in the center creates a warm effect on an end table or as an interesting centerpiece. 3¼"h. x 9½" diam. *Swan ring* 1-21-4022 $34.95

Call Toll-Free 24 hours a day

"HUDSON VALLEY SUNSET" PRINT
The warmth and serenity of the scene executed in exceptionally radiant tones with excellent detail makes this a captivating wall accent for your living or family room. The eye is drawn down the road into the village where a church steeple rises protectively over the homes; on the river a boat sails to rest at the shore. The old-style hardwood frame trimmed with black and gold is ready to hang. 26" x 33½" 1-31-4023 $109.95

SOLID CHERRY COFFEE TABLE & SOFA TABLE
New! Beautifully designed and crafted tables of solid cherry with a very fine handrubbed finish. Classic Queen Anne cabriole legs ending in spoon feet; graceful scalloped aprons and molded table tops will formalize any traditional decor. *Coffee Table.* 17"h. x 45"w. x 23½"d. 3-18-4026 $229.00; *Sofa Table.* 28"h. x 54"w. x 14¼"d. 3-18-4025 $259.00

HANDPAINTED PORCELAIN "COMMON LOON" DECOY
Evocative bird handpainted by Sadek on fine porcelain. An outstanding reproduction with fine detailing. Handsome as a single accent or as a member of your decoy collection. 6" x 6" x 10½" 1-21-4024 $34.95

Figure 11-12 *from Sturbridge Yankee Workshop*

Why Nearly 250,000
Prefer Shopping by Mail with

Taking Customer's Rush Order.

Inside the Computer Room.

Sorting Mail and Processing Orders.

Selecting Wigs for Shipment.

Personal Service

Can a mail order company give you really PERSONAL attention? Yes! Shopping with us by mail or phone can often be a far MORE satisfying experience than trying to deal with indifferent sales clerks in a retail store.

Whether you order by mail or phone, your order receives individual attention. Careful records are kept of your style and color, as well as any special requests you make and the full resources of the company are put toward serving you quickly and completely.

Fast Delivery

This year, Paula Young™ will ship almost ½ million wigs to the women of America . . . 5 to 10 percent of ALL the wigs purchased in this country. And one of the reasons is SERVICE!

From the moment we receive your order by phone or by mail, it is rarely more than one or two days from going out the door, and on its way to you. While other mail order companies make you wait 4 to 6 weeks for shipment, our aim is to get your wig to you in 4 to 6 DAYS!

Keeping You in Fashion

This year we will mail millions of catalo to women all over the U.S., with all the latest fashions, and improvements in w design. As a customer you'll receive ma ings of special offers, new styles, new p ducts . . . everything you need to be a v informed wig wearer. Paula Young brin the wig fashion world right into your li ing room, where you can shop in comfe and at leisure.

2

Figure 11-13 *from Paula Young*

Our 50,000 Wig Warehouse

Out the Door and On Their Way to You.

Wig Selection With YOU in Mind

The style you want in the color you want is ready to be sent to you TODAY! Our warehouse stock of 50,000 wigs, the largest of any consumer wig outlet in the country, enables us to fill the thousands of orders we receive every month with ease.

In addition, we work closely with the leading wig-makers, Eva Gabor and Adolfo, to develop new and improved styles based upon the ideas and suggestions we get from YOU, our customers.

6 Good Reasons:
to Become a
Paula Young Customer

1. GUARANTEE - You MUST be satisfied when you shop with Paula Young. Just read this:

No Risk Guarantee
Everything you order from Paula Young is uncon-ditionally guaranteed. You may return your purchase at any time - for any reason - for credit, exchange, or refund, no questions asked.

2. SELECTION - No store can offer so many different styles and colors for you to choose from — over 600 different styles and color combinations.

3. CONVENIENCE - You can place your order from the comfort of your home, by mail or telephone and have it delivered to your door in a matter of days.

4. ECONOMY - We will NOT be undersold. If you find an EVA GABOR or ADOLFO style offered elsewhere for less than our price, send us the page on which it appears, and we will meet the lower price, and send you a free gift for your trouble!

5. PRIVACY - You may try on your wig at home, taking all the time you need.

6. SERVICE - No waiting. Most orders are shipped within 2 days after recceipt. Full exchange privileges means no problem if you wish to exchange your purchase for a different style or color.

Yes - Six good reasons why nearly 250,000 American women order their wigs form Paula Young™. May we serve you as well?

Cordially,

Paula

3

To Place An Order
Call 1-802-362-1300

If you wish to place a phone order using your Credit Card, or have a question about any product in the catalog, Orvis operators will handle your order promptly and efficiently. Your call will be answered between **8:00 a.m. and 11:00 p.m. Eastern Time, Monday through Friday and Saturday and Sunday between 9:00 a.m. and 4:00 p.m.** At any other hour, you can place an order with our recorded answering service using your Credit Card (Visa, MasterCard or American Express).

For Customer Service
Call 1-802-362-3434

If you wish to check on an order placed previously, inquire about deliveries of orders or for questions about products or special needs, call between the hours of **9:00 a.m. and 4:00 p.m. Eastern Time, 7 days a week.** You will be connected with someone who can help you.

For Technical Questions
Call 1-802-362-3166

If you wish to get some advice on what tackle to take on a fishing trip or order a new fly rod and reel but aren't quite sure of which model or for technical advice of any kind, call our special number **Monday through Friday between the hours of 8:00 a.m. and 5:00 p.m. Eastern Time.**

For Schools or Trips
Call 1-802-362-3900

If you wish to make a reservation for any of our schools (fishing, shooting, etc.) or one of our special fishing or hunting trips, call between **8:00 a.m. and 5:00 p.m. Eastern Time, Monday through Friday.**

GREG COMAR . . . if you have any technical questions on an Orvis product, if you need rod building or fly tying information, or if you're wondering what kind of gear to take on a fishing or hunting trip, call Greg at 1 - 802 - 362-3166.

MARY SPRAGUE . . . heads our Customer Service Department and will answer all your questions about products or special needs. In fact, Mary can handle practically anything . . . call 1 - 802 - 362-3434.

KATHY BACON . . . will be happy to answer your inquiries about orders you have placed or deliveries of orders. Call 1 - 802 - 362-3434.

SUSAN ELWELL or one of our instructors will answer your questions and make reservations for all our Orvis schools and our special fishing or hunting trips. 1 - 802 - 362-3900

How To Order By Mail

Use the inserted order blank or ANY sheet of paper. Be sure your order specifies BY WHOM the order is made and TO WHOM you would like it shipped. Select items and specify QUANTITY, CATALOG ITEM NUMBER, SIZE/PATTERN NO., OTHER INFORMATION and PRICE.

Total order and ADD $3.90 to cover packing, shipping and guaranteed delivery. YOU WILL NOTE that certain heavy or bulky items carry an additional postal amount which should be added to the $3.90 per order charge. For **Special Delivery, ADD $3.00** in addition to the above $3.90. For **Air Service, ADD $5.00** in addition to the $3.90 per address. Total all charges and enclose complete payment: check, money order, or credit card information. Be sure to **sign your name, it is required.** Please, no C. O. D.'s, stamps or currency.

SALES TAX . . . For deliveries in California, add 6% State Tax (6½% in Alameda, Contra Costa and San Francisco counties). For deliveries in Vermont, add 4% State Tax.

ORVIS CATALOG MAILING LIST . . . If your address is incorrect, or if you are moving or are receiving more than one copy at the same time of our catalog, please **send address(es) on your catalog(s) with your instructions regarding changes/corrections/deletions** so you will receive the copies you wish.

MAIL PREFERENCE SERVICE . . . Orvis occasionally makes its customers' names available to carefully selected companies with offers that may be of interest to you. If you prefer not to receive such mailings, please copy your mailing label exactly and send it to: Orvis Mail Preference, 10 River Road, Manchester, Vermont 05254 or note it on your order.

INTERNATIONAL ORDERS . . . **Minimum Order $25.00.** Payment must be made in U.S. funds (checks payable by a U.S. bank) or major credit card. Add 30% to merchandise total to cover documentation and shipping by air. 42" (106cm) length limit. CANADIAN CUSTOMERS . . . no length limit. Add 40% to the total ordered. We PREPAY Canadian duty, Dominion Sales Tax, brokerage fees, postal charges and insure safe delivery direct to your address.

We have representatives in over 20 countries to serve Orvis customers. We would be pleased to provide their addresses. For our British catalog, send direct to: Orvis (UK) Ltd., Nether Wallop Mill. Stockbridge, Hants, SO 20 8ES, U. K.

ORVIS MANCHESTER	ORVIS HOUSTON
Historic Route 7A	5848 Westheimer Road
Manchester, Vt. 05254	Houston, Texas 77057
Tel. 1 - 802 - 362-3434	Tel. 1 - 713 - 783-2111
ORVIS NEW YORK	ORVIS SAN FRANCISCO
45th St. and Madison Ave.	166 Maiden Lane
Entrance on 45th Street	Union Square
Tel. 1 - 212 - 697-3133	Tel. 1 - 415 - 392-1600

– – – – – – – – CUT OFF HERE – – – – – – – –

MAY WE SEND AN ORVIS CATALOG TO A FRIEND WITH YOUR COMPLIMENTS . . . JUST FILL IN AND MAIL TO ORVIS, MANCHESTER, VERMONT 05254.

Name . . . .

Address. . . . .

. . . . .Zip Code . . . .

[ ] Fishing/Hunting Catalogs   [ ] Clothing/Gift Catalogs

Name . . . .

Address. . . . .

. . . . .Zip Code . . . .

[ ] Fishing/Hunting Catalogs   [ ] Clothing/Gift Catalogs

From . . . .

Figure 11-14 *from Orvis*

A FEW THINGS ABOUT ORDERING FROM US.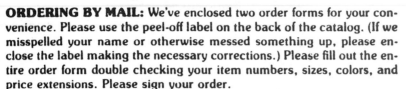

ORDERING BY MAIL: We've enclosed two order forms for your convenience. Please use the peel-off label on the back of the catalog. (If we misspelled your name or otherwise messed something up, please enclose the label making the necessary corrections.) Please fill out the entire order form double checking your item numbers, sizes, colors, and price extensions. Please sign your order.

TELEPHONE ORDERS: Eddie said it would be nice if our customers could call in their orders toll free. I agreed, and we added a new 800 number this year. It's 1-800-251-8600. Alaska, Hawaii, and Tennessee residents should still use (615) 759-7184. (No collect calls please.)

Anyway, before you call, please go ahead and fill out the order form. It'll serve as your order record and help us both to get everything right. We can accept only charge card orders over the phone.

PAYMENT: Eddie and I gladly accept personal checks, certified checks, money orders, MasterCard, Visa, and American Express. We advise you not to send cash through the mails. (Checks should be payable to: Lynchburg Hardware & General Store.) When using a charge card, please include all numbers, expiration date and your signature.

HOW WE SHIP: For the most part, we'll ship your order by United Parcel Service (UPS), although sometimes we do use Parcel Post. That's why it's very important to have a full street address for us to ship to.

FOREIGN ORDERS: We don't mind a bit getting foreign orders. But we do ask this . . . please write to us in English and send your payment in U.S. dollars. If you will add 10% to your total order, that should be good enough to cover the extra postage (not airmail).

Since duties vary from country to country, we suggest you check with your country's customs bureau to find out the duty they will charge you. We have enough red tape with Uncle Sam without having to get involved with other governments.

RETURNS AND EXCHANGES: Our main goal is to have you as a satisfied customer. But every once in a while we do make a mistake. If the mistake is our fault, and you want a refund or exchange, we'll gladly do that. And we'll pay you the postage involved in returning the item to us. But say you ordered a medium shirt and we sent you a medium shirt but you ate too much Thanksgiving dinner and really should have ordered a large shirt and you want to exchange it—well, you return it and we'll do just that.

DUPLICATE CATALOGS: Should you receive more than one catalog, please help us out and pass the extra one(s) along to friends. Also, if you will, please return the duplicate label(s) marking it "Duplicate". It'll save us some money and in turn, it'll save you, our customer, money also.

OUR GUARANTEE: Mr. Lem Motlow said it years and years ago, and Eddie and I still say it today, and we really mean it, "All Goods Worth Price Charged".

Figure 11-15 *from Lynchburg Hardware & General Store*

Why you'll see me in our new stores.

Because pleasing you means everything to us, whether you order by catalog or in person.

I drop into the new stores regularly, to check products, presentations, and test our customer service. That's what you expect, and you'll find whenever you visit us.

Our sales people are friendly product experts. Our carefully-chosen managers share a philosophy with me: That our reputation with you is more important than any profit. Order with confidence, because you must be 100% satisfied—or we'll make it right.

You'll probably see me in San Francisco, Los Angeles, Denver or Houston. Just introduce yourself and tell me what we can do to improve. I'm listening.

Happy shopping!

Richard

Richard Thalheimer
President

P.S. We gladly accept returns. And we appreciate your cooperation in returning items complete with box and packaging materials.

HOUSTON
700 Rusk Street
(at Louisiana)
(713) 224-2412

DENVER
Tabor Center
1201 16th Street
(at Arapahoe)
(303) 534-1636

SAN FRANCISCO
Main Store
680 Davis Street
(415) 445-6100

Sale Store
406 Jackson Street
(discontinued products at sharply reduced prices)
(415) 391-0563

LOS ANGELES
601 Wilshire Blvd.
(at Grand)
(213) 622-2351

RETURN WITH US NOW...

McGonigle by Jeff Danziger ©N.A.S.

Figure 11-16 *from The Sharper Image*

All right, you know how to evaluate your catalog. You know what to look for. You know how to approach and analyze your catalog assignment. You know why certain things are needed to bring the customer into the dialogue. You know how to use AIDA and other formulas, and to keep an eye out for Involvement, Credibility, Offer, and Motivation. Let's hope you also know you can't do all of this alone. Who's missing? You're right; just as before—just as always—your artist, or art director, or designer. Your words are important, but equally important is the look, the design and layout of the catalog. The two of you should work closely from the beginning.

What more do you need? Well, if I were you and about to get a catalog assignment, I'd rush off and order ten to fifteen of the country's top catalogs. You can't find better teachers, or better sources of new ideas. I've made up a list for you at the end of this chapter. It includes many of the newer catalogs as well as some classics. Newcomers have to fight harder to develop an image, so they may be particularly helpful to you.

A Paean to the Catalog

Browsing through catalogs makes one realize what wonderful stores these are! What a joy to shop them, meet their people, learn about new products and improvements, and all sorts of intriguing things from the story of European goose down to the giant Amur fish that took over a fresh water pond.

I wish you a good experience with catalogs, particularly with those that can use your help. You have the equipment to provide this help. Use it. Not many people know how to examine the creative elements of a catalog analytically. You do and can.

Send in for your catalogs; enjoy them and learn from them! Order from them! You'll find it's irresistible!

WHAT TO DO WITH ALL THOSE SUBSCRIBERS

There is only one answer for a direct marketer—renew them! Or if they're new subscribers (first time)—convert them! This is called circulation promotion. It's part and parcel of direct response because it enables you to continue the dialogue you began via your initial prospecting for new subscribers to magazines, newspapers, newsletters, and trade journals.

Over the years, circulation (or the area that pertains to getting the publication distributed—circulated—via the mails) has become increasingly sophisticated. In the 1950s and 1960s most magazine publishers merely sent out a series of notices or letters informing new and old subscribers alike that their subscriptions would soon run out.

Human beings being human, they frequently postponed renewing and let their subscriptions lapse, so publishers and circulation directors decided to give subscribers more time to respond by moving up the notices and increasing the number of efforts. They also began offering incentives and special rates to spur subscribers to act.

Being good direct marketers, the publishers and circulation directors also tracked, tested, and measured. They found that the earlier they started, the more direct mail efforts they sent, the greater the response—particularly if later messages became more urgent in tone. Ultimately, they also tested expired or lapsed subscribers and found that, if offered special low prices, many of these people could be returned to the fold or reinstated.

In a few cases, all of this testing and trying resulted in renewal series of ten to fifteen or more efforts (or mailings). In most cases, only five to seven efforts were used. Whether five or fifteen, renewals always seemed terribly wasteful and irritating to outsiders, but productive to the inside professionals, as no effort was maintained that couldn't pull its own weight in subscriber response. (For example, if an effort cost $300 to mail, it had to bring in at least that much in renewed subscriptions.)

A standard series (a series format that works for most monthly publishers) evolved.

First notice–four months prior to expiration

Second notice–three months prior to expiration

Third notice–two months prior to expiration

Fourth notice (last chance)–one month prior to expiration

Fifth notice–two weeks or a month after expiration

Sixth and final notice (optional)–two months after expiration

By the 1960s, thanks to the computer and its ability to develop and maintain extensive subscriber records, circulation directors knew where a subscriber came from (source), how long a subscriber had been on the books (first time renewal or regular), the kind of offer the subscriber responded to up front (full price, half price, premium, or sweepstakes). They were then able to study subscriber actions as groups, based on where they came from (source).

When you begin to learn all these things about your customers (or subscribers) you also begin to see that not all new subscribers behave the same. And, ultimately, to maximize response, maybe they should be treated differently, according to source.

Situation: Those obtained from TV had a very low first renewal or conversion rate. Those from direct mail consistently did well.

Solution: Concentrate on direct mail-acquired subscribers. Convert television-acquired subscribers with special price or offer.

Situation: Those new subscribers acquired through an up-front offer that included a premium did not convert (or first renew) as well as new subscribers acquired with a standard offer without premium.

Solution: Offer premium-acquired subscribers premiums with first conversion.

Situation: Subscribers acquired through agents that used big national sweepstakes converted poorly, often taking an agent's new sweepstakes offer and starting a new subscription rather than converting as a regular subscriber through the publisher.

Solution: Send these subscribers a very early conversion opportunity loaded with extras such as a publisher's sweepstakes offer or multiple premiums.

From all this "sourcing" several things became apparent, and they now form the basis of the kind of renewal planning you'll encounter today.

1. Direct mail is the best and strongest source of new subscribers.

2. In all groups, subscribers who plan to renew will do so in early efforts (one and two). Later efforts must become more promotional to encourage the waverers.

3. Sweepstakes or premium-induced new customers require like or similar offers to respond well in conversions (premium sold–premium renewed).

4. It is cost-efficient to promote some source groups with only three to five efforts. While stronger, direct-mail sold sources may go profitably for six to twelve or more efforts. Each publication must determine its own exact pattern through testing.

5. A promotional "Early Bird" offer (sent some six months prior to expiration) can hype upfront renewal response considerably. Sometimes, however, it is merely robbing Peter to pay Paul, and the renewal series *overall* response ends up about the same in both test groups when this is split tested.

6. All conversion and renewal efforts seek to upgrade the subscriber to full renewal rates. This can be done quickly with some sources (direct mail) or it may take a couple of years (for some cut-rate and agent-sold subscribers).

7. Net sub value—or the lifetime value of a subscriber—is determined by tracking and costing source groups over a period of years. (Don't worry, there are computer models for this.)

As you may guess, today's renewal planning is no simple thing. A publication can have as many as six or seven sources for new subscribers. Most source group renewal series will vary in length. Some will have varying offers. And offers within any one group may change as expire time approaches and passes

To further complicate this, circulation directors are also testing formats. Many are using the magazine itself as a vehicle for expiration notices through cover wraps (this is your last issue) and bind-in cards and pages (yes, renew my subscription).

Sound complicated? Wait a minute. You're just getting started. Let's review, however, before we jump ahead.

1. Your basic renewals are keyed or broken out into two kinds of renewals—first time (or conversions) and regular. Some publishers, by the way, even break regular renewals into first regular *and* regular.

2. Each *conversion* group is broken out by source: direct mail sold, insert card obtained, agent sold, TV, print ads, and unknowns or write-ins, called *white mail*. (Sourcing is carried in the customer record for many years to track the overall net worth of the subscriber group during its lifetime. But for renewal purposes, it is used only to break out promotional planning in the conversions.)

3. The offer is composed of price and term (number of days, weeks, or months in the subscription), plus any specials such as premiums or sweepstakes. (There are audit control bureaus that limit or supervise price setting and offers.)

4. Offer, term, and price structures are carefully overlaid (and frequently tested) on all conversion source groups to determine the most effective offer structure for each group. *Within* each group, offer variations will be tested as well. Regular renewal groups generally do very little offer testing by comparison.

5. Length of series also varies by source among the conversion groups (when does first effort mail, how many efforts are to be used).

6. Renewal format testing on the entire series is very popular today. Some publishers test wraps and bind-ins in conjunction with direct mail; others, to replace direct mail. (Results are uneven here; a few publishers have had success with a pure wrap series on the four issues prior to expiration, others have had more success with a standard series of direct mail efforts plus a wrap or cover on the last issue prior to expiration.)

Why in the World Am I Telling You All of This?

First, you won't find all this information so easily anywhere else.

Second, you need it to understand how creative development takes place in a highly personalized, very instructive segment of direct response dialogue.

Third, circulation promotion is an excellent learning ground for direct marketing creative people and if you have the chance, you might want to do something here. It is not simple but this chapter will help you dig in and understand what it entails.

Fourth, it's a great place to work in applying the Underlying Law—over and over. Let me explain this one: Circulation directors and publishers get so caught up in segmentation and number crunching that the forest-and-trees syndrome sets in! They're out there in the woods. *You* must stay back and look at the forest.

Your new subscribers are *people*. How is all of this going to sound to them? Remember how you destroy credibility by crying "Wolf" too often? You do the same thing by telling the relatively new subscriber that the subscription is running out a full six months before expiration! Or by saying that this is absolutely, positively the *last* chance when it isn't.

Here are two wonderful tools to help you make sense to your subscribers in planning and dealing with all the offers, source groups, and formats.

Timing and Pacing—The Tools to See You Through

Timing: Let's take timing first as you'll be hanging your pacing from it. Timing? Isn't that the distance between efforts? Like four weeks or a month? Right you are. That's part of it. By the way, do you know why we leave four weeks between most efforts instead of three or seven? Answer—that's the time it takes to get an effort or mailing out (via third-class mail) and back by first-class, with a little time at the end for updating your customer files as to who answered and who didn't. Mail any closer, and you'll suffer huge doses of "crossed in the mail." This irritates customers and creates extra trouble for you.

So why not mail six weeks apart and really update the file before your next mailing? Nope. Four weeks. *If* you want to maximize overall response with as many efforts as are reasonably possible prior to the subscription expiration date of each expire group while *also* minimizing "crossed in the mail" complaints for those you didn't catch in the computer update—four weeks.

Timing in terms of spacing between efforts is only *half* the story however. The other half involves the pacing. This half helps you convey creatively to your customer or subscriber just exactly what is happening, has happened, and will happen to his or her subscription *in real time.*

If it is well done, you'll have a socko series; if badly done—confusion, irritation, and inaction on the part of your subscribers. *That's* how important it is!

Come again? Not clear? Try this.

Situation 1: You send a notice saying "your *final* issue of *Black Snail* is on its way to you. This is absolutely your last chance to renew without a break in service." *This notice is followed by two more issues.*

Situation 2: You send a notice in March telling the subscriber that "your subscription is about to run out." *The computer renewal form shows a July expiration date.*

Situation 3: You use a wrap for the last subscription issue. It says "this is your last issue of *Black Snail*" but your last-chance letter, which states "your *next* issue is your last," *follows this issue-with-wrap by a day or two.*

Subscription service, unfortunately, is not run on a four-week cycle. The subscriber file has to be updated in the computer and this is done on a set date every two, three, or four weeks. Last-minute renewals can't always promise that the customer won't miss an issue, and expired subscriptions are not always cleaned out immediately, but often sent an extra issue or two. What's more, subscriber copies are mailed out on a specific day every week or month. Some publications are received in a day or two, others may take as much as a week to arrive.

All of these factors will affect your renewal credibility *negatively* if you don't take them into account in your planning. To do this you must understand expire policy. How and when subscribers will be dropped, held *and* reinstated, when the customer file is updated, when the issues mail each month or each week, when they are 90–95 percent received.

And you must *overlay all of this* on your timing—whether you have a basic five- or six-part series, a shorter or a longer one. For example: A renewal effort stating "the issue you have just received is your last" is a powerful statement if indeed the last issue has just landed on my desk a few days ago. If, on the other hand, I receive such notice two weeks later or—heaven forbid—two weeks earlier, it is ineffectual, confusing, and irritating.

Good timing that takes all of this into consideration is the first step in formulating a solid renewal series or improving an existing one. The proof of the pudding of course is always "Will this make sense to the subscriber?"

Pacing and Your Creative Strategies

This is not quite the good old proposition, benefits, hypothesis, and approach you've been following all along with customer/subscriber acquisition. If your publication has done its job, you are primarily providing an easy opportunity for satisfied current customers to continue. Those who didn't get the value or involvement they expected are largely lost causes and will fall away regardless of what you say or do.

Your hard work comes in convincing all those waverers and doubters. Those who may or might—or might not—or just don't want to think about it yet.

Your hypothesis still revolves around the benefits of the publication. But instead of throwing all of this into one big direct mail offering, you develop a group or string of efforts paced to tease, coax, and convince—and there is a pattern. You cull out the happy subscribers up front with your first two efforts; you become more urgent and pull in a few more; then just in time to renew without missing an issue—you hit them hard with "Last Chance." This is the high point in your pacing. After expiration you offer a quick reinstate (still time), then at the end either a poignant, involving "how-can-we-serve-you-better/where-did-we-go-wrong" or a hard-hitting, one-time only, last chance price break. Here's a standard creative theme outline that may be helpful; assuming you overlay *real time*, this is paced to build to Effort 4.

Effort #1: *Time to Renew* (Editorial preview—all the great things ahead.)

Effort #2: *Reminder* (Don't forget—time to renew) short effort.

Effort #3: *Hurry up* (Possible edit review of all the past good things or involvement questions; time is running out.)

Effort #4: *Last Chance* (Urgent notice that service is about to be suspended. You are about to get your last issue.)

Effort #5: *Reinstate* (Still time to reinstate your lapsed subscription; won't
you think it over quickly?)

Effort #6: *If Part We Must* (One last opportunity. How might we have
served you better? Or an absolutely one-time chance for the
lowest rates we can offer you.)

How you handle your pacing depends on your publication (consumer or
business magazine, trade paper or newsletter) and its policies (when it runs the
updating, its procedures regarding final issues), its frequency or timing (weekly,
monthly, six times a year), and its renewal rate structures.

Consumer publications usually treat their "worst" or hardest-to-convince
subscribers best, offering the lowest rates at the end of the series. This doesn't
seem fair, somehow but, believe me, a few publishers have reversed this, trying
to inject fairness. They warned laggards that the best rates were *only* for the
early renewers. Humans, being what they are, continued to hold out, and the
series as a whole fell flat on its face.

Who's Talking?

The next step in your renewal planning is your choice of spokesperson.
Nothing is more suitable than a series written by the circulation director and/
or the publisher. There are, however, other opportunities for creativity (and
more fun for you) if you vary your spokesperson.

After all, who might logical spokepersons be for a magazine? The editor is
obvious when you do an editorial sell. The editor or publisher is best on a final
"Part We Must," credibly inquiring how to serve the subscriber better—while
all the time reselling the product. (Crafty, heh?)

The circulation director is good on Last Chance because seeing that
subscribers get subscription service is his or her logical role. Then all sorts of
other staff can be brought in—if you find a logical reason (researchers, writers,
photographers—even news bureau chiefs—well-known experts who contribute
to the publication, and the corporate president or founder). Check the masthead
and use your imagination.

Your Tone and Style

Traditionally, the tone and style of every renewal series should reflect the
publication. If it is a serious, thoughtful publication, its renewal efforts should
be serious and thoughtful. If it is raucous and irreverent, its renewals should
reflect this. A business publication requires a businesslike renewal series—one
that matches its style and tone as well.

Your pacing, of course, should be overlaid on your style. For example: Effort 4 for a business publication would be businesslike and urgent...for a consumer humor magazine it would be light but urgent...for a sports magazine it might incorporate sports competition—use the symbolism of the race—to show urgency...for a drama magazine it could imply that the curtain was falling on the last act, and so on.

You and the Artist—Still Working Together

Just as you work your timing and pacing into the theme along with the style and tone of your publication, so you'll want graphic development that gives you the appropriate visual pacing and theming. For example: Should your Last Chance outer shout? Should it be solid red? Should your second effort *look* like a reminder—a memo copy? Should art work or photography be used? Should the overall feeling be conservative? Want to change the format of the fourth effort? Want to test a postcard on the final effort?

The Generic Renewal Series—A Big Question Mark

You may come across publishers (usually ones with a stable of special-interest magazines) that use what I call a *generic* series.

A generic series follows the standard five-to-six effort theme *and* pacing *without* style or tone. It is basic, informative (if the timing is fine-tuned), and efficient. And one series can be used for all magazines (with a simple change of logotype on the letterhead).

In some cases (largely business and trade publications), renewals even run under a generic letterhead like "Subscription Services" or "Circulation Services." (If the reader sees his or her publication listed in the group at the top under these heads, the reader can assume that's the product they're talking about.)

Such series are indeed economical. They lower renewal costs considerably. But they eliminate editorial reselling, edit previews of features to come, reviews of past highlights, reminders of benefits—all the things that attracted the subscriber in the first place. They eliminate a good part of the dialogue in fact.

You, by now, have come to understand that the more direct, the more personal a promotional communication can be, the more effective it will be. The best direct mail efforts are those that know their prospects well and capitalize on this.

Renewals and conversions are selling efforts—or efforts to resell customers. How can the response be as strong, then, when we treat the customer like a stranger and use only a portion of the knowledge we have? I like to think that generic renewals can't possibly lower promotion costs enough to make up for the subscribers they lose.

SOME HELPFUL POINTERS ON OTHER BACKEND AREAS

If You're Asked to Do a Billing Series on the Side

"Charge it" traditionally increases mail order response by a minimum of 30 percent and sometimes by much more. House accounts, however, are a rarity and publications are the big exception. (The advantages far outweigh the risks for publications, as service can be suspended after a few issues are sent.) Because of this, nearly all publishers offer "bill me" options, and over 80 percent of all subscribers opt to charge. This creates a massive dunning situation for every publication and most of them are handled in much the same way.

You may be called upon to do a dunning series—or to improve an existing one. Please remember, *this is not the same thing as renewals.* Not at all. Don't try to be flamboyantly creative here. Billing has its structure—usually five to six efforts (four weeks apart) with an extra week thrown in between the last two efforts.

Some series are longer (if it pays to continue); others are shorter. All start politely and end up strong—as strong as you can make it without offending or inviting legal action. Always apply the Underlying Law and stick to the facts.

Your series should run something like this (but there are many variations).

Effort 1: Welcome or "thank you," and, by the way, your invoice is enclosed (possibly with an opportunity to take a longer term at an even greater saving).
    —4 weeks—

Effort 2: Reminder.
    —4 weeks—

Effort 3: Second reminder. Is something wrong? Please let us know or take care of this matter now.
    —4 weeks—

Effort 4: This is the fourth notice we have sent and still no word from you (mild threat of discontinuing service).
    —4 weeks—

Effort 5: Strong threat, usually with time limit on service cutoff.
    —5 to 7 weeks—

Effort 6: Last chance—final opportunity to pay and have service reinstated (sometimes with threat of turning unpaid bill over to a collection agency).

Many publishers and circulation directors have tried to improve (or lower) their bad pay by adding style and tone to their copy to coax their recalcitrants. No good. They've added humor and editorial resell. It doesn't work either. On the other hand, most publishers hesitate to get too strong and alienate a prospect for a few dollars.

This is not benefits-to-you time. Billing or dunning is *not* selling. It's serious stuff. Nobody's interested in talk. The bill's primary job is to gain attention and to impress or motivate the recipient to act—now.

And remember, up front you're talking to prime customers. After the second bill, in most cases you're working a group of deadbeats. So make it look and sound serious—official even, as you move along. Use the comptroller or treasurer as spokesperson for final efforts. But not too harsh…here's your chance to play kindly bill collector. And even that can be fun.

Member Mailings—A Good Place to Get Experience

Like publication circulation, book clubs have been known as good training grounds for aspiring direct response writers. It's a fine place to start, because book club backend consists of regular member communications (a package every month, or every twenty-six days or so). You have a chance to do the equivalent of small space ads for books—or small space for whatever else your club is offering. And you may have a chance at a small catalog as well.

Each club has its own procedures for handling members (and rules) which you will learn. But here's something to bring to it, whatever the club: Go back to the Underlying Law. In customer dialogue, remember—*something has gone before* and *something will follow.* Does your assignment fit in and make sense with the big picture—the customer continuity?

Step out of context and *be* a customer. (Make sure you're on the mailing list.) Is it all clear (and positive and promotional)? Does the club project a good image? Does it have an image to project? If so, sustain and strengthen it. If not, see if you can start to develop one (and don't forget your art director).

The book clubs have a job to do, like the catalogs: repeat business, satisfied customers. Your job is to seek, examine, question. *You know how.* You may, in fact, be surprised at how much you know and how few of your fellow workers question established formats and procedures. Don't let that slow you down.

Inquiry Fulfillment—Another Opportunity

This is also a good place to get your feet wet because it's very much like direct mail prospecting, except that the door has already been opened by an inquiry of one kind or another.

In other words, you have a friendly audience. And that's nice. After all, with a good lead-getting program, think of what you know about your prospect! Your first step is to find out, of course, who these prospects are and what you *do* know. Request a copy of the direct response promotion that produced the inquiry. From this you will get the basic data for your fulfillment approach.

Once you determine exactly what you know about your prospects, utilize this information as fully as you can. For example:

- Although you know he or she is interested in the product or service, what is the extent of the interest? This will be determined by the qualification factors in the promotion. (Was it a freeloader's paradise or did it qualify prospects with a tight offer and highly related premium?)
- You now have a correct name and address. If this is a business inquiry, let's hope you also have a title. (Good personalization!)
- Did you get a phone number? They're great for "next steps." ("John Smith, our sales representative in Houston, will call you in a few days.")
- Any other data given? Size of company? Type of service desired? Monies available? Size of investment or loan considered? (Effective inquiry fulfillment will utilize such data in a covering letter along with any promised collateral or premiums.)

Now plan for the next step. Unfortunately, many marketers spend fortunes acquiring leads, yet treat these valuable prospects like second-class citizens when they arrive. Little provision (budget) is made for follow-up and even less good planning for continuing the dialogue! (If, thanks to bad planning, it takes weeks even to get an answer out in the mail, you can forget it, because the prospects have, too, by then.)

It's almost as bad to add "Just call if you have any further questions." (*Further questions?* Who's selling whom?) Of course it's better than *nothing*. Or is it? You put all the responsibility on the prospect's shoulders. (Make 'em work, heh-heh. That'll teach them to respond.) And some inquiry fulfillment does just this.

Wouldn't it be nice (smart) to continue the dialogue—to move the relationship to another level? Sure, you shouldn't have to be thinking of this. Some marketer somewhere has it all worked out. *He or she* knows.

Don't accept this! If (when) such dead-end situations occur, ask for the objectives. (Ask anyway, just to be sure you're doing your part.) Then see if you can find a way to keep the dialogue going. Will a salesman call for an appointment? Do you want the prospect to come in to the salesman and if so, why should he or she? How about getting the prospect to request more specific information? Or outright asking for the order?

If you know the next step—or the basic objectives—you can help work toward this by using response motivators or door openers for the next round:

Fill out and return the enclosed analysis form and our local sales representative will call and deliver the completed profit analysis directly to you within two weeks....

Come in to our local loan offices and bring the enclosed certificate with you for an immediate credit evaluation....

We will send you free of charge a complete specification book on whichever machine is best suited to your plant requirements. We'll send an engineer as well, if you wish. Just look over the preliminary specifications and availabilities here and....

Take this "key" token down to your local Maxi dealer today and enjoy a test drive of the new Maxi and a bottle of wine (to drink when you get home)—on the house....

Two more things (they may seem pretty obvious to you by now, but not to a lot of those other people involved in inquiry fulfillment): (1) Get the envelope opened; and (2) include a letter.

Under the absolutely *worst* of circumstances (no budget), you can capitalize on the inquiry request to maximize your direct mail impact very simply. Merely put "Enclosed, the materials you requested" on your outer. This is no secret. Nor can I believe it's any secret to you as to why it works, every time. And even with a minimal budget, push for a brief letter. You should be able to develop excellent letter formats that can accommodate all the data from each inquiry. (Computer letter typers can handle this. So can word processors or good old-fashioned typists, if the responses are few.)

If the response device in the original promotion was looking for several kinds of inquiry responses, you'll need an equal number of letter versions (one for the large equipment interests, as opposed to the small equipment; one for the bond investors and one for the stock investors; one for the health insurance group and one for the life insurance; and so on).

Remember, it has to make sense, preserve continuity, and embody as much personalization as you can give it. Don't use the too familiar "Here's the information—thanks—goodbye."

There are other kinds of backend—like small flyers or mini brochures that are enclosed in customer or member mailings, gift-giving folders, and referral requests. You can pick up the knack for handling these quickly if they come your way. What you must remember is that all opportunities to talk to customers should make sense and should be handled with loving care. None of this "Yah—they're old friends; no fancy stuff, just give 'em letter #22..."

Direct marketers know that their current customers are their best friends. These customers are crucial to direct marketing success because that's where the profits come from. Yet some marketers spend heavily on the glamorous front end, acquiring prospects and customers, then scrimp with little thought or planning on the real profit center, the backend. How foolish.

Start at the backend and learn to nurture and respect the customers who make your job possible. Maximize sales with those customers by dealing productively on a continuing basis and giving good value and good service. Develop a feeling for the continuing dialogue that's possible thanks to our computer abilities and customer records; see how you can use this to build a customer relationship that's far more personal and more caring and more effective than any relationship in today's retail arena.

That's direct marketing. Nothing else comes close to it.

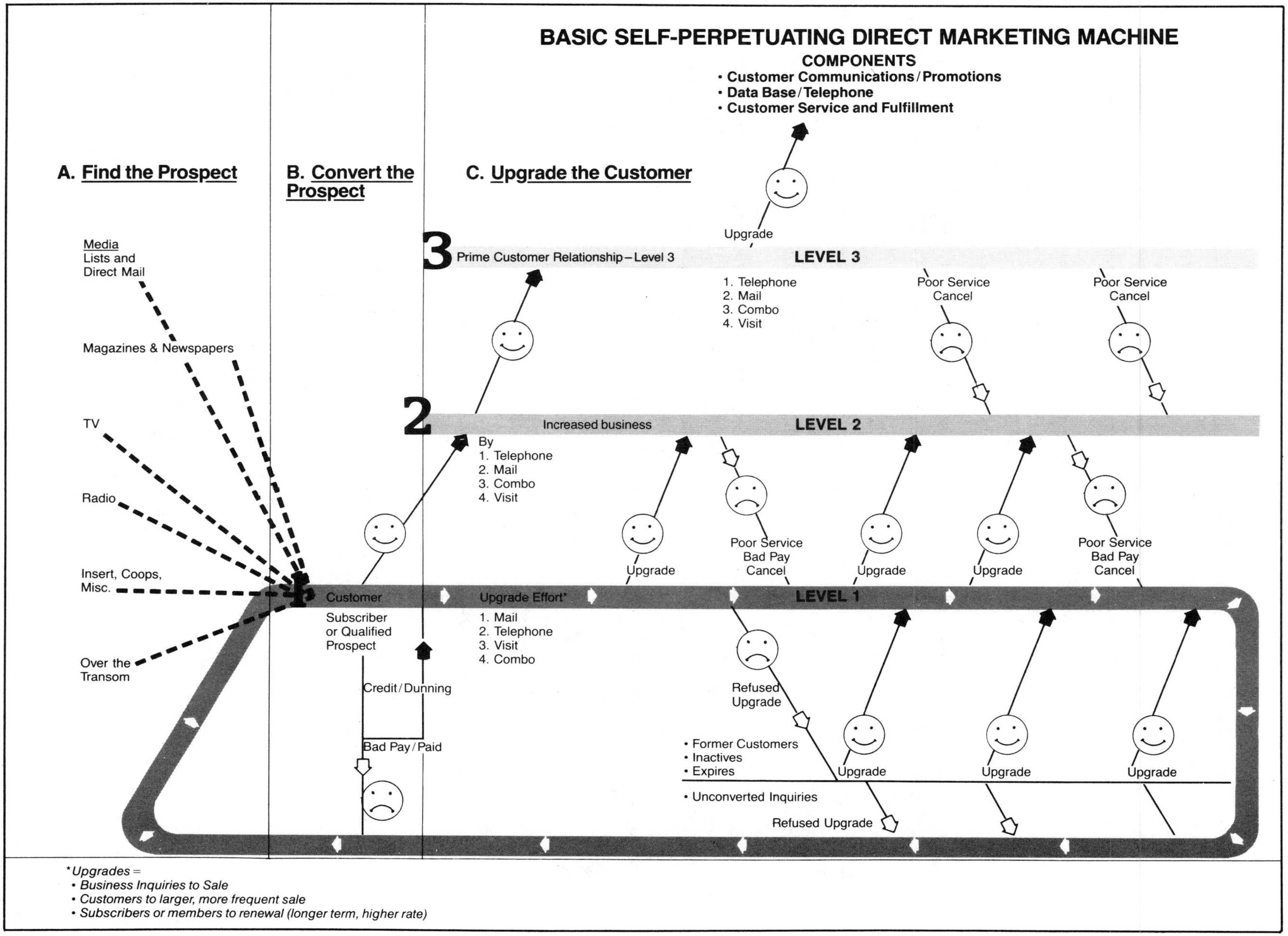

BASIC SELF-PERPETUATING DIRECT MARKETING MACHINE

COMPONENTS
- Customer Communications / Promotions
- Data Base / Telephone
- Customer Service and Fulfillment

A. Find the Prospect

B. Convert the Prospect

C. Upgrade the Customer

Media
Lists and
Direct Mail

Magazines & Newspapers

TV

Radio

Insert, Coops,
Misc.

Over the
Transom

Customer
Subscriber
or Qualified
Prospect

Credit / Dunning

Bad Pay / Paid

3 Prime Customer Relationship – Level 3

Upgrade

LEVEL 3

By
1. Telephone
2. Mail
3. Combo
4. Visit

Poor Service
Cancel

Poor Service
Cancel

Upgrade

Upgrade

2 Increased business

LEVEL 2

By
1. Telephone
2. Mail
3. Combo
4. Visit

Upgrade

Upgrade

Poor Service
Bad Pay
Cancel

Poor Service
Cancel

Upgrade

Upgrade

Upgrade Effort*
1. Mail
2. Telephone
3. Visit
4. Combo

LEVEL 1

Refused
Upgrade

Upgrade

Poor Service
Bad Pay
Cancel

Upgrade

Upgrade

- Former Customers
- Inactives
- Expires

- Unconverted Inquiries

Refused Upgrade

*Upgrades =
- Business Inquiries to Sale
- Customers to larger, more frequent sale
- Subscribers or members to renewal (longer term, higher rate)

Figure 11-17

375

The Self-Perpetuating Machine

Here in Figure 11-17 is a sort of Rube Goldberg sausage machine that illustrates the importance of the backend and how it works. The object is to illustrate the continuing process of

- bringing on new prospects from a wide variety of media efforts
- converting prospects to customers via direct mail, telephone, or an office visit—or combinations of these (losing as few as possible to bad pay, poor service, general inertia, or nonresponse)
- motivating customers to purchase more often and in larger quantities

At all times, while you are upgrading some customers, you will be losing others, but many of them (old or inactive customers) can be activated by repromotion or reinstatement efforts.

Just imagine that everything is moving in this diagram—up, down, across. Nothing stays the same. Customers and prospects come on up front and immediately start to fall away due to failure to pay bills and nonresponse to promotions. At the same time, other customers are buying—each time more and more.

This is a continuing process, for business and consumer prospecting, mail order catalogs, publication subscriptions, and book club memberships. It employs all the media and direct response methodologies to prospect, convert, upgrade, reinstate, repromote and, ultimately, to recycle. Not much is wasted in a good sausage machine. Same goes here!

SOME CATALOGS TO SEND AWAY FOR

The Sharper Image
680 Davis Street
San Francisco, CA 94111

The White Flower Farm
Litchfield, Conn. 06759-0050
(Charge $5 per year by subscription
—and worth every penny)

Smith & Hawken
25 Corte Madera
Mill Valley, CA 94941

The Vermont Country Store
PO Box 3000
Manchester Center, VT 05255-3000

Comfortably Yours
52 West Hunter Ave.
Maywood, N.J. 07607

Lands' End Direct Merchants
Lands' End Lane
Dodgeville, WI 53595

Sir Thomas Lipton's Trading Company
Mail Order Division
PO Box 215
105 Oak St.
Norwood, N.J. 07648

Sunnyland Farms, Inc.
Albany, GA 31703

Early Winters, Ltd.
110 Prefontaine Place South
Seattle, WA 98104

Omaha Steaks International
PO Box 3300
Omaha, NE 68103

NM By Post
c/o Neiman Marcus
P.O. Box 2968
Dallas, TX 75221-9950

The Company Store
1205 South 7th St.
La Crosse, WI 54601

Eddie Bauer
Fifth & Union
PO Box 3700
Seattle, WA 98124

Cuddledown
106 Main Street
Yarmouth, ME 04096

Banana Republic
Box 77133
San Francisco, CA 94107

Wigs from Paula Young
Box 483
Brockton, MA 02403

Lynchburg Hardware & General Store
Lynchburg, TN 37352

Johnny's Selected Seeds
Albion, ME 04910

L.L. Bean, Inc.
Freeport, ME 04033

chapter 12

You Move On

YOUR BACCALAUREATE ADDRESS

Well, here we are at the last chapter. We've been through a lot, you and I, and now it's time for you to graduate—to go it alone. You've probably already guessed that the purpose of this whole thing is to give you the confidence and the ability to make creative judgments, starting with basic common sense—the Underlying Law, of course.

Your ability to apply creative reasoning to your assignments will enable you to make the sound decisions that save you from failed work. Your ability to work with others and develop creative strategies, applying the appropriate formulas and rules, will ensure that your work will be competent and effective. You will plan well and test intelligently.

Your ability to write, be it a letter, small space, or broadcast, will be enhanced if you follow the procedures and guidelines set down for you.

The missing ingredients that no one can give you are personal style and creative genius. The way your writing sounds is your personal style. Writers inject their personalities into their work, whomever they write for, whatever role they act out. They still sound like themselves beneath it all. It's their own particular way of developing dialogue, not necessarily better, just different.

As for style and genius, I suggest you read a small gem called *Becoming a Writer* by Dorothea Brande, published by J. P. Tarcher, Inc., Los Angeles, California. In the foreword John Gardner promises:

> The root problems...are problems of confidence, self-respect, freedom: The writer's demon is imprisoned by the various ghosts in the unconscious.
>
> Ms. Brande points out—with the delightful wit we find everywhere in her book—that for the writer suffering from uncertainty and self-doubt, writing teachers and books about writing, not to mention symposia of famous authors, do to the young (or old) struggling writer just about the worst thing they could do: "In the opening lecture, within the first few pages of his book, within a sentence or two of his authors' symposium, he will be told rather shortly that 'genius cannot be taught'; and there goes his hope glimmering. For whether he knows it or not, he is in search of the very thing that is denied him in that dismissive sentence." Ms. Brande's purpose in

Becoming a Writer is to make available to the writer the very thing usually denied.

   She is right that genius can be taught (once the secret emptiness of that phrase is understood) because in fact genius is as common as old shoes..."[1]

If writing is self-expression for you, if you take joy in creative development, and polishing your work is second nature, the odds are strongly in your favor. You'll be a writer all right. Just believe and keep working at it. You'll find all the "genius" you need.

WHITHER DIRECT MARKETING

Now before you leave, I'd like to give you an idea of where direct marketing is taking you, if you choose to join it and if you plan to stay with it.

   Many of the futurists in direct marketing claim that it is an expanding form of marketing, and will gradually encompass all goods and services, regardless of size or cost, in the future. Giant companies will offer customers a diversity of interrelated products and services—merchandise services, financial services, medical services, even.

   The fact is, direct marketing pretty well achieved this back in 1909! (But people forget.) That was the year Sears Roebuck & Co. first introduced its mail order homes. It sold 100,000 of them (ranging in price from $595 to $5,000) between 1909 and 1937. There were two-bedroom cottages, three-story houses, and even a mansion with Gothic columns, curving staircase, and servants' quarters. The prices were good and the materials were "quality." And many of these homes are still lived in today, cherished collectors' items.

   According to an article in the *Wall Street Journal,*

The pieces for the houses arrived by train, complete with everything required, including the kitchen sink. Rail deliveries were arranged so that each shipment arrived at just the right time in the construction schedule. The lumber for the frame came first, already cut, notched and mitered, and with each piece numbered to identify its place in the house. Then came shipments of window frames, plaster, plumbing, wiring, trim, glass, red-cedar shingles and, finally, enough paint and varnish for three good coatings. Even the nails came from Sears. And the floor plans were marked to show where an extra Sears sofa or Sears piano might be placed.
Financing was also provided by Sears. Monthly payments on a $2500 home might come to about $30—and Sears would even lend $500 in cash to help meet the cost of construction.

   The instructions were bound in leather and bore the new homeowner's name in gold. Creativity was discouraged. "Do not take anyone's advice as to how your building should be erected," the manual said. "This causes more difficulty than all other things put together."

---

[1] John Gardner, "Foreword" to *Becoming a Writer* by Dorothea Brand. Copyright © 1981 by J. P. Tarcher, Inc. Reprinted by permission of Houghton Mifflin Company and J. P. Tarcher, Inc.

Possible pitfalls were highlighted. The instructions warned, for example, that "there are mistakes made in the erection of chimneys which are too numerous to mention." And it called for extra care in the construction of the porch, since "this part of your house is seen first and last!"

"In a 1929 newsletter," The *Wall Street Journal* continues, "Sears had even personified its houses and given them a soothing voice:

> To all in the family, I guarantee contentment, a new sense of stability and independence, and the knowledge that regardless of any vicissitudes of fortune, you will always have one of the prime essentials of civilized life—comfortable, substantial shelter.
>
> After all the philosophies of the ages are condensed, one thing alone remains—the desire for happiness. And, in the final analysis of my offerings, it is Happiness that I present."[2]

Is this direct marketing—or is this direct marketing! 1909—not 2000! And a model for today.

Sadly, the Great Depression finished Sears' modern-homes department in 1931, but it remains one of the best mail order examples on record—*the* big sale (perhaps bigger than any like it today), *plus* financing *and* a clear-cut effort for add-on products in home furnishings. An ongoing dialogue, solid backend efforts, and an outstanding moral imperative/hypothesis are all contained in this example.

We may not be as original today as we think we are, and that leads us to a big problem. Everyone wants to try the "newly discovered" marketing. It's future marketing. It's chic. But as we rush forward, some people are indeed forgetting the lessons of the past (if they ever learned them). And knowledgeable direct marketers are expressing concern.

Direct marketing has been exceeding its bounds while practitioners jostle to define the bulging bounds themselves. The expansionists want direct marketing to be all-encompassing, and often self-interest pushes them to stretch their definitions to any form of advertising that receives a measured response! Some of these expansionists also claim that it's impossible (or unnecessary) to test—that direct response should go into a vast national media mix, all of which must "break" (or reach the market) in time and in tune with general advertising.

The purists (among whom I stand firmly) recognize direct marketing as measured response combined with the establishment (and use) of a database—dialogue marketing (Chapter 2), remember? All the rest is whatever else you choose to call it—sales promotion or response advertising—it is *not* direct marketing.

What difference the definition, you ask? Here's the difference. With the

---

[2]Reprinted by permission of *The Wall Street Journal*, © Dow Jones & Company, Inc. 1985. All Rights Reserved.

lack of a clear, mutually acceptable definition, direct marketing will become diluted and diffuse. It will gradually lose its careful practitioners and stern requirements to test and implement and "roll out," to measure and learn and improve and project. It will cease to work to define and acquire a customer, then to establish a dialogue and cultivate that customer.

It will go for the megabucks of packaged goods and mass sampling instead. And as it does, it will become *nothing*—nothing more than a promotional tool, a coupon that's counted, a "vote" on a national toll-free number, a faceless wave of response or rejection, mass advertising's child. That's why it is important for you to understand what direct marketing is, and has been, and can continue to be—and to keep it pure.

Aside from these threats of dilution and diffusion, there are other challenges to face. For example, if you hang around in direct marketing for a while you're bound to wonder about "the other 98 percent." Direct marketers have been using 2 percent as an acceptable direct mail response for a long time: "Hey, Joe—what do you think we ought to get from this mailing?" "Oh, I guess you could get 2 percent all right."

The real question here is, "What do you need? Are your expectations realistic?" After all, if you're selling a Mercedes or Sears' houses, you don't even need 2 percent response to make a fortune. (CPM—Chapter 4, remember?) If, on the other hand, you have a $10 silk scarf, you'd better get at least 10 percent to turn a profit (and *that* may not be a realistic expectation).

Whether it's 2 percent, or 1 percent, or 5 percent, or more—the question still remains: "What happened to the 98 percent, the 99 percent or the 95 percent that never responded? How do we get them to respond?" Put another way, can you continue to advertise in markets where over 90 percent of your expensive promotion is a dud?

This is a question that will be getting increasing attention in the years ahead—and it will affect you, because in looking for an answer you will be asked to come up with new ways of pulling in or qualifying some of that 98 percent that isn't answering (like testing an offer that allows a prospect to say "maybe" or "not now" instead of "no"). You will be given more and more data about your prospects, as marketers use ever more sophisticated techniques of segmentation and market selection to reduce the 98 percent. (*How you use this data* to strengthen your hypothesis and personalize your copy can mean an important contribution.)

This brings us to another challenge coming up. The more you know about your market, the more effective your advertising will be in this customer-driven form of marketing. But there are bounds and limitations to how much any of us should know about the other guy (without the other guy's permission). There is such a thing as privacy—and if you overstep the bounds of good taste you risk offending and irritating your prospect. Just what these bounds should be, and what the individual has to say about it, is becoming a national issue with a capital *P—Privacy.*

The growing computer information network that helps direct marketers be personal and caring and highly service oriented can also become a weapon to be used against them if it is abused. Be careful how, and to what extent, you use personal data. (You want to make friends but don't be impudent. It's still a customer/business relationship. You're not one of the family.)

It's the old story, if we don't police ourselves here, someone else steps in and does it for us. And Privacy looks like one cause that every state and federal legislator has his or her eye on. Keep your eye on it, too.

Every so often bright, young creative people, or older creative people trying to sound bright and young, deplore the state of the art. They call to task the direct marketing industry for using tired formulas and rules that don't work, employing "hack" writers and weak graphics. Self-examination by the profession can be productive, but consider the improbability of such statements. If you are in a customer-driven business and testing is its basis, how can the feelings, desires, and preferences of the market be ignored? And how can there be rules and formulas that don't work, if you constantly test them? Can these critics possibly be suggesting that we're advertising without the moral imperatives of a well-constructed hypothesis—or (worse still) that we've *stopped* testing?

On the other hand, why not ask, "If there is good advertising, why can't there be better advertising?" And right you are! I think you can see from many of the examples in your mailbox, in magazines, on television, and in this book that we do some very good direct response advertising, and it's getting better. It has to get better if it's going to survive.

One major aspect of creativity is changing—and that is the role of the art director, designer, or artist.

The "Age of the Art Director" may be approaching. Neglected for too long, subordinated to the copywriter in the creative process, the art director is now beginning to come into the limelight.

More often than not these days, the art director is in at the start—and I hope that by now I don't have to spell out the advantages of this for you. But why? Why are art directors becoming more important? Are we making up guiltily for years of artistic suppression? Nope. Business—and particularly advertising—just doesn't work that way.

Look at the market for your answers. The customer drives, remember? Is it not possible that our society today is somewhat more visually oriented than the societies of the past? Fifty years ago when you wanted news, you read a newspaper or listened to a radio. Photography was just replacing *drawings* in many newspapers, magazines, and advertising materials.

Today over 65 percent of the American people take their news by screen. We are far more visually alert or visually oriented than we've ever been. All-type ads used to be popular. Now there are few markets (media) that can support pure type. Such type ads still do best in magazines and newspapers that they resemble, those designed for serious readers.

But even our literati, when they look for a new car, like to *see* it from all angles, and most of our larger market segments require dramatic new graphics to attract *and* hold the prospect's attention (the mailbox, remember?). We are getting more sophisticated graphically.

But because we are customer-driven, direct marketers tend to be reactive; we do not lead. We follow the tastes and dictates of the customer as they may have been established or developed by other forms of advertising and communications that are proactive.

Thanks to modern advertising, art and design, thanks to video-oriented customers, we have new opportunities. How we use these opportunities to develop our own exciting graphics (many of which you've seen here) is something else again. That's why the art director is coming into the picture in a big way. Copywriters can no longer do their best work without an art director or artist by their side. The good copywriters are beginning to acknowledge this now. Unfortunately, good art directors are just as rare as good copywriters.

Which brings us to the next point in Whither Direct Marketing? If it survives diffusion and dissolution and graphic sophistication *and* lack of talent—will it survive in the form or in the media we know today? What about the telephone?

Let's dispense with the telephone quickly. It's here—arrived—a permanent part of the mix. Why mail or write when you can call? The *800* number is instant gratification, order verification, credible communication all in one. It increases response. It can also increase order size.

What took it so long? Studies indicate that the older market held back. (Those who witnessed the first toll-free offers resisted because of conscious or unconscious fears about charges.) That market is almost gone now and the rest of us take toll-free calls for granted. Today business-to-business direct marketers can't function without it, and most consumer companies have found that although it is expensive, it usually pays for itself.

What about video—interactive television, video discs and cassettes? Will these change everything?

First, you have to ask, "Does such a question suggest that reading is (or soon will be) a dead activity?"

Some video futurists might have us think so, but the consensus seems to indicate that we'll be reading for a while yet—certainly through your lifetime and mine. Ordering products and services via video screen and computer is not considered threatening to the catalogers. Most of them feel catalogs can live quite compatibly with this—for now.

We are learning a lot about the video medium and what it can do for direct marketing, but we're learning *gradually.* Here's what it may mean to you: In Chapter 10 you saw how broadcast is creeping in through the basement as part of the media mix, rather than charging in the front door and taking over. This will probably continue, along with other audiovisual forms of direct response advertising to include video kiosks in airports and shopping malls, infomercials and interactive TV on cable at home, video cassettes and video disks. But gradually. You may hardly notice it for several years.

Direct marketers are the conservative advertisers. They wait until the market is ready. They use the medium, the form of advertising, that is most comfortable for the customer. They are not trying to change the customer, but to accommodate him or her. Their first job is to listen carefully and coax response.

It was not until the 1980s that direct marketers began to use space advertising to do more than produce a measured response (witness Lands' End and Spiegel's in Chapter 9). Direct marketers never seriously considered the extra benefits of multimedia efforts until the 1980s either. The effect of one medium on another in multimedia campaigns was virtually ignored because this was hard to measure—and expensive. What's more, few direct marketers had multimedia programs. This is changing.

If there is any one area where you will see changes in the years ahead, it is in the use of more than one medium—the media mix. Direct marketers are learning how to carry successful creative efforts from one medium to another, how to plan multimedia campaigns and use the media to create awareness and build image while it also returns a measured response.

These will be the new trends or movements facing you in the years ahead, not the demise of direct mail or print, or an all video future.

Of course, we change with the times. But it has been said that within the past we find the seeds of the future. Today Sears Roebuck & Company is offering all kinds of credit, insurance, real estate, dental services, and a full array of retail and mail order products. But is this so different from its mail order homes of 1909, with financing and furnishing and the promise of family "happiness"? Think about it.

SOME ADVICE ON COMMENCING

If you are not already gainfully employed in direct marketing—and most particularly as a direct response creative person—here are some tips on getting started.

Originally, I promised you fame, wealth, and power if you mastered the techniques and strategies for creating winning direct response advertising. Let's say you're ready to start practicing in earnest and accumulating a little of that fame, wealth, and power. Now how do you convince others that you've arrived?

Whether you use an employment agency or the local paper, much will depend on where you start. Pickings will be slim in small towns, of course. Cities like New York, Los Angeles, San Francisco, Boston, Chicago, Kansas City, Houston, and Dallas offer the most opportunities. Geography will also determine your selection of types of direct response. Cities like New York and Chicago have a range of direct response agencies, book publishing operations, and magazine circulation departments—a wide variety of direct response entry possibilities.

If you like your local neighborhood and it's not New York, Chicago, Los Angeles, or some other city with a variety of opportunities, research the area.

Look into local publishing operations or catalog companies or regular advertising agencies that may be planning to set up a direct response arm. (I've found lots of these in places like Charlotte, North Carolina; Phoenix, Arizona; Ft. Lauderdale, Florida.)

WHAT TO LOOK FOR WHEREVER YOU ARE

There's a lot of dabbling in direct marketing or *faux* direct marketing procedures going on in companies that are convinced it's fashionable. Some of the larger ones even set up "direct marketing" in their sales promotion or merchandising areas. And a few general agencies put in instant direct marketing departments when their clients ask for it. If you can help it, don't get involved with these people. They may need *you*, but you've little to gain from them. (They'll be shaving off *your* beard.) Here are a few questions to ask to help determine how suitable and serious a company is:

1. Does the company really understand direct marketing? Is it honestly committed to it?
2. Who's in charge of direct response advertising? Is there at least one executive working full-time on direct marketing? Is the executive experienced in direct marketing? What kind of staff is there? How much space does it have? What facilities are available to it?
3. Does the company have a direct response training program?
4. Does it offer its creative people classes or seminars outside the company?
5. Is it a member of local direct marketing groups? Or the national organization, the Direct Marketing Association?

If the group gets poor marks (especially on 1 and 2), beware.

HOW TO GET HIRED AND AVOID CREATIVE CATCH-22

Let's say you've found some honest-to-goodness openings. They need a creative person, and you want them to want you. Now how do you go about it? The best answer is that everything helps—résumé, references, samples, perseverance.

Let's start with the résumé. If you have direct mail or direct marketing experience, flaunt it—whatever it may be. If you have creative experience, flaunt that, too. If the best you can say is that you've worked and you're willing, then show what you've done and tie it in, if you can, with the job's requirements. Last, but not least—what about your education? Did you major in advertising? Have you taken special courses in writing or direct marketing?

Next, *samples*. From day one every writer and artist starts compiling a book of samples. If you already have your collection started, organize your materials so that those showing qualities and executions most important to the job predominate. If you have direct response samples, these will be of primary importance.

What if you have no samples? Should you make up examples—rough copy and layouts for imaginary assignments? It's like chicken soup: It can't hurt if you're willing to work hard and make a professional presentation. But some interviewers aren't impressed with this. They only want to see what you can do by looking at examples of what you've done. Reasonable enough if you have just what they want. Otherwise it's creative Catch-22: "Show us that you have done it and we'll give you the job." "Give me the job and I'll show you what I can do." This happens primarily (1) when you're moving from general advertising to direct response advertising; (2) when you're moving from one kind of direct response advertising to another (remember financial writers or consumer writers versus business-to-business writers in Chapter 2?); or (3) when you're just starting out and have no samples at all.

To overcome the problems, offer to take on a small assignment for them. Act as their free-lancer. Ask your questions, get samples, do your research, draw up your creative strategy, hypothesis, and approach. Do the work professionally, complete with copywriter's dummy or rough. It is not unreasonable to ask them to pay you for the work if they use it, particularly if you've been doing direct response copy. This kind of offer shows two things: your interest and enthusiasm for the job, and your willingness to prove yourself to them. If they are sincere and interested in you, most prospective employers will take you up on the offer because it gives them a chance to see how *you* work, what questions you ask, how you relate to others (creative director, artist), how you take responsibility, how your mind functions as you develop creative concepts, how you meet deadlines, how you present, and how you receive criticism.

One point I mentioned above deserves special emphasis. Regardless of your experience, your samples and your résumé, your interest in and enthusiasm for the job can override a lot of shortcomings.

If you're sincerely excited about the products and services you'll be dealing with, if you're bursting with enthusiasm over the opportunity to do direct response advertising for the interviewer, you'll rack up high marks on attitude. What's more, if you're sincere (and I trust you will be), the odds are strong that you will do good work.

SOMETHING TO KEEP WITH YOU

Once you're hired and settled in, in no time at all you'll remember Tom Collins' words, "Advertising is hard!" You do have to do your homework, plan carefully, write hard, then rewrite and polish, polish, polish, but don't be discouraged. You've also got to keep the Joy Factor going. Otherwise, two things may happen to you that happen to potentially good writers all the time as they grow their wings:

First, you may freeze out all creative fun by the fear of making a fool of yourself. You stick close to the rules and cancel out your own creative emotions with a fearful "That might sound dumb." Second, you can try too hard. This may sound silly coming from me, but you *can* work so hard to excel that you completely lose your perspective. Your work may even become convoluted and obscure. You will see distant reasons and grand, universal patterns behind your thinking, but you will have left the effective, simple solutions behind—along with most of us, sitting back on earth confused and unimpressed.

Don't let these things happen to you. If you continue to be shy, or tense, here's a suggestion that's worked for some of my students. Their creativity is alive and well on assignments or exercises that aren't judged by a supervisor or creative director. All right, take a real assignment and do it two ways—the way you think is more "acceptable" *and* the way you'd like to see it go. Present both to your creative supervisors and explain what you're doing. Enlist their help. They'll appreciate it. Listen. Learn to channel your creative ideas into acceptable formats. Or maybe—just maybe—you'll prove to the world what a genius you are right from the start!

Remember, you are a creative, reasoning human being. You have talent. You can use it wisely. Despite the rules and formulas and strategies, you have the ability to be unique. Don't be afraid. Relax. Concentrate. Now—get lost in the challenge and fun of your project!

Well, it's your turn now. Time to gather your samples, update your résumé, and go out and shake up the direct response advertising business. Direct response needs *your* talent!

So go for it! And good luck. Just put me on the shelf for now. I'll be waiting should you ever need a little reinforcement or friendly support. But don't let me get dusty. See you later...

Index